THE CAMBRIDGE COMPANION TO
CHRISTIAN POLITICAL

Interest in political theology has surged in recent years, and this accessible volume provides a focused overview of the field. Many are asking serious questions about religious faith in secular societies, the origin and function of democratic polities, worldwide economic challenges, the shift of Christianity's center of gravity to the global south, and anxieties related to bold and even violent assertions of theologically determined political ideas. In fourteen original essays, authors examine Christian political theology in order to clarify the contemporary discourse and some of its most important themes and issues. These include up-to-date, critical engagements with historical figures like Augustine, Thomas Aquinas, and Immanuel Kant; discussions of how the Bible functions theopolitically; and introductions to key movements such as liberation theology, Catholic social teaching, and radical orthodoxy. An invaluable resource for students and scholars in theology, the *Companion* will also be beneficial to those in history, philosophy, and politics.

Craig Hovey is Associate Professor of Religion at Ashland University and Executive Director of the Ashland Center for Nonviolence. His publications include *Bearing True Witness: Truthfulness in Christian Practice, Nietzsche and Theology* (2011) and *To Share in the Body: A Theology of Martyrdom for Today's Church* (2008).

Elizabeth Phillips is Tutor in Theology and Ethics at Westcott House, an Anglican theological college affiliated with the University of Cambridge. She is the author of *Political Theology: A Guide for the Perplexed* (2012).

CAMBRIDGE COMPANIONS TO RELIGION

This is a series of companions to major topics and key figures in theology and religious studies. Each volume contains specially commissioned chapters by international scholars, which provide an accessible and stimulating introduction to the subject for new readers and nonspecialists.

Other Titles in the Series

AMERICAN ISLAM Edited by Juliane Hammer and Omid Safi
AMERICAN JUDAISM Edited by Dana Evan Kaplan
AMERICAN METHODISM Edited by Jason E. Vickers
ANCIENT MEDITERRANEAN RELIGIONS Edited by Barbette Stanley Spaeth
KARL BARTH Edited by John Webster
THE BIBLE, 2nd edition Edited by Bruce Chilton
BIBLICAL INTERPRETATION Edited by John Barton
DIETRICH BONHOEFFER Edited by John de Gruchy
JOHN CALVIN Edited by Donald K. McKim
CHRISTIAN DOCTRINE Edited by Colin Gunton
CHRISTIAN ETHICS Edited by Robin Gill
CHRISTIAN MYSTICISM Edited by Amy Hollywood and Patricia Z. Beckman
CHRISTIAN PHILOSOPHICAL THEOLOGY Edited by Charles Taliaferro and Chad V. Meister
CLASSICAL ISLAMIC THEOLOGY Edited by Tim Winter
JONATHAN EDWARDS Edited by Stephen J. Stein
FEMINIST THEOLOGY Edited by Susan Frank Parsons
THE JESUITS Edited by Thomas Worcester
JESUS Edited by Markus Bockmuehl
C. S. LEWIS Edited by Robert MacSwain and Michael Ward
LIBERATION THEOLOGY Edited by Chris Rowland
MARTIN LUTHER Edited by Donald K. McKim
MEDIEVAL JEWISH PHILOSOPHY Edited by Daniel H. Frank and Oliver Leaman
MODERN JEWISH PHILOSOPHY Edited by Michael L. Morgan and Peter Eli Gordon
MOHAMMED Edited by Jonathan E. Brockup
PENTECOSTALISM Edited by Cecil M. Robeck, Jr and Amos Yong
POSTMODERN THEOLOGY Edited by Kevin J. Vanhoozer
PURITANISM Edited by John Coffey and Paul C. H. Lim
THE QUR'AN Edited by Jane Dammen McAuliffe
KARL RAHNER Edited by Declan Marmion and Mary E. Hines
REFORMATION THEOLOGY Edited by David Bagchi and David Steinmetz
RELIGIOUS STUDIES Edited by Robert A. Orsi
FREIDRICK SCHLEIERMACHER Edited by Jacqueline Mariña
SCIENCE AND RELIGION Edited by Peter Harrison
ST. PAUL Edited by James D. G. Dunn
THE TALMUD AND RABBINIC LITERATURE Edited by Charlotte E. Fonrobert and Martin S. Jaffee
HANS URS VON BALTHASAR Edited by Edward T. Oakes and David Moss
JOHN WESLEY Edited by Randy L. Maddox and Jason E. Vickers

THE CAMBRIDGE COMPANION TO
CHRISTIAN POLITICAL THEOLOGY

Edited by

Craig Hovey
Ashland University

Elizabeth Phillips
University of Cambridge

CAMBRIDGE
UNIVERSITY PRESS

32 Avenue of the Americas, New York, NY 10013-2473, USA

Cambridge University Press is part of the University of Cambridge.

It furthers the University's mission by disseminating knowledge in the pursuit of education, learning, and research at the highest international levels of excellence.

www.cambridge.org
Information on this title: www.cambridge.org/9781107633803

© Cambridge University Press 2015

This publication is in copyright. Subject to statutory exception and to the provisions of relevant collective licensing agreements, no reproduction of any part may take place without the written permission of Cambridge University Press.

First published 2015

Printed in the United Kingdom by Clays, St Ives plc

A catalog record for this publication is available from the British Library.

Library of Congress Cataloging in Publication Data
The Cambridge companion to Christian political theology / edited by Craig Hovey, Elizabeth Phillips.
   pages cm. – (Cambridge companions to religion)
Includes bibliographical references and index.
ISBN 978-1-107-05274-1 (hardback) – ISBN 978-1-107-63380-3 (paperback)
1. Political theology. 2. Christianity and politics.
I. Hovey, Craig, 1974– editor of compilation. II. Phillips, Elizabeth, 1973– editor of compilation. III. Title: Companion to Christian political theology.
BR115.P7C234 2015
261.7–dc23   2015022167

ISBN 978-1-107-05274-1 Hardback
ISBN 978-1-107-63380-3 Paperback

Cambridge University Press has no responsibility for the persistence or accuracy of URLs for external or third-party Internet Web sites referred to in this publication and does not guarantee that any content on such Web sites is, or will remain, accurate or appropriate.

Contents

Notes on Contributors page ix

Preface xi

Part I ***The Shape of Contemporary Political Theology***

Mid-Twentieth Century Origins of the Contemporary Discipline

1 European Political Theology 3
JÜRGEN MOLTMANN

2 Liberation Theology 23
MIGUEL A. DE LA TORRE

3 Public Theology 44
HAK JOON LEE

Political Theology and Related Discourses

4 Catholic Social Teaching 67
LISA SOWLE CAHILL

5 Protestant Social Ethics 88
D. STEPHEN LONG

Twenty-First Century Reimaginings

6 Postliberalism and Radical Orthodoxy 110
DANIEL M. BELL JR.

7 Postcolonial Theology 133
SUSAN ABRAHAM

Part II ***Contemporary Questions in Political Theology***

The Contemporary Discipline and Traditional Sources

8 Scripture 157
CHRISTOPHER ROWLAND

9 Augustinianisms and Thomisms 176
ERIC GREGORY AND JOSEPH CLAIR

Issues

10 Liberalism and Democracy 197
CRAIG HOVEY

11 Capitalism and Global Economics 218
PHILIP GOODCHILD

12 Political Theology as Threat 236
WILLIAM T. CAVANAUGH

Ends

13 Good Rule 256
PETER J. LEITHART

14 Eschatology and Apocalyptic 274
ELIZABETH PHILLIPS

Index 297

Notes on Contributors

Susan Abraham is Assistant Professor of Theological Studies at Loyola Marymount University. She is the author of *Identity, Ethics, and Nonviolence in Postcolonial Theory: A Rahnerian Theological Assessment* (2007) and coeditor of *Shoulder to Shoulder: Frontiers in Catholic Feminist Theology* (2009).

Daniel M. Bell Jr. is Professor of Theology and Ethics at the Lutheran Theological Southern Seminary. He is author of several books including *Liberation Theology after the End of History* (2001), *Just War as Christian Discipleship* (2009), and *Economy of Desire* (2012).

Lisa Sowle Cahill is J. Donald Monan, SJ, Professor of Theology at Boston College. Her most recent publications include *Global Justice, Christology and Christian Ethics* (2013), *Bioethics and the Common Good* (2004), and *Theological Bioethics: Participation, Justice and Change* (2005).

William T. Cavanaugh is Director of the Center for World Catholicism and Intercultural Theology and Professor of Catholic Studies at DePaul University. He is coeditor of the journal *Modern Theology* and author of six books, most recently *The Church as Field Hospital* (2015).

Joseph Clair is Director of the William Penn Honors Program and Assistant Professor of Religious Studies at George Fox University. He is coeditor of *Maritain and America* (2009), and author of *Discerning the Good in the Letters and Sermons of Augustine* (2016).

Miguel A. De La Torre is Professor of Social Ethics and Latino/a Studies at Iliff School of Theology, and the author of more than thirty books. He served as the 2012 President of the Society of Christian Ethics and is the current Executive Officer of the Society of Race, Ethnicity, and Religion.

Philip Goodchild is Professor of Religion and Philosophy at the University of Nottingham. Among his books are *Deleuze and Guattari: An Introduction to the Politics of Desire* (1996), *Capitalism and Religion: The Price of Piety* (2002), *Theology of Money* (2007/2009), and, as editor, *On Philosophy as a Spiritual Exercise: A Symposium* (2013).

Eric Gregory is Professor of Religion at Princeton University. He is author of *Politics and the Order of Love: An Augustinian Ethic of Democratic Citizenship* (2008), and various articles in Augustine studies, moral and political theology, and the role of religion in public life.

Notes on Contributors

Craig Hovey is Associate Professor of Religion at Ashland University and Executive Director of the Ashland Center for Nonviolence. He is the author of numerous books including *Bearing True Witness: Truthfulness in Christian Practice* (2011).

Hak Joon Lee is Professor of Theology and Ethics at Fuller Theological Seminary. He has published several books, including *The Great World House: Martin Luther King, Jr. and Global Ethics* (2011) and *Shaping Public Theology: The Max L. Stackhouse Reader* (coedited, 2014).

Peter J. Leithart is President of the Theopolis Institute in Birmingham, Alabama, and author, most recently, of *Gratitude: An Intellectual History* (2014) and *Traces of the Trinity* (forthcoming).

D. Stephen Long is Cary M. Maguire University Professor in Ethics, Southern Methodist University. His work is in the intersection of theology and ethics. His most recent publication is *Saving Karl Barth: Hans Urs von Balthasar's Preoccupatio* (2014). His forthcoming work is *The Perfectly, Simple Triune God: Aquinas and His Legacy*.

Jürgen Moltmann is Professor Emeritus of Systematic Theology at the University of Tübingen. He is author of *Theology of Hope* (1967) and *The Crucified God* (1974).

Elizabeth Phillips is Tutor in Theology and Ethics, Westcott House, Cambridge. She is author of *Political Theology: A Guide for the Perplexed*, and contributor to several volumes on topics including justice in Christian ethics, theological ethnography, and Christian Zionism.

Christopher Rowland was Dean Ireland's Professor of Exegesis of Holy Scripture at the University of Oxford until his retirement in 2014. His recent publications include *Blake and the Bible New Haven* (2011) and, with Christopher Morray-Jones, *The Mystery of God: Early Jewish Mysticism and the New Testament* (2009).

Preface

Three things are undeniable when it comes to discussions of the contemporary state of political theology. First, there is a significant resurgence in interest in political theology within the academy. Increasing numbers of books are being published in the field, and increasing numbers of political theology courses are being offered. Second, this increased interest has not arisen from a single locus, and its motivations and expressions are numerous. Differing inquiries carried out under the same name, "political theology," are specializations within theology, political science, political philosophy, Continental philosophy, Critical Theory, and history of philosophy. An online search for syllabi in political theology brings up courses offered in universities and seminaries, by theologians, political scientists, philosophers, and historians. Third, if there is any way to draw together all these differing types of political theology under one heading, having something vaguely to do with how the theological and the political impinge upon one another, we see that this is not an area of interest limited to the academy. Questions surrounding the political assertions of various fundamentalisms, secularism and secularization, real and perceived conflicts between the political values of the Christian West and global Islam, ongoing rumblings of postcolonial struggles – these and many more – feature routinely in the headlines and in popular conversation. Our historical moment is ripe for the kind of sustained exploration of theopolitical questions we seek to address here.

This slim volume, however, is not an attempt to address the entire breadth of this resurgence or of all the relevant current issues. Nor have we attempted a comprehensive introduction to all the major sources, thinkers, and doctrines of political theology. We commend *The Blackwell Companion to Political Theology*, edited by Peter Scott and William T. Cavanaugh, as an excellent and relatively comprehensive introductory companion of that sort.

In this volume, our particular interest is in political theology as a focus of Christian theology – an inquiry carried out by Christian theologians in relation to the political, where the political is defined broadly to include the various ways in which humans order common life. The structure of this volume is itself meant to make an argument about that field of inquiry. Because of the focus of this argument, many relevant thinkers, movements, and issues have been excluded. We could not hope to make a coherent argument about all of global political theology, and have in reality only addressed those political theologies outside the English-speaking West that have impinged most directly and influentially upon academic theology in the English-speaking West. We have not attended sufficiently to Africa, Southeast Asia, or the political theologies of Eastern Orthodoxy.

In addition, due to the length of this volume, thinkers, movements, and topics that deserve attention in their own right are dealt with in relation to one another. Black theology and feminist theology in particular deserve their own chapters. Including a chapter on eschatology and not on the other key Christian doctrines is also a clear limitation. Finally, due to our own limitations as editors, we are certain that other oversights and unintentional exclusions will be called to our attention in the reception of this volume. We welcome these questions as these are the conversations that keep scholarship moving forward and that make Christian theology a living tradition.

The argument of this volume about the contemporary discipline of political theology relates to how it has emerged over the past century and the types of questions it now addresses in its various forms. In Part I, we explore how the discipline has taken shape in recent decades. We contend that the current shape of political theology is best understood as having been most influenced by three mid-twentieth-century streams: the distinctive political theology of Europe following World War II, liberation theology's prominence in Latin America as well as in the liberative politics of black and feminist theologies, and public theology's quest for wide, popular appeal in the diverse communities of the United States.

Since its ancient beginnings, the political has always been an unmistakable and inextricable thread within Christian theology and practice. Yet, as the various threads of theology were picked apart in the specializations of the modern academy, and as the various settlements of the church and the modern state were negotiated in Christian practice, something of the political thread seemed to have dropped somehow. In the mid-to-late twentieth century, diverse Christian voices began to say that Christianity must regain its political presence in relation to specific problems. German theologians began to question the inwardness of European Christianity, and grappled with the complicity of this Christianity with the politics of the Third Reich. In Chapter 1, Jürgen Moltmann, one of these pioneering political theologians, gives his account of the emergence and task of political theology.

However, from the mid-twentieth century, Europe was no longer the uncontested center of Christian theology in the west. In other locations and contexts, liberative political theologies also arose in roughly the same period. Black theologians in the United States began to question the politics of white Christianity, and to question how Christianity became co-opted to support slavery and segregation. Women theologians questioned the sexism of Christian doctrine and practice, bringing into theology the critical insight of feminism that the personal is the political. And Catholic laypeople and clergy began to question the Christianity of Latin America, which propped up oppressive regimes and was voiceless in the face of extreme poverty and suffering. In Chapter 2, Miguel De La Torre discusses the origins and continuing work of liberation theologies, showing the distinctive ways that these advance from the perspectives of oppressed peoples.

Nearer the end of the twentieth century, new political theologies arose in North Atlantic contexts in response to concerns about secularization, the loss of Christianity's public voice, questions about religious pluralism, and hopes for the revitalization of civil society. In Chapter 3, Hak Joon Lee describes the impetus for public theology, especially its distinctive and determined attempt to shed Christianity's preference for "sectarian" ways of framing social and political issues at the expense of a wider moral consensus.

In each of these three streams – with differing social catalysts, sources, interlocutors, and themes – theologians sought to recapture some dimension of politics that they identified as lost or endangered in the theology and practice of Christianity in their contemporary contexts. Yet the political had never been absent from Christian practice, nor had it disappeared in theology in the preceding century. Political theology must be understood in relation to two related and overlapping discourses. In Catholic thought, politics has been central in Catholic Social Teaching, while in Protestant theology, political issues have been approached through the lens of social ethics. In Chapters 4 and 5, Lisa Sowle Cahill and D. Stephen Long, respectively, relate political theology to these two discourses.

The decades surrounding the turn of the century have seen both a continuation of the three original streams of political theology as well as significant shifts that have changed the agenda for other political theologians. We understand three movements in particular as both the inheritors of the work of the first generation of political theologians in the three streams, as well as key critics of some aspects of that generation's assumptions and agendas: postliberalism, Radical Orthodoxy, and postcolonialism. In Chapter 6, Daniel Bell argues that Radical Orthodoxy is a postliberal political theology. In Chapter 7, Susan Abraham outlines the challenges faced by theologies that attempt to display and reflect on freedom after European colonialism.

There are some questions that cut across all these distinctions between schools of thought, movements of particular moments, and overlapping discourses. We address three types of questions in Part II. First, there are the questions of how contemporary political theologies relate to the traditional sources of the Christian tradition. Primary amongst these is, of course, Christian scripture. In Chapter 8, Christopher Rowland explores the retrieval of the political in biblical studies, focusing especially on eschatology and politics in the New Testament. Outside of scripture, the two most influential, critiqued, and debated sources are the works of Augustine and Aquinas. In fact, many have argued or assumed that there are two basic forms of Christian political theology: Augustinian and Thomistic. In Chapter 9, Eric Gregory and Joseph Clair argue instead that there are important and neglected resonances between the political theologies of Augustine and Aquinas, and propose a contemporary Augustinian-Thomism.

Second, there are the questions raised by the pressing issues of contemporary politics. We address only three of what could be a much more extensive list in a longer volume, which would certainly include contemporary issues related to the environment, race, violence, sexuality, and gender, to name only a few. In Chapter 10, Craig Hovey investigates the theological case for versions of democracy, especially in light of its contemporary liberal forms. In Chapter 11, Philip Goodchild considers the relevance of Christian political teachings to contemporary capitalism and the global economy. And in Chapter 12, William Cavanaugh considers the perspectives of those who consider political theology to be a dangerous threat.

Finally, we argue that political theology must be assessed in terms not only of its diverse approaches and the various issues that it approaches, but in terms of its ends. In Chapter 13, Peter Leithart considers the political *telos* of good rule and the obligations of political sovereignty to use power in service to public rather than private goods. And in the final chapter, Elizabeth Phillips argues for the interrelatedness of eschatology, apocalyptic, and creation in Christian theopolitics.

Part I

The Shape of Contemporary Political Theology

*Mid-Twentieth Century Origins of the
Contemporary Discipline*

1 European Political Theology
JÜRGEN MOLTMANN

WHAT IS THE POINT OF POLITICAL THEOLOGY TODAY?

Isn't the modern world committed to the principle of strict separation of church and state and of religion and politics? Did we not secularize politics, when we made it democratic? Isn't it the case that in democracies "all power originates from the people"? What do the politicians of any country know about religion and what do the authorities of religious communities know about politics? If one speaks of "political theology," is one not advocating that we return to a situation in which theologians intervene politically, like the mullahs in Iran or the cardinals in the *ancien régime* in France, or even a situation in which one might envisage the establishment of a theocracy? How can there even be such a thing as a political theology, if the fundamental conviction of the modern world about politics and religion is that "religion is a private matter"?

My intention in this essay is to sketch a path from the old forms of politicized religion and theology to the New Political Theology of Christianity, which was fully engaged in criticism of public affairs in the tradition of prophets. When the terrorism of National Socialism was raging unabated on the streets of Germany, only a very few Christians protested; most retreated into the sphere of their private lives and obeyed the God-given "constituted authorities"(Rom. 13:1). The New Political Theology was born of this scandalous and shameful episode.

After Auschwitz, Christian faith is no longer a private matter in Germany, and theology belongs in the realm of the public discussion of political freedom, social justice, and the future of the earth. Apartheid was the origin in South Africa of a theology liberated from racism. "The poor" are the origin in Latin America for the development of a political theology of liberation. "Han," the pain and anger of the oppressed, was the origin in South Korea of the political Minjung-theology, a "theology of the people." White racism was the origin in the United States of the public theology of the civil rights movement under Dr. Martin Luther

King Jr. Everywhere in the Christian world new political theologies have arisen, all of them with an ecumenical dimension. I limit myself in this essay to the developments in Europe and concentrate especially on those in Germany, because I have been a part of them.

There are at least four different types of political theology in Europe: (1) the theological formulation of the age-old political religion; (2) the modern conflict between anarchism and political sovereignty, and between terrorism and the politics of safety; (3) the New Political Theology of Christian resistance against privatization of faith and political idolatry; and (4) engagement for social justice, just peace, and the integrity of creation.

POLITICAL RELIGION

The term *political theology* was coined in pre-Christian stoic philosophy as the *genus politikon*: "Panaitius delineated three classes of God-figures: natural powers thought of as persons, the Gods of the state-religion, and the Gods of the myths (genus physikon genus politikon and genus mythikon)."[1] The Roman Marcus Terrentius Varro (116–27 BC) spoke of the "natural theology" of philosophers and the "political theology" of the citizens. Augustine referred to this distinction in *De Civitate Dei*.[2]

What was, and to some extent still is, political religion? According to the ancient doctrine of the state, worship of the gods of city, country, and empire is the state's supreme purpose (*finis principalis*). The state's gods provide for the prosperity and peace of the people, so the citizens must provide for their appropriate worship. The favor of these Gods is won through public sacrifice, but if there are famines, pestilences, natural catastrophes, and wars, they are signs that the gods are angry because of blasphemy, insufficient cultic observance, or the disobedience of the citizens. The people must do penance, as once in Nineveh, make special sacrifices, or slay the wicked who are in their midst.

To ensure the favor of the gods was the preeminent task of ancient rulers worldwide, for they all were priestly kings. The Roman Caesar was the *pontifex maximus* of Rome's state god. The Chinese emperor certainly stood over his subjects as "Son of Heaven," but if he fell into disfavor with heaven and his country was visited by famine, plague, earthquakes, and floods, he could be overthrown. The Moloch of Carthage demanded children as sacrifices; the Aztecs and Mayas offered their Gods still-quivering hearts. These political religions were *do ut des* religions in which the relationship between deity and worshippers was one of contractual exchange.[3] Blasphemy was the worst of crimes, because it was not directed against human beings but against the protecting gods. The blasphemer had to be eliminated and put to death. In the late Roman Empire, Jews and Christians were persecuted whenever misfortunes and disasters happened. They were accused of "atheism" because they did not worship the Caesar cult.[4] As late as 1706 the law and theology faculties in the University of Tübingen declared jointly: "That blasphemy was the most horrible and greatest of crimes, whereby God could easily be moved to wrath and could avenge the outrage on the whole land through famine, earthquake and pestilence."[5]

Political religion embraced not only the human but also the natural world. The human state had to be governed in congruity with surrounding nature. The sovereign was responsible for peace not only in the human world but also in the world of nature. Chinese political religion was founded in the harmony of heaven and earth: in spring the emperor acted as the "first man of the land" at the agricultural altar in Beijing.

In the European tradition the correspondence between the monarchical structure of the cosmos and the political monarchy of the one ruler was observed.[6] Aristotle quoted in his Metaphysics XII a word of Agamemnon in Homer's Iliad ("But the world must not be governed badly: 'The rule of the many is not good; let one be the ruler.'")[7] and turned this political idea into cosmology. The order of the cosmos is: one god – one logos/nomos – one universe. The corresponding political order is: one emperor – one law – one empire. This type of divine monarchy was always imperialistic. This was not limited to European monarchies. A famous word of the Mongol Lord Genghis Khan, reportedly spoken in 1254 to Franciscan monks who tried to convert him, shows that this was a universal political religion from Rome to China and everywhere: "In heaven there is no other than the one, eternal God, on earth there is no other than the single lord Genghis Khan, the Son of God. This is the word being said to you."[8] Monotheism – whether religious or metaphysical – served monarchism and imperialism in politics.

With the Constantinian turn, Christianity changed from a persecuted minority to a tolerated religion (*religio licita*) and finally to the general political religion of the Christian Empire. Byzantium became the center of the world and the mirror of heaven on earth.[9] But the connected imperial claim overcharged the power and the possibilities of the state and was a reason for its decay. The originally critical Christian eschatology was changed into the political ideology of the Christian Empire: the kingdom of Christ has no end. The Christian Empire combined the *Pax Romana* with the *Pax Christi*. The Christian

Caesar represented Christ the *cosmocrator*; his rule was an absolute rule, an *imitatio Dei* and an *imitatio mundi*. Political structure had to be understood as the image of heaven. Ceremony at court was a political liturgy worshipping God and his image on earth. The Christian Caesar was the unique source of power and law in the empire and his role was without limits. The Christian emperor was also the protector of the Christian church. In the name of the political imperial religion he had to unify the various churches and different theologies. Nicaea (325) and Chalcedon (450) were the results. Swords were converted into Christian swords and warfare limited by the criteria of a just war. This idea of a Christian political religion and theology was alive in Moscow, "the Third Rome," until 1917.[10] The symphony of religion and politics in this form is traditional Orthodox "political theology" until today. Constantine and Helena are saints and the last tsar and his family, killed in 1917, are venerated as holy by the Russian Orthodox Church and the Russian people.

However, the Constantinian turn did not only create a Christian imperial religion but also – in opposition – a monastic movement. Beginning with Antonius in Egypt, Christians turned away from the world seeking the "beyond" in eremitic or monastic life.[11] Since that time we have, on the one hand, the Christianity of the world and, on the other hand, the Christianity of the religious orders; political secularization was answered with a religious desecularization.

On the theoretical level this was discussed between Erik Peterson and Carl Schmitt. The church historian Erik Peterson wrote his famous treatise "Monotheismus als politisches Problem" (1935) against the *Political Theology* of Carl Schmitt (1922, 1934) and defended the provocative theses: (1) The doctrine of the divine monarchy was already wrecked on the Trinitarian dogma, and (2) the *Pax Romana* idea failed the transcendent character of Christian eschatology. With these developments in Christian theology "monotheism as political problem" is "finished" and Christian faith was "liberated" from the political pressure of the Roman Empire.[12] Christian proclamation of the gospel can no longer be misused to justify political power: the mystery of the Trinity is only in God, not in a creature, and only God can give the peace Christians seek – no Caesar can do this.

Peterson wrote this treatise with salient reference to the year 1933 in Hitler's Germany. Carl Schmitt answered in 1970 with a small book, *Politische Theologie II: Die Legende von der Erledigung jeder Politischen Theologie*.[13] His argument was that theological critique does not do away with the theory and phenomenon of political religion;

political theology is not only possible (contra Peterson) but is necessary until Christ's return. Neither Peterson nor Schmitt discussed a political theology of the crucified Christ, though Jesus was crucified in the name of the *Pax Romana*.

ANARCHISM/TERROR VERSUS SOVEREIGNTY/SAFETY

The modern concept of "political theology" was introduced into a now worldwide debate by the German professor of constitutional law, Carl Schmitt. His American partner was Leo Strauss. Schmitt took this term for his doctrine of political sovereignty from the Russian anarchist Mikhail Bakunin who wrote the book *Gott und der Staat* (1871) with the famous slogan: "Neither God nor state" (ni Dieu – ni maître). Bakunin condemned any domination of humans over humans in state and society and proclaimed liberation from divine and human authority. "If God is, man is a slave; now man can and must be free; then God does not exist."[14] Satan was the first rebel, free thinker, and world liberator because he persuaded human beings to disobey God and eat the fruit of knowledge. Bekunin was a strong materialist: the human being is an animal and the brain a machine.

For Carl Schmitt, God and state constitute that sovereignty that is able to suppress Bakunin's "neither God nor state" anarchism. Schmitt did not borrow the term *political theology* from the ancient world but from Bakunin, who used the phrase as a derogatory label for the work of his opponent, Mazzini. Schmitt argued that "all significant concepts of the modern theory of the state are secularized theological concepts."[15] In his own political theology he referred to Catholic philosophers of the counterrevolution in the nineteenth century: Bonald, de Maistre, and Donoso Cortes. There is no medium between catholicity and atheism, and so there is no medium between authority and freedom. But what is sovereignty? "Sovereign is he who decides on the state of exception."[16] Thus article 48 of the Weimar Constitution in Germany declared a "dictatorship of the president of the Reich."[17] Schmitt defended the dictatorship of Hitler in 1933 as a legitimate act of political sovereignty: "The will of the Fuhrer is law" because he believed *"non veritas sed auctoritas facit legem."*

Schmitt saw the conflict between the sovereignty of the state and anarchy against the background of the apocalypse of world history. He believed in the apocalyptic idea of the final battle at Armageddon of God against Satan, which was the reason, in his opinion, that the world was already engaged in a permanent civil war. He proclaimed the "friend-or-foe-relationship: whoever is not for us, is against us" and called this the existential political category. The archetype for this friend-or-foe distinction is the distinction between God and Satan, which is heading for a decisive battle.[18] God's revelation inaugurates this decision between those who believe and those who become enemies of God. Unbelief is blasphemy and rebellion against God. The fact that we have not yet reached this apocalyptic end of history is due to a mysterious *katechon* (2 Thess. 2:7). The power of delaying the end of the world by restraining evil is the sovereign authority of the state: "I believe in the *katechon*; for me he is the sole possibility for a Christian to understand history and find it meaningful."[19] The *katechon* is the evil-suppressing state and is for Schmitt the only explanation of the delay of the *parousia* of Christ.

The modern politics of safety against terrorism is very much like Carl Schmitt's doctrine of unlimited sovereignty of the state against revolution and anarchy. Schmitt's ideas are influential for conservatives and "neocons" in America, where his friend Leo Strauss popularized his thought. American politics reacted to the terror of 9/11 in 2001 with the Patriot Act, allowing the president to act as in a permanent state of exception. The results are suspension of civil liberties for American citizens, an illegitimate prison in Guantanamo, the unlimited surveillance of the world by the National Security Agency, and the killing of terrorists by drones where ever they may be found. "America is at war," declared President George W. Bush. The friend-or-foe distinction suits the political doctrine of the United States. Since its inception there has been a dualistic doctrine of friend and foe, good and evil, apocalyptically oriented on the millennial role of "one country under God," the "redeemer nation"[20] for the rest of the world.

THE NEW POLITICAL THEOLOGY

The New Political Theology emerged in Germany under the shock of Auschwitz. We survivors of World War II associated with the Shoah of the Jewish people not only the moral catastrophe of our own people but also the shame of Christianity. Why was there so little resistance? We found two patterns of behavior in the Catholic and Protestant political traditions, which apparently led to the failure of churches and Christians. First was the widespread opinion of the middle class that religion is a private matter and has nothing to do with public life and politics – an inward emigration that allowed external crimes to happen on the streets. Second was the Lutheran tradition of two kingdoms – the separation between spiritual and worldly powers that asserts that Christians are free in their faith but obedient to the given political power (Rom. 13). Only when the Nazis attacked the churches, forcing obedience to their ideology, did some Protestant congregations resist in the Confessing Church, whose Barmen Declaration of 1934 stated, "The Church must remain the Church." But there was no protest on behalf of persecuted Jews.

After a century-long antimodern defense strategy, the Roman Catholic Church opened itself to the world in Vatican II (1962–5). *Gaudium et Spes* and *Populorum Progressio* were influential for the famous *aggiornamento*. They demanded a new theology with its face to the world. Catholic fundamental theologian Johann Baptist Metz began with a "theology of the world," and saw the relationship of church and world in the light of a "political theology."[21] He established political theology not as a special theological discipline in ethics or social teaching, but rather as the public consciousness of church and theology in modern times. In *Theology of the World*, Metz touched on two points: (1) Political theology is the critical correction of the privatization of modern religion ("Religion is a private matter") and of modern theology as transcendental, existential, or personalistic. (2) Political theology is a formulation of the eschatological Christian message under the condition of modern society. The church must become a "social-critical institution," and theology must be a liberating account of faith and hope.

Metz came to political theology through his teacher and friend Karl Rahner. Rahner had introduced the "anthropological turn" into modern Catholic theology. Metz went one step further: "The attempt to interpret theology in a totally existential or personalistic way is an important accomplishment of theology.... This existential-anthropological theology, however, easily becomes isolated from the world and history, when eschatology is not seen to be more basic to theology. Only in the eschatological horizon of hope does the world appear as history."[22] Because he understood my *Theology of Hope* so well at this point, I gladly took up his challenge ("Every eschatological theology must become a political theology which is a socio-critical theology"), and became the second representative of the New Political Theology in Germany.

What distinguished the New Political Theology from the old political theologies was the determining subject: the subject of the old political theologies was the political religion of the power of the state or of revolutionary movements; the subjects of the New Political Theology are the church and Christian communities in society. This is an important difference, because at the center of Christian faith stands not the divine monarchy, but the resurrection of the Christ who died on the Roman cross. For Metz, the cross of Christ is the reason why the scandal and the promise of salvation are public, not private or purely religious. Christ did not die between two candles on an altar but outside of the city, executed at Golgotha. Metz went on to develop his political theology further as a theology of the world of suffering and compassion.[23]

The Kirchenkampf (church struggle) of 1934 to 1945 and the Confessing Church protest against the Nazi dictatorship left Protestant theologians after the war with the need for a political theology. Dietrich Bonhoeffer joined the military resistance and was murdered on April 9, 1945 at Flossenbürg.[24] Paul Tillich emigrated to New York in 1933. Karl Barth was forced to return to Switzerland in 1936. The first problem discussed was political preaching: Must the preacher avoid politics or must he or she prophetically address public questions? Does she or he know more about political solutions as every informed citizen, or must she or he address those who suffer under political power and those who are disoriented by those powers?

After the end of the alliance of throne and altar, the Protestant church was no longer a state-church. The church was to use her new freedom for prophetic public declarations and had to develop a public or political theology of her own. Apartheid, atomic rearmament, hunger in Africa, and homelessness in Germany became questions of Christian faith and ethics, and the answers were often different from the German government. Lutheran theologians revised their age-old doctrine of two kingdoms and became engaged in the public field for justice, peace, and the integrity of creation. But old state-church Christianity on the European continent had problems with democracy and civil liberties that developed in free-church contexts in America or in French *laicité* (secularism).

I began my contribution to this conversation with a political theology of the cross.[25] With Pontius Pilate, a politician came into the Christian confession of faith. Jesus of Nazareth was condemned and executed as an enemy of the Roman Empire. The inscription on the cross told the reason for his execution: INRI, *Jesus Nazarenus Rex Judaeorum*. Whether this was an error or not is irrelevant. The empire condemned Jesus, but God raised the crucified one from the dead and elevated him to his kingdom. The Roman Empire is condemned by God, the Father of Jesus Christ.[26] What the state intended as shame received the highest glorification of God. Those who believe in the resurrection of the crucified one see the divine glory on the face of Christ and no longer in the face of the politically powerful. For those who believe in the glory of the crucified one, every divine legitimation is withdrawn from political power. All that is left is the human legitimation of political power. The Christian martyrs who died in Roman arenas because they refused the Caesar cult knew this and died "with Christ."

The crucified Christ has a strong idolatry-critical power for those who follow him. Power enables idolatry of the worst and most dangerous kind. Whoever touches the political idols of the powerful must die.[27] This was the case in the religious nationalism of the nineteenth and twentieth centuries: the "holy Fatherland" demanded millions of victims. This was even more the case in the totalitarian dictatorships of fascism and Stalinism in the twentieth century where opponents and dissidents were eliminated. This is also the case in the globalized capitalism of the twenty-first century, which impoverishes the many to make a few rich. The natural feeling of empowerment is divine; the feeling of powerlessness creates anxiety and is degrading. All human idols are fixed on power. The resurrection of the powerless Jesus shows that God's weakness is stronger than "all rule, authority and power" of this world (1 Cor. 15:24).[28] Following the crucified one is the power of the powerless.

Political and civil religions serve the symbolic integration of a nation. They also serve the self-righteousness of the people. The critic of this self-idolization of nations serves the humanization of men and women and the universalism of the kingdom of God. If there is no theological affirmation of a religious justification of political power "from above," the political field is free for a legitimation of political power "from below," from the people instead of from the gods or the beyond. "Give to God what is God's and to the Caesar what is Caesar's" – this word of Jesus separated God from Caesar, reducing Caesar to a human being. In the long run this paved the way from divine political monarchy to democracy and a "government of the people, by the people and for the people," as Abraham Lincoln said in his famous Gettysburg address. Political power is to be separated, given only limited time, and must be used according to the law and the constitution, the covenant of the citizens. Wherever government rule is illegal, illegitimate, or against human rights, resistance is a duty. According to article 14 of the Scottish Confession of Faith (1560), Christians have "to repress tyrannie, to defend the oppressed" as part of their love of neighbor.[29] Today capitalism must be democratized. "The cross is our political critic; the cross is our hope for a politics of freedom. The memory of the crucified Christ is our reason for political theology."[30]

The most well-known and most controversial prophetic voice of the New Political Theology of postwar Germany was Dorothee Sölle. She was a protester and a poet, a praxis-oriented and experience-grounded theologian. Political praxis precedes theology as much as the experience of God. She combined mystical spirituality and political resistance in a unique way. She became the theologian of groups protesting against nuclear rearmament and environmental destruction, against capitalism and socialist dictatorship. Her theology arose from the "death of God" movement and started with a book on Christ "after the death of God."[31] Through the Kölner Nachtgebet (evening prayer at Cologne, 1969–71) for the "politization of the conscience" she became famous for political prayer and an actualization of the Psalms. In 1971 she departed from Rudolf Bultmann's existential hermeneutics: "Theology must reflect her own social and political situation in the conflict of her time."[32] Bultmann's hermeneutic was apolitical: his religion was a private matter, and he refused to join the movement against atomic weapons in the 1950s. The New Political Theology was, however, only one the first step for Sölle. When Latin American liberation theology became widely known after 1972, Sölle joined this way of doing theology for the poor and the oppressed. She would also go on to identify with feminist theology, seeking the liberation of women from age-old patriarchal domination into full autonomy and equal human rights. But at the end of her life she returned to mystical spirituality, for which she had written an early book, Hinreise.[33]

Mysticism is the "longing for God," who is the "mystery of the world." Mystical spirituality is in all world religions, and, at the same time, above all religious institutions as "the anti-authoritarian element." Mysticism is the true unity of all different religions and secular longings. In her 1997 book *Mystik und Widerstand: "du stilles Geschrei,"* she "democratized" the otherwise often elitist mystical experience.[34] Mystical experience can happen every day to everyone. United with the mystery that is named "God," one's self is liberated from the ego, possessions and violence, and greed and anxiety. This is the best preparation for resistance against a wasteful, consumerist society and an alternative life: "A different world is possible." Dorothee Sölle's ideas are similar to Thomas Merton's "contemplation in a world of action" (1965) and Roger Schutz and the Taize-spirituality of "lute et contemplation." Her last and unfinished book, *Mystik des Todes,* is on the mystery of death. This is no longing for dying but for a full and free life in God, as we can experience it in mystical moments of the *nunc aeternum*.

A sociocritical theology of the world will meet other critical movements and theories in society. In the Western world this was Marxism and the Critical Theory of the Frankfurt School. The New Political Theology was often interpreted as socialist theology, while the traditional theologies of churches and universities remained conservative. It was in 1968 that the student revolts in Paris and Berlin, in Berkeley and Mexico City reached a climax. These were young people's revolts, a cultural revolt, a radical democratic movement, and a socialist experiment. It was out of this student revolt that Helmut Gollwitzer's socialist theology emerged.[35] Gollwitzer was a strong Barthian and a pastor of the resisting church during the Nazi dictatorship, but it was the students in Berlin who convinced him of the "capitalist crime against humanity" and a "revolution of life" that was required. Capitalism was going to end in the downfall of humanity, unless there was a turn to life. In this conversion from destructive greed to love for life he saw the dawn of the kingdom of God in this perverted world. His "Theses on Revolution as a Theological Problem" were passed from hand to hand. He tried to find an authentic location for the church in the so-called class struggle of the present. His colleague Friedrich-Wilhelm Marquardt found a combination of theology and socialism in the early writings of Karl Barth.[36] The Lutheran Ulrich Duchrow combined anticapitalism with antiimperialism.[37] George Casalis in Paris proclaimed a "planetary class struggle" between the poor and oppressed people of Third World countries and the rich nations in the First World. He went to Nicaragua to join the Sandinistas against the Somoza dictatorship. Richard Shaull in Brazil was the first to introduce "revolution" into ecumenical theological debates. Many Catholic theologians who had studied in Europe developed in Latin America revolutionary and Marxist theories and joined the struggle of the people for liberation. There was a lively exchange of ideas between political theologies in Europe and Latin America, though not without conflict. Marxism became en vogue through the religious neo-Marxism of Ernst Bloch and the sharp social criticism of the Frankfurt School of Max Horkheimer, Theodor W. Adorno, Herbert Marcuse, and Jürgen Habermas. This New Left movement in the West was not supported by the Stalinists in the Soviet world or the Maoists in China, but rather feared. The outcome in Latin America was liberation theology, started by Gustavo Gutiérrez.[38] In Europe it was a radical democratic political theology of human rights and the rights of nature. That is to say, the critique of capitalism and imperialism of Karl Marx was taken over, while the Stalinist form of socialism was refused. In

Protestant theology, a new materialist exegesis emerged: so-called socioeconomic hermeneutics. The Marxist presupposition is that the economic context makes the religious text; one must therefore interpret the religious text in the given sociohistoric context and conflicts in order to bring the readers of the religious text into the struggle to overcome capitalism and colonialism today. Sociohistorical hermeneutics may be the only lasting fruit of the socialist theology of the 1970s.

I now conceive of the term *political theology* more broadly than Metz and I did in the beginning, as a designation for theological reflection on the concrete political practice of Christianity. Christians participate in the public affairs of their societies and the world because they hope for the kingdom of God and anticipate the justice and peace of the new earth as much as they can. *Kairos*, context, and community shape the political hermeneutics of the Christian message.

POLITICAL THEOLOGIES OF JUST PEACE AND ENVIRONMENTAL JUSTICE

A divided Germany was always the center of military confrontations between the superpowers. Around 1980 the situation heated up through the mutual arms race. Nowhere in the world were so many atomic bombs warehoused as in West and East Germany. The people responded to this with a large peace movement. Human chains stretched from Stuttgart to Ulm and continual protests in Mutlangen and other military installations indicated resistance on a massive scale. The Protestant Church in West Germany published a position paper on peace, and the Reformed Church called out for a *status confessionis*: "Either atom bombs or Christ."[39] Historic peace churches such as the Mennonites were the role model for everyone who decided "to live without armaments." In the demonstrations against the nuclear terror, which was called "mutual deterrence," nonviolence was practiced. Jesus's Sermon on the Mount became a guideline for protesting Christians, and because evoking it became dangerous, West German politicians dabbled in political exegesis. The Federation of Protestant Churches in East Germany repudiated solemnly "the spirit, logic and practice" of the weapons of mass destruction.[40]

In Leipzig's Nikolaikirche there was a small group who met every Monday for peace prayer beginning in 1980. In the fall of 1989 this peace circle served as the initial spark for the massive demonstrations that toppled the East German socialist dictatorship. It was a nonviolent triumph against violence. With the cry, "We are the people," Germans struggled for the first time in their history for democracy. It was the first successful revolution in Germany, and a nonviolent one. Peaceful change from dictatorship to democracy was possible. The downfall of the Soviet Empire followed as well as other revolutions throughout Eastern Europe. In Latin America military dictatorships gave way to democratic governments.

It was clear to me how Christians should respond to violence: do not turn swords into Christian swords, and do not be satisfied with only Christian plowshares, but turn the swords into plowshares.[41] This is a politics of disarmament while building up just peace. This is the conversion of the war industry into a peace industry. Peace in a violent world can be achieved through confidence-building measures. Peace is not the absence of violence, but the presence of justice. Peace is not a given situation, but a process of reducing violence and constructing justice in the social and the global relationships of humankind.[42]

The long European Constantinian era thus comes to an end. The time of Christian swords is over. The Church becomes an ecumenical church of peace independent of the state and the political interests of the powerful. There is no valid theological doctrine of a just war anymore but only the new theological doctrine of just peace, as it was decided in the International Ecumenical Convocation on Peace in Kingston, Jamaica, in 2011.[43]

Alongside the new political theology of just peace, there has arisen a new political theology of nature.[44] The universal ecological crisis demands a complete reform of Christian theology and spirituality: We need not only peace on earth, but also peace with the earth. We stand at the end of the modern age and at the beginning of the ecological future of our world, if our world is to survive. A new paradigm is in the process of developing, which links human culture and the nature of the earth differently from the way they were linked in the paradigm of modern times. The modern age was determined by the human seizure of power over nature and its forces. This domination and exploitation of nature have come up against their limits.

As early as 1962, Rachel Carson published *The Silent Spring* and awakened environmental awareness in America and beyond. The Club of Rome demonstrated *The Limits of Growth* in 1972.[45] The Chernobyl disaster of 1986 made large parts of Belorussia uninhabitable and took more than 140,000 human lives. Finally, the Fukujama catastrophe of 2012 in Japan warned the world. Universal climate change is producing man-made natural disasters of typhoons, tsunamis, and the rising water level of the oceans. Yet people seem to be paralyzed by a kind of ecological numbing, and the world conferences of the United Nations are not very effective against national interests.

Why do we need a new theology of all things? Because it was modern theology in the West that determined the human relationship to nature and the concept of human lordship over the earth – the concepts of *dominium terrae* and *imago Dei*.[46] It was a concept of God without the world and of a world without God. The monotheism of a transcendent God cleared the path for the mechanistic view of nature. As God is the omnipotent lord and owner of the universe, man as his image must become the mighty lord and owner of the earth: "Subdue the earth and have dominion over every living thing" (Gen. 1:28).

A new picture of the human being is emerging: from the center of the world to a cosmic integration, and from the arrogance of world domination to a cosmic humility.[47] Anthropocentric anthropology gives way to integral anthropology: before human beings can "subdue the earth" they are part of the nature of the earth, and whatever the special human position may be, they are members of the great earth-community of living beings.[48] In theological terms, before human beings are *imago Dei* they are *imago mundi*, creatures of the earth, "earthlings" (Gen. 2:7). Before human beings assume any rule over the earth, or any responsibility for creation, the earth cares for them. It is not that the earth is entrusted to us; we are entrusted to the earth. The earth can live without human beings, but we cannot live without the earth. The Earth Charter says rightly, "Humanity is part of a vast evolving universe. Earth, our home, is alive with a unique community of life."[49] And, as ecofeminism has noted, this integral anthropology would also end the domination of the soul over the body and the domination of men over women.

Modern theology has always seen the earth only as something that human beings are supposed to subdue, but many premodern cultures and religions have said the earth is "our mother" (Eccles. 40:1). Can one subdue one's own mother?[50] Modern ecological theology starts with the assumption that the earth is our home.[51] What is the earth? New astro-sciences have shown the interactions between the nonliving and the living spheres of the earth. The result is the idea that the earth's biosphere, together with the atmosphere, the oceans, and land masses, forms a unique and complex system that has the capacity to bring forth life and create habitats. This is James Lovelock's much-discussed and influential Gaia theory.[52] This theory corresponds to the wealth of biblical traditions about the earth: the earth is a creative creature and "brings forth living creatures ..." (Gen. 1:24); there is a direct covenant of God with the earth (Gen. 9:13); the divine Spirit is the earth's creative life power (Isa. 32:14); the Messiah is a fruit of the earth (Isa. 4:2); and God has reconciled the cosmos through the risen Christ (Col. 1:20).[53]

Modern theology has made a strict distinction between God and the world: God is unworldly – the world is not divine but secular.[54] Ecological theology is moving from this godless world to the world in God and God in the world with the help of Trinitarian thinking: God the Father created the world through the Son/Logos in the energies of the Spirit. It follows that the world is seen as a nondivine being interpenetrated by God through the energies of the Spirit. God is present in every created being. Some call this panentheism, others prefer to speak of the cosmic *schechina* of God or the *perichoresis* of God in the world and the world in God (see 1 John 4:16).

Christian spirituality was and is mostly a spirituality of the soul and the beyond. The redeemed go to heaven and leave the earth behind. They were only guests on earth. The new spirituality will be an earth spirituality. Human beings are earthlings and the earth is our home.[55] The new spirituality is seeking contact with the cosmic Christ through the spirit of the earth.

Like socialist theology and the theology of just peace, ecological theology aims to stir up Christians to participate in these initiatives and in them to realize their own visions. By contrast, like the other movements, ecological theology also brings the problems of society and a globalized world into the church, so that the Christianity is present in the promise and the sufferings of human beings and the nature of the earth.

CONCLUSION

At the end of our investigation we must ask about the limits of political theology. A theology that faces toward the world will not see in that world only politics, and the politics that it sees is no longer the omnipotent power it once seemed to be. Rather politics now seems increasingly to have to follow along behind economics and must take account of ecology. This is the reason for the proposal that has recently been made in the United States to speak of "public theology" rather than "political theology." Political theology, on this conception, should be understood as an important part of public theology, but is not the only part. Public theology treats issues that arise from the globalization of the media, of the economy and finance, and from world politics. Christian theology was always ecumenically oriented, that is directed to the whole of the inhabited globe, just as the Christian Church has always understood itself as a Catholic Church. The more globalization makes us more aware of the universality of Christian theology and of the Christian Church, the more theology and the Churches must self-critically free themselves from nationalism and from the forms of imperial colonization of the world by the "Christian" nations of Europe and America. Only by doing that can Christian theology become a source of the power of life for all humans. These should be the tasks of political and public theology in the future.

One must keep in mind that every Christian theology has its political causes and its political effects. The task of political theology is to make theology aware of these and to judge them in the light of the gospel.

Notes

1 Max Pohlenz, *Die Stoa*, Vol. I (Gottingen, 1964), p. 198. All translations from German texts are my own.
2 Ernst Feil, "Von der 'politischen Theologie' zur 'Theologie der Revolution'?" in *Diskussion zur "Theologie der Revolution,"* ed. E. Feil and R. Weth (München Mainz, 1969), pp. 113–17; Siegfried Wiedenhofer, *Politische Theologie* (Stuttgart, 1976); Alfredo Fierro, *The Militant Gospel* (London, 1977); Alisdair Kee, ed., *A Reader in Political Theology* (London, 1971).
3 Jürgen Moltmann, *Ethics of Hope* (London: SCM Press, 2012), pp. 169–77, 191–4.
4 Adolf von Harnack, "Der Vorwurf des Atheismus in den ersten drei Jahrhunderten," in *Texte und Untersuchungen zur Geschichte der altchristilichen Literatur*, XXVIII, 4 (Heft, 1905), p. 10.
5 Ansgar Skriver, *Gotteslasterung?* (Hamburg, 1962), p. 24.
6 Erik Peterson, "Monotheismus als politisches Problem (1935)," in *Theologische Traktate* (München, 1951), pp. 49–105; Dazu A. Schindler, *Monotheismus als politisches Problem? Erik Peterson und die Kritik der politischen Theologie* (Gutersloh, 1978).
7 Homer, *The Iliad*, 2:204, quoted in Aristotle, *Metaphysics*, XII:X.
8 Michael de Ferdinandy, *Tschingis Khan. Steppenvolker erobern Eurasien* (Hamburg, 1958), p. 153.
9 Franz Geog Maier, ed., *Byzanz. Fischer Weltgeschichte Band 13* (Frankfurt, 1973), pp. 31–43.
10 Hildegard Schaeder, *Moskau – das Dritte Rom. Studien zur Geschichte der politischen Theorie in der slawischen Welt* (Darmstadt, 1963).
11 Hans Conrad Ziegler, *Als die Religion noch nicht langweilig war. Die Geschichte der Wustenvater* (Koln, 2001).
12 Peterson, "Monotheismus als politisches Problem (1935)," pp. 104–5; Carl Schmitt, *Political Theology II: The Myth of the Closure of Any Political Theology*, trans. Michael Hoelzl and Graham Ward (Cambridge: Polity Press, 2008).
13 Recently translated into English: see note 12.

14 Michael Bakunin, *God and the State* (New York: Dover Publications, 1970), p. 17.
15 Carl Schmitt, *Political Theology: Four Chapters on the Concept of Sovereignty* (Chicago: University of Chicago Press, 1985), p. 36.
16 Ibid., p. 6.
17 Carl Schmitt, "The Dictatorship of the President of the Reich According to Article 48 of the Weimar Constitution," in *Dictatorship: From the Origin of the Modern Concept of Sovereignty to Proletarian Class Struggle*, trans. Michael Hoelzl and Graham Ward (Cambridge: Polity, 2014), pp. 180–226.
18 Heinrich Meier, *Carl Schmitt and Leo Strauss: The Hidden Dialogue* (Chicago: University of Chicago Press, 1995); *The Lesson of Carl Schmitt: Four Chapters on the Distinction between Political Theology and Political Philosophy* (Chicago: University of Chicago Press, 1998).
19 Meier, *The Lesson of Carl Schmitt*, p. 162.
20 Ernest Lee Tuveson, *Redeemer Nation: The Idea of America's Millennial Role* (Chicago: University of Chicago Press, 1968); Jürgen Moltmann, "Die 'Erlöser-Nation.' Religiose Wurzeln des US-amerikanischen Exzeptionalismus, in Die Friedens-Warte," *Journal of International Peace and Organization* (2003), Band 78, Heft 2-3/2003, S. 161–173; Francis Schüssler Fiorenza, "Prospects for Political Theology in the Face of Contemporary Challenges," in *Political Theology: Contemporary Challenges and Future Directions*, ed. Francis Schüssler Fiorenza, Klaus Tanner, and Michael Welker (Louisville, KY: Westminster John Knox, 2013), pp. 37–60.
21 Johann Baptist Metz, *Zur Theologie der Welt* (München-Mainz, 1968); *Theology of the World*, trans. William Glen-Doepel (New York: Scribner, 1969); H. Peuckert, Diskussion zur "politischen Theologie," (München-Mainz, 1969).
22 Metz, *Theology of the World*, p. 90.
23 Johann Baptist Metz, *Mystik mit offenen Augen. Wenn Spiritualitat aufbricht* (Freiburg, 2011); *Memoria Passionis. Ein provozierendes Gedachtnis in pluralistischer Gesellschaft* (Freiburg, 2006).
24 Eberhard Bethge *Dietrich Bonhoeffer, A Biography* (Minneapolis, MN: Augsburg Fortress, 1999).
25 Jürgen Moltmann, "Theologische Kritik der Politischen Religion," in *Kirche im Prozess der Aufklarung*, ed. J. B. Metz, J. Moltmann, and W. Oelmuller (München-Mainz, 1970), pp. 11–51; Moltmann, *On Human Dignity: Political Theology and Ethics*, trans. M. Douglas Meeks (Philadelphia: Fortress Press, 1984).
26 G. W. F. Hegel, *Philosophie der Religion*, Werke Band 16, 2, 198.
27 Jon Sobrino, *Sterben muss, wer an Gotzen rührt. Das Zeugnis der ermordeten Jesuiten in San Salvador* (Freiburg, 1990).
28 Paul expected these powers and authorities of the world to be "annihilated" (1 Cor. 15, 24), while Eph. 1, 10 and Col. 1, 20 see them "reconciled" and "integrated" into the reign of Christ the cosmocrator.
29 Karl Barth, *The Knowledge of God and the Service of God According to the Teaching of the Reformation* (London: Hodder and Stoughton, 1960), p. 124.
30 Moltmann, *Kirche im Prozess der Aufklärung*, p. 51.

20 Jürgen Moltmann

31 Dorothee Sölle, *Stellvertretung. Ein Kapitel Theologie nach dem "Tode Gottes"* (Stuttgart, 1965); *Christ the Representative: An Essay in Theology after the "Death of God,"* trans. David Lewis (Philadelphia: Fortress Press, 1967).
32 Dorothee Sölle, *Politische Theologie. Eine Auseinandersetzung mit Rudolf Bultmann* (Stuttgart, 1971); *Sympathie. Theologisch-politische Traktate* (Stuttgart, 1979); *Aüfrustung tötet auch ohne Krieg* (Stuttgart, 1982); D. Sölle and F. Steffensky, eds., *Politisches Nachtgebet in Köln*, Vol. I (Stuttgart-Mainz, 1971); *Politisches Nachtgebet in Köln*, Vol. II (Stuttgart-Mainz, 1972).
33 Dorothee Sölle, *Hinreise. Zur religiösen Erfahrung. Texte und Uberlegungen* (Stuttgart, 1975); *The Inward Road and the Way Back*, trans. David L. Scheidt (Philadelphia: Fortress Press, 1978).
34 Dorothee Sölle, *Mystik und Widerstand. "Du stilles Geschrei"* (Hamburg, 1997); *The Silent Cry: Mysticism and Resistance* (Philadelphia: Fortress Press, 2001).
35 Helmut Gollwitzer, *Die kapitalistische Revolution* (München, 1984); *Forderungen der Umkehr. Beitrage zur Theologie der Gesellschaft* (München, 1975); *Krummes Holz – aufrechter Gang. Zur Frage nach dem Sinn des Lebens* (München, 1979).
36 Friedrich-Wilhelm Marquardt, *Theologie und Sozialismus. Das Beispiel Karl Barths* (München, 1972); George Casalis, *Correct Ideas Don't Fall from the Skies: Elements for an Inductive Theology*, trans. Jeanne Marie Lyons and Michael John (Maryknoll, NY: Orbis, 1984); Helmut Gollwitzer, *An Introduction to Protestant Theology* (Philadelphia: Westminster John Knox Press, 1982).
37 Ulrich Duchrow, *Alternativen zir kapitalistischen Welt wirtschaft* (Gutersloh, 1994).
38 Gustavo Gutierrez, *Teologia de la liberacion* (Salamanca, 1972); *A Theology of Liberation* (New York: Orbis, 1973; repr. 1988).
39 *Das Bekenntnis zu Jesus Christus und die Friedensverantwortung der Kirche, Eine Erklarung des Moderamens der Reformierten Kirche* (Gutersloh, 1982).
40 B. Klappert and U. Weidner, ed., *Schritte zum Frieden. Theologische Texte zu Frieden und Abrustung* (Wuppertal, 1983).
41 For a transformative ethics because of a transformative eschatology cf. Jürgen Moltmann, *Ethics of Hope*, trans. Margaret Kohl (London: SCM Press, 2012). For the separatist option cf. Stanley Hauerwas, *The Peaceable Kingdom: A Primer in Christian Ethics* (Notre Dame, IN: University of Notre Dame Press, 2002).
42 Still worth reading is Immanuel Kant, "Zum ewigen Frieden. Ein philosophischer Entwurf," in *Werke Band VI*, ed. W. Weischedel (Darmstadt, 1964), pp. 191–251.
43 Konrad Raiser and Ulrich Schmitthenner, *Gerechter Friede. Ein ökumenischer Aufruf zum gerechten Frieden, Ökumenische Studien 39* (Munster, 2012).
44 This is the title of Peter Scott, *A Political Theology of Nature* (Cambridge: Cambridge University Press, 2003).

45 Donella and Dennis Meadows, *The Limits to Growth* (London: Pan Books, 1972).
46 Jürgen Moltmann, *Man: Christian Anthropology in the Conflicts of the Present* (Philadelphia: Fortress Press, 1974).
47 Richard Bauckham, *The Bible and Ecology: Rediscovering the Community of Creation* (London: Darton, Longman and Todd, 2010).
48 Larry Rassmussen, *Earth Community Earth Ethics* (Maryknoll, NY: Orbis, 1996).
49 Earth Charter International, "The Earth Charter," http://www.earthcharterinaction.org/content/pages/Read-the-Charter.html.
50 Leonardo Boff, *Ecology and Liberation: A New Paradigm* (Maryknoll, NY: Orbis, 1995).
51 Geiko Müller-Fahrenholz, Heimat Erde. *Christliche Spiritualitat unter endzeitlichen Lebensbedingungen* (Gütersloh, 2013).
52 James E. Lovelock, *Gaia: A New Look at Life on Earth* (Oxford: Oxford University Press, 1979); Rosemary Radford Ruether, *Gaia and God: An Ecofeminist Theology of Earth Healing* (New York: HarperCollins, 1983); Sallie McFague, *The Body of God: An Ecological Theology* (Minneapolis, MN: Augsburg Fortress, 1993).
53 Matthew Fox, *The Coming of the Cosmic Christ* (New York: HarperCollins, 1988).
54 Bill McKibben, *The End of Nature* (New York: Random House, 1989).
55 Celia Deane-Drummond, *Creation through Wisdom: Theology and the New Biology* (Edinburgh: T&T Clark, 2000); Jürgen Moltmann, *The Spirit of Life: A Universal Affirmation* (Minneapolis, MN: Fortress Press, 1992); Michael Welker, *God the Spirit* (Minneapolis, MN: Augsburg Fortress, 1994); Larry Rassmussen, *Earth-honoring Faith* (Oxford: Oxford University Press, 2013).

Further Reading

Metz, Johannes Baptist, *Theology of the World*, trans. William Glen-Doepel. New York: Scribner, 1969.
Moltmann, Jürgen, *The Spirit of Life: A Universal Affirmation*. Minneapolis, MN: Fortress Press, 1992.
  The Ethics of Hope, trans. Margaret Kohl. London: SCM Press, 2012.
Rassmussen, Larry, *Earth-honoring Faith*. Oxford: Oxford University Press, 2013.
Ruether, Rosemary Radford, *Gaia and God: An Ecofeminist Theology of Earth Healing*. New York: HarperCollins, 1983.
Schmitt, Carl, *Political Theology: Four Chapters on the Concept of Sovereignty*. Chicago: University of Chicago Press, 1985.
  Political Theology II: The Myth of the Closure of Any Political Theology, trans. Michael Hoelzl and Graham Ward. Cambridge: Polity Press, 2008.
Scott, Peter, *A Political Theology of Nature*. Cambridge: Cambridge University Press, 2003.

Sölle, Dorothee, *Christ the Representative: An Essay in Theology after the "Death of God,"* trans. David Lewis. Philadelphia: Fortress Press, 1967.
The Inward Road and the Way Back, trans. David L. Scheidt. Philadelphia: Fortress Press, 1978.
The Silent Cry: Mysticism and Resistance. Minneapolis, MN: Fortress Press, 2001.

2 Liberation Theology

MIGUEL A. DE LA TORRE

We live in a world where from 2010 to 2012, 850 million people (12.5 percent of the population) were hungry and malnourished.[1] By 2010, of the seven billion earth inhabitants, about 1.75 billion in 104 countries, consisting of about a third of their population, lived in multidimensional poverty. The 2008 Great Recession only exasperated the situation, pushing 64 million more people under the $1.25 a day poverty threshold. In Africa alone, it is estimated that an additional thirty thousand to fifty thousand children died as a direct result of the 2008 financial crises.[2] Underdevelopment at the global periphery, liberationist theologians will argue, is a by-product of the development of the global European center.

We live in a world where the global economic policies known as neoliberalism produce much of the dispossession, destitution, and disenfranchisement experienced by the least among us. What was once colonialism, where world powers occupied other's lands to extract natural resources and human labor, has been replaced with a modern form of global exploitation. The gluttonous consumption of the world's resources by First World nations is not only morally indefensible, but also, according to liberationist thinkers, the root cause of much of the present global political instability. This instability is a breeding ground for violence, fertilizing the mind-set that birthed the 9/11 terrorist attacks. Former UN general secretary Kofi Annan, reminds us: "No one in this world can feel comfortable or safe while so many are suffering and deprived."[3]

Global oppression exists. But does a religious response uttered from the depths of inhuman condition also exist? Liberationists argue that ignoring the world's oppressed borders on idolatry, replacing materialism for spirituality. Resistance to the powers and principalities of this world responsible for so much global misery becomes foundational to what will eventually be termed *liberation theology*. In fact, any spiritual movements (not necessarily Christian) that seek to dismantle the global social structures responsible for causing so much poverty and

23

oppression can be called *liberative*. I argue a subtle difference exists between liberation theology and liberative theologies. Liberation theology is rooted within Christian faith (originally Catholic), while liberative theologies need not be Christian. Liberative religious movements can be found among Muslims, Hindus, Buddhists, or even Humanists.[4]

LIBERATION THEOLOGY'S ORIGINS

Resistance exists whenever and wherever oppression rules. When this resistance is based on the people's spirituality, it could be understood as a liberative response to the political. In the Western hemisphere, this liberationist spirit can be traced to those originally considered heathens. As Christians massacred indigenous people, a voice of resistance arose in the form of a chieftain named Hatuey who carried out guerrilla-style warfare against the invaders. Eventually captured and condemned to death, a Franciscan friar attempted to convert Hatuey with the promise of heaven and the threat of hell. Prior to lighting the faggots that would burn the Indian leader alive, the friar promised mercy in the form of strangulation if Hatuey converted. Hatuey apparently asked whether Christians would be in heaven. Upon hearing an affirmative response, the condemned warrior chose death for he did not want to go where he would be with such cruel people. Although not a Christian, Hatuey is probably the first liberative figure to resist oppression in the Western Hemisphere. Hatuey, and many others like him, stood in solidarity with the subjugated by struggling against the European Christian forces responsible for causing systematic oppression.

Nevertheless, Bartolomé de Las Casas is considered to be the first predecessor to liberation theology. Gustavo Gutiérrez writes, "Among those with the keenest interest in Bartolomé de Las Casas today are Latin America's liberation theologians, who have recognized in the Dominican friar a prophetic forerunner of the church's radical 'option for the poor.'"[5] Renouncing riches and slaves, Las Casas joined the Dominican order, dedicating his life to seeking justice for Indians. Becoming Christ's witness to so-called heathens, Las Casas realized that it was he, the priest and missionary, who was living without God. By equating salvation with the establishment of social justice, Las Casas understood that unjust treatment of the Indians placed the conquistadores' salvation in jeopardy. For Las Casas, and liberationist theologians who would follow, Jesus Christ was the "least of these," the one suffering hunger, thirst, nakedness, alienation, infirmity, and incarceration (Matt. 7:21–27). Conversion became the process in which one comes to know Christ as one of the disenfranchised, and the action taken to develop a lifestyle of solidarity with the marginalized.[6] Although Christian conquerors defined Indians like Hatuey as "unbelievers," the Indians' humanity makes them sacred because they possess the *imago Dei* (the image of God).

The Native American scholar George Tinker critiques the liberation theologian's forerunner, insisting Las Casas "was in the final analysis thoroughly committed to european colonialism and the exploitation of Indian lands and labor. His concession to his christian conscience was to promulgate 'a greater conquest' conducted by the church on behalf of his royal majesties in Spain."[7] Even though Las Casas protected Indians from bodily genocide, he remained complicit in cultural genocide, extinguishing and substituting indigenous culture with European centered value systems.

The early 1800s saw the rise of Latin American nationalistic fervor which birthed independence wars. Emerging nations sought to maintain the same control over the church previously held by Spain. Christendom, the space carved out by royal ruling power, provided religious legitimacy to existing political social structures. When local elites sought independence, the Church, usually the largest landholder and main conservative political force, was perceived to be an enemy. Most local bishops sided with the crown, as popes made proclamations against independence movements. Although the dispossessed took up arms, their plight remained unchanged once independence was achieved. Rather than submitting to crown and church, they were now subjugated to the commercial class and local landholders.

Independence brought laws confiscating land from those whom local elites viewed as backward, specifically the lands of the church, religious orders, and Indians. In time, the church aligned itself with the interests of the landowning class to counter the rise, in the latter 1800s, of Liberals with their anticlerical Enlightenment views. Although independence was declared, Latin America soon found itself dependent on the economic power of first the British Empire, and then the United States.[8] Conditions of economic subjugation throughout Latin America were created, especially in Central America, eventually giving rise to a spiritual and religious movement called liberation theology.

LIBERATION THEOLOGY'S BIRTH

Liberation theology was influenced by the works of educator Paulo Freire, specifically his concept of *conscientização*, or consciousness raising. Liberation theologians attempt to move away from Christendom's complicity with political and economic oppressive structures that contribute to the people's false-consciousness. Through praxis, understood as action, those who are oppressed move from being objects toward subjects of their own destiny. Although false-consciousness and praxis have roots in Marxist theory of social class, Freire and the liberationist thinkers that followed him emphasize false-consciousness as myth responsible for keeping the oppressed silent, accepting through socialization, religion, and education, a false reality that benefits oppressors' privileged space. Rather than the Marxist move of dismissing religion as an opiate, the liberationist's task is to raise consciousness through faith convictions, calling for radical praxis that can transform political structures responsible for repression.

Freire argues that "the radical, committed to human liberation, does not become the prisoner of a 'circle of certainty' within which reality is also imprisoned. On the contrary, the more radical the person is, the more fully he or she enters reality so that, knowing it better, he or she can better transform it."[9] The liberationist's radical belief in Jesus's promise of an abundant life in the here-and-now, not just some afterlife (John 10:10), rejects anything that prevents realizing this promise. Abundant life, this process of humanization, is not limited to the oppressed; it also exists for oppressors also living under false-consciousness. They too need liberation. Hence, liberation theology is not simply a political movement to free the marginalized from oppressive structures; it is a religious movement striving to bring salvation – liberation – to those falling short of God's will to live abundant and fruitful lives.

U.S. foreign and economic policies and the multinational corporations whose interest the U.S. protects (e.g., the United Fruit Company) have been a major cause of poverty throughout Latin America that denies many the promise of abundant life. Resources and raw material flow from the periphery toward the center to ensure supremacy of the world's elite. Oppression is institutionalized to maintain the privileged position of the so-called developed. The response must thus move beyond charity. Dom Hélder Câmara, a Brazilian archbishop, said it best, "When I give food to the poor, they call me a saint. When I ask why the poor have no food, they call me a communist."

Liberation theology began with Christian Base Communities (*comunidades eclesiales de base*, CEBs) in the late 1950s. CEBs' aims were pastoral, not political. The dispossessed gathered to discover how to turn their Christian conviction into a liberative reality. Until then, many within Christendom were taught that poverty was God's will. Now they learned that poverty was caused by oppressive political and economic structures. At CEBs, Freire's model of *conscientização* facilitated the poor to become active agents. Priests served as advisors, training the laity to lead discussions, usually around a methodology known as "see-judge-act." They learned to implement the gospels' liberating message within their lives, as they sought salvation – understood as liberation from all sins (communal and individual). Within normative theological discourse, theology is understood to be a first act upon which praxis, as second act, is based. Liberation theology turned this methodology on its head by making theology a second act, a reflection of praxis, or actions, taken by the poor.

The 1959 Cuban Revolution contributed to the rise of liberation theology. For the first time in Latin America, a Catholic nation fell to an anti-Catholic communist regime. But the revolution was first and foremost a Third World rebellion against U.S. subjugation and the passive role Christendom played. Rural guerrilla movements, inspired by the Cuban example, sprung up throughout Latin America. In response, Pope John XXIII invited missionaries to Latin America in 1961, asking North American and European religious orders to send 10 percent of their clerics. Fearing advances made by "Marxists," some representatives from European and U.S. churches who went to serve the poor became radicalized when they encountered the depths of their new parishioners' poverty.

Papal literature also contributed to liberation theology in the form of Catholic Social Teaching, which focused on the church's response to political, economic, and social concerns, culminating with the Second Vatican Council (1962–5). Moving away from hierarchical societal control, the Church redefined itself as being on pilgrimage with humanity. The Church moved away from Christendom and its alignment with the powerful and committed itself to service and to be in solidarity with the oppressed. Probably the most important document developed at Vatican II was *Gaudium et Spes*, which called the Church to identify with the hopes, joy, grief, and trials of humanity. The document asserted the Church's independence from political and economic structures while maintaining responsibility for passing moral judgment on such matters.

In the midst of the Vatican's new progressive thoughts, Latin American political regimes became more oppressive, as illustrated by the 1964 Brazilian military coup. Religious leaders disappeared; those who didn't became radicalized as they witnessed the disappearance of the parishioners and colleagues. Many fled, taking their progressive liberationist ideas with them, cross-fertilizing the new communities in which they sought refuge. Some chose a different path and fought back. Dealing with repression in his own homeland, Camilio Torres, a Colombian priest, found it difficult to carry out his duties within the official Church's power structures. Hanging up his holy vestments in 1965, he chose to align himself with the church's poor and join the Columbian guerrilla revolutionary forces. In 1966, he died a violent death during battle; nevertheless, his radicalization inspired other young leftist revolutionaries.

About six hundred bishops from Latin America attended Vatican II's opening session. Upon their return, several began to wrestle with how to implement the council's conclusions in the Latin American context. To that end, the General Conference of the Latin American episcopacy (CELAM II), also known as the Medellín Conference, was held in 1968. Attended by 146 bishops and their staff, the conference proclaimed that "[t]he Latin American bishops cannot remain indifferent in the face of the tremendous social injustices existent in Latin America, which keep the majority of our people in dismal poverty, which in many cases becomes inhuman wretchedness."[10] The conference pondered how the Church can remain faithful within the context of U.S.-backed right-wing military dictatorships and asked what God's response is to the suffering of the poor. By the end of the conference, those attending realized that involvement in controversial political programs and movements was faithfulness toward a radical option for the poor. Those participating in the economic development conversations that arose from the Medellín conference rejected the language of development and instead chose the proactive word *liberation*. Probably the most important publication, and what became the definitive description of liberation theology, was a book written by Gustavo Gutiérrez titled *Teología de la liberación* (1971), published in English as *A Theology of Liberation* (1973). The book described a grassroots, praxis-based theology committed to the poor.

LIBERATION THEOLOGY'S MESSAGE

Liberation theology is a spiritual response to the everyday sociopolitical realities of oppressed people. Liberation thinkers argue that liberation is salvation, using both terms interchangeably. More than simply liberation from sin, personal or corporate, salvation is achieved through the consciousness-raising process of learning how oppressive structures prevent the abundant life promised by Christ. Theology is more than simply creating, expanding, or sustaining doctrinal beliefs. Understood as a reflection of praxis, theology must respond to inhuman conditions experienced by the majority of humanity. A salient characteristic of liberation theology is its ability to reconcile the theoretical and theological with pastoral concerns, rooted with the people's daily experience of disenfranchisement. From the underside of power and privilege, a religious view is developed from which to address structural injustices.

Liberationists argue that *all* theology is contextual (including Eurocentric-based theologies), because they're rooted in the social location of those seeking faith-based responses to their situation. If true, then different contexts produce different theological expressions. Not all who are disenfranchised have similar experiences. How African Americans understand theology that emphasizes racism differs from how Latin American women wrestle with theology's response to sexism. Hence, there cannot be one liberation theology, but many. While the starting point of liberative theological reflection remains the marginalized existential experience, the ultimate goal remains liberation from the reality of societal misery. Liberation theology is a praxis-centered methodology recognizing that, before theology can be done, connecting the spiritual with material realities is the first liberative act.

Implementation of liberation theology follows a "see-judge-act" paradigm (borrowed from the 1930s Young Christian Workers). Liberationists "see" the oppression occurring. Through consciousness-raising they "judge" the causes of oppression; finally they commit themselves to "act." This action is a reflective praxis rooted on the oppressed social and political context. Such praxis brings us back to "see," where the impact of action is evaluated. This inductive methodology argues that theology is the second step as orthodoxy (correct doctrine) flows from orthopraxis (correct action). By contrast, Eurocentric theology is usually deductive – starting from some purported universal truth (e.g., the Bible or church teachings) and moving toward an act as a second step – thus, orthopraxis flows from orthodoxy. Only through justice-based praxis, engaged in transforming society, can individuals come closer to understanding God's will and revelation. Although the Catholic model of seeing, judging, and acting is helpful, I propose an ethical paradigm that expands this model to five basic steps forming a wider hermeneutical circle and therefore serving as the methodology for seeking justice.

The first step is observation, an attempt to understand why the present moral dilemma exists. To observe seriously considers the historical situation responsible for the oppressive circumstances faced by the marginalized. Understanding the disenfranchised social location requires exploring why, how, and when present oppressive structures were created and how they are normalized and legitimized. To observe is to consciously seek the disenfranchised voices, which are often excluded from history. An attempt is made to "see" through the dispossessed eyes of the poor, maltreated, and suffering, recovering their voices so as to provide a critique of the prevailing powers.

While the first step focuses on "seeing" the historical, how did we arrive to these present oppressive structures, the second step focuses on reflecting upon what is seen, an attempt to understand how social structures maintain oppression. Society cannot be transformed without first doing social analysis. Social sciences provide a means to collect raw data that can elucidate the marginalized reality. To show how social mechanisms maintain institutionalized oppression is to uncover the dominant culture's sin. No adequate response to oppressive structures can be made if the disinherited fail to fully understand how society created and preserved the economic, social, and political subjugation of the world's marginalized.

The third step, prayer, is an attempt to understand what should be the faith community's responsibility. Prayer is not limited to a private conversation with the Creator of the universe. Prayer encompasses a communal act by which marginalized faith community members stand in solidarity during trials and tribulations. Prayer establishes communities where the oppressed stories are critically listened to and where commitment to work in solidarity for full liberation, both spiritual and physical, takes place. To pray, for purposes of how it is being used within this hermeneutical circle, is to discern God's will. One way of discerning God's will is through a critical application of the biblical text to the moral dilemmas faced by those relegated to history's underside. To read the Bible as a community is to fuse the biblical narrative with the everyday experiences of marginalization, producing a biblical witness capable of addressing oppression.

The fourth step is praxis, a response based on what Christians claim to believe. Regardless of how sincere and noble those from the dominant culture appear, theorizing about justice changes nothing. Liberative theology from the margins is to *do*, not simply to *theorize*. Praxis moves beyond paternalistic "charity" toward actions that dismantle social structures detrimental to the majority of humanity.

The fifth and final step is reassessment, an attempt to insure that the action taken is faithful to the gospel message of liberation/salvation. This step asks if the implementation of praxis brought more abundant life to disenfranchised communities. If so, what additional praxis is required? If not, what should be done to replace the previous praxis with new and more effective actions? It is through the analysis of the effectiveness of actions taken that creates theology.

Reflecting on praxis leads to more correct doctrine. Praxis therefore forms doctrine, informs scriptural interpretations, and transforms ethical systems.[11]

To do liberation theology is to do it with and from the oppressed material perspectives. Liberationists seldom struggle with God's existence; they struggle with God's character. Whoever God is, God imparts and sustains life while opposing death. God is *presente* (present) wherever lives are threatened with oppression. This God hears the cries of the enslaved Hebrews, physically enters history, and leads God's people to the Promised Land. Entering history and standing in solidarity with the oppressed means that God takes sides over and against the rich and powerful, not because the marginalized are somewhat holier, but because they are oppressed. God makes a preferential option for the poor and oppressed, over and against the pharaohs of this world. This is the God whom the Hebrews called *Go'el*, the one who provides justice for the weak, makes a home for the alien, becomes a parent to the orphans, and comforts the widows – biblical shorthand for society's most vulnerable. The type of worship that best honors this God, where God finds pleasure, is in the doing of justice (Isa. 1:10–17).

Making a preferential option for the poor and oppressed means that God can never belong to the oppressors – mainly because Jesus is one of the oppressed. The last shall be first, the center shall be the periphery. In Matthew 25:31–46, Christ returns to earth to judge between those destined for the reign of heaven and those who are not. The blessed and the cursed are separated by what they did or did not do to the least among us. Specifically, did they feed the hungry, welcome the alien, clothe the naked, and visit those infirm or incarcerated? So that there is no confusion about God's preferential option, Jesus clearly states, "Truly I say to you, inasmuch as you did it to one of these, the least of my people, you did it to me."

The church is called to make the same preferential option God makes by identifying and standing in solidarity with the oppressed. To stand apart from marginalized faith communities is to exile oneself from hearing and discerning the gospel message of salvation – a salvation from the ideologies that mask power and privilege and the social structures responsible for their maintenance. José Comblin was among the first to insist that liberation theology must change to meet the new century's challenges. He realized that the Brazilian poor left rural lives of poverty, finding "liberation" by moving into urban areas to seek employment. This migration weakened the CEBs already decimated by decades of bloody rural repression. CEBs had been successful in outlying barrios, but not among middle-class traditional churchgoers within the parish center, nor among the very poor of the city and surrounding countryside. Economic changes as well as migration have since brought the CEBs to a standstill. Even people still struggling for land live in the city. And should they obtain land, they may choose to work it for a while but inevitably return to the city.[12]

Scholars such as Philip Berryman do not see the future belonging to the CEBs. Some CEBs have become a type of tourist spot where North American religious liberals can go to experience liberation theology in action, what Marcella Althaus-Reid calls the creation of theological Hollywood or Disney-churches for North American consumption.[13] Ironically, according to a popular Latin American saying, "While liberation theologians made a preferential option for the poor, the poor made a preferential option for evangelicalism." For Berryman, the future belongs to evangelical Protestantism, particularly in its Pentecostal form. The explosive growth of these non-Catholic groups is contributing to a new face of religious reality in urban Latin America. The emphasis that some evangelical Protestant groups place on prosperity theology makes this new religious movement more compatible with capitalist tenets. This new religious focus on personal piety and prosperity is not likely to challenge neoliberalism.

The miracle of the incarnation is not that God became human, but rather that God became poor. Jesus suffered oppression on the cross as a divine commitment to stand against injustices; a stance believers are called to emulate. While many Eurocentric theologians focus on Jesus's death as salvific, most liberationist view Jesus's entire existence as liberative – not solely his crucifixion. The crucifixion has less to do with a single act that produces atonement for sinners, and has more to do with being an act of solidarity. Through Jesus's ultimate act of solidarity with all being crucified, God knows what it means to exist in solidarity with all who today are crucified on the crosses of sexism, racism, ethnic discrimination, classism, and heterosexism.

Jesus taught that God's reign is for the here and now, not only some future hereafter. Nonetheless, the world's oppressed have heard countless sermons that it is "God's will" that they suffer in this life for rewards that await them in the next. Spiritualizing Christ's crucifixion ignores that his death was a political act. Crucifixion recognizes that death-dealing acts are the usual response from the authorities protecting their power and privilege. Seeking salvation/liberation strives toward establishing justice as God's reign on earth.

Leonardo Boff, a Franciscan priest, reminds us that what social analysis calls "structural poverty" faith calls "structural sin." And what analysis calls the "private accumulation of wealth" faith calls "the sin of selfishness."[14] Sin has a communal dimension. Western Eurocentric theology, in most cases, has made sin and its redemption personal. Conversion, however, is never personal; it must encompass social transformation. Because socioeconomic structures cause death, they are sinful – hence, the critique of capitalism. But is liberation theology Marxism in religious garb?

Critics have linked liberation theology with socialism or Marxism. It is true that most (if not all) liberation theologians express opposition to capitalism and multinational corporations. It is also true that a few liberation theologians have considered themselves to be Marxist (although several moved away from this self-identification). Marxist economic theories have been helpful in explaining the plight of the poor. Even though an overreliance on such theories has been employed, other aspects of Marxism are discarded, for example, Marx's rejection of God or his failure to consider sin. Nevertheless, liberationists insist on employing whatever social scientific methodologies best elucidate the causes of oppression. During the late twentieth century, that methodology was Marxism. Likewise, some liberationists today employ postcolonial and/or postmodern methodologies.

Liberation theologians have consistently argued that their commitment has always been for liberation, not to Marxist thought. Marxist economic theories may be helpful in explaining the plight of the poor, but they are only some of many conversation partners. The liberationist is more influenced by the Gospel of Mark than the Gospel of Marx.

LIBERATION THEOLOGY'S EARLY PROPONENTS

In the midst of Latin American carnage throughout the 1960s, 1970s, and 1980s, church leaders and thinkers risked their lives to articulate a theological reflection rooted in the plight of the oppressed, forging a theology where the blood of martyrs was routinely spilled. The early discourse was shaped by a willingness to stand in solidarity with the many being crucified. While not everyone can be mentioned, the following are some of the more prolific shapers of the discipline.

Gustavo Gutiérrez, a diocesan priest of indigenous ancestry is responsible for drafting many of the movement's early primary documents. His works provide a pastoral answer to the question of how

Christians can live a life faithful to God and the neighbor manifested as the poor. He sought a theology relevant and liberative at the underside of history. The goal of theology no longer was to understand the world, but to change it by liberating/saving humanity, the church, and society from idolatry, ideology, and alienation.

Leonardo Boff responds to the challenges faced by the church by accenting the communal aspect of the faith community. His major contribution has been creating a Christology "from below." For Boff, Jesus is foremost a liberator from all forms of sin and oppression, seeking nonviolent liberation from unjust political, social, and economic structures. This is a Christ rooted in the oppressed experiences, in open dialogue with the world, in seeking liberation for the voiceless from the structural evils that transcend individual evils, and in emphasizing liberation-in-act over liberation-in-thought.

Juan Luis Segundo was a Jesuit, considered to be one of the main architects of liberation theology. Theology for him was a reflection of everyday believers' experiences, not academic disciplines claiming neutrality or objectivity. Liberationists recognize that there exists no value-free perspective. Even though neutrality or objectivity is claimed, it still remains contextual. By focusing on the disenfranchised experiences, the church, committed to transforming oppressed reality, accomplishes its mission of serving the people through praxis that radically challenges the so-called objective worldview.

Claims by liberation theologians that they simply are articulating the theological reflections emerging from the grassroots faith community have been challenged by indigenous groups and non-Catholics because their theological articulations appear to be very Eurocentric and Catholic (as is evident in the footnotes of Gutiérrez groundbreaking work *Teología de la liberación*). When we consider that most of the poor are a mixture of races and cultures, we are left to wonder where the indigenous elements of the people's faith are incorporated. Some, like Vine Deloria and George Tinker, would argue that any liberation theology based on Catholic and European thought is destructive to indigenous cultures, for it continues the participation of "colonial" discourse hostile to native people. Missing from liberation theology are the faith-based reflections of the poor whose beliefs are shaped by non-European cultures and non-Christian faith traditions.

Segundo was the prominent thinker in the development of the hermeneutical circle, which interprets the biblical text in light of oppressed situations. The first step of the hermeneutical circle emphasizes an ideological suspicion of what is determined to be objective and normative. Second, ideological suspicion is applied to the entire ideological superstructure, attempting to "deideologize" theology. Third, experiencing reality leads toward suspicion of prevailing biblical interpretations for not considering all-important contexts based on the present reality. This leads toward a new hermeneutic, a way of interpreting scripture with new information in hand.

Jon Sobrino, a Jesuit from Spain, spent more than fifty years teaching and ministering in El Salvador, including during its civil war. He emphasized close parallels between Jesus's social location and the contemporary context of Latin Americans, hence the need to do Christology from the "underside of history," that is, the poverty into which Jesus was born and under which he lived, as well as his life under the imperial rule (Rome for him, the United States for Latin Americans). The oppressed are today's crucified people who, like Jesus, provide an essential soteriological perspective on history. Sobrino insists that God chooses those oppressed in history and makes them the principal means of salvation, just as God chose the "suffering servant," the crucified Christ, to bring salvation to the world. Sobrino taught and published with Ignacio Ellacuría, another Jesuit who served as rector of Central American University and focused on liberation theology's philosophical foundations. Along with six others, Ellacuría was martyred by the Salvadorian military on November 16, 1989.

José Porfirio Miranda, a Marxist philosopher, economist, ex-Jesuit, and biblical scholar emphasized the communal practices of the first Christians: selling their possessions and holding everything in common so that each could have according to their needs (Acts 2:44–45). To enter God's kingdom, one first had to renounce private property (Mark 10:21, 25); thus, only the poor could enter (Luke 6:20). No one can serve both God and capital (Matt. 6:24), forcing all, according to Miranda, to choose between the capitalism prominent in this world, or the communism advocated by the Bible.

Among Protestants, Enrique Dussel is a theologian, historian, and primary founder of the theme *philosophy of liberation*, which analyzes alienation caused by more than five centuries of colonization and imperialism. He explores the legitimization of the universal knowledge expounded by the ruling elites, paying close attention on how power, domination, and Eurocentric thought become identical. José Miguez Bonino, a Methodist minister, stresses that liberationists are not socialist or Marxist ideologues, but rather "a new breed of Christians" committed to form a new society comprised of liberated humans.

During the height of political repression, many liberation theologians avoided controversial issues like women's ordination, birth control, abortion, sexual orientation, or clerical celibacy (for Catholics). Missing from liberation theology was a feminist social critique. Elsa Tamez, a Methodist, is among the first to show how sexism is a major form of oppression. Among liberation theology's early proponents, one was hard pressed to find women contributing to the discourse, specifically as theologians. Those who did were usually relegated to what was considered the domain of women, like Mariology or an essentialized celebration of motherhood.

Not surprisingly, a backlash from the Roman Catholic Church occurred, as the Vatican sought to delegitimize liberation theology. Newly elected Pope John Paul II began to denounce some of liberation theology's tenets, even while speaking against social, political, and economic injustices. Cardinal Joseph Ratzinger (later Pope Benedict XVI), as prefect of the Congregation for the Doctrine of the Faith, launched a systematic persecution of liberationists. In early 1984, both Gutiérrez and Sobrino were investigated for possible unorthodoxies; Clodovis Boff and six other priests were removed from their teaching posts; and Leonardo Boff was silenced for one year.

During the 1980s, military dictatorships gave way to elected civilian governments. With the collapse of Communism and the election of leftists and a few former guerrillas to public office, some began to question liberation theology's relevance. Another consequence of the collapse of Communism was the globalization of "free markets." The rise of neoliberalism contributed to a series of economic and political changes both in Latin America and in the international arena. Faced with a new world order, many of the original statements and discussions of liberation theologians during the 1960s and 1970s were no longer relevant to present economic challenges.

These global changes led Gustavo Gutiérrez to declare during the 1996 American Academy of Religion conference that he did not believe in liberation theology; rather, he believed in Jesus Christ. Because liberationist thinkers believe theologies are contextual to a specific place and time, they insist theologies should be abandoned when they no longer address the needs of the faithful. Still, the poor and oppressed will continue to exist, and liberation theologians will continue to look to them when describing theological perspectives of marginalized faith communities. How then does liberation theology liberate itself from a social context that no longer exists?

NORTH AMERICAN LIBERATION THEOLOGY

Liberation theology argues that because it is contextual, it is unable to be exported into a different geographical or social location as if it were some sort of commodity. Nevertheless, conversations among different marginalized communities influence each other as they struggle with similar oppressive structures. Although influential, it would be erroneous to think liberation theology migrated from Latin America to North America. Theological perspectives always existed among the disenfranchised, explaining the different manifestations of liberation theologies formed in the north.

In 1975, twenty-five Latin American liberationists met with about 175 North Americans to discuss the significance of liberation theology within the United States. The "Detroit Conference" explored liberationist theological reflections from the global south perspectives, recognizing that even in the heart of the United States, areas of the "global south" exist. Members of U.S. disenfranchised communities, specifically feminists, African Americans, Latino/as, and Asian Americans attended. While these different groups shared commonalities by occupying marginalized spaces and struggling against the imposition of a dominant Eurocentric theological "norm," there also existed dissimilarity that pitted groups against each other, due mainly to their unexamined biases.

Feminists showed how Latin Americans ignored gender issues. African Americans were concerned about the lack of racial analysis. In return, the Latin Americans were critical of both groups for failing to do rigorous economic analysis. Feminists were challenged for not examining their white middle-class privileges. Women of color uncovered how their white sisters failed to scrutinize their racism, and how their ethnic and racial brothers failed to scrutinize their sexism. Missing were voices from what is now referred to as the LGBT community. It seemed that those oppressed in certain situations benefitted from oppression in other situations. Although similarities exist in theological perspectives among different marginalized communities, different contexts lead to different perspectives that, at times, conflict with other disenfranchised groups. This section will concentrate on some of these differences.

U.S. Feminist Theologies during the 1960s infused elements of Christianity ignored by dominant theological reflections with the reality of androcentrism – how being male becomes normative for all humanity. Feminist theologians challenged how Christianity legitimizes and normalizes male superiority. Feminist theologies can be understood as revolutionary, reformist, or reconstructionist.[15] Revolutionary feminist theology believes Christianity is beyond reform and advocates a post-Christianity that turns toward goddess traditions. Reformists do not advocate abandoning Christianity, but rather reforming the tradition by questioning the established role to which the church and society have relegated them. Finally, reconstructionists agree with the reformist commitment to Christianity; however, they make a liberationist call to transform both the faith and society. Reconstructionists, while not apologizing for Christianity's patriarchy, nonetheless recognize a liberative Christian message capable of dismantling faith and society's structural androcentrism.

Early feminists responded to sexism by interpreting the biblical text to show women's presence in early church life, serving as apostles, theologians, ministers, missionaries, and prophets. St. Paul was seen as patriarchalizing the new faith, making it more compatible with the sexism of his time. Applying a hermeneutics of suspicion, women scholars showed how men read their theology and gender biases into the text. Women's stories were recovered to reveal their wisdom and insight in doing theology, revising and reshaping the tradition so that it could be more liberative for all, women as well as men.

Bell hooks critiqued white feminist liberationists by calling for a theoretical expression rooted in the social location of nonwhite privileged women. Women of color need to respond to their community's sexism and to the racial, ethnic, and class prejudice existing within Anglo-feminist communities that ignore the fundamental ways white women benefit from the oppression of women of color. Moving beyond a male-female strategy that weakens a unified struggle for liberation, they remain concerned with the men of color who dismiss white feminism as a Eurocentric project incongruent with the ethos of their communities.

Black Theologies are a product of 250 years of slavery and a century of Jim and Jane Crow segregation. During the 1950s and 1960s, the civil rights movement was led by Christian liberationists like Martin Luther King Jr. and Muslim liberationists like Malcolm X. King stressed the freedom African Americans can achieve because God, working through black churches, stands in solidarity with them. Malcolm X sought liberation of colonized minds that reinforced subjugation to a white ideal that promoted black self-hatred. Black theologians and religious leaders stressed a God who willed freedom from racism and the social structures it undergirds. In 1969, James Cone published *Black Theology and Black Power*, synthesizing King's call for the black church to engage in radical institutional social change and Malcolm X's call for black self-love. The development of womanist (black women pastors and theologians) thought in the mid-1980s contributed to both feminist and black theology. Womanist theology can be understood as "the systematic, faith-based exploration of the many facets of African-American women's religiosity ... based on the complex realities of black women's lives."[16]

Hispanic Theologies are not an outgrowth of Latin American liberation theology; rather, its roots can be traced to before there was a United States. The present manifestation begins in the 1970s and 1980s with the founding of *Las Hermanas*, the 1972 establishment of the Mexican American Cultural Center, the 1981 publication of *Apuntes* – the first Hispanic scholarly religious journal – and the 1988 creation of the Academy of Catholic Hispanic Theologians of the United States (ACHTUS).

Despite Latina/o diversity, certain theological concepts are common. Among them is *lo cotidiano*, translated as "the everyday," which focuses on Hispanic daily existence and struggles. A survival theology emerges that attempts to ascertain the God's character in the midst of struggle, a character that provides guidance as to what type of praxis is to be undertaken *en conjunto*, that is, within community. Latino/a theologies become a praxis-centered theology of *acompañamiento*, of accompanying, making a preferential option for the oppressed. It should be noted that while some of these Spanish terms appear on both sides of the border – some are used differently, some are not accentuated on one side, while others are very U.S. based; thus a deference in emphasis exists depending on inter- and intrageography expressing the *mestizaje*, the mixture, of the Hispanic social location.

Latina/o liberation theology is done from the context of *nepantla*, an indigenous term that connotes being in the middle. To be in the middle means neither denying the indigenous Hispanic customs and traditions, nor denying the new religions and concepts brought about by the vicissitudes of conflicting cultures. The Hispanic *mestizaje* – that is the cultural, political, religious, social, and physical "mixing" birthed from the pain and anguish of continuous conquest – contributes to a notion of *nepantla* that describes the recognition that within most Latino/a's veins flow the blood of both the conquerors and the conquered. To be in *nepantla*, living on the borders between marginality and acceptance, is to struggle for one's daily bread, to fight for one's family's basic human dignity. Even those minor privileges taken for granted by the dominant culture (such as never having to be reminded of one's ethnicity) is a constant *lucha*, struggle for Hispanics. *La lucha* for survival not only describes the Hispanic social location, but also provides the means by which Latina/os develop their worldview, learn to maneuver the consequences of ethnic discrimination, and begin to construct a more liberative understanding of themselves. For Latin American, the struggle has been focused on the consequences of U.S.-backed dictatorship and economic imperialism fueled by multinational corporations. This differs for Latino/as who place the focus on internal cultural and ethnic social structures that reinforce U.S. oppression.

Asian American Theologies represent multiple national origins, within which diverse cultural groups exist; nevertheless most, like other minoritized groups, are disproportionately disenfranchised. Physiognomic features (e.g., eye shape), regardless of how many generations within the United States, relegate those of Asian ancestry to "forever foreigners." Experiences of multiple marginalities caused by unbearable injustices developed an inexpressible pang in the pits of their stomachs called *han*. *Han* encompasses the feelings of resentment, helplessness, bitterness, sorrow, and revenge that are felt deep in the victim's guts. Religious pluralism is also an important theme. Asian and Asian American scholars remind us that to accept one religion neither rejects nor demonizes other religions. For thousands of years, religious pluralism has been a natural way of spiritual living in the homelands of Asian Americans; where an eclectic mixture meant that no one soteriological claim had a hold over and against other faiths. Many Asian American Christian scholars employ a liberative approach through the use of a "third-eye" theology. A "third eye" allows Christianity to turn to the abundant indigenous stories, legends, and folklore of the people.

Asian American liberative theology of marginality is based on the experience of living on the margins of an American and Asian world, living in-between (neither American nor Asian) and in both (both American and Asian) worlds. An attempt is made to indigenize the Christian faith by focusing on Asians' daily experiences. Relying on an autobiographical methodology, the Bible is understood through other traditions (e.g., Buddhist culture), hence the importance of advocating for an inclusive and multicultural church sensitive to plurality, diversity, and the bonds of solidarity that unite all believers.

BEYOND LIBERATIVE THEOLOGIES

Since the 1960s when liberation theology began to take shape, the situation for the oppressed has worsened as the rich have become wealthier and the poor have sunk into greater poverty. This led Ernesto Cardenal, priest and former Nicaraguan Sandinista rebel, to exclaim: "[L]iberation theology is in crisis. Capitalism won. Period. What more can be said?"[17] Faced with a new, neoliberal world order, many of the original discussions concerning liberation theology cease to be relevant to today's economic challenges. Some scholars, especially from the dominant culture, began to view liberation theology as an irrelevant fad. Yet oppression continues that still requires a religious response. Maybe it is time to move beyond liberation theology so as to meet new challenges.

Among the many who are contributing to new discussions is José Comblin, the first to question how theology must change to meet the new century's challenges. He realized the newly rich are no longer the old bourgeoisie *patrones* who felt paternalistic toward those under them. The new elite are "executives" who accumulate wealth through commerce instead of production, feeling little obligation to the poor.[18] Scholars like R. S. Sugirtharajah, Fernando F. Segovia, and Kwok Pui-Lan began rereading scripture through postcolonial eyes, unmasking how its words are not always liberating.[19] Postcolonial criticism exposes how Eurocentric biblical interpretations remain complicit with oppression, specifically, how the Bible been used to enforce and reinforce colonial structures.

Voices systematically ignored from the liberative discourse have been those of lesbians, gays, bisexuals, and transgender folk. Including their voices or perspectives was considered indecent. Marcella Althaus-Reed calls for this indecency as she seeks a sexual theology arising from liberation theology. To counter decency, she calls for doing theology with "one's panties off," for proper behavior usually masks oppressive relationships detrimental to sexual outcasts.[20] I also argue for an indecent approach to praxis. Believing global successes of neoliberalism make hope for liberation from oppressive economic systems unrealistic, I call for an ethics *para joder* (an ethics that screws with). When the oppressive structures cannot be overturned, the only ethical response is to screw with the structures, creating disorder and chaos. Corrupt social structures that legitimize the privilege of the few are hopelessly beyond reform. By calling for disrupting normative social oppressive structures, new possibilities can arise that might lead toward a more just social order.[21]

CONCLUSION

At its best, liberation theology is not just another theological perspective struggling with ethereal concepts concerning eschatology or ecclesiology. As religions of resistance, theologies of liberation become a source of strength for persecuted people searching for means of survival while challenging forces of oppression. Liberative praxis and thoughts by persecuted people render a counterhegemonic challenge to the prevailing social order, offering a critique of Western political and economic structures.

Notes

1 Food and Agriculture Organization of the United Nations, *The State of Food Insecurity in the World* (2012), p. 8.
2 UN Development Programme, *The Real Wealth of Nations* (2010), pp. 78, 80, 96.
3 Tim Weiner, "More Entreaties in Monterrey for More Aid to the Poor," *New York Times*, March 22, 2002.
4 See Miguel A. De La Torre, *The Hope of Liberation in World Religions* (Waco, TX: Baylor University Press, 2008).
5 Gustavo Gutiérrez, "Foreword," in *Witness: Writings of Bartolomé de Las Casas*, ed. George Sanderlin (Maryknoll, NY: Orbis, 1992), pp. xi, 46–8.
6 Ibid.
7 George E. "Tink" Tinker, *American Indian Liberation: A Theology of Sovereignty* (Maryknoll, NY: Orbis, 2008), pp. 11–12. Tinker intentionally uses lowercase letters for the words *European* and *Christian*.
8 See Tulio Halperín Donghi, *The Contemporary History of Latin America* (Durham, NC: Duke University Press, 1993); Andre Gunder Frank, *Capitalism and Underdevelopment in Latin America: Historical Studies of Chile and Brazil* (New York: Monthly Review, 1969); Alfred T. Hennelly, ed. *Liberation Theology: A Documentary History* (Maryknoll, NY: Orbis, 1990); and Pablo Richard, *Death of Christendoms, Birth of the Church: Historical Analysis and Theological Interpretation of the Church in Latin America* (Maryknoll, NY: Orbis, 1987).
9 Paulo Freire, *Pedagogy of the Oppressed*, trans. Myra Bergman Ramos (New York: Continuum, 1993), p. 21.
10 Second General Conference of Latin American Bishops, *The Church in the Present-Day Transformation of Latin America in the Light of the Council* (Secretariat for Latin America, 1973), 14:I:1.
11 Miguel A. De La Torre, *Doing Christian Ethics from the Margins* (Maryknoll, NY: Orbis, 2004; repr. 2014), pp. 58–69.
12 See José Comblin, *Called for Freedom: The Changing Context of Liberation Theology* (Maryknoll, NY: Orbis, 1998).
13 Marcella Althaus-Reid, *Indecent Theology: Theological Perversions in Sex, Gender and Politics* (New York: Routledge, 2000), p. 31.
14 Leonardo Boff, "Salvation in Liberation," in *Salvation and Liberation: In Search of a Balance between Faith and Politics*, ed. Leonardo Boff and Clodovis Boff, trans. R. R. Barr (Maryknoll, NY: Orbis, 1979; repr. 1984), p. 9.
15 See Anne M. Clifford, *Introducing Feminist Theology* (Maryknoll, NY: Orbis, 2000), p. 32.

16 Stephanie Y. Mitchem, *Introducing Womanist Theology* (Maryknoll, NY: Orbis, 2002), p. ix.
17 Juan O. Tamayo, "Rethinking Option for Poor: Liberation Theology Barely an Echo in Old Stronghold," *The Miami Herald*, January 31, 1999.
18 See Comblin, *Called for Freedom*.
19 See R. S. Sugirtharajah, *Asian Biblical Hermeneutics and Postcolonialism: Contesting the Interpretations* (Maryknoll, NY: Orbis, 1998); Fernando F. Segovia, *Decolonizing Biblical Studies: A View from the Margins* (Maryknoll, NY: Orbis, 2000); and Kwok Pu-lan, *Postcolonial Imagination and Feminist Theology* (Louisville, KY: Westminster/John Knox, 2005).
20 Althaus-Reid, *Indecent Theology*.
21 Miguel A. De La Torre, *Latino/a Social Ethics: Moving beyond Eurocentric Moral Thinking* (Waco, TX: Baylor University Press, 2010).

Further Reading

Althaus-Reid, M., *Indecent Theology: Theological Perversions in Sex, Gender and Politics*. London: Routledge, 2000.
Boff, L., *Jesus Christ Liberator: A Critical Christology for Our Times*, trans. Patrick Hughes. Maryknoll, NY: Orbis Books, 1978.
Cone, J. H., *Black Theology and Black Power*. New York: Seabury Press, 1969.
De La Torre, M. A. *Latina/o Social Ethics: Moving Beyond Eurocentric Moral Thinking*. Waco, TX: Baylor University Press, 2010.
Deloria, V., Jr., *Custer Died for Your Sins: An Indian Manifesto*. New York: McMillan, 1969.
Ellis, M. H., *Toward a Jewish Theology of Liberation: The Uprising and the Future*. Maryknoll, NY: Orbis Books, 1987.
Engineer, A. A., *Islam and Liberation Theology: Essays on Liberative Elements of Islam*. New Delhi: Sterling Publishers, 1990.
Freire, P. *Pedagogy of the Oppressed*, trans. Myra Bergman Ramos. New York: Continuum Publishing, 1970.
Gutiérrez, G., *A Theology of Liberation*, trans. Sister Caridad Inda and John Eagleson. Maryknoll, NY: Orbis Books, 1973.
Kwok, P., *Postcolonial Imagination and Feminist Theology*. Louisville, KY: Westminster John Knox Press, 2005.
Sugirtharajah, R. S., *Asian Biblical Hermeneutics and Postcolonialism: Contesting the Interpretations*. Maryknoll, NY: Orbis Books, 1998.

3 Public Theology
HAK JOON LEE

The term *public theology* may appear odd or suspicious to many people. What kind of theology is it? How does it differ from other, more familiar forms of theology, such as systematic theology or biblical theology? What exactly does the adjective *public* mean in this case? Is it theology that promotes specific government policies? Or is it a theology of a politically motivated group that tries to impose its morality upon the public? In an era of specialization and overly politicized religion, "public theology" may either sound like another hypertechnical term that does not deserve our attention or raise suspicions of religious radicalism and authoritarianism.

The term *public* is highly controversial and even misleading in our postmodern culture because it quickly brings to mind a liberal secular ideology that separates fact from value and relegates personal opinions and religious beliefs to the private realm. However, the meaning of *public* in public theology is different from its secular liberal counterpart. Rejecting the modern dichotomy of fact and value, as well as that of the religious and the civic, public theology advocates for a constructive public role for religious discourse in a pluralistic society, neither suppressing religious expressions nor dismissing democratic values such as human rights, tolerance, and equality. *Public* refers not so much to a locale as a posture of doing theology, namely the dialogical openness to everybody in pursuing the common good of a society. Specifically, the adjective *public* in public theology connotes at least three core intentions: (1) a concern for the well-being of a society, (2) the discovery and communication of the public meaning and import of religious symbols and creeds through dialogue, which is related to (3) a critique of the "private," "sectarian," or "authoritarian" expressions of religion that either reduce religion into individual or parochial matters or refuse to validate its truth and moral claims to its members or outsiders with warrants and evidences.[1] Public theology claims that theology need not be esoteric or parochial, but rather can be communicated to others in its interpretation of religious canons, symbols, and rituals, as well as its search for truth and justice.

Public theology is a relatively recent genre of theology. The term first appeared in 1974 in Martin Marty's article on Reinhold Niebuhr's thought. Marty introduced the term because he was unsatisfied with terms often employed in scholarship and the media to describe public engagement with religion – terms such as *public religion* and *civil religion*. He believed that those terms are too general to capture believers' religious identity, affiliation, and commitment to their specific religious traditions and institutions – such as churches, synagogues, and mosques – in focusing on religion's influence on broader society and politics.

On a deeper sociocultural level, however, the rise of public theology as a specific theological genre was a response to a large religious and moral sea change slowly taking place in postwar U.S. society. The rise of material prosperity, religious pluralism, immigration, and secularization challenged the traditional place and integrative role of Christian values in U.S. society. Social institutions and popular culture became increasingly indifferent, if not outright hostile, to religion. The place and role of Christianity in public life became fragile and uncertain, even relegated to the private realm. Additionally, the erosion of spiritual and moral values under rapidly spreading materialism, utilitarianism, and moral relativism posed a threat to the common welfare. Society was losing its spiritual moral anchor. Public theology, in seeking the renewal of the common life in U.S. society, was a response to these challenges.[2]

This essay studies the central features, core theological and ethical convictions, and practices of public theology. Starting with a brief overview of the historical background and impetus of public theology in the United States, the essay discusses the distinctive features of public theology – especially its understanding of the task and methodology of theology, as well as the scope and means of political change – in comparison with three other major contemporary theological approaches: European political theology, Latin American liberation theology, and postliberal theology. The focus of the analysis will be public theology's understanding of the communicative and ethical task of theology, especially articulating the religious meanings and moral groundings of human existence. Finally, the essay explores the current challenges, growing significance, and future promise of public theology in a global society that is highly interdependent and mobile yet disorganized. It should be noted that due to the introductory nature of this essay and space limitations, my discussion of the four theologies is limited to their general characteristics and distinctive emphases, leaving the more complex nuances and internal divergences of each theology untapped.

HISTORICAL IMPETUS OF PUBLIC THEOLOGY IN THE UNITED STATES

Contrary to the relatively recent introduction of its terminology, the historical root of public theology is old and deep, running throughout Judaism and Christianity. In fact, care for common life and concern for justice reflect the very character of God, the Creator who governs the universe with love and justice. From the exodus event, including the gift of the Law, prophetic outcry against corrupt rulers and unjust legal systems, to Jesus's and his apostles' confrontation with religious and political powers, concern for protecting and promoting the common good and social justice permeates scripture. This prophetic stance and caring for the public good have continued throughout Christian history in different forms and emphases by diverse Christian communities.

After the Reformation, this impetus took a grassroots popular form with a more democratic tone and pluralistic sensibility. An inchoate form of public theology developed energetically with increasing sophistication and confidence in the Protestant soil of America. Beginning with the settlement of the Puritans in the colonial era, and moving through the Declaration of Independence and the Revolutionary War to the birth of the republic, Protestant Christianity (in particular its Reformed branch with its distinctive emphasis on sin, covenant, moral law, etc.) has played a significant role in shaping the identity, cultural ethos, political system, and institutional structure of the nation. Just as the ecclesiology of free churches (in particular the governance of the laity) informed the development of popular sovereignty and democracy, the Christian notions of the sanctity of human life, natural law, and natural right have influenced the shape of the modern ideas of constitutional democracy, human rights, and the rule of law, without countenancing the modernist assumptions of individualism and contractualism.[3] For the forerunners of public theology, human rights are not entitlements bestowed upon individuals by the state but rather are grounded in the biblical conviction of human beings as bearing God's image. Laws are not the result of human fiat but of divine origin; therefore social contract is bound by the higher law of God.

The impulse of public theology in the United States, however, was not only theological, but also practical. From the beginning, the nation faced the challenge of pluralism – religious, cultural, and ethnic – which continued to accelerate with an ongoing influx of immigrants. The radical diversity of racial, ethnic, and religious groups was perceived to be a threat to the existence of the republic, for fear of potential conflicts – in particular among religious groups. This threat prompted Christians to seek a creative solution to the challenge of how to encourage diverse religious expressions while maintaining national unity. The concept of religious freedom (bound up with the separation of church and state) was a response to this challenge: that is, the state should neither enforce a particular religious belief nor protect the special privilege of a particular religious group at the expense of others. This arrangement allowed religious groups to work for the commonwealth of the nation while maintaining their doctrinal and liturgical differences.

Once established, this constitutional arrangement has made an indelible impact, setting the tone and pattern for later religious groups arriving from other shores. That is, the principle of religious freedom and democratic arrangements have put pressure on new religious groups or movements to adapt to these moral ideals and institutional values as they seek public recognition, and theologically engage with these institutions and ideals. The result of this experimentation is that the United States has been an exceedingly religious nation with a largely successful system of democracy and a vibrant civil society that has avoided the tyranny of fascism, Nazism, communism, and religious theocracy.

Throughout U.S. history, the public strand of Christian theology provided the vision, direction, and energy for the advance of democracy and its institutions, despite occasional setbacks and mistakes. The impulse of public theology emerged at major turning points of U.S. history, renewing or redirecting the nation and revitalizing religious and civic organizations: the abolitionist movement of Frederick Douglass, the temperance movement of Lyman Beecher and Justin Edwards, the Social Gospel movement of Walter Rauschenbusch and Washington Gladden, the Christian realism of Reinhold Niebuhr, and the civil rights movement of Martin Luther King Jr.

CATHOLIC PUBLIC THEOLOGY

The tradition of public theology within Protestantism has deeply influenced the rise of a specifically Catholic form of public theology in the United States. Traditionally, Catholic theology has enjoyed rich resources of its own for public theology: an articulate theory of reason and natural law and Catholic social teaching (the Papal Encyclicals). However, the Catholic Church in Europe experienced difficulty in the face of modernity; the Church initially rejected modernity – especially the idea of religious freedom – as the epitome of all heresies, believing that it marginalized the church from the public realm. A breakthrough from the grave doubt about the notion of religious freedom surprisingly occurred in the United States, a land primarily Protestant in character.

The Catholic Church's embrace of religious freedom in the United States was a response to external and internal forces; externally, the Catholics needed to overcome the suspicion of Protestants about their perceived loyalty to the Vatican. Internally, as the Catholic Church was engaging with U.S. society, many Catholic theologians began to appreciate the American experimentation – its model of the church-state relationship that is different from the modern continental (especially French) model.

John Courtney Murray was a major intellectual figure who helped the Catholic Church embrace religious freedom, democracy, and social pluralism. Murray worked out an articulate form of public theology on the basis of the Catholic natural law tradition, making an indelible contribution to the Second Vatican Council's adoption of religious freedom. Accepting religious pluralism as an unavoidable element of the social context of Catholic ministry, he argued that the ideas of democracy, human rights, and religious freedom are neither anti-Catholic nor completely secular. Murray saw the contact point between the Catholic natural law tradition and the U.S. Constitution and social creeds in terms of respect for reason, concern for the public life, and the idea of a religiously informed transcendental moral order.[4]

Vatican II opened wide a door for further exploration of public theology in cross-fertilization with Protestant theology and other religious traditions. Capitalizing on its rich tradition of natural law and fundamental theology, Catholic public theology has made substantial contributions in the areas of theological method, economic justice, war and peace, human rights, ecology, sexuality, and so forth.[5] For example, David Tracy builds the premise of Christian theology on the public nature of theological claims by contending that "all theology is public discourse" and the public nature of theology is not one of many facets but the very heart of Christian theology.[6] In defending his thesis, he specifically draws upon the idea of a "classic": that is, religious canons should be understood as classics (like classic works of art and literature) whose disclosive meaning and transformative power are enduring and transcultural – thus *public*.[7] Furthermore, he proposes the idea of the "three publics" (church, society, and academia) – each with its own distinctive focus, criteria, intellectual modality, and audience – as the core areas of theological investigation. Today, Catholic public theology is strong and vibrant. Sociologist John Coleman, ethicists David Hollenbach and Dennis McCann, feminist theologian Lisa Sowle Cahill, and others continue to expand public theology in global, pluralistic social contexts. They embrace biblical symbols and theological doctrines in a more explicit and extensive way than the natural law tradition as they engage the Catholic tradition of the common good, teleology, human dignity, and subsidiarity with various public concerns and philosophical issues.

Currently public theology is embraced and promoted by many ecumenically oriented Protestants, progressive evangelicals, and Catholics in diverse forms. Those who study public theology gain insights and wisdom not only from scripture but also from the Patristics (e.g., Augustine), Thomas Aquinas, Reformers such as Calvin and Luther, Jonathan Edwards, Abraham Kuyper, Jacques Maritain, Karl Barth, Paul Tillich, Reinhold Niebuhr, Martin Luther King Jr., and other theologians. They defend and articulate the truth and social meaning of the gospel for the common life in a fresh way, in response to newly arising needs, questions, and challenges in their societies.

The river of public theology is growing deeper and wider throughout the world today. Public theology receives broad, substantial attention in both religious and secular schools, among scholars and the general public, and in Christian and non-Christian contexts. Increasingly, public theology courses are taught in college and graduate schools, books and articles are published, and research centers have been established in Australia, the United Kingdom, and South Africa.[8]

WHAT IS PUBLIC THEOLOGY? CENTRAL FEATURES AND CORE PRINCIPLES

Public theology is not monolithic; it is a dynamic, complex, and divergent theological movement: public theologians continue to debate among themselves the meaning, nature, and scope of the "public," the audience, criteria, and practices of public theology. Despite their difference in doctrinal foci, ethical emphases, and moral nuances, most descriptions of public theology share several core moral convictions and characteristics:

(1) Public theology has an apologetic character. It is grounded in the simple but powerful desire of every religious person to offer a "reasonable" account of why she believes what she believes to those

outside her faith community. From the beginning of their history, Christians faced this question from inside and outside the church: Who is Jesus and what does it mean that he is the Lord and the Messiah? Many early Christian writings were written for apologetic purposes, and public theology continues today under the same compelling impulse. Public theology does not impose particular religious assumptions and perspectives upon others; nor does it reduce religious differences into minimal moral denominators. Its posture is neither hegemonic nor reductive, but rather dialogical; it communicatively engages with other religious and philosophical traditions for mutual understanding and the betterment of a common life.

While grounded in a particular religious tradition, public theologians are willing not only to communicate their religious convictions and beliefs to the public, but also to demonstrate the validity and relevance of an individual religious belief in ways that others can understand and adopt as well. Conceiving the relationship of reason and faith as "mutually enriching and mutually corrective for each other,"[9] rather than mutually exclusive, public theology rejects any privileged or fideistic claims in articulating God's truth and justice. In particular, unlike some fundamentalists or Pentecostals who draw on literalist interpretations of the Bible or personal subjective experiences as the only sources of moral authority, public theology values intelligible, coherent, and truthful arguments validated by warrants and evidences, and respects a free, equal, and discursive process in discerning truth and morality. It claims that not all theological arguments, religious expressions, and practices are equally valid; they need to be assessed in light of universal norms and values, as well as their relative capacity to illuminate deep moral concerns and offer guidance for complex human interactions in a global society.

While defending the validity of the truth and moral claims of a particular religious community, public theology simultaneously argues that major religious traditions, when properly interpreted, provide valuable spiritual and moral guidance for the common life. Religious moral convictions, symbols, and doctrines are not esoteric; they have public meanings and significance.

Public theologians argue that Christian doctrines of creation, sin, redemption, eschatology, covenant, and ecclesiology are informative for our understanding of the nature, meaning, and destiny of human life. When properly interpreted, these doctrines assist the members of a society in deciphering the deeper meanings and complex nature of human life that scientific knowledge and liberal philosophies cannot provide on their own.

This claim is based on its belief in the constitutive nature of religion for human life. Advocates of public theology believe that humans are essentially religious (*homo religiosus*); religious aspirations and expressions are found in every place, constituting the deepest foundation of human existence and common life, and shaping human values, beliefs, and sensibilities in the most basic and powerful sense.[10] For this reason, religious beliefs cannot be relegated to the private realm, and laws and public policies should not be formulated solely on a secular basis without accounting for a religious dimension of human existence; doing so significantly disadvantages any society.

(2) Relatedly, public theology is critical of the naturalistic or humanist basis of liberal ethics and philosophy. It offers a compelling theological critique and revision of the liberal ideas of freedom, human dignity, justice, and human rights. In public theology, for instance, freedom does not mean self-sufficiency or autonomy. Rather, it is relational in character and cannot be separated from obligations; persons are not isolated individuals, just as society is not the aggregation of those individuals. Therefore, the Christian concept of rights stresses mutual obligations and duties as well as individual entitlements. Democracy requires a deep understanding of the good with a strong communal ethos and habits that cannot be generated by liberalism. In short, liberal norms, insufficient by themselves to be fully functional, require the deeper theological ground and vision that public theology provides.

(3) Unlike the postmodern philosophies and postliberal theologies that we will discuss later, many proponents of public theology, especially Catholic and mainline theologians, believe in the existence of certain universal moral norms that bind all of humanity, despite their diverse historical manifestations and interpretive possibilities. This belief is based on the observation that every society has certain rules regarding lying, stealing, murder, greed, violence, honoring parents, the purity of marriage, justice, the golden rule, and so on. These moral norms are closely associated with the functional requisites of basic social institutions, such as the family, the economy, and the judiciary system. Without them, the maintenance of a minimal social order and the flourishing of its members are inconceivable. This implies that variances in religious practices and

narratives do not necessarily indicate the differences in their underlying values and norms. For example, although the Buddhist idea of compassion and the Christian concept of love are based on different religious assumptions, they still describe a similar attitude of a person toward others – goodwill and care. For public theologians, these norms are not mere human constructs, just as this transcultural overlap is not accidental. Termed as natural law, creation order, or first principles, these norms have a protological basis. God, whose sovereign moral will is reflected in the order of the universe, and is discernable by every human being through the use of reason, is the ultimate source of the moral norms. That is, the knowledge of God's moral will is not confined to scripture and the Christian community; as the Apostle Paul stated, humans are born with some principles of right and wrong "written on their hearts" (Rom. 2:15). Although this rational capability is distorted by sin, it is not completely erased; it can be further improved when sanctified by God's grace and properly guided by scripture. Reformed theologians call this positive moral force "common grace" that accounts for the possibility of public moral discourse and agreement among people with different religious beliefs.

According to public theologians, these universal norms are critical for the well-being of a society and its members because they constitute the moral foundation of the common life. Every society needs a shared moral core for its survival and thriving. These norms guide human choices about the pursuit of vocations, the use of power, the establishment of laws and public policies, the ordering and arrangement of institutions, and the distribution of resources and goods.

Without this core, civilization would suffer from internal decadence, endless conflicts, and/or the incapacity to cope with external threats; laws and public policies would lose their authority because they would be perceived merely as the invention of the powerful.

(4) Relying on these norms and the other authoritative sources (scripture, tradition, philosophy, and social sciences), public theology seeks to discern God's will in various social, cultural, and historical contexts. That is to say, it carefully studies how the *logos* of *theos* (the truth of God) is manifested in various social contexts and institutions while attending to contextual distinctiveness, mindful of the power of sin that affects human knowledge, moral understanding, and action (including the exercise of power by the authorities). In the process of discerning the *logos* of *theos*, pluralism in

interpretation is inevitable as scripture provides a rich and complex view of the divine reality and the understanding of the world. Christian symbols and narratives constantly invite new interpretations in response to new social and cultural issues. Public theology discriminates between multiple competing interpretations through communicative exchanges of validity claims in light of criteria such as consistency, relevance, faithfulness, and comprehensiveness – in short, the plausibility and cogency of interpretation for addressing urgent social cultural issues.

COMPARISON: PUBLIC THEOLOGY, POLITICAL THEOLOGY, AND LIBERATION THEOLOGY

The distinctive characteristics of public theology become clear when they are compared with other genres of contemporary Christian theology, especially European political theology and liberation theology, which are equally passionate for justice and the active participation of Christianity in social transformation.

The three theologies share several common features and interests: all three are critical of certain aspects of modernity – particularly instrumental reason, a utilitarian economic ethos, and materialism with its detrimental impact on moral formation, culture, and the environment. They reject the modern premise of secularization – the separation of secular and sacred, fact and value, history and eternity. They also agree that the gospel is concerned with issues beyond individual piety, as it is social and political in nature; therefore the church has a prophetic responsibility to promote social justice and peace. The three theologies rely on some form of a correlation method, as they critically engage God's reign with sociopolitical experiences of poverty and exploitation (liberation theology), the condition of radical pluralism (public theology), and the crisis of modern technological civilization (political theology).

DIFFERENCES

Despite their similarities, however, the three theologies differ considerably in their understanding of the task and methodology of theology, the role of the state, the nature of knowledge, and the Christian stance regarding liberal democracy and capitalism.[11] Understandably, their differences reflect the historical and cultural differences arising from their German, Latin American, and U.S. contexts. The radical politics of liberation theology reflect the painful and oppressive realities of Latin America and the failure of political systems there. Similarly, political theology is rooted in the German experience of the colossal failure of the system during the Holocaust. By contrast, public theology has thrived in the United States, maintaining relative stability and even achieving some significant, though incomplete, internal reforms such as rights for women and minorities through democratic processes and movements within the bounds of the Constitution.

(1) One finds a major difference between public theology and the other two theologies in their primary goal and scope. Liberation theology seeks liberation from oppression, while political theology pursues the radical interruption and transformation of society in the eschatological anticipation of God's future; public theology, by comparison, strives for a new social consensus and the moral renewal of civilization. In their striving for social changes, the goals and horizons of liberation and political theology are more radical, revolutionary, and totalistic than public theology because they are compelled by a deep sense of crisis – a threat to the sanctity of life – and because their political visions, projects, and social practices are informed by a fervent eschatology and Marxist or neo-Marxist theories. In contrast, public theology is far more tempered in its social analysis and its political proposals. It is neither revolutionary nor millenarian but reformative as it aims at gradual transformation of social order through the reinvigoration of society's moral fabric and the vocations of institutions and individuals. Public theology is suspicious of any totalistic social vision and utopian political programs or movements because no human power should be sovereign or claim exemption from public scrutiny and institutional checks and balances. Such a reservation is based on a healthy realism – an awareness of the depth of sin, the danger of institutional monopoly of power, and the moral pretense of millenarian politics that often results in more injustice and pain. With a pragmatic sensibility for the complex, pluralistic institutional reality in a postindustrial society, it carefully navigates between the entrenched reality of sin and the possibility of human freedom in seeking social progress.

(2) The three theologies noticeably differ on the nature of human knowledge. Public theologians seek the validity of theology's truth and moral claims in public discourse, employing rational warrants and evidences, whereas liberation and political theologies assume that theology is not a neutral but an interested language that reflects

specific social locations and cultural backgrounds. Public theology refuses to claim any privileged status or divine authority for itself. Similarly, it hesitates to reduce human knowledge and truth claims to their social contexts because such an intellectual posture is not public enough but rather smacks of authoritarianism. Public theologians believe that no human group, including the oppressed, can claim privileged access to truth and justice at the expense of mutual checks and balances and criticism in the pursuit of truth and justice.

(3) The differences in their political proposals and sociological principles, and epistemological assumptions are also reflected in the three theological movements' stances toward any dominant political and economic system. Political and liberation theologies in general are markedly critical of liberal democracy and capitalism, while public theology strives for moral progress and political reform within the system; liberal democracy is flawed, yet it nevertheless contains reformative potentials. This modest, reformist attitude of public theology is disclosed in its view of modern institutions. Compared to political theology, public theology more actively explores a constructive synthesis between theology and modern democratic values and institutions. It does not regard bureaucracy, technology, science, the critical use of reason, and other modern projects (e.g., constitutionalism, human rights, democracy) as intrinsically evil. In fact, they can make positive contributions to humanity by bringing convenience, increasing productivity and problem-solving capacity, and prolonging life expectancy; therefore the primary question should concern harnessing and guiding them with a proper theological vision and ethical perspective, rather than simply condemning them.

(4) In comparison to public theology, political theology and liberation theology tend to give more weight to the state than to civil society as the primary locus (or instrument) of social change. They approach politics, with the state at its center, as a defining integral force even over human life. Dorothee Sölle, for instance, writes: "Political theology is a theological hermeneutic which, in distinction from a theology that interprets reality from an ontological or existentialist point of view, holds open a horizon of interpretation in which politics is understood as the comprehensive and decisive sphere in which Christian truth should become praxis."[12] On the contrary, public theology affirms the legitimate place of the state in the context of civil society, even while always remaining wary of its

pretense to absolute claims and intrusive power over civil society and its institutions.

Public theology is critical of the inflated sense of politics in political theology and liberation theology that often confound the state and civil society. The distinction between the *public* and the *republic* is critical in public theology, a major point of distinction from political theology. This stance is based on the understanding that the public realm is more inclusive than and prior to the political. Constituting the fabric of civil society, the public is more decisive of and normatively more important for the common life than is politics. Stackhouse's metaphor is very apt in describing the difference between public theology and the other two:

> Politics in human affairs makes great waves, like a hurricane or typhoon on the top of the ocean – often with great and fateful consequences; but these massive storms seldom change the deeper tides, currents or dominant wind patterns. At deeper social levels, fundamental alterations of the structures that channel the flows of energy, the powers and principalities of life, make a much greater difference over time, and even determine what political storms get played out.[13]

In general, one may say, public theology is more concerned about the danger of a collectivistic or authoritarian state, while political and liberation theologies are more about the threat of unbridled capitalism and its technocratic control.

(5) The three theologies' respective positions on the state and modern social institutions reflect the different social scientific theories on which they rely. Liberation and political theologies are sympathetic to Marxist and neo-Marxist social theories (e.g., the critical theory of the Frankfurt School) or a Hegelian philosophy, while public theology distances itself from these theories, relying instead on a variety of social theories and academic disciplines, whose choice depends on specific social institutions or issues it studies. This posture is consistent with its pluralistic sensibility embodied in associational pluralism. In general, political theology and liberation theology serve more as social-political criticism than as a pragmatic political project. Their audience is consequently quite selective – a closed circuit of churches, theological schools, and progressive religious and civic organizations – and their narrow social analysis and policy proposals make it difficult to address the complex cultural

situations of postindustrial society, with its institutions and social relationships.

In summary, although all three theologies take the church's political engagements and commitment to social justice seriously, they display considerable differences in their respective understanding of the nature and task of theology, the mission of the church in particular in relation to the state and civil society, and the Christian stance on liberal democracy, capitalism, and Marxism. However, despite their differences, the ongoing critical conversations among the three theologies are important for not only the enrichment and strengthening of each theology but also for the Christian witness in a global society.

POSTLIBERAL THEOLOGY

Another form of theology that currently competes with public theology in the United States is postliberal theology. Postliberal is a form of theology that began in the 1980s, initiated by scholars closely affiliated with Yale Divinity School, notably Hans Frei, Paul Holmer, David Kelsey, and George Lindbeck. These, in turn, had been significantly influenced by the theological and philosophical works of Karl Barth, Clifford Geertz, and Ludwig Wittgenstein.

As its adjective indicates, postliberal theology presents itself as an alternative to the entire program and influences of liberalism, in both its secular and theological expressions – its theory, its practices, and even its institutional achievements, such as democracy, justice, and human rights. Whereas public theology is willing to critically engage with liberal society for its moral sanctification, the primary concern of postliberal theology is neither social change nor improvement, but rather safeguarding the distinctiveness of a Christian tradition from liberal cultural influences and protecting the church from their fragmenting and disintegrating forces.

For postliberal theologians, modernity is the attempt to establish the objective, impartial foundation of knowledge, truth, and morality apart from any particular tradition and community. The Enlightenment's appeal to a "universal rationality" and liberal theology's assumption of common religious experience are invalid because all religious experiences and truth claims are historically embedded and epistemologically mediated by a particular tradition, narrative, and set of communal practices.

It would not be much of an exaggeration to say that postliberal theology is the nemesis of public theology, as it is critical of almost everything that public theology stands for.[14] Although some theologians, such as Ronald Thiemann, seek constructive rapprochement between two theologies by granting public theology a relatively limited apologetic scope and adjudicative possibility while emphasizing the significance of ecclesial practices, most postliberals believe that public theology commits the same fallacy as modernism; the project of public theology is an attempt to "secure the intelligibility of theological discourse" for a general description of the human condition and moral experiences.[15] They charge that the apologetic endeavor of public theology to translate theological convictions into a neutral philosophical and moral idiom, together with its endorsement of liberal democracy and morality, inevitably make the church's social life indistinguishable from secular voluntary associations. From a perspective of postliberals, public theology, a form of theological liberalism, is the product of a long undesirable habit of the Constantinian Christianity – the project to be palatable to the dominant philosophical and moral mind-sets and worldviews of a society. In particular, public theology's commitment to "public" or "universal morality" such as natural law or human rights inevitably undermines the Christian identity and basic convictions by subordinating them to general, abstract moral categories and criteria that are alien to Christians. Furthermore, intolerant of ethical differences, natural law and human rights justify sanctions against their dissenters, using violence if needed, in the name of universal morality and order.[16]

Calling for a clear sense of identity for a Christian community, postliberal theology certainly offers an attractive option for those Christians who struggle with fragmentation, anomie, and confusion in their social life. It imparts a strong sense of boundaries and commitment for Christian churches, consistently reminding them of the danger of uncritical assimilation to liberalism.

However, from the perspective of public theology, postliberal theology generally tends to be confessional or fideistic in nature and relativistic in its moral implications because it rejects the idea of universal norms and the public adjudication of Christian truth and moral claims. This fideistic tendency is especially prominent in Stanley Hauerwas, a leading postliberal ethicist. Hauerwas argues that Christian ethical life is intelligible only in the context of the church; outside the church, Christian ethics loses its proper meaning and content. Such a claim makes it hard to avoid the charge of fideism because it makes Christian truth and moral claims self-referential.

Although some postliberal theologians cautiously embrace the idea of ad hoc apologetics or the adjudication of Christian claims on a local level, their scope is far from encompassing.[17] In particular, in the area of ethics, postliberal theology faces the difficulty of addressing the question of a social order and common morality in a pluralistic society. Public theologians ask: Can an increasingly interdependent global society survive without any shared morality? Does the demise of foundationalism mean that the idea of a common moral order is implausible? Is it impossible to establish such an order on a nonfoundational basis, such as an overlapping consensus?

Unlike postliberal theologians, public theology – without necessarily acceding to liberal assumptions – sees some compatibility between liberal norms and Christianity. Although liberal values are not substantive enough to guide Christian lives, they are nevertheless useful for the public life, especially in a pluralistic society. For example, Max L. Stackhouse contends that some aspects of liberal thought, such as suspicion about uncritical allegiance to authority and tradition, are not alien but actually intrinsic to Christianity. He says, "Christianity has a liberal element at its core. Following Jesus, Christians have been willing to challenge tradition when it becomes legalistic, ethnic, or impervious to prophetic insight."[18] So for public theologians, the demise of a philosophical foundation of liberal values (such as democracy, human rights, tolerance, fairness) does not mean the loss of their practical values in a global, pluralistic society. This critical stance of public theology toward liberalism is more reasonable than its complete rejection because if liberalism is a particular form of the good rather than a universal ethics (as postliberals contend), then a critical dialogue with and incorporation of liberal ethics is possible (just as some postliberals engage in ad hoc apologetics with other religious traditions).[19]

Similarly, public theology may answer the postliberal criticism that it is a new form of theological liberalism or Constantinian Christianity by pointing to associational pluralism (a pluralistic theory of "public") that it espouses. Public theology conceives of a society as a symbiotic entity consisting of multiple publics or spheres (e.g., church, academia, education, politics). David Tracy argues that each public maintains its own distinctive logic and subject matter even in its interactions with other publics, and Christians pursue the discursive redemption of their claims fitting to the logic and subject matter of each public. This means that Christians can be rooted in a particular tradition without necessarily being self-enclosed within it. Through the aid of public theology, they may actively engage in their professional contexts and the larger society out of their own particular beliefs and convictions while exercising sensitivity to a distinctive subject matter and the good of each sphere.[20] For public theologians, the questions of religious identity and social relevance, narrative and public justice, do not have to be mutually exclusive; the danger is rather in reifying only one dimension at the expense of the other. They rather find a creative role for theology in mediating and coordinating the activities of various publics in order to avoid unnecessary conflicts and confusions between them.

CHALLENGES FOR PUBLIC THEOLOGY

What is the practical viability of public theology in the West where moral emotivism has become a fad, the middle class (the backbone of liberal democracy) and public trust in the government are declining, and a Christian historical heritage is rapidly waning? Is the fear of moral relativism that worried John Courtney Murray and other public theologians being realized now? Is public theology – its vision, basic convictions, and methodology – still sustainable today in a society? I believe that the significance and necessity of public theology extends even further today for the following reasons.

First, public theology is indispensable for the ordering of our common life in a religiously and culturally pluralistic society. Our current political and cultural polarization shows how much our society suffers when it lacks some form (even a minimal one) of common moral language and norms. Society needs a shared moral vision, language, and norms that can guide individuals and institutions, serve as the criteria of evaluation and adjudication, and bind diverse groups toward a common purpose. Without them, society disintegrates, government becomes dysfunctional, and individuals are vulnerable to corporate and governmental abuses.

Second, public theology, through its emphasis on dialogue and universal moral norms, is instrumental for interreligious dialogue and ecumenical work among diverse religious groups in the pursuit of global justice and peace. Far from withering away, religions are surging and spreading in many parts of the world today, and their passions and imaginations need to be channeled and directed toward constructive purposes. As Hans Küng warned, there is no world peace without peace among religions; the price of religious violence and conflicts is too high. The method of public theology helps each religious group avoid religious conflicts and engage in common social issues out of its own religious tradition. As much of the future of humanity and our planet depends on how we create a just, sustainable, and cooperative global society, religious communities need to rise up and meet the challenges on the basis of a competent public theology. This means that public theology must travel beyond its Western context and apply its vision and practices to global civil society and issues, such as global trade, ecology, terrorism, and immigration, in order to protect human rights and to enhance the common good in an era of high mobility and interactions. Perceiving the necessity for social cooperation among religions and in the face of political corruption, ecological crisis, and economic inequality, many religious communities are more actively engaging in the public realm. They endeavor to critically incorporate the ideas of democracy, human rights, and freedom, justice, and equality into their own religious and cultural frameworks.[21]

Third, public theology is instrumental in anchoring the complex emerging civilization in stable moral ground. Fortunately, the ideas of common morality and social consensus are gaining new attention on a global level out of practical necessity, for example in coordinating national policies on climate change and terrorism. Public theology is appreciated as a mechanism for addressing the challenge of pluralism because globalization confronts all humans with larger concerns and issues that affect all of humanity and the planet. For example, the project of global ethics points toward this direction as the leaders and practitioners of various religions work to find common moral norms that can address common threats and challenges. It reminds us that every society is obliged to treat every human fairly and justly, as stipulated by the shared norms of the global community.

These observations lead us to believe that instead of retreating or contracting in the face of postmodernism, public theology needs to expand its realms and partnerships beyond its traditional geographical or ecclesiastical boundaries and topics. In the United States, public theologians need to invite and share their experiences with evangelicals and Pentecostals for the collective task of public theology, and it is encouraging that there is already a growing movement toward this direction among evangelicals as one sees in the works of Ronald Sider, David Gushee, and Jim Wallis, among others. Similarly, public theology, limited thus far mostly to white theologians, needs to listen to the voices of black theology, feminist theology, Latino and Mujerista theology, and Asian American theology, learning from their discussions of historical experiences, bicultural identities, and diaspora social practices. These theologies challenge the nature, function, and procedure of theological discourse in various publics of the United States, asking whether their discourses are genuinely public, and whether their common concerns are *common* enough to include the voices of the poor, women, and people of color.[22] Beyond that, these theologies and their relevant communities could assist public theology's global outreach as the bridge builders between different civilizations and continents. This expanded dialogue will facilitate the internationalization of public theology and enrich the conversations among Christians in the global south and north, and one sees such a positive development in the work of the *International Journal of Public Theology* and others.

Public theology needs to take seriously the interlocking crises of agency, depletion of trust, disintegration of institutions, and confusion of identity, which are unfortunately symptomatic of most contemporary industrialized societies. Globalization and the popular use of communication and transportation technology are eroding the fabric of societies, disintegrating their institutional structures, and disrupting the process of socialization in primary institutions (family, church, and neighborhood). Assisting in the formation of a holistic moral agency that respects both religious conviction and civility is a major psychological and social challenge.

At the same time, the condition of secularization and postmodernity compels public theology to engage not only in the intellectual and cognitive dimensions (the explication of the *logos* of *theos*), but also at a practical level – how to nurture public virtue and Christian agency, revitalizing Christian congregations and institutions. That is to say, public theology needs to pay attention to the basics of Christian life: worship, liturgy, arts, and evangelism. In a post-Christian society, the discipleship and public virtues of individual Christians and churches can no longer be taken for granted. As the gap between the *ecclesia* and other social institutions grows through the progress of secularization, public theology needs to help Christians develop their public witnesses in a way that remains integral to their personal character and spirituality. This task requires a new kind of theological creativity that engages not only philosophy and the social sciences but also liturgy, the arts, and communal practices. Without a deep ecclesial basis and communal embodiments, public theology may end up being an elitist discourse for professional theologians.

CONCLUSION

Through its rigorous search for a third way beyond the dichotomy of secularism and sacralism, cosmopolitanism and sectarianism, public theology offers a competent theological framework that addresses emerging global social needs and complex cultural issues. Public theology rejects narrow forms of religious expressions that avoid or forfeit constructive public engagements (e.g., dogmatism, sectarianism, and privatism) and a secular truncation of the public sphere that excludes religions. It reminds secularism of the religious foundation of human existence and civilization, while assisting in channeling religious passion and energy constructively to the common task of justice and peace. However, public theology is more than a theological rhetoric or a religious fad; it is rooted in deep human aspiration for the enduring and perfect truth, beauty, and justice that only God can provide.

In the time of rapid erosion of public virtues and the rise of radical religions, Christians and other people of goodwill can greatly benefit from public theology as they seek God's reign in history and work together to protect and promote the common well-being of humanity and the planet.

Notes

1. For similar or other related concepts, such as public philosophy, public ethics, or public religion, see E. Harold Breitenberg Jr., "To Tell the Truth: Will the Real Public Theology Please Stand Up?," *The Journal of the Society of Christian Ethics* 23.2 (2003): 55–96.
2. Robert McElory, *The Search for an American Public Theology: The Contribution of John Courtney Murray*. Mahwah, NJ: Paulist, 1989: pp. 15ff.
3. H. Richard Niebuhr, *The Kingdom of God in America*. New York: Harper and Row, 1937.
4. McElory, *The Search for an American Public Theology*, pp. 97ff.
5. Notable are the U.S. Conference of Catholic Bishops' two pastoral letters, "The Challenge of Peace: God's Promise and Our Response" and "Economic Justice for All," issued in the 1980s.
6. David Tracy, *The Analogical Imagination: Christian Theology and the Culture of Pluralism*. New York: Crossroad, 1998: p. 2.
7. Ibid., p. 108.
8. E. Harold Breitenberg Jr., "What Is Pubic Theology?," in *Public Theology for a Global Society: Essays in Honor of Max L. Stackhouse*, ed. Deirdre Hainsworth and Scott Paeth. Grand Rapids, MI: Eerdmans, 2010: p. 4.
9. David Hollenbach, *Justice, Peace, Human Rights: American Catholic Social Ethics in a Pluralistic World*. New York: Crossroad, 1988: p. 75.
10. Cf. Max Stackhouse, *Creeds, Society and Human Rights: A Study in Three Cultures*. Grand Rapids, MI: Eerdmans, 1984.
11. For the comparison among the three theologies from a Catholic perspective, see Gaspar Martinez, *Confronting the Mystery of God: Political, Liberation, and Public Theologies*. New York: Continuum, 2001.
12. Dorothee Sölle, *Political Theology*. Minneapolis, MN: Fortress, 1971: p. 59.

13 Max L. Stackhouse, "Civil Religion, Political Theology and Public Theology: What's the Difference?," *Political Theology* 5.3 (July 2004): 275–93 (see p. 285).
14 Ronald Thiemann, *Constructing a Public Theology: The Church in a Pluralistic Culture.* Louisville, KY: Westminster John Knox, 1991.
15 Stanley Hauerwas, "On Keeping Theological Ethics Theological," in *The Hauerwas Reader*, ed. John Berkman and Michael Cartwright. Durham, NC: Duke University Press, 2001: p. 63.
16 Stanley Hauerwas, *Peaceable Kingdom: A Primer in Christian Ethics.* Notre Dame, IN: University of Notre Dame Press, 1991: p. 61.
17 William Placher, *Unapologetic Theology: A Christian Voice in a Pluralistic Conversation.* Louisville, KY: Westminster John Knox Press, 1989; Alasdair C. MacIntyre, "Moral Relativism, Truth and Justification," in *The MacIntyre Reader*, ed. Kelvin Knight. Notre Dame, IN: University of Notre Dame Press, 1998: pp. 202–20.
18 Max L. Stackhouse, "Liberalism Dispatched vs. Liberalism Engaged," *Christian Century* 112.29 (1995): 962.
19 Michael Quirk, "Beyond Sectarianism?," *Theology Today* 44 (April 1987): 78–86 (see p. 83).
20 Cf. Michael Walzer, *Spheres of Justice: A Defense of Pluralism and Equality.* Boston: Basic Books, 1984. Several public theologians, such as Richard Mouw, Max Stackhouse, and John Bolt, rely on Dutch theologian Abraham Kuyper's theory of sphere sovereignty in articulating this point.
21 For a detailed discussion of public theology and interreligious exchanges and cooperation, see my book, *The Great World House: Martin Luther King, Jr. and Global Ethics.* Cleveland, OH: Pilgrim, 2011: ch. 5.
22 Cf. David Tracy, *On Naming the Present: God, Hermeneutics, and Church.* Maryknoll, NY: Orbis, 1996.

Further Reading

Bene, Robert, *The Paradoxical Vision: A Public Theology for the Twenty-First Century.* Minneapolis, MN: Fortress Press, 1995.

Cady, Linell E., *Religion, Theology, American Public Life.* Albany: State University of New York Press, 1993.

Himes, Michael, and Kenneth Himes, *Fullness of Faith: The Public Significance of Theology.* New York: Paulist Press, 1993.

Hollenbach, David, *The Global Face of Public Faith: Politics, Human Rights, and Christian Ethics.* Washington, DC: Georgetown University Press, 2003.

Kim, Sebastian, *Theology in the Public Sphere: Public Theology as a Catalyst for Open Debate.* London: SCM Press, 2011.

Paeth, Scott, E. Hal Breitenberg, and Hak Joon Lee, eds., *Shaping Public Theology: The Max L. Stackhouse Reader.* Grand Rapids, MI: Wm. B. Eerdmans Publishing Co., 2014.

Stackhouse, Max L., *Public Theology and Political Economy: Christian Stewardship in Modern Society.* Lanham, MD: University Press of America, 1991.

Storrar, William, and Andrew Morton, eds., *Public Theology for the 21st Century*. London: T&T Clark, 2004.
Thiemann, Ronald, *Constructing a Public Theology: The Church in a Pluralistic Culture*. Louisville, KY: Westminster John Knox, 1991.
Tracy, David, *The Analogical Imagination: Christian Theology and the Culture of Pluralism* New York: Crossroad, 1981.

Political Theology and Related Discourses

4 Catholic Social Teaching
LISA SOWLE CAHILL

Catholic Social Teaching (CST) refers primarily to a series of papal encyclicals authored from 1891 (Pope Leo XIII's *Rerum novarum*) to the present (Pope Francis's *Laudato Si'*, 2015). Secondarily, it includes other papal teaching documents (such as Pope Francis's apostolic exhortation *Evangelii Gaudium*, 2013), conciliar documents (Vatican II's *Gaudium et spes*, 1965), publications of governing bodies of the Vatican (e.g., the *Compendium of the Social Doctrine of the Church*, released in 2004 by the Pontifical Council for Justice and Peace), statements from episcopal synods (*Justitia in mundo*, 1971), and local episcopal conferences (such as the African bishops' 2009 *Message to the People of God*, addressing conflict, corruption, and the status of women).[1]

Yet the acronym for Catholic Social *Teaching*, CST, also stands for Catholic Social *Thought* and Catholic Social *Tradition*. As a historical reality and development, CST assumes, depends on, and incorporates the *thought* of theologians and other theorists, just as it inspires further intellectual reflection and refinement. Moreover, CST is shaped and borne forward not only by popes and bishops, but also by a practical and living *tradition* of pastors and teachers, activists and organizers, and workers and government officials who live out the implications of Christian faith in daily life, cooperating with other "people of goodwill." The authors of the encyclicals in fact rely upon "a small band of ghostwriters, advisors, consultants, and pastoral ministers in the formulation of these documents." Conversely, the documents have influence because they are "'translated' into sermons, lectures, public programs, social movements, acts of charity, just deeds, and peacemaking."[2] Magisterial teaching and the process of intellectual and practical interpretation are "part of the same tradition of reflection and practice," with no strict separations.[3] This essay will first place CST as a distinctive type of political theology, and then situate the development of CST historically, with specific examples from the Catholic encyclical tradition.

CST as political theology is marked by at least three characteristics. First, CST is constructive and universalist, calling "all people of goodwill" (to paraphrase the opening address of John XXIII's *Pacem in terris*) to respect human dignity and the common good, and to take action against evils such as war and world poverty.

Second, while the encyclicals name and assess specific forms of injustice in social terms, the Church's most distinctive role is to stress gospel-based values and concerns. Key among these are the preferential option for the poor and solidarity; the realities of sin and suffering; and the spiritual basis of the power to transform social conditions.

Third, CST is in some ways similar to and in others different from modern liberal politics. CST can be an ally of liberalism, yet it brings to the latter important qualifications and critiques. Like CST, liberal thought is egalitarian regarding human moral worth, universalist in its approach to human rights and the rule of law, and meliorist in its view that social institutions can be improved. CST and liberalism both endorse the dignity of the individual person. However, whereas liberalism asserts the freedom and autonomy of the individual over against the demands of any collectivity, CST affirms the sociality of the person as equally basic to freedom. While liberals stress toleration as the response to difference, CST stresses solidarity. While liberals stress equality before the law, CST stresses as well the material and social conditions that allow freedom and equality to be realized at the practical level. CST also sees tradition-based values, including religious values, as appropriate candidates for public debate, while liberalism tends to see public reason as "secular" and tradition free. While CST progressively has learned to endorse human rights, liberalism has incorporated the value of distributive justice. While Catholicism needs to make progress in its commitment to democracy, liberalism needs more consistently to affirm the common good and the full participation of all members of society.[4]

UNIVERSALISM AND THE NATURAL LAW TRADITION

Addressed to a potentially universal audience, CST does not rely on biblical, theological, and ecclesial sources alone, but also on the tradition of "natural law" paradigmatically elaborated by Thomas Aquinas.[5] Natural law is grounded theologically by Aquinas in terms of laws of human nature established by the Creator as part of divine providence for the common good of the whole creation. The natural law is in fact "the rational creature's participation in the eternal law."[6] Thus, while Aquinas's explication of natural law makes frequent reference to scripture and to theological authorities (especially Augustine), reference to Christian faith or revelation is not necessary to grasp its basic content, because practical reason as such *participates* in the eternal law or wisdom of God. Thus all people in principle can discern the basic requirements of justice.

For Aquinas, divine positive law, or revelation, is necessary to direct human nature to its supernatural destiny, union with God in friendship, and to correct limits and distortions deriving from finitude and sin. But the basic obligations of the natural law still may be inferred from the experience of certain goods as essential to human fulfillment and flourishing. As examples, Aquinas offers the goods of life and its preservation; of sex, reproduction, and education of children; and of cooperative social life.[7] Aquinas's perception of goods and obligations was undoubtedly influenced by his medieval European Christian worldview; especially regarding specifics in such areas as just war, sex and marriage, women's roles, and government. Nevertheless, Aquinas provides the basis on which CST later proposes the universal intelligibility of the dignity of the person and the common good, as requiring participation, mutual rights and duties, subsidiarity, solidarity, and preferential action on behalf of the poor. Although God is the final end or ultimate "common good" of all human beings, the common good is also a temporal form of flourishing, good in itself, through which human sociality, practical reasonableness, moral agency, and finite love are expressed.

A primary virtue Aquinas identifies for social ethics is justice. Aquinas sees justice as an acquired habit of the will that allows the person to choose and then to act in accordance with what the intellect discerns to be just in relation to other persons. Justice is the standard for CST, and includes the dignity of the individual, the common good, and the fair participation of all.

Aquinas has a strong view of the inherent sociality of persons, and of the responsibilities of individuals to the good of the whole. Therefore "the virtue of a good citizen is general justice, whereby a person is directed to the common good."[8] The dignity and good of individuals is not entirely subsumed by the "body politic" because the ultimate purpose of human existence is unity with God.[9] Yet Aquinas describes the relation of persons to the common good as integral, a relation of part to whole. Following suit, CST holds in balance the interdependent dignity of the person and the common good.[10] The association of all persons in the temporal common good is an inherent and not merely instrumental good.

For CST, participation in the common good goes beyond receiving protections and benefits; it entails contributing to the good of others and to the common life, proportionately to the capacities of each, in solidarity with others. David Hollenbach calls this "contributive justice."[11] *Gaudium et spes* affirms that justice, love, and the common good are fulfilled only when all contribute to "the public and private institutions dedicated to bettering the conditions of human life."[12]

In Aquinas's ethics, charity and the other theological virtues (faith and hope) confirm and inspire the virtue of justice. Yet these do not override its requirements,[13] except in limited cases, such as religiously motivated fasting (instead of temperate eating), and the courage of martyrdom (rather than preservation of life). For example, Aquinas recognizes the contrary force of the Sermon on the Mount in his discussion of war, but still argues that war can be justified if necessary for the common good.[14]

CATHOLIC SOCIAL TEACHING, POLITICS, AND SIN

CST as political theology recognizes that evil and sin mar the created universe and the human creature's role in it. This makes politics both the art of the possible (Otto von Bismarck) and a realm of frequent compromise and occasional "justified" inequity or violence. The items on Thomas Massaro's list of key themes in CST connote underlying evils, the remedies for which are controversial, both at the level of international agreement and that of local application. The themes are the dignity of every person and human rights; solidarity, common good, and participation; family life; subsidiarity and the proper role of government; property ownership in modern society; the dignity of work, rights of workers, and support for labor unions; political self-determination and economic development; peace and disarmament; and option for the poor and vulnerable.[15] One could easily add other issues, such as the rights and roles of women, racial equality, and the conservation of the natural environment.

These values and goals are specified in view of the prevalence of their opposites: violations of human rights, family disruption, tyranny, unemployment, destitution, economic exploitation, and neocolonialism. An honest and effective Christian politics presumes radical self-examination and conversion from our own complicity in or causation of the suffering of others, so that we may "imagine alternatives to the way things are."[16] CST recognizes that such evils will always be a threat to justice, but refuses to concede that they cannot be penetrated by concerted political action.

THE ECCLESIAL AND POLITICAL
SPHERES: DISTINCTION WITHOUT SEPARATION

The ongoing historical contradiction of the gospel by myriad and profound evils poses a question that no political theology can avoid: What is the proper relation of "the church" to "the world"? Elizabeth Phillips poses this question in terms of God's eschatological reign as advanced by the church, and the potential of human government to order life according to God's wisdom even though that reign is "an already-but-not-yet reality."[17]

In the perspective of CST, the Church prophetically denounces unjust social norms, but is not limited to being a contrast society. CST participates in the public, political realm, imbuing it with values and practices that more closely cohere with the gospel. Ideally speaking, the political sphere is the place where a democratic consensus is formed and institutions built favoring just and transparent government, the rule of law, the good of the whole society, and the guarantee of individual rights. What the church especially brings to the table is a persistent and prophetic emphasis on values such as compassion, reconciliation, care for the poor, and solidarity. Catholic leaders, laity, and organizations are politically involved as Catholics; Catholics also belong to governments, legislative bodies, judiciaries, and a variety of politically active groups not specifically identified as religious. William Cavanaugh is right that there is no absolute divide between the "religious" and the "secular," for the boundaries are not only "contingent and fluid,"[18] they are interactive and interpenetrating.

For Catholic political theology (CST), a synergy between the ecclesial and political realms, even between Catholicism and liberalism, does not necessarily degrade Christian identity and its witness. Daniel Bell, representing a strand of political theology associated with postliberal theologians such as Stanley Hauerwas, John Milbank, and Oliver O'Donovan, accuses other political theologians of ceding the public square to a modern, liberal "*mythos* of politics as statecraft," while reducing the church to a mere "guardian of abstract values."[19] To the contrary, CST engages modern liberalism without ceding its distinctive voice, and certainly without speaking only in abstractions.

Popes, bishops, Vatican representatives, theologians, educators, and the vast array of Catholic organizations, movements, and activists, have taken very specific stances for and against particular laws, policies, and military ventures. These stances are backed and implemented by innumerable forms of concrete social action, from interventions at the United Nations in Geneva by the Vatican ambassador and the programs of Caritas Internationalis and Jesuit Relief Services to the political messages, symbolic actions, and voter education efforts of local bishops' conferences and Catholic nonprofits. These initiatives reflect some values shared with liberalism, such as equality and rights; but they also prioritize the common good, the preferential option for the poor, and the power of Christ and the Spirit to inspire historical, political change.

Proponents of CST would agree with Stanley Hauerwas that the church "is a social ethic"[20] in that it embodies justice as grounded in salvation from God in Jesus Christ. However, they would not agree with Hauerwas that the church does not "have" a social ethic, if by that is meant that the church has nothing explicitly to say about strategies for achieving more just forms of the common life. For CST, the social existence of the church *as church* implies the obligation – or better stated, the inevitability – of Christian political participation, both by the institution and by individual members. As *Gaudium et spes* teaches,

> The Church and the political community in their own fields are autonomous and independent from each other. Yet both, under different titles, are devoted to the personal and social vocation of the same men [and women]. The more that both foster sounder cooperation between themselves with due consideration for the circumstances of time and place, the more effective will their service be exercised for the good of all.[21]

Sometimes CST enters political discourse with a biblically and theologically backed "humanistic" vocabulary like common good, dignity, rights and responsibilities, and solidarity.[22] At other times, it is expressed through biblical narratives such as the parable of the Good Samaritan or symbolic actions such as John Paul II's visit to the Western Wall in Jerusalem, or Pope Francis's Vatican prayer vigil to avoid military intervention in Syria. The interaction of specifically religious sources in a wider public sphere is a flexible and ongoing question, opportunity, and project necessarily contoured to specific occasions and cultures.[23]

In CST since Vatican II, the amenability of cultures to religiously inspired insights, and of Christian politics to cooperation with other political traditions, is bolstered by the theological idea that grace is universal. This proposal is associated with the theologies of Henri de Lubac and Karl Rahner, both of whom were *periti* (expert advisors) at the Council. While de Lubac helped draft *Gaudium et spes*,[24] Rahner's highly influential theology of the "anonymous Christian" (a good person saved without explicit faith) is reflected in the Council document *Lumen Gentium*.[25]

As Kristin Heyer says of CST as political theology in the United States (which she terms "public theology"), faithfulness to Christian distinctiveness and the theological tradition must stand in a mutually corrective relation to other resources necessary to understand and address complex social problems. A "fully theological and fully public approach" avoids a false opposition between charity and justice, between Christian witness and advocacy for social reform, between protecting the identity of the church and cooperation with others "toward a more just society."[26]

For CST, "a political rendering of the claim that Christ is Lord"[27] neither equates to nor absolutely opposes political liberalism. CST sees a political role for religion that some liberals deny. With liberalism, CST endorses the personal rights and civil liberties guaranteed by modern democracies. Equally important, CST rejects the excessive individualism, greed, and consumerism that produce social exclusion and misery for the world's majority. Liberal autonomy and market capitalism must be limited by the reciprocal rights and duties of all in the common good. All citizens must be committed to more just "juridical-political structures" and to electing competent governments and leaders who take responsibility for "the commonwealth."[28]

Thomas Massaro invokes a pilgrimage metaphor to convey the dual religious and political identity of Christians moving toward the fullness of God's reign. Pilgrims feel deeply connected to the path they travel, as well as drawn forward by their holy destination. Christian pilgrims "give their full attention to the deliberate action of walking along the way of life," hoping that "by working together to improve the present age, the ultimate justice of God's kingdom will be reflected a bit more clearly through the attainment of greater social justice in the world we share."[29]

THE POLITICAL THEOLOGY OF CATHOLIC SOCIAL TEACHING IN VARIED HISTORICAL CONTEXTS

Although modern CST began in the nineteenth century, the origin of "political theology" proper is often considered to lie in the twentieth century, after the two world wars.[30] Mid-century political theology decries the political failure of the churches in the era of World War II, as owing to the idea that salvation concerns only the individual's immortal soul. The resulting politics was impotent in the face of monstrous social evil. For the political theologians, to be a Christian is to be committed to the gospel in the world and to the reordering of the world in light of the radical message of the gospel. These convictions also typify CST.

The leading political theologians, Jürgen Moltmann, Dorothee Sölle, and Johann Baptist Metz, all German, had experienced at firsthand the all too easy capitulation to, and even embrace of, the Nazi ideology by a supposedly "Christian culture." As teenagers during the war, the three struggled with the meaning and existence of divine goodness and power; with the meaning of Christ and salvation; and with the authentic social identity of the church.

Although the social commitment of these three is not generated from within the same grassroots experience of oppression that lies behind later theologies of liberation, they are far from armchair academics. Sölle was known for her activism. Metz and Moltmann were drafted into Hitler's army before they were twenty. Moltmann repeatedly laments the guilt and despair he suffered in belatedly realizing the enormity of the crimes he had indirectly supported.[31] All three are motivated by the responsibility of middle-class Christians, including academics, to be intelligent, critical, prophetic, and politically engaged.

For these theologians, as for CST, theology and politics are connected by the gospel. To live the gospel is to live forgiveness, reconciliation, sacrifice, and justice both in the community of disciples and in carrying out one's more expansive social roles. Christian particularity is not stripped away for the sake of a universal politics. To be a Christian is to practice Spirit-bestowed virtues that sensitize the agent to the priority of love, compassion, and inclusion; maintain these priorities despite obstacles, defeat, and suffering; and act with practical commitment and realistic hope. These political theologians trust that common action can be taken with advocates in other rich and "thickly" experienced traditions. The shared or universal dimensions of the human condition are known in and through particularities, at a level of depth within them. Common political values and goals are forged through the engagement of particular believers and traditions around common problems, not in abstract theories or in some illusory tradition-free zone.

CST, thought, and tradition likewise expect that other human beings, groups, and societies have sufficient capacity for straight thinking and goodwill to discern from within and among their specific identities the goods basic to human and social flourishing, and to act in favor of these goods a significant proportion of the time. According to CST, the distinctive role of the Church and the disciple of Christ is consistently to proclaim in word and deed the dignity of the person, the common good, and the priority of the poor, fought for in full recognition of the suffering that will result in a world marked by sin and evil.[32]

CST as political theology changes shape over time, responding to sociopolitical circumstances and to theological and ecclesial visions. The themes enunciated by Massaro are framed in a way reflecting a post–Vatican II, liberation-theology-informed sensibility, poising the Catholic Church and its members to act on a global stage. Yet key elements such as dignity of the person, common good, advocacy for the poor, cooperation of all persons and traditions in pluralistic societies, cooperation of church and state or government, social and legal rights and duties, democratic participation and rule of law remain in place throughout the tradition. Moreover, from *Rerum novarum* onward, the encyclicals are occasioned by the same issues: unjust economic disparities, the tendency of capitalists to exploit the working classes and the have-nots, and the ease with which the former manage to do so. However, the era of the Second Vatican Council brings a shift in emphasis, visible already in the encyclicals of John XXIII. While earlier encyclicals foregrounded the responsibilities of heads of state, legislators, and other elites within a hierarchical yet essentially just social order; later encyclicals are ever more critical of the vices that infect "First World" leadership and increasingly call entire populations and international institutions to account for worldwide poverty and structural violence.

LANDMARK ENCYCLICALS

To understand CST as political theology, it is useful to look at illustrative encyclicals, keeping in mind this growing concern with global social issues and the need to mobilize all levels of church and society. Not only do the popes respond differently to the problems of their era, their biblical-theological framework changes as they are informed by the demands of new social problems, and by the social vision, agenda, or strategy of the pope in question.

RERUM NOVARUM

When *Rerum novarum* appeared in 1891, it was preceded by efforts of a vast array of church officials, theologians, and grassroots leaders to respond to social questions including the movement from an agricultural to an industrial economy, and related dilemmas of family, politics, and culture. In the first half of the nineteenth century, the Catholic Church contended with the introduction of liberalism into European intellectual life and politics as a result of the Industrial Revolution. Emergent liberal values included free enterprise and democratic government, as well as freedom of conscience, publishing, teaching, and association. Liberal Catholic intellectuals met resistance and even condemnations from the Vatican; Pius IX mobilized Catholic resistance to liberal reforms across several nations, especially civil marriage and state control of education.[33] Then, as today, traditionalists were wary of change and loss of identity, transformationists began visionary local reforms to deal with immediate problems, and cosmopolitans hoped for international momentum toward social justice. In 1862, a French bishop wrote a pastoral letter condemning U.S. slavery as a violation of universal human rights.[34]

More important than Pius IX's specific political goals, however, is the fact that, even as he advanced the centralization of doctrine and ecclesial organization, he energized the social activity of lay Catholics, resulting in the creation of hundreds of new movements, associations, and organizations.[35] These "diverse and abundant expressions of Roman Catholic social thought," all sought to "enrich the Catholic imagination" and respond to "the shocking changes and enormous complexities of their world."[36]

Rerum novarum broke into a social situation burdened not only by social ills such as long work hours, dangerous work conditions, child labor, starvation wages, and inadequate housing, but also by the threats to civil and ecclesial authority posed by liberal, democratic, and Marxist solutions. Social reformers favoring the working class emerged in France, England, Switzerland, and Germany. With a paternalistic bent, they relied on charity rather than structural reforms to relieve the workers' plight.[37]

Rerum novarum reminds "the State" to protect the rights of property owners, without neglecting to keep "wage workers" and "the great mass of the needy ... under its special care and foresight."[38] Leo XIII handles worker justice as a duty of "rich men and employers," yet calls for measures by the "public authority" to ensure compliance.[39] Rulers must "make sure that the laws and institutions, the general character and administration of the commonwealth, shall be such as to produce of themselves public well-being and private prosperity."[40]

Nevertheless, *Rerum novarum* takes for granted that inequality is part of the natural order, necessary to society's harmonious operation,[41] though all are of equal spiritual standing before God. Class distinctions are not absolute; workers have a right to join workers' associations. The right of private ownership is asserted for all, from the factory owner or big industrialist down to the worker saving to improve his family's lot.

Some class mobility is envisioned. The rights of the poor are a matter of distributive justice, and are necessary to avoid class warfare. (Pope Leo overlooks the fact that for Aquinas, private property is actually not a natural right, or demanded by the natural law; though it can be justified on the basis of practical necessity, it is limited by the right of the poor to have basic needs met.[42])

Rerum novarum manages to call for structural reforms, maintain the weight of authority on the top side of the ecclesial and social order, and guard Christian revelation against encroaching philosophical systems, by turning to the neoscholastic theology and philosophy derived from the thought of Thomas Aquinas, whose work was formally sanctioned by Leo XIII in the encyclical *Aeterni Patris* (1879). According to one of the drafters of *Rerum Novarum*, a "sound scholastic philosophy" would "overcome ... false modern notions of liberty and authority."[43]

Anniversary Encyclicals: Quadragesimo anno, Mater et magistra, and Octogesima adveniens

In 1931 and 1971, Popes Pius XI and Paul VI wrote forty-year anniversary commemorations of *Rerum novarum* (*Quadragesimo anno* and *Octogesima adveniens*, respectively), with John XXIII taking up similar themes in *Mater et magistra* in 1961, after only thirty years. These later encyclicals reflect a less hierarchical social vision, increasingly champion the economic and social rights of the poor, and reflect a growing biblical-theological orientation, focused on the gospel. In the seventy years between the first and last of these encyclicals, democratic governmental reforms spread across Europe. After World War II, the global process of decolonization was irreversible. These developments affected the church, as theologians and the *magisterium* aligned with the legal and social recognition of democracy and human rights, and with discoveries of modern science. Within the church, these same currents shaped the Second Vatican Council. The social encyclical tradition increasingly accentuated the equality and unity of all members of society in the common good, and called for structural reforms, especially justice for the excluded.

Notable for introducing the concept "social justice" into the encyclical tradition, and for articulating the so-called principle of subsidiarity, Pius XI decisively names the need for all to participate actively in the common good. Though to be kept in the perspective of humanity's eternal good, justice demands equitable distribution of created goods.[44] (The socioeconomic rights of women are subsumed under those of the male wage earner, however; and the rights and duties of "man" are not nuanced to account for special barriers posed by racism and cultural difference.) The principle of subsidiarity responds to the threats of socialism and collectivism. It warns that "it is an injustice and at the same time a grave evil and disturbance of right order to assign to a greater and higher association what lesser and subordinate organizations can do."[45] Subsidiarity limits the power of government, while validating local institutions, grassroots community action, and labor organizations.

Pius XI's theological backing does not reference Jesus's mission to the vulnerable. In fact, the pope is more concerned with the spiritual welfare of the wealthy classes than with the material deprivation of the exploited. He appeals to the gospel and Christ to remind readers that they risk their "eternal salvation" if they are overly and unjustly attached to temporal goods, commending "the spirit of the Gospel, which is the spirit of Christian moderation and universal charity."[46] However, the connections among social justice, social charity that supports and enlivens it, and the common good in *Quadragesimo anno* "adumbrate relationships among common good, justice and solidarity developed later in the century by Pope John Paul II,"[47] who did foreground preferential love and justice for the poor. *Quadragesimo anno* proposes that the socioeconomic order be organized around the values of Roman Catholicism as the one true religion; yet it is forward looking in advocating social justice, the common good, and subsidiarity; denouncing huge economic disparities; and mandating serious structural reforms.[48]

The social vision of John XXIII's pre–Vatican II *Mater et Magistra* is already leaps and bounds beyond *Quadragesimo anno*. The encyclical opens a new era in Catholic social thought with its attitude of openness and dialogue. It addresses the issue of developing nations for the first time, and invites the laity to put CST into action by employing the method of "see, judge, act."[49] Gone are the running battles with liberalism and socialism, the suspicion of participatory democracy, the aspiration to establish Catholicism's authority over the civil order, and the ambition to suppress other religious faiths.

After the devastations of the Great Depression and World War II, many European societies turned to the welfare state to protect workers, some by means of socialist redistribution of property through high taxation. Though not going so far as to endorse socialism, *Mater et magistra* turns *Quadragesimo anno* on its head by redefining subsidiarity as the power and duty of "public authorities to reduce imbalances" and "intervene in a wide variety of economic affairs," when necessary for the common good.[50] The encyclical's methodology of "see, judge, act" gave rise to regional theologies beginning from the situation of the poor. Dom Helder Camara, then auxiliary bishop of Rio de Janeiro, called for implementation of *Mater et Magistra* to bring world peace and rebalance the relation between the industrialized and underdeveloped countries. Official recognition of the method encouraged local and regional appropriations of the Church's social message by bishops' conferences, including CELAM (Conference of Latin American Bishops).[51]

AFTER VATICAN II: POPULORUM PROGRESSIO

In 1967, just two years after the closing of Vatican II, Paul VI authored another social encyclical, *Populorum progressio*, on international development. This encyclical, building on John XXIII, consolidates a shift in the orientation and style of CST's social analysis. Despite the outward and onward-looking vision of Vatican II, the 1960s were shadowed by the Cold War, the battle for civil rights, and the division of the globe into different political and economic spheres: the so-called First World (prosperous industrialized nations), the Second World (the Soviet Union and nations it controlled in Eastern Europe, and Communist China), and the Third World (developing countries in Asia, Africa, and Latin America). In the face of these realities, *Populorum progressio* continues the social vision of *Gaudium et spes*, stressing Christian humanism, human dignity, dialogue, and solidarity in the universal common good. However, there is now an even more critical approach to the global effects of market capitalism, and a special emphasis on the dignity, needs, rights, and participation of the "less developed" peoples.[52]

Concerted global action must deal with the reality that "in whole continents countless men and women are ravished by hunger, [and] countless numbers of children are undernourished, so that many of them die in infancy."[53] *Populorum progressio* warns, "[I]t is not enough to recall principles, state intentions, point to crying injustice and utter prophetic denunciations; these words will lack real weight unless they are accompanied for each individual by a livelier awareness of personal responsibility and by effective action."[54]

More than pre–Vatican II encyclicals, *Populorum progressio* refers specifically to the transforming effect of the gospel as embodied in Jesus's ministry, in order to remind, chastise, and motivate readers. Jesus's special concern for the poor is a model for the Church's mission that is at the same time emerging in liberation theology, and that will increasingly inform magisterial teaching. "True to the teaching and example of her divine Founder, Who cited the preaching of the Gospel to the poor as a sign of His mission, the Church has never failed to foster the human progress of the nations to which she brings faith in Christ."[55] Paul announces a "global vision" of "integral development," consisting in the "full flowering" of "the good of every man and of the whole man."[56]

JOHN PAUL II

One more commemorative encyclical on *Rerum novarum* (*Centesimus annus*, 1991) is authored by John Paul II on its 100th anniversary. *Centesimus annus* does not renounce the system of democratic capitalism that first inspired the modern social tradition, yet resonates with the justice message of John XXIII. First, John Paul II accepts the possibility in principle that markets can be moral, and that the productivity they inspire can serve the good of individuals, the common good, and the poor. Second, *Centesimus annus* is cognizant of post–Vatican II debates about liberation theology and its alliance with Marxist analysis, the neoconservative defense of market capitalism, and specific responses to economic issues by local bishops' conferences.[57] While John Paul elaborates a defense of private property, he also insists that the market come under social and legal control, in order that the basic needs of all are met, and all have the opportunity of participation.[58]

Importantly, this encyclical incorporates the virtue of solidarity, earlier elaborated in John Paul's *Sollicitudo rei socialis* (1987), to be discussed in the following section. Categorizing solidarity with Leo XIII's friendship, and Pius XI's social charity, John Paul goes further in aligning solidarity with the "preferential option for the poor," an option defined as a "special form of primacy in the exercise of Christian charity." Solidarity requires national and international action to relieve economic, social, and political evils comparable to those caused by industrialization.[59]

ANNIVERSARY COMMEMORATIONS OF POPULORUM PROGRESSIO

Even though John Paul II in *Centesimus annus* adds to the series honoring the first papal social encyclical, he also begins a new tradition, one that marks twenty-year anniversaries of *Populorum progressio*. This commentary tradition had been initiated with *Sollicitudo rei socialis*, published four years before *Centesimus annus*. In the earlier work, John Paul II defines solidarity as "a firm and persevering determination to commit oneself to the common good."⁶⁰ Like *Populorum progressio*, *Sollicitudo rei socialis* is an encyclical on development that denounces the economic and social "mechanisms" exploited by more developed countries to "increase the wealth of the rich" and "increase the poverty of the poor." In the pope's view, private property is under a "social mortgage," with its use accountable to the common good.⁶¹ John Paul II targets unemployment, lack of housing, and international debt as symptoms of structures of global interdependence not framed by ethical criteria.⁶² These are in fact "structures of sin," to be overcome only through "human and Christian solidarity," and "the option or love of preference for the poor" manifest in the life of Christ.⁶³

It is *Populorum progressio*, not *Rerum novarum*, that becomes the touchstone of the political theologies of John Paul II's successors, Benedict XVI and, at least from early indications, Francis. *Populorum progressio*, along with *Sollicitudo rei socialis*, is at the start of the twenty-first century, the major articulation of CST on global economic justice. These encyclicals approach the matter in terms of solidarity of the privileged with the two-thirds world in the process of integral human development.

The 2009 commemorative encyclical of Benedict XVI, *Caritas in veritate*, illustrates the ongoing development of CST as political theology, as well as the challenges this tradition faces in an era in which Catholic social teaching, thought, and tradition are carried forward by teachers, thinkers, and practitioners in the Global South.⁶⁴

As a rendition of CST, *Caritas in veritate* should be considered in light of Benedict's 2005 encyclical *Deus caritas est*. The latter reflects Benedict's long-standing concern to reinvigorate the Christian identity of a secularizing Europe, and to raise the Roman Catholic Church's countercultural voice. Backing this encyclical is a theology of Christ as the incarnate Word, whose world-transcending identity enables a personal relation to God. Social justice is distanced from theological charity, with the former consigned to the laity and the latter designated the mission of the church as such. Thus, "building a just social and civil order" is not "the Church's immediate responsibility" but a "political task."⁶⁵

The drafting of *Caritas in veritate*, however, was in process at the same time as preparation for the 2009 Second Synod for the Bishops of Africa. The themes of *Populorum progressio* had to be tailored to the depth and complexity of current problems in the Global South, including those the African bishops were urgently addressing.⁶⁶ In contrast with *Deus caritas est*, *Caritas in veritate* portrays "integral human development and authentic development" as "the heart of the Christian social message."[67] Work for justice as structural change is demanded by Christian love, not as a secondary task of lay Christians in nonecclesial roles. Indeed, charity inspires "courageous and generous engagement in the field of justice and peace."[68] Solidarity in this encyclical is defined as "gratuitous" concern for one's neighbor, and extends to international responsibility, justice, and the common good.[69] Envisioning the partnerships that effective change assumes, Benedict asserts that God's presence is seen in all those who work for justice, not in Christians or the church alone.[70]

Despite this reorientation of perspective by Benedict, African theologians have raised a number of questions about the adequacy of CST for Africa. When social analysis begins in the continent, the perspective on CST as "political theology" looks rather different. Africa's main social problems are not liberal individualism, secularism, or excessive attachment to the luxuries available to few. Africa's more urgent agenda is postcolonial liberation of "masses of Africans from their subservience to a collective oppressive mentality and memory."[71] Economic development models adopted in the CST tradition range from modernization theory (*Gaudium et spes* and *Populorum progressio*) to dependency theory (*Octogesima adveniens*, *Justitia in mundo*, and *Evangelii nuntiandi*), and recently to a more complex cultural analysis (*Sollicitudo rei socialis*) favoring "integral development." Yet even the new model runs the risk of blaming the predicament of Africa on African culture.[72] CST must engage more deeply with African traditional values, appropriating African resources for justice and peace, HIV/AIDS, transparent governance, human rights, and poverty reduction, in specific local cultures.[73]

Even a concept so integral to contemporary CST as "solidarity" works differently as "political theology" in Africa. Intended by the popes to inspire commitment across classes, cultures, and nations, "solidarity" in the African context can have an unfortunate resonance with the ethnic and clan loyalties that have in fact validated corruption and violence.[74] Along these lines, CST could present a salutary redefinition of family identity with Pauline imagery of a new, inclusive family in Christ. Still, critical awareness is needed of the ways that traditional African religion and culture, and the Catholic Church, oppress women in families, denying women the familial, social, and ecclesial roles they deserve.[75]

African CST, and other versions from the two-thirds world, will not be mere duplicates or straightforward applications of the political theologies of the North. While recognizably similar to such criteria as the common good, dignity of the person, and solidarity, they bring fresh and creative insights and practices from which multiple cultures can learn. Agbonkhianmeghe Orobator offers an African model for the resulting political theology: palaver.

> Rather than a dialogue of like-minded inquirers, producing a sanitized chorus of theological formulas, this methodology creates a shared intellectual space allowing theologians to expand the horizon and frontier of their understanding of God, faith, and the community called church.[76]

This space and process will need to incorporate practical experience, extend beyond senior elites and males, and lead forward as a concrete, on-the-ground and transformative politics. "[T]he vision of Catholic social thought is grounded in a ... radical unity of the human family ... and challenges us to build a community of solidarity," in line with the gospel.[77] Yet it is equally true that the politics of and the theology behind CST are shaped by the particular contexts in which CST has its roots and effects, and it is in these that the politics of salvation in Christ and the Spirit find their ultimate expression.

CONCLUSION

CST embodies an evolving tradition of political theology with certain enduring characteristics: the dignity of the person, the common good, reciprocity of governments and citizens, democratic rule and just laws, advocacy for the marginalized, and alliances among Christians and others to improve social life. While official CST still refers primarily to papal and episcopal documents, the present Argentinean pope, Francis, travels extensively to encounter the realities of church and politics in multiple cultural contexts. He goes beyond statements, addresses, and encyclicals to include symbolic actions, liturgies, and informal interviews as media of expression. These seem to invite further interaction to define and refine the church's political presence.

Returning to the three distinctive characteristics of CST, we see *first*, that the universalist and constructive outlook of CST has since Vatican II given increasing attention to global responsibility for violence, war, and economic injustice. *Second*, CST has begun, if more slowly, to grasp that the option for the poor has to become an option *of* and *by* the poor, framed from the poor's perspective. The future of CST as political theology calls for more decentralized forms of creativity and leadership. *Third*, CST's alliances with liberalism in Europe and North

America will need to make room for equally prophetic and constructive relationships to the cultural-political heritages of other peoples and continents.

Notes

1. Official documents are available at the Vatican website, www.vatican.va.
2. Kenneth R. Himes, O.F.M., "Introduction," in *Modern Catholic Social Teaching*, ed. Kenneth R. Himes (Washington, DC: Georgetown University Press, 2005), p. 3.
3. Johan Verstraeten, "Rethinking Catholic Social Thought as Tradition," in *Catholic Social Thought: Twilight or Renaissance?*, ed. J. S. Boswell, F. P. McHugh, and J. Verstraeten (Leuven, Belgium: Peeters, 2000), p. 63.
4. R. Bruce Douglass, "Introduction," in *Catholicism and Liberalism: Contributions to American Public Philosophy*, ed. R. Bruce Douglass and David Hollenbach (Cambridge: Cambridge University Press, 2006), pp. 10, 12.
5. Francis P. McHugh, "Muddle or Middle-Level: A Place for Natural Law in Catholic Social Thought," in *Catholic Social Thought*, pp. 35–57.
6. Thomas Aquinas, *Summa Theologiae*, I-II.Q91.a 2.
7. Ibid., I-II.Q94.a2.
8. Ibid., II-II.Q58.a6.
9. Ibid., I-II.Q21.a4.ad3.
10. *Gaudium et spes*, no. 26.
11. David Hollenbach, S.J., *Common Good and Christian Ethics* (Cambridge: Cambridge University Press, 2002), p. 198. See also pp. 9, 69–70, 81, 196. David Matzko McCarthy reinforces this same point in "Modern Economy and the Social Order," in David Matzko McCarthy, *The Heart of Catholic Social Teaching: Its Origin and Contemporary Significance* (Grand Rapids, MI: Brazos, 2009), p. 135.
12. *Gaudium et spes*, no. 30.
13. ST.II-II.Q104.a6.
14. Ibid., .II-II.Q40.
15. Thomas Massaro, S.J., *Living Justice: Catholic Social Teaching in Action* (Franklin, WI: Sheed and Ward, 2000), pp. 113–65.
16. Maureen H. O'Connell, *Compassion: Loving Our Neighbor in an Age of Globalization* (Maryknoll, NY: Orbis, 2009), p. 169.
17. Elizabeth Phillips, *Political Theology: A Guide for the Perplexed* (London: T&T Clark, 2012), p. 57.
18. William T. Cavanaugh, "The Invention of the Religious-Secular Distinction," in *At the Limits of the Secular: Reflections on Faith and Public Life*, ed. William A. Barbieri Jr. (Grand Rapids, MI: Eerdmans, 2014), p. 121.
19. Daniel M. Bell Jr., "State and Civil Society," in *The Blackwell Companion to Political Theology*, ed. Peter Scott and William T. Cavanaugh (Oxford: Blackwell, 2004), pp. 429, 431.
20. Stanley Hauerwas, *The Peaceable Kingdom: A Primer in Christian Ethics* (Notre Dame, IN: University of Notre Dame, 1983), p. 99.

21 *Gaudium et spes*, no. 76.
22 Slavika Jakelić, "Engaging Religious and Secular Humanisms," in *At the Limits of the Secular: Reflections on Faith and Public Life*, ed. William A. Barbieri Jr. (Grand Rapids, MI: Eerdmans, 2014), pp. 305–30.
23 William T. Barbieri, "Introduction," in *Limits of the Secular*, pp. 13–14; and the collection as a whole.
24 Kevin E. Miller, "The Gift and Mission of Love: The Theological Dimension of Catholic Social Teaching," in *Catholic Social Thought: American Reflections on the Compendium*, ed. D. Paul Sullins and Anthony J. Blasi (Lanham, MD, and Boulder, CO: Rowman and Littlefield, 2009), pp. 3–13.
25 *Lumen Gentium*, no. 15.
26 Kristin E. Heyer, *Prophetic and Public: The Social Witness of U.S. Catholicism* (Washington, DC: Georgetown University Press, 2006), p. 203.
27 Bell, "State and Civil Society," p. 436.
28 *Gaudium et spes*, no. 75, on "Political Participation."
29 Massaro, *Living Justice*, p. 49.
30 Phillips, *Political Theology*, pp. 42–4; and Michael Kirwan, *Political Theology: An Introduction* (Minneapolis, MN: Fortress Press, 2009), pp. 6, 126, 129–39, 171–5, 182–3, 192; John K. Downey, ed., *The Political Theology of Johann Baptist Metz* (Harrisburg, PA: Trinity Press International); J. Matthew Ashley, "Johann Baptist Metz," in *Blackwell Companion*, pp. 241–55; and O'Connell, *Compassion*, pp. 120–47.
31 See, e.g., *Jesus Christ for Today's World*, trans. Margaret Kohl (Minneapolis MN: Fortress, 1994), pp. 2–3.
32 See David Hollenbach, S.J., "Social Ethics under the Sign of the Cross," in *The Global Face of Public Faith* (Washington, DC: Georgetown University Press, 2003), pp. 54–71.
33 Vera Negri Zamagni, "The Political and Economic Impact of CST since 1891," in *The True Wealth of Nations: Catholic Social Thought and Economic Life*, ed. Daniel K. Finn (Oxford: Oxford University Press, 2010), p. 98.
34 Michael J. Schuck, "Early Modern Roman Catholic Social Thought, 1740–1890," in Himes, *Modern Catholic Social Thought*, p. 101.
35 Zamagni, "Impact of CST," pp. 98–9.
36 Schuck, "CST, 1740–1890," pp. 118–19.
37 Thomas A. Shannon, "Commentary on *Rerum novarum* (*The Condition of Labor*)," in Himes, *Modern Catholic Social Thought*, pp. 131–2.
38 *Rerum novarum*, no. 54.
39 Ibid., no. 38.
40 Ibid., no. 26.
41 Ibid., no. 15.
42 ST.II-II.Q66.a2.
43 Matteo Liberatore, S.J., as cited by Shannon, in "Commentary on RN," p. 133.
44 *Quadragesimo anno*, nos. 57–8.
45 Ibid., no. 79.
46 Ibid., nos. 130, 138.
47 Christine Firer Hinze, "Commentary on *Quadragesimo anno* (*After Forty Years*)," in Himes, *Modern Catholic Social Thought*, p. 167.

48 Ibid., p. 171.
49 Marvin L. Mich, "Commentary on *Mater et magistra* (*Christianity and Social Progress*)," in Himes, *Modern Catholic Social Thought*, p. 191.
50 *Mater et magistra*, nos. 53–4.
51 Mich, "*Mater et magistra*," p. 211.
52 Alan Figueroa Deck, "Commentary on *Populorum progressio* (*On the Development of Peoples*)," in Himes, *Modern Catholic Social Thought*, p. 297.
53 *Populorum progressio*, no. 45.
54 Ibid., nos. 31, 51.
55 Ibid., no. 12.
56 Ibid., nos. 13–14.
57 Daniel K. Finn, "Commentary on *Centesimus annus* (*On the Hundredth Anniversary of Rerum Novarum*)," in Himes, *Modern Catholic Social Thought*, pp. 439–40.
58 *Centesimus annus*, nos. 35, 48, 58.
59 Ibid., nos. 10–11.
60 *Sollicitudo rei socialis*, no. 38; and *Centesimus annus*, no. 49, respectively.
61 *Sollicitudo rei socialis*, no. 42.
62 Ibid., nos. 16–20.
63 Ibid., nos. 40, 42.
64 Daniel McDonald, S.J., ed., *Catholic Social Teaching in Global Perspective* (Maryknoll, NY: Orbis, 2010).
65 *Caritas in veritate*, nos. 28–9.
66 Message of the Second Special Assembly for Africa of the Synod of Bishops "Africa, Rise Up and Walk!," AsiaNews.it, http://www.asianews.it/index.php?l=en&art=16681 (accessed October 25, 2009); and Agbonkhianmeghe E. Orobator, S.J., ed., *Reconciliation, Justice and Peace: The Second African Synod* (Maryknoll, NY: Orbis, 2011).
67 *Caritas in veritate*, no. 13.
68 Ibid., no. 1.
69 Ibid., no. 38.
70 Ibid., no. 78.
71 A. E. Orobator, "*Caritas in Veritate* and Africa's Burden of (Under) Development," *Theological Studies* 71.2 (June 2010): 320–34 (see p. 323).
72 Uzochukwu Jude Njoku, "The Influence of Changes in Socio-Economic Thinking on the Development of Post-Vatican II Catholic Social Teaching," *Political Theology* 8.2 (2007): 235–48.
73 David Kaulemu, "Building Solidarity for Social Transformation through the Church's Social Teaching," in McDonald, *CST in Global Perspective*, pp. 36–80. See also David Kaulem, "The African Synod for Those of Us Who Stayed Home," in Orobator, *Reconciliation, Justice and Peace*, pp. 143–55.
74 Orobator, "*Caritas in veritate*," p. 328.
75 Ibid., pp. 330–1; and Teresa Okure, "Church-Family of God: The Place of God's Reconciliation, Justice and Peace"; Anne Arabome, "'Woman, You Are Set Free!' Women and Discipleship in the Church"; and "Come, Let Us Talk This Over: On the Condition of Women Religious in the Church," all in Orobator, *Reconciliation, Justice and Peace*, pp. 13–24, 119–30, 131–42.

76 Orobator, "Introduction: The Synod as Ecclesial Conversation," in *Reconciliation, Justice, and Peace*, p. 5.
77 Meghan J. Clark, *The Vision of Catholic Social Thought: The Virtue of Solidarity and the Praxis of Human Rights* (Minneapolis, MN: Fortress, 2014), p. 146.

Further Reading

Barbieri, W. A., Jr., *At the Limits of the Secular: Reflections on Faith and Public Life*. Grand Rapids, MI, and Cambridge: Eerdmans, 2014.

Beyer, G. J., "The Meaning of Solidarity in Catholic Social Thought," *Political Theology* 15.1 (January 2014): 7–25.

Clark, M. J., *The Vision of Catholic Social Thought: The Virtue of Solidarity and the Praxis of Human Rights*. Minneapolis, MN: Fortress, 2014.

Coleman, J. A., and W. F. Ryan, eds., *Globalization and Catholic Social Thought: Present Crisis, Future Hope*. Ottawa, ON: Novalis, 2005.

Himes, K. R., O.F.M., et al., eds., *Modern Catholic Social Teaching: Commentaries and Interpretations*. Washington, DC: Georgetown University Press, 2005.

Hollenbach, D., S.J., *The Common Good and Christian Ethics*. Cambridge and New York: Cambridge University Press, 2002.

Massaro, T. J., S.J., *Living Justice: Catholic Social Teaching in Action*. Franklin, WI: Sheed and Ward, 2000.

McCarthy, D. M., ed., *The Heart of Catholic Social Teaching: Its Origins and Contemporary Significance*. Grand Rapids, MI: Brazos Press, 2009.

McDonald, D., S.J., ed., *Catholic Social Teaching in Global Perspective*. Maryknoll, NY: Orbis, 2010.

Orobator, A. E., S.J., ed., *Reconciliation, Justice and Peace: The Second African Synod*. Maryknoll, NY: Orbis, 2011.

Phillips, E., *Political Theology: A Guide for the Perplexed*. London: T&T Clark, 2012.

Pontifical Council of Justice and Peace, *Compendium of the Social Doctrine of the Church*. New York: Bloomsbury, 2006.

Pope, S. J., ed., *The Ethics of Aquinas*. Washington, DC: Georgetown University Press, 2002.

5 Protestant Social Ethics
D. STEPHEN LONG

ORIGINS OF PROTESTANT SOCIAL ETHICS

Although Protestant Christianity always had a concern for ethics, "Protestant social ethics" identifies something narrower within this ongoing concern, a preoccupation with ethics that emerged within liberal Protestantism when subjectivity, moral experience, and historical mediation became central themes. These themes challenge previous metaphysical certainties and make ethics rather than metaphysics the "first philosophy" upon which theology works. "Protestant social ethics" has a history that begins among German Protestants and then gets transplanted to various parts of the world, especially England and North America. Because "Protestant social ethics" in the twenty and twenty-first centuries is unintelligible without this history, attention must be paid to the foundations laid in the eighteenth and nineteenth century. Those foundations begin with Immanuel Kant (1724–1804).

The Emergence of Liberal Protestantism: Precursor to Protestant Social Ethics in the Eighteenth and Nineteenth Centuries

As Gary Dorrien so aptly puts it, "The modern departure in religious thought begins with the unavoidable figure in modern philosophy, Immanuel Kant.... Enlightenment rationalism had a critique of authority religion before Kant came along, and it advocated using reason to its utmost. But it had no theory of the creative power of subjectivity or the grounding of religion and freedom in moral experience."[1] Kant shifted the questions theology posed. Prior to Kant, Roman Catholic scholastic theology and much of Protestant orthodoxy began by asking, "who is God?" and "does God exist?" Theology began with the speculative or contemplative task. The true and the beautiful were as important as the good. Kant's arguments against the proofs for God's existence in his first critique, *The Critique of Pure Reason*, persuasive or not, changed the questions, making questions of epistemology and morality foundational. Roman Catholic scholastic theology and Protestant orthodoxy could no longer begin with the confidence they previously had. If they still claim metaphysical answers to the questions "who is God?" and "does God exist?," they were nonetheless forced to defend their answers in the face of Kant's critique. However, Kant did not categorically reject proofs for God's existence, nor did he reject metaphysics. He revised both, and in the process made "ethics" more central than it had hitherto been. For the liberal Protestantism that emerged Kant's moral proof for the existence of God provided a way forward, especially as Kant translated Christianity into an ethics that emphasized the Kingdom of God.

Kant's moral proof for God's existence in his second critique, *The Critique of Practical Reason*, brought together, in part, what he divided in his first critique – freedom and nature. He claimed in his first critique that causation could be explained equally well by assuming human creatures were free agents or that natural forces determined them. Pure reason could not resolve this antinomy. Practical reason, however, could. Moral responsibility requires that we assume human freedom. Otherwise, human creatures would be no more responsible for their actions than a force of nature. If we are to assume humans are free agents, then something other than nature alone must provide the conditions for that freedom. Moreover, if humans were free agents acting morally, and nature did not always support their morality by making them happy, something other than nature had to be posited to bring about the happiness of persons' freely accomplished moral actions – a happiness often denied in this life. God, Kant argued, could be postulated as the most plausible source for human freedom and the moral law, and the judge who would bring about the required happiness in the Kingdom of God. The Kingdom of God became central to his moral philosophy, but he meant something specific by it that did not fit well what Jesus announced in the Gospels.

Kant distinguished the Kingdom of God as an "ethical commonwealth" from the state as a "juridico-civil society."[2] The Kingdom of God is more universal. It is based on divine law, but it is a law that each person also affirms by exercising her or his moral autonomy and responsibility. The Kingdom of God surpasses the church with its "ecclesiastical faith," and assumes a higher reality of "moral" or "pure religious faith."[3] As Kant put it, "The gradual transition of ecclesiastical faith to the exclusive sovereignty of pure religious faith is the coming of the Kingdom of God."[4] Jesus is the embodiment of "pure religious faith" because he lives exclusively from his "moral idea of reason," overcoming his Jewish parochial history.[5] The Kingdom of God is then the ethical commonwealth that is coming, which is distinct from the state and the church, although they both point to it. It becomes a regulative ethical ideal that allows a deontological ethic that, although it cannot guarantee happiness in this life, nonetheless provides a purely moral or religious faith that each individual should seek to embody by treating every person with dignity as an end and not a means. If there is a continuous thread throughout "Protestant social ethics," it is the Kingdom of God as its goal.

While affirming the freedom Kant made central for liberal Protestantism, G. W. F. Hegel (1770–1831) offered an alternative to Kant. He set the course for Protestant social ethics for at least three reasons. First, like Kant, he was convinced that only Protestantism preserves the freedom necessary for moral and political action. Second, and unlike Kant, he located subjectivity in sociohistorical contexts. Ethics is more than an individual standing before a moral law required to fulfill duties; it is found in the intersubjectivity of *Sittlichkeit* ("ethical life"). Hegel set *Sittlichkeit* against Kant's *Moralität*. As Charles Taylor notes, Hegel found Kant's morality empty because it always set morality and freedom against nature. Kant's "kingdom" could never be embodied because it could not be found in nature; it lacked a substantive politics. Hegel turned to the historical mediation of customs (*Sitten*) in particular communities. Spirit moves through these mediations becoming ever more rational, reconciling freedom and nature.[6] Third, Hegel drew on the Christian doctrine of the Trinity, developing it as a historical movement of Spirit, to overcome the nature/freedom split Kant bequeathed. Hegel maintained much more of the content of historical Christianity than did Kant, but like Kant he understood the historical church as transitional. Revealed religion is "picture religion" that must give way to Spirit as Absolute Knowing, which will be found in a rational state.[7] As Charles Taylor persuasively argues, Hegel was no lackey for the Prussian state, nor is he a source for fascism.[8] He does, however, see the outcome of the historical mediation of Spirit(s) as a free and rational state.

Hegel's development of Protestant theology emphasized historical mediation. The move to historical mediation defines liberal Protestantism. However, neither Kant nor Hegel rejected metaphysics for a purely historical orientation. That move was made by Albrecht Ritschl, who reinterpreted the historical significance of Jesus as the value he gave to the Kingdom of God.[9] Ritschl's historical approach influenced in varying degrees Harnack, Herrmann, Troeltsch, and

Rauchsenbusch. The move to history also led to historical quests for the real Jesus, who often turned out to be a modern, ethical teacher or a failed apocalyptic prophet, which is to say, he announced a Kingdom of God that never came. If this was Jesus, what were Christians to do? Protestant social ethics is what happens when Jesus is either understood as an ethical teacher who proclaimed the Kingdom as an ethical commonwealth or is understood as a failed apocalyptic prophet whose Kingdom never came, and thus his failed Kingdom is replaced with the ethical commonwealth. When Jesus is understood as a failed apocalyptic prophet, then rather than being abandoned as was the case with some such as David Friedrich Strauss (1808–74), he must be reconceived by emphasizing new aspects of his life that had previously gone unrecognized such as his religious personality, consciousness, or ethical teaching on the Kingdom of God without the eschatology, which is what occurs in Ernst Troeltsch (1865–1923) whose influential work sets the bar for Protestant social ethics.

As Gary Dorrien notes, "Hegel's fluid, spiraling, relational panentheism changed the debate in theology about how God might relate to the world," which "paved the way for Troeltsch."[10] Troeltsch so emphasizes the historical nature of religion that he is often accused of relativism.[11] Unlike Kant and Hegel, Troeltsch interprets Jesus as failed apocalyptic preacher. Jesus's failure is not ultimately decisive for Christianity. His eschatological preaching is not important; what matters are his "personality" and its influence. In itself, Jesus's personality is neither social nor political. In order to become such, it must merge with some other ethical system.

Troeltsch's colleague Max Weber (1864–1920) encouraged him to address the "social question."[12] He did so and published a watershed work for Protestant social ethics in 1911, *The Social Teaching of the Christian Churches*. Troeltsch argued that Christianity has no politics or social ethic because it provides no blueprint for "society." It did not ask the "social question," but was "purely religious." Jesus proclaimed the Kingdom of God, but Troeltsch stated, "This Message of the Kingdom was primarily the vision of an ideal ethical and religious situation, of a world entirely controlled by God, in which all the values of pure spirituality would be recognized and appreciated at their true worth."[13] As with Kant and Hegel, for Troeltsch, Christianity becomes ethical only with its contribution to the Kingdom of God, where the Kingdom is understood as an ethical commonwealth that must be mediated to society. By "society" Troeltsch meant the following: "the social relationships which result from the economic phenomena."[14] Christianity contains no intrinsic social teaching because it provides no specific platform for the economic distribution of goods and services. There is at most a "Christian ethos," which Troeltsch defined as "absolute individualism and absolute universalism." Nonetheless, Christianity developed social teachings that could address the social question. Here is how he understood the task: "If we admit that the State and the Society, together with innumerable other forces are still the main formative powers of civilization, then the ultimate problem may be stated thus: How can the Church harmonize with these main forces in such a way that together they will form a unity of civilization?"[15] The question of social ethics becomes the question of the church's contribution to some greater whole – "civilization."

If Weber gave Troeltsch the impetus to address the social question, he also provided an ethical framework that has lasting influence on Protestant social ethics. In 1918 Weber gave a famous speech at the University of Munich entitled "Politics as a Vocation," in which he distinguished an "ethics of ultimate ends" and "ethic of responsibility." They represent "two fundamentally and irreconcilably opposed maxims," which can guide moral action. The former is not identified with "irresponsibility," but Weber stated, "there is an abysmal contrast between conduct that follows the maxim of an ethic of ultimate ends – that is, in religious terms, 'The Christian does rightly and leaves the results with the Lord' – and conduct that follows the maxim of an ethic of responsibility, in which case one has to give an account of foreseeable results of one's actions."[16] Because the "decisive means for politics is violence," only an "ethic of responsibility" can be political; for it alone allows agents to eschew perfection and take up the sword. Weber wrote, "No ethics in the world can dodge the fact that in numerous instances the attainment of 'good' ends is bound to the fact that one must be willing to pay the price of using morally dubious means or at least dangerous ones – and facing the possibility or even the probability of evil ramifications."[17]

Troeltsch, like Weber, constructed a typological answer to the form of the relationship between the church and other social formations by examining historical movements, abstracting an ideal essence from them and setting forth those abstractions as ideal types. Three ideal types constructed his answer to the social question: the church type, the sect type, and the mystical type. The first two mirror Weber's ethics of responsibility versus ethics of ultimate ends. Briefly put, the church type contributes to other social formations by adopting a social ethic from the culture at large. It chooses responsibility over faithfulness.

Medieval Christianity primarily accomplished this through the adoption of the stoic natural law. The sect type refused accommodation with the larger culture and maintained its religious purity. In so doing it became politically irrelevant. It chooses faithfulness over responsibility. The mystical type emphasized a noninstitutional form of Christianity that privileged individual freedom. Troeltsch clearly thought that this third type embodied the direction modern Protestantism would, and should, pursue.

The Twentieth and Twenty-First Century

Troeltsch and Weber led the transition to twentieth-century Protestant social ethics. Twentieth- and twenty-first-century Protestant social ethics is an ongoing debate about the legacy Kant, Hegel, Troeltsch, and Weber bequeathed us. The legacy is vast and complicated, but its focus is often on how we should understand the "Kingdom" (or Realm) "of God." Is it an ethical commonwealth to which the church and its ecclesiastical faith should be subordinate? If so, how? What is the role of the nation, the state, culture, and economics in this Kingdom of God? Is the ethical commonwealth more directly tied to the church and its ecclesiastical faith? If so, how? Is the church a social ethic or politics? Answers to these questions fall along a continuum (perhaps) between two poles. At one pole are those who would subordinate the church *to* the ethical commonwealth. At the other pole are those who understand the church *as* an ethical commonwealth. For the first pole, the church will need to look to "society" and find a way to mediate its essentially religious idea. For the second pole, no neutral or pure "society" exists. The church is a society among others constantly negotiating its mission through witness and service.

POLE I: CHURCH AND ECCLESIASTICAL FAITH IN
SERVICE TO THE ETHICAL COMMONWEALTH

Other than "death of God" theologians (left-wing Hegelians for whom "God" is nothing more than an immanent spirit embodied in communal practices), no Protestant social ethicist would dissolve the church into the ethical commonwealth. However, some find the primary task of social ethics is to serve the Kingdom of God by using it as an ideal to guide "society" toward a progressive betterment. The church points away from itself and toward a more universal ethical commonwealth. Jesus's eschatological teachings, and his formation of the church, are less significant that the universal ideals of dignity or human rights that can be culled from his unique personality or his ethical teachings.

A Social Gospel and Human Progress

Walter Rauschenbusch (1861–1918) explicitly argued that ethics should replace eschatology. He developed a tradition known as the "Social Gospel" that took the ethical ideals of the gospel and applied them to the "social," which are institutions of governance and economics. Rauschenbusch's *Christianizing the Social Order* perpetuated Troeltsch's answer to the social question by finding the vocation of the church was to "mould our public opinions and our institutions from the foundation up."[18] By "our" Rauschenbusch meant the American nation. It was the formative civilizing power such that the church's response to sociopolitical matters depended upon its ability to mold the opinions of national institutions. Some Protestant churches adopted this same strategy by setting forth a Social Creed in 1908. The Social Creed was a progressive political platform calling for equal rights, a living wage, the abolition of child labor, an end to sweatshop labor, and a limit to the workweek. It remains a powerful expression of a social ethic that accords with similar movements toward "social justice" occurring in Roman Catholicism during this time.[19] Although the courage and witness of the Social Gospel against exploitative economic practices should be affirmed and celebrated, it also carried within it the assumption found in liberal Protestantism that Christianity was neither social nor political but primarily religious. In other words, Christianity becomes a "social ethic" when something not constitutive of it, but to which it contributes, mediates it to the "social." The essence of Protestant Christianity remained what it had become in modernity, a private transaction of salvation between God and the individual, which then needed mediation through a discourse or practice external to Christianity if it were to become a social ethic.

The Methodist theologian and first woman to teach theology in a U.S. seminary, Georgia Harkness (1891–1974), reflects well the themes of Protestant social ethics within the liberal Protestant tradition. She acknowledges Jesus was Jewish, and identifies three strands of Judaism – nationalism, legalism, and apocalypticism. Jesus rejects the first two but was influenced by the third. His apocalypticism poses a problem for Christian ethics because the apocalypticism of Jesus's day was "pessimistic and fatalistic." However, Jesus differed from it in that his apocalypticism was "centered in a serious, but joyous and confident, reliance on God." Persons would inherit the Kingdom based on their "treatment of one's fellow man." Despite Jesus's lack of concern with "political schemes or plans for immediate social amelioration," Harkness argued that ethical principles could be abstracted from his apocalyptic teaching, and such principles would be "adaptable to all times."[20]

Although Harkness clearly represents liberal Protestantism, her hymns set forth substantive Christological convictions. Her "Hope of the World" continues to have profound influence in mainline Protestant Churches. She wrote:

> Hope of the world, Thou Christ of great compassion;
> Speak to our fearful hearts by conflict rent.
> Save us, Thy people, from consuming passion,
> Who by our own false hopes and aims are spent.
>
> Hope of the world, God's gift from highest heaven,
> Bringing to hungry souls the bread of life,
> Still let Thy Spirit unto us be given
> to heal earth's wounds and end our bitter strife.

Harkness presented Christ as the "Hope of the World." As Kenneth Oakes has demonstrated, liberal Protestantism was often Christocentric. Knowledge of God comes through Christ's revelation.[21] But how Christ relates to ethics remained unrelated to any dogmatic claims that the church traditionally ascribed to him. He influences us through his religious personality or his consciousness. It provides us with what we need to enact the ethical commonwealth. Notice the last line in the hymn in the preceding text that requests the Spirit be given so that we "heal earth's wounds." Ethics replaces eschatology. In fact, some contemporary inheritors of liberal Protestantism find that the dogmatic tradition and Christian eschatology pose a threat to Protestant social ethics. Catherine Keller, a Methodist theologian, expresses this well. After rejecting most of the traditional teaching on God and its correlative eschatology, she concludes, "It is not up to God to right our moral wrongs, to fix our injustices and correct our oppressions. That doesn't happen. To depend on God to intervene, to justify 'himself,' to operate as the just patriarch is to abdicate our own moral responsibility for the earth."[22] But is this what Harkness asserts in the last line of her hymn? Is it Christian hope or human moral progress?

Niebuhrian Realism

A contemporary of Georgia Harkness, Reinhold Niebuhr (1892–1971) skewered what he thought was an unwarranted optimism in liberal Protestantism. Although he held many similarities with it, he denied its affirmation that the Kingdom of God would come in history. Niebuhr was much less Christocentric in his version of Protestant social ethics. He found the incarnation to be "logical nonsense"; someone historically conditioned (Jesus's humanity) could not be the eternal unconditioned (Jesus's divinity.) [23] But Niebuhr thought liberal Protestantism neglected the all-pervasive character of sin, which resulted in a too easy call for the realization of the Kingdom. He retrieved an "Augustinian" sense of sin. Robin Lovin notes that Niebuhr opposed "one fundamental confusion" in liberal Protestantism: "the moral vision of the New Testament is treated as a 'simple possibility.' It becomes a key point of Christian Realism that the ethics of Jesus cannot provide a social ethics."[24] If Jesus does not provide a social ethics, then, of course, a social ethic will need to be adopted by Christianity. Niebuhr found such an ethic in Max Weber's (and Adam Smith's) doctrine of unintended consequences. Good moral action always brings with it unintended consequences. If those consequences are not taken into account, then pursuing the good through an ethic of ultimate ends can do more harm than acknowledging that in history the best that can be accomplished is the relative good of an ethic of responsibility.

If Niebuhr characterized the Social Gospel correctly, if it did have the progressive optimism he identified, then his sense of the tragic helps describe what occurred in the twentieth century. What began as hope for the "Christian century," ended in a sober recognition that Christianity's failures resulted in a post-Christian era. The Kingdom of God as an ethical commonwealth did not arrive. Instead, Christianity confronted world wars, revolutionary upheaval against colonialism, and rebellions against economic disparities. Cornel West identifies the benefit he gained from Niebuhr as his "sense of the tragic, rejection of perfectionism, and sober historicist orientation."[25] Niebuhr teaches us to be skeptical of human efforts to attain the good.

Church-Sect-Mystic: Troeltsch's Legacy
Reinhold Niebuhr's brother, H. Richard, noted that Reinhold's God never "acted in history."[26] God was never incarnate; he exists only at history's edge. If Reinhold adopted Weber's doctrine of unintended consequences, H. Richard mediated Christianity more through Troeltsch's "social teachings." Troeltsch's typology influenced Protestant social ethics in North America through H. Richard Niebuhr's *Christ and Culture*. Niebuhr wrote his dissertation on the "religious a priori" in Troeltsch, and followed Troeltsch in crafting the language many social ethicists use to explain the relationship between the church and other social

formations. Niebuhr claimed an "enduring problem" presented itself for theological reflection, which was the relationship between Christ and culture or between Christianity and civilization. By "Christ" Niebuhr primarily meant the mediator between God the Father and human creatures, between eternity and time.[27] In his definition of culture, Niebuhr relied upon Troeltsch's work, where culture is understood as the free creativity of human creatures in art, literature, technology, and science.[28] Niebuhr defined culture as "that total process of human activity and that total result of such activity to which now the name *culture*, now the name *civilization*, is applied in common speech."[29] Christianity could best be mediated to culture by working upon it and transforming it. Culture, like society, exists before Jesus arrives.

For all the vast differences in the previous discussions of Protestant social ethics, what they hold in common is some version of the "social question." Christianity is not a social ethic; it needs to adopt one by finding some means to mediate Christianity to the "social." What it does offer is the Kingdom of God as an ethical commonwealth, which either functions as a regulative ideal that critiques all human efforts to attain it (Kant, R. Niebuhr) or as a actualized reality working itself out in history (Hegel, Social Gospel).

POLE 2: CHURCH AS AN ETHICAL COMMONWEALTH OR SOCIAL ETHIC

Although liberal Protestantism could be very Christocentric, its social ethics was nonetheless borrowed from sources external to Christianity. For that reason, it held little place for the church as a social ethic. A significant revision of Protestant social ethics occurred by the inheritors of Karl Barth's theology. Barth (1886–1968) had studied with Harnack and Herrmann and remained influenced by the latter's Christocentrism. Nonetheless, when Barth began to develop ethics in the late 1920s, he distanced his own position from that of his teachers. Prior to those developments, Barth recognized that "ethics" had become a problem.

Karl Barth's Rendering of Ethics as Problematic

Barth's important essay, "The Problem of Ethics Today," was not his idea. He was given the topic for a ministers' conference at Wiesbaden, September 1922. The essay, however, proved to be decisive for a more theological approach to ethics. Consistent with his work on Romans, Barth sees the "problem" as a crisis. This crisis is, in fact, the crisis of

Western culture, and in particular that of liberal Protestantism. Barth finds it no longer credible. It substituted ethics for dogmatics, thinking that the former was the heart of Christianity. Ethics meant the continuation of progress and civilization, of our culture. The crucial question was whether philosophy or theology would best advance it. Barth writes, "Fundamentally, it was a matter not of asking *what* to do, as if that were not known, but rather of finding out whether philosophy or theology, Kant or Schleiermacher, provided the more illuminating formula for the obvious – for it was obvious that what to do was to further this infinitely imperfect but infinitely perfectible culture."[30] Here is the context for Barth's ethical question: "What shall we do?" Crisis originates the question.[31] We no longer know what to do. Neither Kant nor Schleiermacher provides the answer. The fact that we must now ask, "What shall we do?" means something significant has changed. "Our" ethics no longer works.

For Barth the question of the good marks a "crisis," a recognition that all is not well. We do not know what to do. For this reason, rather than a counsel of despair, the question is part of the solution. The question ruptures the security of the "towers" and "high places" our ethics had built. Barth writes, "The problem of the good calls in question all actual and possible *forms* of human conduct, all temporal *happenings* in the history both of the individual and of society. *What* ought we to do? is our question; and this *what*, infiltrating and entrenching itself everywhere, directs its attack against all that we did yesterday and shall do tomorrow."[32] Barth made an identical claim two decades later when he published *Church Dogmatics* II.2.[33] Barth's important revision – or perhaps better said: *rupture* – with liberal Protestantism is a refusal to make ethics Protestantism's first philosophy. Instead, "church dogmatics" is the foundation for ethics.

American Revisions of a Barthian Ethic: Yoder, McClendon, Hauerwas

John Howard Yoder (1927–97) took courses at the University of Basel in the 1950s, working with Barth and others. He was by no means an unreconstructed Barthian; in fact he wrote a book criticizing Barth on war, which he presented to Barth while Yoder was still a student in Basel. Yoder did, however, take up a Barthian position that related theology and ethics much more closely than did the more mediating version of liberal Protestantism. He directly took on the tradition of Weber and Troeltsch that denied Christianity had a "social ethic." His influential *Politics of Jesus*, originally published in 1972, set forth "an understanding of Jesus and his ministry of which it might be said that such a Jesus would be of direct significance for social ethics."[34]

Yoder critiqued "mainstream ethics" for refusing to make Jesus its "norm" through its badly informed biblical interpretations.[35] They could only conceive of Jesus as a failed apocalyptic prophet whose radical ethic was for a brief interim. They reduced Jesus to a "simple rural figure" who knew nothing about global responsibility. He only served the interests of a small, "witnessing community," whose success in the fourth century required a new social ethic. Or Jesus was not concerned with social ethics at all; he was only concerned with existential or dogmatic matters.[36] In opposition to all these efforts Yoder interpreted Jesus as bringing a specific politics and ethics that was inextricable from the community he formed, the church.

He found a "Messianic Ethic" in scripture that related Jesus's mission and work directly to political and economic realities. Rather than setting eschatology and ethics in opposition, Yoder pointed out their necessary relationship. Consistent with Jesus's eschatology is his gathering of his disciples and creating the church. Jesus establishes a people whose common life is to witness to the reign of God as it comes in Christ. Christian ethics did not need to choose between apocalyptic in-breaking and the church's ongoing, instituted life.

In one sense, Yoder worked within the tradition of Protestant social ethics. Their concerns were his concerns. He had little to no interest in the metaphysics of the Protestant scholastics, nor did he take much interest in the dogmatic tradition. He worked primarily within questions animated from the "good," and seldom addressed questions of truth or beauty. Like Protestant social ethics, he was willing to revise much of the tradition, and felt little commitment to traditional doctrine or ethics. Some have raised the question whether or not Yoder's theology, like much of liberal Protestantism, was heterodox.[37] If his theology is not heterodox, elements of his ethical practice were. Yoder's self-deceived attempts to create a new sexual ethic for Christianity produced his greatest failure and left an inexcusable history of abuse against women. Yoder challenged Protestant social ethics by changing the question. Following Barth's lead, he found reducing theology to its ethical significance unsustainable. He no longer asked how Christianity could contribute to the "social," as if it were a neutral identifiable space to which Christianity comes – and always too late because it has already been inhabited by some other ethic. He asked instead how Christianity, as itself a social reality, cohered and differed from other social realities. He opposed Troeltsch and H. Richard Niebuhr's social ethics because they required a singular answer to the "social question": Christianity's relation to the social. Yoder stated, "[Y]ou must either withdraw from it all, transform it all, or keep it all in paradox. Niebuhr cannot conceive of, much less respect, a position which would not make a virtue of such consistency."[38] If, as Yoder taught, Christianity is a social reality existing amidst other social realities then the question shifts depending upon which social reality it confronts. A Christian social ethic, grounded in Jesus's politics, will take on different forms given different social configurations. In an accommodated fourth-century empire, it might need to take to the desert. In a violent sixteenth-century Europe, it might need to seek the peace of the cities ensconced in warring madness through offering specific political wisdom. In twentieth-century liberal democracies, it might need to affirm the good of the freedoms offered and be critical about the violent security apparatus that affirms those goods. In a post-Christian society, it is even possible for Yoder, albeit unlikely, that some form of "Constantinianism" would be defensible.[39] In setting forth how the Christians should witness to the state, Yoder admonishes his readers not to be *a priori* closed to Constantinianism. He writes:

> Our minds should remain open to the possible rational or biblical arguments of those who might claim that the attainment of a privileged social position by the church in the fourth century called for changes in morals, ecclesiology, and eschatology; thus far it must be admitted that clear and cogent arguments for this have not been brought.[40]

For Yoder, a Christian social ethic is not a singular answer to a perennial question, but the discernment as to how Jesus's specific politics located in the social reality of the church and found primarily in scripture interacts with other social formations. Jesus remains present to his church and has already waged the "war of the Lamb" by which the world is to be set right. Christian social ethics, then, means to live as people who witness this victory until it is complete and in so doing serve the common good.[41] Ethics does not replace eschatology; eschatology makes ethics possible.

James William McClendon (1924–2000) and Stanley Hauerwas develop Christian ethics through the questions Yoder raised, which make them, like Yoder, ambivalently related to the tradition of Protestant social ethics. McClendon accepted neither Troeltsch nor Niebuhr's depiction of the options for a Christian social ethics in terms of a church, sect, or mystic typology, for they all implicitly accept Weber's account of the political as necessarily violent. If to be political and responsible entails violence, then the discussion is finished before it begins; no discernment as to how the church relates to various social formations can get off the ground.

McClendon, like much of liberal Protestantism, begins theology with ethics. But unlike it, his ethics does not subordinate the church to a greater ethical commonwealth. Nor does he only develop ethics in terms of the church. He writes, "The church is a society that embodies powerful practices, among these are the practices of evangelism and the practice of worship. The church also fitfully embodies the ministry or practice of peacemaking." These practices "constitute the moral life of Christians in community as well."[42] The "as well" here matters. The church does not exclusively constitute Christian ethics for the church always exists within a threefold structure, that of the "natural order" where we are biological, organic bodies; a "social world" constituted in part by the church; and an *"eschatological* realm." He draws on the metaphor of a three-corded rope to express this structure, which he respectively names "the *body*, the *social* and the *resurrection* strands or spheres of Christian ethics."[43] McClendon's "social ethics" proper (the second strand) cannot exist without attention to the bodily and eschatological strands. Like Yoder, eschatology entails ethics, but McClendon has more of a place for everyday bodily practices in the answers he provides to the "social question."

If Yoder changed the question, Hauerwas changed the answers. While McClendon emphasized the biological and natural more so than Yoder, Hauerwas draws more on philosophy, especially Aristotle and Wittgenstein. Hauerwas's work begins with an unapologetic commitment to the Christian faith. An exchange with the political theorist Rom Coles demonstrates this point. Coles states:

> [Y]ou have defended orthodoxy – which risks a kind of hierarchy – and I think you do so out of a sense that it is a crucial condition for engendering a people who don't fear death and who might resist the politics of empire, capitalism and the megastate (and the cultures that come with these). Do you end up with a paradox here? Namely, that undemocratic institutions linked to orthodoxy often would be the condition of radical democracy?

Hauerwas responds, "The first thing I need to say is that I defend 'orthodoxy' because I think the hard-won wisdom of the church is true."[44] The first task of Christian social ethics is not to figure out how to mediate the gospel to the state, but to know what the gospel entails. The good is wedded to what is true.

The church remains central for Hauerwas's version of "social ethics" as it was for Yoder and McClendon. It is not subordinated to an ethical commonwealth, or mediated to some putative neutral "social" space. For Hauerwas the church does not have a social ethic; it is in itself a social ethic. He closely links Christology and ecclesiology. He is well known for saying, "The church makes Jesus possible." What he means by that is found in his *Cross Shattered Church* in which he stated that "the Gospel is not a truth that can be known without witnesses.... No Jesus; no God. No Church; no Jesus."[45] Christian ethics is the church's witness throughout time to the truth found in God's creation and redemption of the world in Jesus Christ. Nothing more universal or catholic than that exists.

"Augustinian" Alternatives at the Second Pole

Yoder, McClendon, and Hauerwas share a family resemblance in their development of a Christian social ethic. They are, of course, not the only option to, or within, its development out of liberal Protestantism. There are other significant U.S. and British theologians who fit closer to pole two than pole one, but who nevertheless maintain a distance from the Anabaptist inclination of Yoder, Hauerwas, and McClendon. These theologians represent a more self-consciously "Augustinian" version of social ethics.

The American Methodist Paul Ramsey (1913–88) brought Catholic norms into what he feared had become a Protestant "wasteland" of utilitarianism. His central concept was "love transforming the natural law." More so than Yoder, Hauerwas, and McClendon, he acknowledged creaturely patterns in nature that entailed universal moral principles, perhaps even exceptionless ones. Although he was a lifelong Methodist, Ramsey never fit well within liberal Protestantism because he refused to replace eschatology with ethics or jettison theological orthodoxy. Ramsey influenced the Anglican moral theologian Oliver O'Donovan, who also develops the eschatological significance of Christian ethics. Rather than finding it at odds with national political structures as do Yoder, McClendon, and Hauerwas, he finds Christ's victory in his Resurrection and Ascension to be the reestablishment of political order (although he remains critical of the modern, liberal nation-state).[46]

John Milbank is an important Anglican theologian whose 1990 publication *Theology and Social Theory* changed the nature of the debate over "social" ethics. Originally intended as a textbook for seminarians to navigate the relationship between theology and the social sciences, it was a magisterial achievement that traced the historical development of what made "the social" possible as an object of a science. It begins with the claim that modern theology suffers the "pathos of a false humility," allowing it always to be positioned by some other discourse, especially those claiming to be "social."[47] Theology must critically engage all other disciplines without assuming that they provide a neutral analysis free from theological judgments.

Although his work resembles much that is found in Yoder and Hauerwas, Milbank rejects their constructive proposal in favor of "Augustinian compromise." They rightly recognize an ethics of virtue and a catholic ecclesiology as the necessary conditions to embody Christ's peace. He does not accuse them of being apolitical or sectarian, a common charge brought against them by Niebuhrians and others. Milbank also wants to distance his own position from Niebuhrian realism, which he has done since his essay, "The Poverty of Nieburhianism."[48] But he worries about a perfectionism he finds in their work that prevents Christian theology from a viable rule in political establishment. In the end, for Milbank, the church must make alliances with "contaminated, compromised coercive power" grounded in a "secular justice."[49]

CONCLUSION

Protestant social ethics shifted from the dominant tradition of liberal Protestantism that held sway over much of the nineteenth and twentieth centuries, in which ethics replaced eschatology, the church pointed to something more catholic than itself and Jesus remained central but largely because of his unique ethics, religious personality, or God-consciousness. It shifted to a more traditional Christology, catholic ecclesiology, and eschatological foundation for ethics. Ethics remained important, but no longer functioned as first philosophy. Ecclesiology and eschatology returned creating a new set of questions that had largely been sidelined. Even the best of the liberal Protestant tradition found in Gary Dorrien's important work addressed the changed circumstances and realized a "conservative" defense of liberal Protestantism no longer remained viable.[50]

Perhaps the future of Protestant social ethics will be a conversation primarily among those found closer to poll two. As the culture becomes more and more secular, the strategy of mediating Christianity through established institutions in the West becomes less convincing. There are voices that challenge the shift in the conversation. James Davison Hunter calls for a "new city commons" through a "theology of faithful presence." He thinks that the "neo-Anabaptists" (Yoder, Hauerwas, and other such theologians) cannot answer the "vocation" to such a faithful presence because they only have a "world-hating theology." He writes, "*In effect*, theirs is a world-hating theology. It is not impossible but it is rare, all the same, to find among any of its prominent theologians or popularizers, any affirmation of good in the social world and any acknowledgement of beauty in creation or truth shared in common with those outside of the church."[51] Such a criticism is mystifying. Yoder, Hauerwas, and McClendon's critique of the modern security state results from the good they find in the social world, the beauty in creation, and truths shared among diverse social realities. Related, but more sober criticisms are found in the left Hegelian Jeffrey Stout and the Niebuhrian Eric Gregory. Stout finds Hauerwas's, Yoder's, and Milbank's ecclesially centered ethic deeply problematic. He writes, "The traditionalist story that a particular religious tradition in fact functions as a community of virtue over against the sinfulness of the surrounding social world strikes me as extremely dubious as well as exceedingly prideful."[52] He continues, "Many of Hauerwas's readers probably liked being told that they should care more about being the church than about doing justice to the underclass."[53] Is this why Hauerwas's work has become so influential? If so, it will need to incorporate the very concerns Stout identifies. Likewise Eric Gregory finds Hauerwas and Milbank losing the important tradition of "civic virtue" in Augustine and Niebuhr. He writes, "I will argue that [Reinhold Niebuhr's] critics swing too far in an opposite direction by allowing ecclesiology to overwhelm Augustinian political theology (especially an ecclesiology that subsumes both Christology and pneumatology)."[54] Jean Bethke Elshtain offered a related criticism.

Sorting out who agrees with whom over what remains an unfinished (and most likely an unending) task for Protestant social ethics. The relationship between it and liberal Protestantism raises questions that remain unanswered. Is the dominance of ethics and practical reasoning the fruit of Kant's critiques over metaphysics? Should the "good" have this kind of dominance over speculative theology, over the true and beautiful or fitting? Does it among those who are critical of liberal Protestantism? Are the common criticisms of the ecclesial-centered ethic simply a rearguard reaction of the earlier dominant liberal Protestantism or are they something different? Are these concerns in harmony with criticisms of theology brought by liberation, feminist, and postcolonial theologians? Is there more sanguinity between the two poles than has been thought, or is the "continuum" broken, ruptured by the new questions and answers Yoder, McClendon, and Hauerwas raised? What relationship does Roman Catholic moral theology now have to Protestant social ethics? Has Catholic social ethics adopted, post–Vatican II, the tradition of Protestant social ethics, which the second pole may have brought to an end? These questions and many more will press upon Protestant social ethics, whatever it is, for the foreseeable future.

Notes

1. Gary Dorrien, *Kantian Reason and the Hegelian Spirit* (Oxford: Wiley-Blackwell, 2012), p. 23.
2. Immanuel Kant, *Religion within the Limits of Reason Alone*, trans. Theodore M. Greene and Hoyt H. Hudson (New York: Harper Torchbooks, 1960), p. 87.
3. Ibid., pp. 101–3.
4. Ibid., p. 105.
5. Ibid., p. 109. Kant understands Christianity as "completely forsaking the Judaism from which it sprang, and grounded upon a wholly new principle, effecting a thoroughgoing revolution in doctrines of faith." It created the universal conditions for a "purely moral religion in place of the old worship" (p. 118).
6. See Charles Taylor, *Hegel* (Cambridge: Cambridge University Press, 1975), pp. 376–8.
7. G. W. F. Hegel, *Phenomenology*, trans. A. V. Miller (Oxford: Oxford University Press, 1977), p. 764.
8. Taylor, *Hegel*, pp. 374–8.
9. Dorrien, *Kantian Reason and the Hegelian Spirit*, p. 318.
10. Ibid., p. 13.
11. For a persuasive defense of Troeltsch against this accusation see Sarah Coakley, *Christ without Absolutes* (Oxford: Oxford University Press, 1988).
12. Dorrien, *Kantian Reason and the Hegelian Spirit*, p. 354.
13. Ernst Troeltsch, *The Social Teaching of the Christian Churches, Vol. 1*, trans. Oliver Wyon (Chicago: University of Chicago Press, 1981), pp. 39–40.
14. Ibid., p. 30.
15. Ibid., p. 32.
16. Max Weber, "Politics as a Vocation," in *From Max Weber: Essays in Sociology*, ed. Hans Heinrich Gerth and Charles Wright Mills (New York: Oxford University Press, 1958), p. 120.
17. Ibid., p. 121.
18. Walter Rauschenbusch, *Christianizing the Social Order* (New York: MacMillan, 1912), p. 7.
19. Pius XI mentioned "social justice" nine times in *Quadragesimo anno*. He meant something specific by this term. Worker's wages should not be determined simply by market demand, but a sufficient wage should be provided for each worker that he (and later she) could provide for a family and make a contribution to the common good. See *Quadragesimo anno*, #57.
20. Georgia Harkness, *The Sources of Western Morality* (New York: Charles Scribners' Sons, 1954), pp. 221–3. Reprinted New York, AMS Press, 1978.

21 Kenneth Oakes, *Karl Barth on Theology and Philosophy* (Oxford: Oxford University Press, 2012).
22 Catherine Keller, *Faces of the Deep: A Theology of Becoming* (London: Routledge, 2003), p. 140.
23 Reinhold Niebuhr, *Nature and Destiny of Man* (Louisville, KY: Westminster John Knox, 1996), 2:61.
24 Robin Lovin, *Reinhold Niebuhr and Christian Realism* (Cambridge: Cambridge University Press, 1995), p. 5.
25 Cornel West, *Prophetic Fragments* (Grand Rapids, MI: Eerdmans, 1988), p. 152.
26 Richard Fox, *Reinhold Niebuhr: A Biography* (New York: Pantheon Books, 1985), p. 134.
27 H. Richard Niebuhr, *Christ and Culture* (New York: Harper and Row, 1951), pp. 28–9.
28 Troeltsch defined culture as "the sum of all that has spontaneously arisen for the advancement of material life and as an expression of spiritual and moral life – all social intercourse, technologies, arts, literature and sciences. It is the realm of the variable free, not necessarily universal, of all that cannot lay claim to compulsive authority." Ibid., p. 33.
29 Ibid., p. 32.
30 Karl Barth, "The Problem of Ethics Today," in *The Word of God and the Word of Man*, trans. Douglas Horton (Gloucester, MA: Peter Smith, 1978), p. 145.
31 Ibid., p. 139.
32 Ibid.
33 "If the What? Is seriously meant, every answer that we and others may have given is continually questioned again" (*Church Dogmatics*, II.2, p. 645).
34 John Howard Yoder, *The Politics of Jesus*, 2nd ed. (Grand Rapids, MI: Eerdmanns, 1994), p. 11.
35 Ibid., p. 4.
36 Ibid., pp. 4–8.
37 See Paul Martens, *The Heterodox Yoder* (Eugene, OR: Wipf and Stock, 2012).
38 Glen H. Stassen, D. M. Yeager, and John Howard Yoder, *Authentic Transformation: A New Vision of Christ and Culture* (Nashville, TN: Abingdon Press, 1996), pp. 54–5.
39 Yoder is well known for his critique of Constantinianism, which is associated with the Emperor Constantine's conversion to Christianity and the changes he effected in the Roman Empire. But it is also a trope for any form of Christianity that considers its first task is to control history from the perspective of domination and rule. See Yoder's "The Constantinian Sources of Western Social Ethics," in *The Priestly Kingdom* (Notre Dame, IN: University of Notre Dame Press, 1984), pp. 135–47.
40 John Howard Yoder, *Christian Witness to the State* (Newton, KS: Institute of Mennonite Studies Series, No. 3, Faith and Life Press, 1964), p. 56.
41 Yoder could give directions to states based on Christ's odd political triumph on the cross. He wrote, "The Reign of Christ means for the state the

obligation to serve God by encouraging the good and restraining evil, i.e. to serve peace, to preserve the social cohesion in which the leaven of the Gospel can build the church and also render the old aeon more tolerable." Ibid., p. 5.
42 James Wm. McClendon Jr., *Systematic Theology: Ethics* (Nashville, TN: Abingdon, 1986), p. 188.
43 Ibid., p. 66.
44 Stanley Hauerwas and Romand Coles, *Christianity, Democracy and the Radical Ordinary* (Eugene, OR: Cascade, 2007), pp. 323–4.
45 Stanley Hauerwas, *A Cross Shattered Church: Recovering the Theological Heart of Christian Preaching* (Grand Rapids, MI: Brazos, 2009), p. 23.
46 See Oliver O'Donovan, *Resurrection and Moral Order: An Outline for Evangelical Ethics* (Grand Rapids, MI: Eerdmans, 1994); *The Desire of the Nations: Rediscovering the Roots of Political Theology* (Cambridge: Cambridge University Press, 1999); and *The Ways of Judgment* (Grand Rapids, MI: Eerdmans, 2005).
47 John Milbank, *Theology and Social Theory* (Oxford: Basil Blackwell, 1990), p. 2.
48 See John Milbank, *The Word Made Strange* (Oxford: Blackwell Publishers, 1997), pp. 233–57.
49 John Milbank, "Power Is Necessary for Peace: In Defense of Constantine," ABC Religion and Ethics, http://www.abc.net.au/religion/articles/2010/10/29/3051980.htm (accessed October 29, 2010).
50 See not only his important work, *Kantian Reason and the Hegelian Spirit* (Oxford: Wiley-Blackwell, 2012) but also his earlier *Soul in Society* (Minneapolis, MN: Fortress, 1995) and *Reconstructing the Common Good: Theology and Social Order* (Maryknoll, NY: Orbis, 1992).
51 James Davison Hunter, *To Change the World: The Irony, Tragedy and Possibility of Christianity in the Late Modern World* (Oxford: Oxford University Press, 2010), p. 174.
52 Jeffrey Stout, *Democracy and Tradition* (Princeton, NJ: Princeton University Press, 2004), p. 84.
53 Ibid., p. 158.
54 Eric Gregory, *Politics and the Order of Love: An Augustinian Ethics of Democratic Citizenship* (Chicago: University of Chicago Press, 2008), p. 18.

Further Reading

Coakley, Sara, *Christ without Absolutes*. Oxford: Oxford University Press, 1988.
Dorrien, Gary, *Social Ethics in the Making: Interpreting an American Tradition.* Oxford: Wiley-Blackwell, 2011.
Kantian Reason and the Hegelian Spirit. Oxford: Wiley-Blackwell, 2012.
Gill, Robin, ed., *The Cambridge Companion to Christian Ethics*. Cambridge: Cambridge University Press, 2012.
Hauerwas, Stanley, and Samuel Wells, eds., *The Blackwell Companion to Christian Ethics*, 2nd ed. Oxford: Wiley-Blackwell, 2007.

Long, D. Stephen, *Christian Ethics: A Very Short Introduction*. Oxford: Oxford University Press, 2010.

O'Donovan, Oliver, *Self, World and Time: Ethics as Theology, Vol. 1*. Grand Rapids, MI: Eerdmans, 2013.

Stassen, Glen H., D. M. Yeager, and John Howard Yoder, *Authentic Transformation: A New Vision of Christ and Culture*. Nashville, TN: Abingdon Press, 1995.

Troeltsch, Ernst, *The Social Teaching of the Christian Churches, Vols. I and II*, trans. Olive Wyon. Louisville, KY: Westminster John Knox Press, 1992.

Werpehowski, William, *American Protestant Ethics and the Legacy of H. Richard Niebuhr*. Washington, DC: Georgetown University Press, 2002.

Twenty-First Century Reimaginings

6 Postliberalism and Radical Orthodoxy

DANIEL M. BELL JR.

INTRODUCTION

The late twentieth century saw the emergence of a theopolitical vision known as Radical Orthodoxy (RO). To modern ears this moniker strikes a rather discordant note. As John Caputo puts it, RO is "in the strictest and most rigorous terms, incoherent, for the 'radical' strains against and bursts the seams of the 'orthodox.'"[1] The burden of this chapter is to make sense of RO as political theology by answering the suspicion that its politics is really little more than wistful antimodernism.

Our journey begins with a simple but illuminating contrast presented by two essays in political theology. In "Capitalism Versus Socialism: Crux Theologica,"[2] the noted Latin American liberation theologian Juan Luis Segundo throws down the gauntlet for political theology, charging that the most urgent contemporary theological task is that of making the choice between two political options, in this case, capitalism and socialism. In "Materialism and Transcendence,"[3] John Milbank, a leading voice of RO, argues that political theology begins not with a political choice but with ontology. He then proceeds to articulate a nonreductive materialist ontology, which not incidentally requires transcendence precisely to keep said materialism from collapsing nihilistically upon itself, with political consequences currently on display around us.

Put simply, although not yet clearly, the difference between these two essays marks both that which makes RO a radically political theology and what it contributes to understanding what political theology is today. RO does not begin the task of political theology with a political choice that correlates theological values with secular options. To begin the task of political theology with a political choice is to start too late and in the wrong place, thereby ensuring that the gospel in its original, that is, political sense is neither heard nor seen.

RO is a radical political theology because it begins not with politics but with ontology. More specifically whereas modern political theologies share a common ontology and only diverge, if they diverge, at the level of political choice, RO is radical precisely in its ontological divergence, which in turn reveals the political radicality of orthodoxy.

This difference can be schematized in the following manner. Behind politics lies ontology. Modern political theology embraces liberal, secular politics. (This includes options for Marxist socialism, which is fully at home in political liberalism.) This politics stands upon a univocal ontology that cannot found genuine sociality or communion. RO embraces an ecclesial politics underwritten by a participatory ontology that founds genuine community and so politics.

ROOTS OF RADICAL ORTHODOXY

Unpacking this scheme and positioning RO in relation to the dominant strands of political theology begins with consideration of the roots (*radix*) of RO.

What Is Radical Orthodoxy?
Immediately one encounters a difficulty, for it is not obvious what RO is or who it encompasses beyond the eponymous book series. It might be regarded as a school or movement spawned by the series editors John Milbank, Catherine Pickstock, and Graham Ward. The editors suggest that it is deeply indebted to and has strong ties with Cambridge University, past and present. Some have suggested that it was spawned by Milbank's 1990 publication, *Theology and Social Theory*, making RO a kind of Milbankian movement.

The figures most readily associated with RO reject the designation of RO as a school or formal movement. Pickstock argues that RO is not a discrete edifice or stronghold with sharp boundaries that would clearly distinguish it from other tendencies within what might be called postsecular theology but rather is best approached as "a hermeneutic disposition and a style of metaphysical vision; and it is not so much a 'thing' or 'place' as a 'task.'"[4] Elsewhere she calls it "a loose tendency."[5] Ward, likewise, distances RO from any kind of formal movement saying, "RO has no program, it has no headquarters, it has none of the definitiveness of, say, the Yale School." He continues, "I prefer to call RO a theological sensibility, a sensibility shared to a greater or lesser degree with several other contemporary theologians."[6] Among the theologians whom he names are Rowan Williams, Fergus Kerr, Nicolas Lash, Stanley

Hauerwas, David Burrell, and Peter Ochs.[7] Milbank, in turn, associates RO with a shared horizon and ethos, "which certainly does not spring from the thoughts of one person alone or even three people alone."[8]

The point is that notwithstanding the way RO is capitalized as if it were a formal movement with a clear membership and program, RO is better understood as radical orthodoxy, lowercase, that is, as a sensibility. Articulating the nature and political form of that sensibility remains the task of this essay. Yet we begin by acknowledging that radical orthodoxy names a sensibility rather than a formal movement in order to properly place it as an expression of postliberal theology.

Postliberal Theology

Postliberal theology is a diverse movement in English-speaking theology[9] that is most often associated with the work of Hans Frei and George Lindbeck and is frequently referred to as the "Yale School," although as time passes and the emphases associated with that school are more widely dispersed, tracing postliberal theology becomes less a matter of genealogy than discerning family resemblances. What are these family resemblances? They are variously summarized[10] but all accounts recognize that postliberal theology draws deeply from the work of Karl Barth to resist the correlationist habits of modern theology, yet adds to Barth's fideism a linguistic turn prompted by Wittgenstein. The result is a theological vision that eschews construing theology as a symbolic register of universal human experience (Lindbeck's "experiential-expressivist" model of theology) in favor of understanding theology and doctrine as a kind of grammar or cultural linguistics that is founded on the realistic narrative of scripture, understood not as a mine of meaning but as a plotline, which the church extends by means of its creative/interpretive performance of that narrative in the world. Central to this theological vision is a postcritical redeployment of premodern sources in engagement with contemporary insights from philosophy, sociology, and literary theory that focus on nonfoundationalist epistemologies, the interrelation of language, identity and community, and an ad hoc apologetic approach to engaging other discourses and communities. As evidenced by its rejection of correlation, embrace of metanarrative realism, understanding of theology as cultural linguistics, program of *ressourcement*, and insistence on linking the theopolitical task to its ecclesial setting, RO reflects its affinity with the postliberal theological family, an affinity that is reinforced by its direct engagement with the likes of Lindbeck and Frei as well as those associated with the "Yale School," such as Stanley Hauerwas.

Hauerwas is of particular significance for positioning RO within postliberal theology. Hauerwas brought to this postliberal vision the anti-Constantinian sensibilities of the Anabaptist John Howard Yoder as well as an interest in the virtue ethic of Thomas Aquinas. Hauerwas's development of postliberalism is significant for the development of RO in particular as postliberal political theology for several reasons. First, as previously noted, he has been one of the feeders of the radically orthodox sensibility both through his direct engagement with Milbank and by means of several of his students who have contributed to and are identified with RO. Second, postliberalism is a significant theological development that does not necessarily become political theology. Thus, while many theologians have embraced the methodological moves associated with postliberalism, not all have gone on to develop these theological insights in an overtly political direction. Moreover, even when postliberal methodological moves do take form in an explicitly political theology, the result is not necessarily postpolitical liberalism. For example, Ronald Thiemann, widely regarded as a postliberal theologian for his narrative and communitarian emphases, articulates a public theology that is entirely at home in political liberalism. Hauerwas, drawing heavily on the work of Alasdair MacIntyre, brings to postliberal theology a political edge that is decidedly postpolitical liberalism. Third, as we shall see, Hauerwas's anti-Constantinian sensibility, along with a rejection of violence, is central to some of the political diversity that characterizes radical orthodoxy.

The radically orthodox sensibility incorporates insights garnered from other sources as well. Indeed, Milbank has spoken of a kind of convergence of postliberal theologies, referring to not only the Yale School and Hauerwas but also developments associated with the Irish Catholic philosopher William Desmond, certain French and German Thomists, the French Catholic phenomenologist Jean-Luc Marion, and the *nouvelle théologie* of Henri de Lubac, Yves Congar, and Hans Urs von Balthasar.[11]

With regard to understanding RO as a postliberal political theology, *nouvelle théologie* is most immediately relevant. Central to the political vision of RO is the overcoming of the nature/grace distinction that appears in the late medieval theological tradition and colludes with the advent of political liberalism by positing the existence of a pure nature that in time becomes the basis for the invention of the "secular." And it is the *nouvelle théologie* of de Lubac and Balthasar that supplies the clearest guidance in this regard, providing as it does a *ressourcement*, a recovery of a patristic and medieval ontological vision that overcomes the distinction and paves the way for a genuinely postliberal political theology.

But what of the neo-orthodoxy of Karl Barth, which is well known for resisting secular encroachment on the theological? While influential on radical orthodoxy – through the Yale School and Hauerwas as well as the British neo-orthodoxy of Donald MacKinnon – Milbank suggests Barth is not radical enough. He writes, "Radical Orthodoxy considers that Henri de Lubac was a greater theological revolutionary than Karl Barth, because in questioning a hierarchical duality of grace and nature as discrete stages, he transcended, unlike Barth, the shared background assumption of all modern theology. In this way one could say, anachronistically, that he inaugurated a postmodern theology."[12] In other words, even as Barth resisted the encroachment of the secular and any cultural mediation of grace, he did not so much overturn the distinction as reinforce it.

BEYOND POLITICAL THEOLOGY

Modern Christian political theologies are devoted to overcoming the dualisms that forestall faith-based political action.[13] The political theologies that emerged in the last fifty years are devoted to the premise that there is no "pure nature," and in particular no political sphere that is devoid of theological depth and so immune from theological direction. To the contrary, human nature, and so every dimension of human life, is always already imbued with transcendent depth. Consequently, it is not possible to cordon off social and political concerns from more conventionally theological concerns like salvation and eternal life.

Nature and Grace, Religion and Politics

In terms more immediately relevant to political theology, the precipitating challenge is how to overcome the divide between religion and the political that characterizes modern life. What distinguishes RO from the dominant political theologies is *how* the divide between nature and grace (or religion and politics) is overcome. As Milbank explains, modern political theologies seek to overcome the separation of nature and grace along the lines prepared by Karl Rahner's Transcendental Thomism (which has its Protestant parallels, whether in Bonhoeffer's dialectical paradoxes of secularization or Tillich's idealism). Transcendental Thomism attempted to "naturalize the supernatural."[14] That is, it sought to overcome the divide between nature and grace by interiorizing grace, locating the encounter with grace at the margins of each individual's knowing.

In this way, grace becomes a correlate of anthropology or epistemology. No longer is grace dispensed by an ecclesiastical hierarchy; instead it is accessible to every human subject qua human subject.

The implications of this naturalizing the supernatural for the development of modern political theology are multiple and momentous. First, by being always already imbued with theological depth, the secular political realm is valorized as a legitimate sphere of Christian action. No longer is the conventionally "spiritual" or "religious" privileged as the primary arena for the expression of faith. Second, and perhaps more importantly, secular knowledges, especially the social sciences, are validated as true accounts of reality and social-political processes. Thus modern political theology will rely upon the social sciences in a manner (it is claimed) not unlike prior generations drew from philosophy. Third, the secular and secular knowledges are affirmed in a manner that shields them from ecclesiastical interference. This is to say, even as the secular is infused with transcendent depth, its autonomy from the ecclesial is preserved.

In other words, the dominant currents of political theology overcome the *cordon sanitaire* between theology and political action not by abolishing the distinction between nature and grace or religion and politics. Rather, they bridge the division by means of correlation. The theological is not political. The distinction of planes remains, serving to protect the political from the interference and incompetence of the church. But the theological has political implications insofar as it elevates values and ideals, such as justice, equality, human rights or the "preferential option for the poor." And these values, ideals, and options can and should be correlated with insights drawn from secular knowledges and the agendas of secular political movements. Recall, for example, Segundo's way of setting forth the contemporary political challenge for theology: correlating Christianity with either socialism or capitalism.

Political Theology and Political Liberalism

What is noteworthy for positioning RO as political theology is that this overcoming is not an undoing. The secular is not undone; the dominant forms of political theology are not postsecular. Instead they effect a *rapprochement* with the Enlightenment and its politics. They are self-consciously efforts to complete the promise of modernity and its (liberal) politics. They embrace the secular, seeking to advance its promise.

This is evident in several characteristics of contemporary political theology. First, it is seen in political theology's commitment to what Steve Long calls the *analogia libertatis*. Modern political theology is founded upon the notion that in the human striving for modern freedoms, we gain access to knowledge of God.[15] The quest for freedom that characterizes modernity and its politics is endowed with transcendent depth.

Thus public theology, in both its more progressive and neoconservative wings, is deeply committed to the advance of modern liberty, particularly as that freedom has taken shape in North America, with its democratic capitalist system of ordered liberty. Likewise, European political theology heralds the church as an institution of "critical freedom" that constantly highlights the manifold ways the promised freedoms of the Enlightenment remain unfulfilled; a theme picked up by their southern cousins, Latin American liberationists, who in particular observe that the modern quest for freedom has not yet advanced in the economic realm as far as it has in the political.

As a corollary of the modern advance of freedom, these political theologies embrace the depoliticization of the church. While they lament and seek to overcome the church's utter spiritualization or privatization, they nevertheless laud modernity's stripping the church of direct political agency. Indeed, the political deprivation of the church is regarded as a major component of the advance of freedom in history insofar as it is a crucial step in the recognition of the integrity and autonomy of the secular.

But, it is worth emphasizing, the depoliticization of the church is not a privatization. The church continues to have an important public role to play. The church under the sign of modernity is relegated to an *indirectly* political role as the custodian of values and ideals and perhaps a cultural ethos or spirit that should inform, inspire, and animate action in the secular political realm amidst secular political options. So understood, the political task of political theology is fundamentally that of correlating the values and ideals that arise in theological traditions, texts, and practices with the analysis of the social sciences for the sake of clarifying political options, as Segundo does.

Insofar as modern political theologies embrace the Enlightenment narrative of freedom and configure the political task of theology as that of correlating theological values with secular sciences, it should be unsurprising that they embrace as well modern secular politics. Specifically, they embrace political liberalism and politics as statecraft.

Political liberalism is the vision of politics that emerges in the wake of the collapse of medieval Christendom and its robust sense of a common good. With the depoliticization and fracturing of the church, the common good was dispersed as the private goods and interests of individuals. Thus political liberalism is a vision of social atomism, of life that revolves around autonomous individuals struggling to acquire and protect (by means of the assertion of "rights") the resources necessary to pursue their private interests.

Part and parcel of this politics is statecraft. The modern vision of politics as statecraft is a vision of political sovereignty that holds that the realm where individuals come together in a polity, a politics, is properly overseen by and finds its highest expression in the state. It is the investiture of the state with sovereignty over society and, consequently, privileging the state as the fulcrum of social and political change.

The commitment to politics as statecraft is evident in the dominant forms of political theology. It is most transparent in public theology, which openly celebrates modern Western liberal democracy and whose theological politics amount to sustaining while reforming that politics either in a conservative or progressive direction, the former tending to emphasize the organs of civil society while the latter tend to emphasize governmental initiatives.[16] The commitment to politics as statecraft is not as immediately self-evident in political theology because it has a more revolutionary edge. Nevertheless, its vision is embedded in politics as statecraft for even as it criticizes the bourgeois theology that privatizes the church, it does not recognize the church as directly political. To the contrary, any assertion that the church is a fully political agent that might challenge the state's hegemony is denounced as a pernicious "political religion" from which modernity rightly emancipated us.[17] Likewise, neither does liberation theology depart from politics as statecraft, whether that takes the form of the oppressed assuming control of the organs of state or of the oppressed influencing the state through civil society.[18] Moreover, a church or theological politics that refuses its apolitical status is denounced as a "politico-religious messianism."[19]

The Counternarrative of Radical Orthodoxy

As a postliberal political theology, RO narrates the rise of modernity and secular politics differently than the dominant strands of political theology. As Graham Ward notes, perhaps explaining the prevalence of genealogy as political discourse in RO, "The politics of Christian discipleship is about first unmasking the theological and metaphysical sources of current mythologies and revealing the distortions and perversions of their current secularized forms."[20] This counternarrative has three dimensions: not freedom, but a new master; not autonomy, but an iron cage; not peace, but endless war.

RO challenges the narration of modernity's arrival as the advent of liberty. This narrative is well known. Secular modernity, with its political liberalism and sovereign state, was born as a reaction against an oppressive and authoritarian church that was not above unleashing great violence to secure and maintain its privilege. Thus modern politics emerged in the wake of the "wars of religion," whose conclusion with the Peace of Westphalia established the contours of modern politics, where society consists of a collection of individuals who are free to pursue their own vision of the good, limited only by their talents and the rights of other similarly striving individuals. Society is thus conceived of as a collection of individuals presided over by a sovereign state that maintains the peace between these individuals by securing rights through a monopoly on the use of violence.

The counternarrative of RO asserts that this standard story of modernity's rise is actually a myth that serves the sovereign modern state, which did not arrive on the scene as a benign savior to deliver us from wars over confessional differences. Rather, as William Cavanaugh argues, the wars of religion are more accurately remembered as the birth pangs of a modern state struggling to break free of the medieval order and subsume all social bodies under its authority.[21] Furthermore, Cavanaugh argues that modern political space is not a space of freedom from sacralized authority but rather represents a migration of authority from the church to the state. In other words, contrary to the commonplace narrative, modernity is not a space of liberty but the territory of a new lord and master, with a new discipline.[22] And, we might add, a new theology. This is to say that the secular is not theologically neutral but is theologically invested, with the state now functioning as a kind of secular savior enacting political liberalism as a kind of secular soteriology.[23]

As previously noted, a concomitant of the modern political soteriology is the depoliticization of the church and subsequent reconfiguration of the task of political theology as correlation. Affirming the legitimate protest against the hierarchic politics of a church ruled by sacred hierophants, RO is nevertheless deeply concerned with this depoliticization of the church. Indeed, as Graham Ward argues, depoliticization is the key issue for political theology because if we cannot act politically, we cannot counter the enemies of dehumanization.[24]

Of course, political theology asserts that we can act politically but its correlationist politics dilutes the political force of faith. As Milbank writes concerning modern political theology, "[I]nsofar as salvation is 'religious', it is formal, transcendental and private; insofar as it is 'social' it is secular. What is occluded is the real practical and linguistic context for salvation, namely the *particular society* that is the Church."[25] In other words, modern political theology insists that theology is at best only indirectly political, that theology and its correlates, like church, are not immediately social and political forms; rather, it is secular knowledges and secular agents who are recognized as immediately social and political.

This brings us to the second dimension of RO's counternarrative, which associates modernity not with autonomy and freedom but with an iron cage. Modern political theology embraces the depoliticization of the church in the hope of nurturing human agency, more specifically the marginalized and oppressed becoming artisans of their own destiny. Yet, RO suggests, a depoliticized church locks us in the iron cage of the merely human politics of political liberalism.

Earlier it was suggested that behind every conception of politics, and so of every political theology, there stands an ontology. Thus the lock on the iron cage of political liberalism is forged not at the level of political choice (i.e., modern individuals freed from an oppressive church choosing their own form of government) but of ontology.

The fateful ontological move is a shift in the late medieval world away from a metaphysics of participation in favor of the univocity of being. This, Milbank suggests, is "the turning point in the destiny of the West."[26] How so? The univocity of being provides the metaphysical foundation for modern secular politics by establishing a dualism of nature and grace, which underwrites the separation of religion and politics and forges the bars of the iron cage of merely human politics. More specifically, univocal being acquires a kind of autonomy and self-subsistence that renders theology and transcendence either an intrusion or an overlay. Modern political theology is committed to transcendence, but as already suggested, it is also deeply committed to the autonomy of the secular; this commitment to autonomy rules out transcendence as a (supernatural) intrusion. Therefore transcendence must appear as a kind of overlay or supplement along the lines of Transcendental Thomism. Milbank describes the vision of transcendence that results: "Either the transcending impulse remains essentially individual in character, and merely provides motivation and creative energy for social and political action which retains its own immanent norms. Or else the social process itself is identified as the site of transcendence, of a process of 'liberation' which is gradually removing restrictions upon the human spirit."[27]

Put simply, modern political theology is erected upon a univocal ontology that precludes human participation in the divine in such a way that we might expect more than political liberalism can deliver. The ontology that underwrites the depoliticization of the church strips the political of the hope or expectation of anything more than what fallen humans can craft either under the inspiration or motivation of transcendence or as they join the historical process.

This brings us to the third dimension of RO's counternarrative. The hoped for end of political liberalism is peace. Indeed, the modern *mythos* holds that we already experience that peace insofar as we have been released to pursue our private goods under the protection of a sovereign state guarding our rights. Yet, RO argues, genuine peace cannot be the outcome of any politics founded on a univocal ontology. Rather, the end of modernity's march toward freedom is in fact endless conflict.[28] For univocal being unleashes an ontological violence that precludes the peaceful harmony of differences, if by peace is meant more than the absence of open conflict, more than the benign indifference of self-satisfied individuals doing their own thing, more than the soft hum of cash registers, assembly lines, and a warming globe in the commercial war that is capitalism.[29] As political liberalism makes clear, univocal being, with its discrete individuals, can manage relations only in the modes of neglect (indifference), conflict, or conquest. After all, because all that is is in the same way (i.e., univocal being), difference and distinction can be maintained only by distance. To draw near on behalf of a shared or common good, in genuine communion, is to risk the loss of difference, of identity. Thus political liberalism is not about sharing in the good but about managing the conflict of individual rights and private goods, with unfortunate effect:

> The "modernity" of liberalism has only delivered mass poverty, inequality, erosion of freely associating bodies beneath the level of the state and ecological dereliction of the earth – and now, without the compensating threat of communism, it has abolished the rights and dignity of the worker, ensured that women are workplace as well as domestic and erotic slaves, undermined working-class family structure, and finally started to remove the ancient rights of the individual which long precede the creed of liberalism itself ... and are grounded in the dignity of the person rather than the "self-ownership" of autonomous liberal man [sic].[30]

What is needed is a truer liberality, a politics of generosity supported by societies united not by contract but by mutual generosity and gift exchange. To RO's political vision of liberality beyond liberalism we now turn.

ESCHATOLOGY AND ECCLESIALITY

According to the theological tale that RO tells, to the extent that modern political theology embraces political liberalism, its aspirations for a sociality of peace and justice cannot be realized. Established on a metaphysics of univocity, even theological transcendentalism is unable to reconnect the Creation and Creator in such a way to stop the descent of secular political life into the violence of perpetual conflict.

Herein lies the significance of the *nouvelle théologie* for RO's articulation of a postliberal political theology. Instead of bridging the nature/grace distinction, theologians like de Lubac and Von Balthasar sought to dismantle it by means of what Milbank calls "supernaturalizing the natural."[31]

Whereas modern political theology has opted for a transcendental vision that locates grace and transcendence in anthropology and specifically epistemology, which produces abstract values, options, and motivations that must be correlated with secular, political practices, the proponents of the *nouvelle théologie* insisted that grace is encountered "in the confrontation with certain historical texts and images which have no permanent 'place' whatsoever, save in their original occurrence as events and their protracted repetition through the force of ecclesial allegiance."[32] This is to say, revelation is not first and foremost a matter of epistemology, which is but a subset of anthropology. Rather, revelation is primarily a political category. Grace and transcendence are not found unmediated in the interior recesses of the soul but through the encounter with very public material objects, persons, and practices. Supernaturalizing the natural leads to a genuinely postliberal political theology, although Milbank concedes it is not a path that the proponents of the *nouvelle théologie* took.[33] To RO's journey down this path we now turn.

Placing Radical Orthodoxy

Thus far I have indicated some of the ways RO distances itself from political theology within the limits of political liberalism. It remains to be seen if in resisting political liberalism, RO's constructive project amounts to a medieval restoration or to a genuinely postliberal political theology.

The authors associated with RO reject the charge that their political vision is restorationist. Graham Ward observes without regret that "Christendom is over; and with it Christian hegemony."[34] While there is diversity (which will be addressed momentarily) among those identified with RO regarding the role of the state and its relation to the church, with thinkers like Milbank appearing to be more favorably inclined toward Christendom, and while RO unapologetically draws upon the theological vision of the premodern church and associates the adjective "radical" in RO with this return to roots (*radix*), RO refuses labels such as traditionalist, medieval, or conservative.[35] Indeed, as we shall see, RO's return to roots is not uncritical and this criticism includes Christendom.

In rejecting the restorationist charge, RO also rejects the claim that it is wholly antimodern. As Milbank, Ward, and Pickstock note, because the Enlightenment was at least in part a critique of a decadent Christianity, it is possible to learn from it.[36] Indeed, the critique of modernity and secularity proffered by RO is first and foremost a critique of the church, and specifically theological developments, which were the condition of possibility for modernity and political liberalism. For example, Milbank identifies the clericalism of the late medieval church, which failed to sufficiently incarnate Christianity in the lay orders, along with voluntarist theological trends, as the midwives of modernity and liberalism.[37] Thus the *ressourcement* RO advocates is a critical one, one that does not simply repeat the tradition against modernity. As Milbank writes, "[RO] is also a radicalism which regards orthodoxy, in theory and practice, as a project always to be completed, and certainly not as perfected within pre-modernity."[38] Indeed, he goes so far as to suggest that RO seeks to "save modernity," espousing not the premodern but an alternative modernity,[39] a claim that will be borne out momentarily.

Is RO better placed as postmodern? For many of the theologians associated with RO, postmodernity, particularly continental philosophy, serves as an aid to cultural analysis and critique. In particular, postmodern thinkers are deemed helpful in unmasking the illusions of secular reason and politics, revealing them to be not the road to freedom but new forms of discipline established on an ontology of violence. Positively, postmodernity's interest in signification, social semiotics, and the interaction of difference has given impetus to RO's theological *ressourcement*, creating an opportunity for a recovery of a participatory ontology that enacts the relations of difference as peace.

Nevertheless, RO is not properly placed as postmodern without remainder. At best, RO finds in postmodernity a "momentary ally."[40] For even as postmodernity unmasks the nihilistic heart of modernity, it does not know what to do about the void it exposes and so celebrates. As such, postmodernity does not transcend but deepens modernity; it is hypermodern.[41] According to RO, a consistent postmodernity would be postsecular in the sense that it would recognize that Being is not self-sustaining, and so requires an analogical understanding of Being, a metaphysics of participation. For this reason, Ward suggests, RO is best positioned as within and beyond postmodernism.[42]

Eschatology

At the heart of RO's postliberal political theology is an analogical worldview founded on an ontology of participation. Perhaps the easiest entry into this worldview and ontology, as well as the politics RO derives from it, is provided by Graham Ward's foundational claim, "A true political theology can commence only with eschatology, for eschatology examines the God of history, the God in history.... [A] political theology begins with the sovereignty of the one God and the operations of that sovereignty in and across time."[43]

Unlike currents of political theology that challenge the status quo on the basis of a memory of the past and hope of a future, RO challenges the contemporary status quo on the basis of God's sovereignty in history here and now. Furthermore, also unlike much contemporary political theology, RO refuses to locate God in the transcendental margins of epistemology. Instead, RO espouses an "operative messianism."[44] Christ is with us, in keeping with the insights of the *nouvelle théologie*, here and now through the encounter with particular material texts, practices, and people.

In other words, RO is a politics not of correlation but critical mediation. The task of political theology is not that of correlating religious values with secular politics but of identifying and explicating the encounter with grace in the political configurations of material reality. Central to this mediation is the recognition that there is no privileged site of transcendence distinct from purely immanent or secular sites but rather, as Aquinas noted, all of material reality is a vehicle of grace and capable of disclosing transcendence.[45]

This recognition is behind the notion of "suspending the material" that is a hallmark of RO's theopolitical vision. Whereas modern secularity rests upon a univocal ontology that instantiates a dualism between nature and grace, the medieval and patristic analogical worldview reclaimed by RO embraces an ontology of participation, whereby created Being is neither the same as nor utterly different from the being of God but rather by grace participates in divinity. The material is in a sense "suspended" from transcendence. As a result, whereas modernity assumes that the material world is self-sufficient, self-revealing, and self-validating, RO recognizes that the visible, material world is always suspended from the infinite and eternal, that the material exists only by virtue of sustained participation in the infinite. Accordingly there is more to the material than what is visible to the human mind and subject to human grasp.

This returns us to Ward's emphasis on eschatology. Emphasizing eschatology is another way of articulating the "suspension of the material" or the "supernaturalizing the natural." Ward distinguishes between the eschatological *remainder*, which animates RO, and what is sometimes called the eschatological *reserve* or *proviso*. Whereas a "reserve" or "proviso" implies an absence, a lack, or a holding back, which can reinforce the nature/grace dualism by suggesting grace is held back in reserve leaving a naked or secular time/space and thereby a secular politics, the eschatological remainder suggests not an absence but an excess or surplus that abolishes the dualism by flooding the world with more than human possibilities.[46] RO as political theology begins with the reenchantment of the world, which is accompanied by a robust sense of divinization, deification, or sanctification.[47]

What this means is that political possibility is not exhausted by the reach of secular reason, even when that reason is transcendentally enhanced. Even here and now more than political liberalism is possible. And that "more" includes the possibility of genuine peace and communion, of the harmonic sociality of difference that is analogically and not univocally related.[48]

The question is, how is this analogical vision and participatory ontology politically visible? An answer entails turning to what Ward calls "ecclesiality."

Ecclesiality

Nothing incites the suspicions of RO's critics more than the substantive political claims RO advances for the church. Ward claims that in the church God offers us "a new and better politics, a new and better sovereignty."[49] Such sentiments are echoed with some frequency in the RO corpus. "Only the church has the theoretical and practical power to challenge the global hegemony of capital and to create a viable politico-economic alternative,"[50] writes Milbank, followed by the claim that "*ecclesia* names a new sort of universal polity."[51]

Yet as previously noted, RO renounces aspirations for a restored Christendom. This is so in part because of the way Christendom is imagined under modernity, as a kind of ecclesial statecraft where the church either joins or replaces the modern nation-state exercising its monopoly on the use of violence, and RO, as a postliberal political theology, even as it asserts the political character of the church, rejects political liberalism's construal of political space and political actors, including both the state and the church. While there is some divergence regarding the character of the state and the use of violence among thinkers associated with RO, RO uniformly rejects the modern conception of politics as statecraft. Whatever can and should be expected of the state, a Christian political imagination should not anoint the state as the pinnacle of social space and the fulcrum of social change.[52]

Likewise, RO's political theology is not a call for an absolutist church. Granted RO displays a complex relationship with the notion of theocracy. As Cavanaugh writes, "Strictly speaking, the world is a theocracy: it is ruled by God."[53] Ward makes a similar claim when he writes, "[T]he kingdom of God *is* a theocracy and theocratic politics is what Christians are about."[54] Such claims make sense in light of the analogical worldview that confesses the material to be suspended from transcendence, that confesses there is no secular in the sense of pure nature.

However, the analogical worldview need not result in an absolutist church. Indeed, RO decries that in the history of the church, recognition of God's rule has erroneously merged with absolutism and monarchy.[55] In fact, theocracy understood as an absolutist church is only possible where the problematic dualism of nature and grace has been erected, and because RO rejects that dualism, its embrace of theocracy cannot be equated with an absolutist church.[56] Furthermore, RO opposes the "simple" space of secular politics with its absolute sovereign center; instead, RO advocates for complex space where, in keeping with the Catholic political principle of "subsidiarity," authority is dispersed and decentralized.[57]

Making sense of a nonabsolutist theocratic politics requires consideration of Ward's claim for ecclesiality and the significance that Augustine's vision of the two cities holds in RO's theopolitical vision. *Ecclesiality* is Ward's term for the complex space of the church, whereby the church names not a political entity identifiable by spatially discrete boundaries enforced by a sacred hierarchy but is instead "what this body of Christians do" in an ever-expansive web of sociality spun by an array of intermediate associations and relations.[58]

Ward connects this with Augustine's account of the two cities, describing a "theology of commingling."[59] Cavanaugh describes the commingling this way as well. Augustine offers a complex vision of political space that is crossed by multiple, overlapping, and competing authorities, of which the church marks one authority (the love of God) while earthly cities mark others.[60] Thus the church is not distinguishable as a separate and distinct political actor controlling a well-defined space in the modern Weberian sense but is characterized by a certain performance ("ecclesiality") that occurs on a complex political space populated by other political agents enacting other performances.

Of particular significance is the manner in which this vision blurs the boundaries of the church. In contradistinction with an absolutist church, RO's political ecclesiology acknowledges the porous, fluid boundaries of the church. The boundaries are permeable because, in keeping with RO's participatory ontology, the operations of grace are not limited to the church. Christianity recognizes that the entire truth about reality is dispersed harmoniously amongst the body of Christ and, eschatologically, the entire human race and cosmos.[61] Furthermore, to the extent that the church is neither self-grounding nor self-governing it must remain open to receiving the truth. Paradigmatically, Catherine Pickstock argues, this reception happens in the Eucharist where the church receives its social embodiment from outside.[62] Moreover, this openness includes receptivity to outsiders (Matt. 25); indeed, as Augustine's vision of the commingled cities suggests, it is not always clear in this time between the times who are insiders and who are outsiders.[63] Consequently, a certain provisionality attends the church and its claims. After all, it, no less than the world, lives under the promise of eschatological remainder that always exceeds appearances.

Democracy, Socialism, and the State

The twofold emphasis on eschatology and ecclesiality brings to the fore how RO is indeed a post- and not preliberal political theology. RO's commitment to eschatology and ecclesiality amounts to a consistent supernaturalizing of the natural that gives rise to a democratic impulse, simultaneously distancing RO's political vision from medieval Christendom and justifying the assertion, made previously, that RO could be construed as a kind of alternative (postsecular) modernity.[64]

As Milbank says, the ultimate bias of Christianity is democratic.[65] This is the case because the truth is not closed up in a sacred realm distinct from a naked secular realm, nor is it revealed only to enthroned sacred hierophants but rather is dispersed. He writes, "[T]he only justification for democracy is theological; since the people is potentially the *ecclesia*, and since nature always anticipates grace, truth lies finally dispersed amongst the people (although they need the initial guidance of the virtuous) because the Holy Spirit speaks through the voice of all."[66]

This bias for democracy, however, is postliberal and postsecular in that it recognizes as well the political necessity of monarchic and aristocratic dimensions. The monarchical dimension is associated with a reassertion of the quest for the shared love that is the common good and absolute transcendence. In other words, this democracy is not the agonistics of clashing opinions that always gives way, if surreptitiously, to power but rather is a form of discerning the truth that is dispersed.[67] The aristocratic dimension pertains to the initial guidance of the virtuous mentioned in the preceding text, by which is meant the educational task. As such, there is in this politics a place for hierarchy, albeit a self-canceling one. In contrast with the hierarchies of liberalism that are little more than competitions for power, this hierarchy is educative and revolves around excellences that can be shared.[68]

In terms of economics, many figures associated with RO have stated an affinity with socialism, albeit a Christian socialism or "socialism by grace" that differs in important ways from Marxist socialism, which does not escape from the problems of secular reason and political liberalism.[69] Consistent with the commitment to an ontology of participation, this economic vision revolves around a theologic of gift exchange that abolishes neither private property nor the market but insists that both function in a manner that extends communion and participation in the good.[70]

Among those most readily identified with RO perhaps the most visible point of contention concerns the institution of government or the state, although the divergences here are easily misinterpreted and overblown. For instance, it is tempting to approach RO looking for an ahistorical prescriptive theory of the state as such. To extract such a theory, however, would be an error. When RO discusses the state, it is always the state specifically situated in time and place, and it is never pursuant to a theory of (a reified) church and state. Indeed, the reflexive equation of "political community" and "the state" is a problematic modern habit of mind that RO's theopolitical vision seeks to break.

Thus, when RO speaks of the state it is referring to the modern nation-state that claims sole sovereignty over political community and exercises empty secular power to enforce that sovereignty. The authors associated with RO share a desire to "unthink" the necessity of the kind of centralized political sovereignty and secular power that the modern nation-state embodies,[71] hence the strong claims made for the church and ecclesiality as directly and immediately political practice. Thus, it is a mistake to distinguish a more anarchist strand in RO over against a more Constantinian or Christendom strand. The complex political space for which RO advocates neither denies the benefits of political order and political community nor insists that political sovereignty reside only in the church. Where a given author may incline in a more anarchist or Christendom direction, it is not on behalf of an ahistorical theory of church and state but as part and parcel of the attempt to interrogate and articulate the intersection of vision and deed, principle and performance in the present moment.[72]

Having said this, Milbank observes that "the *British* members of RO (including myself) are less hostile to the institution of the state *tout court* than are the American ones, even though this is a matter of degree."[73] What rests behind this difference is the issue of state-sanctioned violence and the difference is less that of nationality than of influence. Those associated with RO who are most hostile to the modern nation-state are those deeply influenced by the Christological pacifism of Stanley Hauerwas.

Yet here too significant differences can be overblown, thereby obscuring the point that this difference is, as Milbank suggests, a matter of degree. After all, both Milbank and Ward have penned criticism of the nation-state every bit as hostile as anything written by those trained by Hauerwas. Furthermore, Milbank's justification of violence is both cautious and limited and in no way an endorsement of the violence unleashed in defense of a threatened American hegemony.

CONCLUSION

RO is a postliberal political theology. It is postliberal in its theological lineage and in its attempt to articulate what political theology looks like after the end of the church's accommodation to Western political liberalism. It is neither medieval nor antimodern but an alternative modernity in its supernaturalizing of the natural, which acknowledges the theological appropriateness of democratic politics. It is a postsecular democratic vision insofar as it is a theocratic politics, recognizing that humanity finds its beginning and end in a shared love and so seeks a politics ordered toward the common good.

What does RO tell us about the character and task of political theology in the early twenty-first century? Modernity's dualism of nature/grace and religion/politics cannot be bridged by means of correlations and transcendentalist epistemologies. Rather, political theology must proclaim the postsecular, proclaim the dissolution of those dualisms, and assist the church in its work of ecclesiality, mediating grace, and strengthening the participation of all in the communion of love that is the blessed Trinity from which all is suspended.

Notes

1. John D. Caputo, "What Do I Love When I Love My God? Deconstruction and Radical Orthodoxy," in *Questioning God*, ed. John D. Caputo, Mark Dooley, and Michael J. Scanlon (Bloomington: Indiana University Press, 2001), p. 306.
2. Juan Luis Segundo, "Capitalism versus Socialism: Crux Theologica," in *Frontiers of Theology in Latin America*, ed. Rosino Gibellini (Maryknoll, NY: Orbis, 1979), pp. 240–59.
3. John Milbank, "Materialism and Transcendence," in *Theology and the Political*, ed. Creston Davis, John Milbank, and Slavoj Žižek (Durham, NC: Duke University Press, 2005), pp. 393–426.
4. Catherine Pickstock, "Reply to David Ford and Guy Collins," *Scottish Journal of Theology* 54 (2001): 406; Catherine Pickstock, "Radical Orthodoxy and the Mediations of Time," in *Radical Orthodoxy? A Catholic Inquiry*, ed. Laurence Paul Hemming (Burlington, VT: Ashgate, 2000), p. 63.
5. Pickstock, "Reply to David Ford," p. 405.
6. Graham Ward, "In the Economy of the Divine: A Response to James K. A. Smith," *PNEUMA: The Journal of the Society for Pentecostal Studies* 25.1 (Spring 2003): 117.
7. Ibid., p. 115.
8. John Milbank, "Foreword," in James K. A. Smith, *Introducing Radical Orthodoxy* (Grand Rapids, MI: Baker Academic, 2004), p. 11.
9. See James Fodor, "Postliberal Theology," in *The Modern Theologians*, 3rd ed., ed. David Ford with Rachel Muers (Malden, MA: Blackwell, 2005), pp. 229–48.
10. See ibid.; George Hunsinger, "Postliberal Theology," in *The Cambridge Companion to Postmodern Theology*, ed. Kevin J. Vanhoozer (New York: Cambridge University Press, 2003), pp. 42–57; Ronald T. Michener, *Postliberal Theology: A Guide for the Perplexed* (New York: Bloomsbury, 2013).
11. See John Milbank, "The New Divide: Romantic versus Classical Orthodoxy," *Modern Theology* 26.1 (January 2010): 26–38; and John Milbank, "The Programme of Radical Orthodoxy," in *Radical Orthodoxy? A Catholic Inquiry*, ed. Laurence Paul Hemming (Burlington, VT: Ashgate, 2000).
12. Milbank, "Programme," p. 35.
13. What follows is drawn from John Milbank, *Theology and Social Theory* (Cambridge, MA: Blackwell, 1990), pp. 206–9. Hereafter *TST*.
14. Ibid., p. 207.
15. D. Stephen Long, *Divine Economy* (New York: Routledge, 2000), p. 6.
16. Max Stackhouse makes much of the difference between government and civil society in "Civil Religion, Political Theology and Public Theology: What's the Difference?," *Political Theology* 5.3 (2004): 275–93. For an explanation of how both constitute politics as statecraft, see Daniel M. Bell Jr., "State

130 Daniel M. Bell Jr.

and Civil Society," in *The Blackwell Companion to Political Theology*, ed. Peter Scott and William T. Cavanaugh (Malden, MA: Blackwell, 2004), pp. 423–38.
17 See, e.g., Jürgen Moltmann, *God for a Secular Society* (Minneapolis, MN: Fortress Press, 1999).
18 For more detail, see Daniel M. Bell Jr. *Liberation Theology after the End of History* (New York: Routledge, 2001) and Long, *Divine Economy*.
19 Gustavo Gutiérrez, *A Theology of Liberation*, rev. ed. (Maryknoll, NY: Orbis, 1990), p. 132.
20 Graham Ward, *Politics of Discipleship* (Grand Rapids, MI: Baker Academic, 2009), p. 165. Hereafter *POD*.
21 William T. Cavanaugh, "A Fire Strong Enough to Consume the House: The Wars of Religion and the Rise of the State," *Modern Theology* 11.4 (October 1995): 397–420; William T. Cavanaugh, *The Myth of Religious Violence* (New York: Oxford University Press, 2009).
22 William T. Cavanaugh, *Migrations of the Holy* (Grand Rapids, MI: Eerdmans, 2011).
23 On this secular soteriology, see William T. Cavanaugh, "The City: Beyond Secular Parodies," in *Radical Orthodoxy*, ed. John Milbank, Catherine Pickstock, and Graham Ward (New York: Routledge, 1999), pp. 182–200.
24 Ward, *POD*, p. 262.
25 Milbank, *TST*, pp. 245–6.
26 John Milbank, *The Word Made Strange* (New York: Blackwell, 1997), p. 44.
27 Milbank, *TST*, p. 229.
28 See Milbank, "Programme," p. 45.
29 See Daniel M. Bell Jr., *The Economy of Desire* (Grand Rapids, MI: Baker Academic, 2012).
30 John Milbank, *The Future of Love* (Eugene, OR: Cascade, 2009), pp. 249–50. Hereafter *FOL*.
31 Milbank, *TST*.
32 Ibid., p. 208.
33 Ibid., p. 209; John Milbank, *The Suspended Middle* (Grand Rapids, MI: Eerdmans, 2005), pp. 104–8; John Milbank, "An Essay against Secular Order," *Journal of Religious Ethics* 15.2 (Fall 1987): 199–224.
34 Graham Ward, *Cities of God* (New York: Routledge, 2000), p. 257.
35 Milbank et al., "Introduction," in *Radical Orthodoxy*, ed. John Milbank, Catherine Pickstock, and Graham Ward (New York: Routledge, 1999), pp. 2, 4; Pickstock, "Reply to David Ford," p. 405.
36 Milbank et al., "Introduction," p. 2; Milbank, "Programme," p. 44.
37 John Milbank, "The Gift of Ruling: Secularization and Political Authority," in *After Modernity?*, ed. James K. A. Smith (Waco, TX: Baylor University Press, 2008), pp. 25, 27.
38 Milbank, "Programme," p. 44.
39 Ibid., p. 45.
40 D. Stephen Long, "Radical Orthodoxy," in *The Cambridge Companion to Postmodern Theology*, ed. Kevin J. Vanhoozer (New York: Cambridge University Press, 2003), p. 129.
41 Ward, *Cities of God*, p. 81.

42 Ibid., p. 70; Ward, *POD*, p. 13.
43 Ward, *POD*, p. 166.
44 Ibid., p. 170.
45 Ibid., p. 198.
46 Ibid., p. 166.
47 Ibid., p. 13. See treatment of the Christian act by ibid., pp. 181–204.
48 See Milbank, *TST*, pp. 278–325.
49 Ward, *POD*, p. 180.
50 Milbank, *FOL*, p. xi.
51 Ibid., p. 256.
52 Ibid., pp. 246, 256.
53 Cavanaugh, *Migrations of the Holy*, p. 5.
54 Ward, *POD*, p. 296.
55 Ibid., p. 296. See also Milbank, "Programme," pp. 36–7; Cavanaugh, *Migrations of the Holy*, p. 5; Milbank, *Being Reconciled*, p. 175.
56 Milbank, "Programme," pp. 36–7; Milbank, *Being Reconciled*, p. 175.
57 See Milbank, *Word Made Strange*, pp. 268–92.
58 Ward *POD*, p. 202.
59 Ward, *Cities of God*, p. 229.
60 See Cavanaugh, *Migrations of the Holy*, pp. 55–67.
61 Milbank, *Future of Love*, p. xiv. See also Ward, *POD*, pp. 202–3, 259–60; Ward, *Cities of God*, pp. 180, 233, 247, 258.
62 Catherine Pickstock, *After Writing* (Malden MA: Blackwell, 1998), pp. 158–66; see also Frederick C. Bauerschmidt, "Aesthetics: The Theological Sublime," in *Radical Orthodoxy*, ed. John Milbank, Catherine Pickstock, and Graham Ward (New York: Routledge, 1999), pp. 214–16.
63 Ward *POD*, p. 259.
64 Unpacking the complex and myriad understandings of the relation of modernity to postmodernity exceeds the scope of this essay.
65 Milbank, *FOL*, p. xiv.
66 Ibid., p. 245.
67 Ibid., pp. 260–1; 248.
68 Milbank, *Being Reconciled*, pp. 182–4; Milbank, *FOL*, pp. 248–9.
69 See Milbank, *FOL*, pp. 63–132; Milbank, *TST*.
70 See the previously cited works on theology and economics by Bell, Cavanaugh, and Long.
71 See Cavanaugh, *Migrations of the Holy* and Milbank, *FOL*, pp. 223–41.
72 See Milbank, *Word Made Strange*, p. 270.
73 Milbank, "Foreword," p. 18.

Further Reading

Bell, D. M., Jr., *Liberation Theology after the End of History*. New York: Routledge, 2001.
  The Economy of Desire. Grand Rapids, MI: Baker, 2012.
Cavanaugh, W. T., "A Fire Strong Enough to Consume the House: The Wars of Religion and the Rise of the State," *Modern Theology* 11.4 (October 1995): 397–420.

The Myth of Religious Violence. New York: Oxford University Press, 2009.
Migrations of the Holy. Grand Rapids, MI: Eerdmans, 2011.
Long, D. S., *Divine Economy.* New York: Routledge, 2000.
"Radical Orthodoxy," in *The Cambridge Companion to Postmodern Theology,* ed. Kevin J. Vanhoozer. New York: Cambridge University Press, 2003: pp. 126–45.
Milbank, J., *Theology and Social Theory.* Cambridge, MA: Blackwell, 1990.
"The Programme of Radical Orthodoxy," in *Radical Orthodoxy? A Catholic Inquiry,* ed. Laurence Paul Hemming. Burlington, VT: Ashgate, 2000: pp. 33–45.
"Materialism and Transcendence," in *Theology and the Political,* ed. Creston Davis, John Milbank, and Slavoj Žižek. Durham, NC: Duke University Press, 2005: pp. 393–426.
"The Gift of Ruling: Secularization and Political Authority," in *After Modernity?,* ed. James K. A. Smith. Waco, TX: Baylor University Press, 2008: pp. 17–43.
The Future of Love. Eugene, OR: Cascade, 2009.
"The New Divide: Romantic versus Classical Orthodoxy," *Modern Theology* 26.1 (January 2010): 26–38.
Milbank, J., C. Pickstock, and G. Ward, eds., *Radical Orthodoxy.* New York: Routledge, 1999.
Pickstock, C., *After Writing.* Malden, MA: Blackwell, 1998.
"Radical Orthodoxy and the Mediations of Time," in *Radical Orthodoxy? A Catholic Inquiry,* ed. Laurence Paul Hemming. Burlington, VT: Ashgate, 2000: pp. 63–75.
Smith, J. K. A., *Introducing Radical Orthodoxy.* Grand Rapids, MI: Baker Academic, 2004.
Ward, G., *Cities of God.* New York: Routledge, 2000.
Politics of Discipleship. Grand Rapids, MI: Baker Academic, 2009.

7 Postcolonial Theology
SUSAN ABRAHAM

Reflection on human freedom as a central task of Christian theology emphasizes that human freedom is a divine gift to be used in the context of human living. Contemporary postcolonial theology similarly asks how we can understand the divine gift of freedom in the aftermath of modern European colonialism. At an intuitive level "postcolonial freedom" refers to Asian, African, and American political and national independence and liberation from colonial power in the modern era. The nation, its cultural particularity, and its struggle to provide a humane life to its inhabitants after the colonial authority departs, is postcolonial freedom. Postcolonial freedom therefore can be said to be an account of liberation from colonialism in postcolonial theology. A very complex picture of freedom emerges out of these reflections. One, for a number of postcolonial thinkers, the very category "postcolonial" does not bring about liberation because it does not decolonize, especially in the way that the category is misused in the Western academy. Another issue has to do with right-wing nationalist narratives that now oppress minority cultural, ethnic, or religious groups in the nation; the "post" of "postcolonial" did not decolonize. A third issue is the newly colonizing force that contemporary forms of neocolonialism and neoliberal capitalism exert on postcolonial nations curbing individual and social freedoms in those contexts. No simple definition of postcolonial theology exists; freedom in diverse political contexts like South Asia, East Asia, Africa, and North and South America, in the aftermath of modern colonialism, is visible in complex forms of decolonization.

Reflection on nation and culture marked the first forms of postcolonial studies. Starting in the mid-1990s, the postcolonial lens, which had up until then been limited to secular literary and cultural studies, began to show up in Christian theology as a form of political analysis. Because the methodology of postcolonial theory was akin to literary and cultural analysis, scholars of biblical literature were among the first to shape the theological discourse of postcolonial theology. Here,

R. S. Sugirtharajah's contributions are unparalleled.[1] Sugirtharajah represents a critical change of voice because he attempted to bring a unique cultural analysis to biblical theology. However, he soon changed such an emphasis on cultural identity because he and other postcolonial theorists realized that writing from a particular cultural perspective had the unfortunate effect of affirming a marginal status. "Other" cultural perspectives functioned in a binary[2] relationship to dominant cultures. In fact, it became clear to many that postcolonial theology could not engage in simplistic claims of unique knowledge, or what is called *epistemic privilege* based on cultural identity, because these claims were assigned to the negative half of the binary. Similarly, Kwok Pui-Lan's well-known *Postcolonial Imagination and Feminist Theology*,[3] is an initial attempt to describe a colonial history together with constructive feminist theological proposals. For many contemporary postcolonial thinkers, identity claims offer limited gains. Some have even begun to talk about going "beyond" postcolonial theory arguing that its many methodological and philosophical strands simply cannot be thought of as a singular strategy. Others argue that postcolonial studies have to track the continuities and discontinuities between older forms of colonial practices and newer ones. A crucial task that contemporary postcolonial studies attempt to undertake, therefore, is to limit the use of the binary of the "West" and the "Rest" in solely *cultural* terms without sidelining the homogenizing effects of economic globalization. Identities such as "Asian," "black," and "Latino/a," are all discursively constructed in a system that covertly replicates former colonial relations because these identity categories represent the "Rest." Another way to dismantle the binary is to show that simple oppositions and antagonisms of identity or cultural difference fail to track the other than oppositional configurations of modernity and tradition in postcolonial contexts. It is not that the "West" is modern and the "postcolonial" is premodern; postcolonial contexts (and the West) are instead multiple and complex negotiations between contending modernities and traditionalisms. What does freedom and liberation look like in such complex contexts?

Consequently, this essay presents in two parts, a multifaceted reading of postcolonial freedom arguing that cultural identity is only one of its markers. The first part demonstrates the difficulty of naming "postcolonial" through two contrasting analyses, both drawing on Immanuel Kant's notions of freedom, but each making a distinct argument for the inclusion of cultural identity. Two political and postcolonial theorists – Gayatri Chakravorty Spivak and Pheng Cheah – contribute a dense and complex analysis of postcolonial theory's continuity and discontinuity with Western modernity, dismantling the binary of "West" and "Rest." They do so through a very particular reading of Immanuel Kant and his notion of freedom, subjecting it to a deconstructive critique. Deconstruction is a hallmark of some forms of postcolonial theory. It is a method drawn from Jacques Derrida's analyses of binaries in language and philosophy and dismantles any metaphysics of Self and not-Self by arguing that the assumed difference of the two halves is better understood as *différance*.

Next, I present what freedom, liberation, and autonomy might mean for critical and constructive political theology in Musa Dube's Southern African postcolonial feminism and Andrea Smith's postcolonial Native American Evangelical feminism. Exploring the concept of freedom in these diverse thinkers identifies the many concerns of postcolonial politics: the legacy of modern colonialism, the emergence of the nation-state, and the effect of globalization and neoliberal capitalism on nations and its inhabitants.

RHETORICAL FREEDOM

For Gayatri Chakravorty Spivak, postcolonial theory is caught in a bind because it has to speak of freedom and its allied concept autonomy from inside Western modernity's metaphysics of Self and not-Self.[4] The very title of her book *A Critique of Postcolonial Reason* alerts us to her unease with the idea of "postcolonial" even though she is immediately identified as one of the most prolific and important voices in postcolonial studies. Spivak is, by her own admission, a deconstructive feminist Marxist and resists any ontology of the postcolonial, that is, a postcolonial metaphysics of "Self" and "Other." This does not mean that she is resistant to the idea of the postcolonial Subject, but that she is resistant to a postcolonial metaphysics that is a binary relationship to Western ontology. Her work, which is also influenced in a major way by Jacques Derrida, argues that the notion of Subject has to be discursively presented; the postcolonial Subject is visible as *différance*. Freedom then has to be recast as resistance to forms of neocolonial imperialism, a decolonizing move. Decolonizing freedom in such a view is to resist the replication of the "West" and the "Rest" and an opening up of the metaphysics of "Self" and "Other."

Spivak's method in critiquing postcolonial reason is that of deconstruction, or a form of postcolonial hermeneutics that attempts to decolonize knowledge systems including academic disciplines such as philosophy and history. As Spivak asserts, a deconstructive reading is "unaccusing, attentive, and situationally productive through dismantling"[5] and reads Kant not to simplistically overturn Kant or replace his Western and modern notion of freedom with a differently culturally grounded idea of freedom. Why would a South Asian postcolonial theorist read Kant? Spivak argues that contemporary forms of critique like postcolonial theory are too "thoroughly determined by Kant, Hegel and Marx"[6] to reject these Western thinkers as simple imperialists. Because there is continuity between Enlightenment notions of freedom and autonomy, postcolonial theory cannot simplistically reject the Western philosophical tradition. Neither can it avoid the discontinuities: "I concentrate more on mainstream texts even as I try to probe what subaltern is strategically excluded from organized resistance."[7] It is the legacy of exclusion that Spivak probes in the project of the Enlightenment. The missing subaltern, or, as Spivak emphasizes, the "gendered subaltern" is the excluded and silent figure in the master texts of European philosophy. Spivak and other postcolonial thinkers employ specialized vocabulary to signal the complexity of identity. Here, the term *gendered subaltern* challenges the idea that simpler terms such as *colonized native woman* grasp the complex history of colonization, exclusion from the after colonial projects, and continuing subjugation under neocolonial practices.

Nevertheless, Spivak is less interested in pointing out Kant's obvious class, race, and gender privilege through which he develops his idea of "transcendental" freedom. Western philosophers such as Kant also have used specialized vocabulary. The term *transcendental*, peculiar to Kant, refers to the necessary preconditions that exist in order for thought to be possible. While Kant does admit for the presence of transcendental freedom in all people, his argument also rhetorically enacts a "foreclosure." Spivak is not interested in castigating Kant for being a Western white male. To do so would only create a "reversal" of the Kantian model, reinforcing the binary of colonial oppressor and postcolonial victim. She provides an analogical reading rather than a historical reading of Kant's presentation of freedom and the role of the "native" in that presentation to show how Kant's notion of the autonomous subject is anchored by the native's lack of autonomy. Consequently, she argues that the great modern conceptualizations of freedom rhetorically performed the violence of "foreclosure" of the native subject. *Foreclosure*, a term borrowed from Lacanian psychoanalysis is the "rejection of an affect."[8] Here the native subject is not erased or ignored, but spoken of in a way that creates an affective response of rejection and disgust. Such an affective response to people who are "different" than the European subject becomes the site of postcolonial political and ethical responsibility. Investigating the Kantian aesthetic for its affective foreclosures is Spivak's deconstruction in action: affect is what makes *différance* clear. An emphasis on social, cultural, or racial *difference* instantiates binary thinking and is dependent on a metaphysics of Self and not-Self. As a feminist political thinker, Spivak emphasizes that the "typecase" or prime example of the foreclosed native is the poorest woman of the South, the gendered subaltern, and it is this (disgusting) figure of *différance* that haunts postcolonial studies.

Another perspective on affect as the site of postcolonial ethics and responsibility is evident in her analysis of how the category "culture" is understood by Kant. Arguing that in *The Critique of Judgment* "culture" is a rational faculty – a receptivity to the Sublime and a natural possibility of the "programming of determinate humanity"[9] – Spivak notes that even as Kant emphasizes that judgment is programmed in nature, there is a resulting subtle argument to exclude those who are "naturally alien" to culture.[10] Thus, it is primarily cultivated and educated men who are able to make rational judgments or respond to the Sublime. The Sublime does not come to some people. Moral ideas are developed in the crucible of culture even though the receptivity to ideas and moral feeling are available to all human beings. But the uncultured man, or in Kant's words, "the raw man," in the absence of the development of moral feeling or ideas, simply experiences the sublime as "terrible." Many thinkers have pointed out[11] that for Kant, the term *raw* has generally meant "uneducated." The uneducated, of course, are children, the poor, women, and native others. The adjective *raw* signals an affective response. In this nuanced criticism of Kant, Spivak's point is not that he performs exclusions of the native informant through a simplistic erasure but rather that Kant uses the native informant negatively in relation to his ideal, "cultured" man, a binary construction through the foreclosing mechanism of affect. The foreclosing of the native in this manner has not been studied by Kant scholars because the effect of foreclosing trickles down the system continuing the systemic foreclosing.

Instead of an accusing reading of Kant, however, Spivak's deconstructive reading exposes a productive tension in the European canon that challenges the notion of freedom as instrumental reason. Spivak therefore shines a laser beam on Kant's invocation of the "natural man ... the New Hollanders or the inhabitants of Tierra del Fuego."[12] Here, argues Spivak, the raw man of the Analytic of the Sublime is named as a "casual object of thought," not a paradigmatic example. He is "not only *not* the subject as such; he also does not quite make it as an example of the thing or its species as natural product."[13] Why does Kant refer to these "geopolitically differentiated" people? The relegation of the *aboriginal* to the natural reveals for Spivak that the aboriginal "cannot be the subject of speech or judgment in the world of the Critique" even as the aboriginal is "the representative example" of the kind of determinant judgment that Kant's reflective judgment corrects.[14] This is the foreclosure, the legible trace of the native informant whose self-determination or freedom has no part to play in the late eighteenth century's philosophical notions of freedom, including Kant's. The deconstructive move therefore discerns both the limits Kant places on the modern notion of freedom through the category of culture, but also deconstructs his racial anthropology that undergirds his philosophical project. It also hints at the impossibility of using Kant to develop decolonizing discourses on freedom in its relation to *culture*.

While it is true that the foreclosed native informant, on whom is built a "relationship without a relationship," inserts an interruption into Kantian universalism, Spivak's criticism is not merely the criticism of classism, racism, or sexism. As she writes: "Quite apart from Kant's expressed opinion on race and colonization, I am noting here the mysterious working of the savage and the named savage in the *central* text on *the* subject's access to the rational will and its consolidation as the transcendental subject."[15] What makes Kant problematic for postcolonial theory is that the key idea of rational will in Kant rests on the figure of the "savage." Any postcolonial analysis that celebrates its "marginal" status is simply mimicking that original Kantian assessment.

For postcolonial theology, what is important is not whether or not Spivak is a secular thinker or even what Kant says about religion. What is important is to track how postcolonial studies, in mimicking the original Kantian foreclosure of the native subject performs complicity. When postcolonial studies or postcolonial theology are solely concerned with contemporary identity, or speak about colonialism as if it were securely in the past, they reproduce neocolonial foreclosures. Postcolonial theology, therefore, has to exert great reflexivity on how it is complicit with neocolonial knowledge. Spivak's rhetorical strategy alerts us to the notion that theology is a discourse, shot through with rhetorical power plays between different groups that become ever more invisible in a globalized political economy. Freedom, one of theology's central concerns, cannot be simplistically presented as a constitutive feature of postcolonial cultural identity. Instead, as Spivak suggests, it is to be tracked in the manner that subject positions come into view in discursive contexts that lead to contemporary forms of imperialism.

HAUNTING FREEDOM

A form of postcolonial discursive freedom is nationalism, which often enacts new violences against minoritized groups within the new nation. Often postcolonial analyses while disparaging Western Enlightenment dismiss nationalism as a form of complicity with European colonialism. As we saw in the preceding text, Spivak would argue that nationalist discourses perform complicitous violence of foreclosing the gendered subaltern. But she would also disagree that nationalism is simplistically a form of cultural essentialism. Postcolonial studies need not jettison nationalist discourses if they also engage in critiques of continuing imperialism. Such a view is to be seen in the postcolonial assessment of Kant's notion of freedom by Pheng Cheah, a Vietnamese American scholar of rhetoric, who tracks the "organismic" nature of freedom in German eighteenth-century philosophy and its association with "revolutionary postcolonial nationalism."[16] Organismic vitalism is a Kantian and German idealist concept that understands individuals and groups as interrelated wholes. As a metaphor for the organic body and life, it remains critical to nationalist discourses. Kant remains important for Cheah too because other parts of Kant's thought, such as the core belief in the right of all people to possess human freedom in historical contexts, remain important for postcolonial contexts. Kant also argued that human beings were "citizens of the world," a cosmopolitan view that Cheah finds useful. Cheah's critique explicitly takes on global capitalism and financialization, which he terms the "haunting of capitalism." Here, like Spivak, Cheah draws on Derrida, particularly, Derrida's work entitled *Specters of Marx*,[17] where the specter is the figure of deconstruction. Whereas Spivak wants to talk about the Southern Women, or, the "gendered subaltern," to critique imperialism, Cheah creatively draws on Derrida's specter to point out the limitations of the organismic metaphor for nation and the actualization of the nation-state. To draw the distinction between nation and nation-state, Cheah makes use of the specter, arguing that the specter as a figure of death, contamination, and undecidability and as a reminder of the impossibility of a pure and definitive being, is a more "apposite figure for freedom today."[18] Thus, nationalist myths of homogeneity and pure stories of origin are challenged by the specter's presence that signals historical heterogeneity in nation contexts as result of colonialism, genocide, war, and commerce.

Cheah's writing is dense and difficult and he uses a number of technical terms that scholars of philosophy use. His explicit stance is that the organismic foundation for freedom is inadequate for postcolonial contexts even though, as the basis of *ontopology* (a term that combines *ontology* and *politics*), it has provided foundational ways to narrate identity, nation, race, and ethnicities. That is, nationalist narratives present culture as the organic outcome of "nation." Ontopologies presume that there is an ontological and organic basis to any assertion of identity and freedom. Cheah argues instead that the actualizing of freedom is what postcolonial studies ought to focus on because such a "vitalist ontology" falsely opposes metaphors of life (nation, native, natality) to death metaphors. In other words, Cheah is critical of the metaphysics of presence that undergirds vitalist ontologies. The opposition of life and death metaphors are clear in the manner that some forms of postcolonial studies present freedom as the teleology of decolonization. Freedom and decolonization are not sequential; freedom instead is a constant openness to past, present, and future time. Here, acknowledging the specter would permit a more creative way to think of nation as a form of resistance to the ravages and excesses of global financialization.

Many nationalist narratives depend on organismic vitalist arguments that sequence time progressively.[19] One reason why organismic vitalism is so attractive to nationalists and postcolonial thought is that it presupposes that freedom is the overcoming of finitude and existential limitation. Such a "purposive endeavor" is inspiring especially in its contrast to nature, which does not demonstrate such purposiveness. Purpose presumes rationality, a quality of human beings that the Enlightenment in Western modernity highly valued. In a manner of speaking, nature is arational: cause and effect are not purposeful. Purposiveness belongs to human beings who stand outside the natural and causal order, a feature of Kant's philosophy. Cheah admits that even as Kant thus makes a good argument for the possibility of freedom, his argument for its actualization creates a problem. That is, precisely because Kant makes a clear distinction between the world of nature and the world of human beings – the sensible world and the intelligible world – it is not clear how freedom is manifested in the sensible world if purposive freedom cannot exist in it. Another way to ask the question is, can freedom be objectively real?

To make that argument, Cheah argues that organic life is invaded by heteronomy,[20] made clear in the manner that *physis* (organic) and *techne* (artifice) operate in Kant's scheme. This point reveals Cheah's discontinuity from Kant. For Kant, autonomy, or freedom cannot be contaminated by heteronomous elements. For Cheah, the contamination of organic autonomy by heteronomous elements is unavoidable.

Thus, while it is true that the objective reality of freedom is to be found in nature, it does not account for a "postcolonial" narrative of freedom. Organic life, for example, is invaded by human *techne* (human making or doing) because nature in Kant's argument is only an instrument of practical reason and subordinate to human practical reason. Cheah's argument is that even as Kant presents the view that "culture" is the rational medium through which human beings incarnate freedom, the particularity of culture cannot be explained solely through the organic metaphor. *Techne* creeps back in, that is, Kant seems to be asserting that we can only understand organismic causality as an act of the will. Furthermore, he points out, even as Kant seems to be foregrounding the projection of human purposiveness onto nature, there are also a number of instances where Kant seems to concede that it is nature that prods and prompts us to experience, without developing the auto-causality of nature. Cheah is unwilling to sideline nature's role in human freedom. It is not that Kant wants to deliberately efface the impulse of nature he argues, but that Kant seems to prefer to conceptualize the impulse of nature in epistemological terms. Hence Kant anthropomorphizes the impulse and limits it to the workings of human beings. Cheah in contrast argues that nature's impulse is more than the human – it is in inhuman (in a manner of speaking). It possesses a radical alterity that cannot be limited as human thought. Human *techne*, that is human making and doing, may be prompted by nature as Kant says, but freedom's heteronomy guarantees that human *techne* of actualizing freedom is not a result of *just* human causality. Nature and its otherness play a very important role in actualizing human freedom. Opposing *physis* and *techne*, as many postcolonial analyses unwittingly do,[21] leads to the false dichotomy of life versus death. The oppositional metaphors can be seen as the difference between nation-people and nation-state. A postcolonial view of freedom is best grasped in a deconstruction of the opposites of organic body and alien state and between life and death.

Postcolonial studies that dismiss nation-state are only conceiving of the nation-state in terms of death metaphors. Cheah argues instead that nation-people and nation-state both are contaminated by life-in-death. "Postcolonial" in view of the heteronomy of freedom depends not just on life metaphors, but also on death metaphors, because "a discourse on death necessarily involves a rhetoric of borders."[22] Freedom is not birthed simply as a reaction to oppressive contexts; the argument for freedom from oppression can backfire by reinforcing the victim status of colonized cultures. Nor is freedom a feature of modernity. Instead, argues Cheah, Kant's model of transcendental freedom for the nation fails insofar as it does not chart the excess of nature. Such an excess to nature confounds the Kantian assertion that it is modernity that confers freedom. The Eurocentricism of many nationalist discourses that bespeaks the nation-state as the pinnacle of modern achievement is dismantled in such a reading. Cheah makes room for the possibility of other than Western modernity framing the claims of nation-people and nation-states.

Nature's spectral basis for postcolonial freedom intensifies postcolonial narratives of freedom by emphasizing that ethics and responsibility is more than the individual self's (or, by extension, the nation's) autonomous will in the present modern moment. His complex argument therefore overturns nativist nationalist narratives what are unable to engage a simultaneous critique of imperialism. Freedom is basic to human beings, precisely because it encompasses more than their will. Like Spivak, what Cheah wants to do is to move the discourse of postcolonialism away from "a fixation on the crisis of culture"[23] to the cry for freedom that is more than the colonial relation or even its resistance. In so doing he attempts to move freedom beyond its ideological and presentist construction by nationalist elements. Further, Cheah is able to show that the survival of the nation-people is also influenced by the presence of global capital; the one haunting the other. Unlike Spivak, whose archival emphasis is South Asian literature, Cheah's use of Javanese author Pramodeya Ananta Toer, who writes in Malay, and Ngũgĩ wa Thiong'o, who writes in English and Gikuyu, demonstrates the heterogeneous nature of postcolonial thought. Instead of a homogenous understanding of postcolonialism as an analysis of a crisis of culture, Cheah explicitly moves to an analysis of freedom in culture as it arises in the complex negotiations of nation-people and nation-state.

In what follows, I have chosen two examples of postcolonial theological accounts of negotiation as examples that make clear the complex moves necessary for postcolonial theology to dismantle cultural, political, and historical binaries. As we shall also see, the disciplinary and methodological plurality demonstrated by the two examples reveals that it is impossible to name "postcolonial" as one half of the binary colonial/postcolonial.

BIBLICAL RHETORICS OF FREEDOM

The rhetorical context of biblical literature is the backdrop against which Musa Dube presents her *Postcolonial Feminist Interpretation of the Bible*.[24] In a twofold move of critical literary analysis, Dube attempts to mine the biblical tradition, encompassing both the narrative within the Bible as well as its reception, for ways in which the Bible has been used both to empower colonization and to overcome colonialism. She argues that colonialism circulates through the "reproduction of recognizable literary-rhetorical constructions" to justify colonialist agendas,[25] meaning that colonialism (and resistance to colonialism) is best discerned through a literary-rhetorical method. The intent to explore the rhetorical constructions of sacred texts reflects the methodological emphasis similar to Spivak's rereading of the Kantian text. While Dube and Spivak represent dichotomous stances in their choices of texts and theological emphasis, a parallel reading of the methods of each author permits a view of the complex strategies of decolonization being attempted in the academic context. First, both present a constructive rereading of the canon, whether philosophical or theological. Neither is committed to a simplistic dismissal of influential texts that have considerable impact on political thought today. Second, both are committed to the central problem that gendered identities represent in colonial and postcolonial politics and thus committed to postcolonial subjectivity in *différance*. Freedom in both is wrought through the method of deconstruction by examining the rhetorical contexts of influential texts. Finally, both are committed to dismantling binary logics in charting a critical complicity between colonizer and colonized.

Dube accomplishes her decolonial strategy by pointing to the ambivalence of biblical texts. The ambivalence of texts, even as they make normative claims, is captured in Dube's reading of the book of Exodus. The narrative world of the text, its ideological apparatus, and the history of the text in the present world form its rhetorical background. Here, even as Exodus begins with the mighty works of God in saving and liberating the Israelites from Pharaoh's slavery, it also chronicles how easily history's victims become its oppressors. In other words, Spivak's caution that the new postcolonial migrant not perform the failed strategy of the reversal is upheld in Dube's constructive reading. Dube points out that the text presents such an insight: "victimized losers" become "victimized winners"[26] when the exodus of the Israelites leads them to lands already inhabited by "the Canaanites, the Hittites, the Amorites, the Perizzites, the Hivites and the Jebusites."[27] Thus, an antiimperial narrative in which God liberates the people from Egypt's Pharaoh, now becomes a colonizing rationale. *Liberation* and *freedom* have different meanings here. The liberating formula of "Let my people go" is also juxtaposed with the promise "I will bring you up out of the misery of Egypt, to the land of the Canaanites." Why does God not care about the Canaanites? It is this ambivalence that is captured by Dube's postcolonial rhetorical analysis.

The theological legitimation of the biblical text's insistence that it is God who commands the liberation of the people is also clearly the legitimation of the enslavement of others importantly, in Dube's reading, for the colonial takeover of land. Dube's deconstructive instinct leads her to point out the binary arrangements that postcolonial theory has identified as the colonial schema – identities constructed as dualistic opposites – operating in the biblical text. Critically for Dube, anti-imperial and colonizing narratives rest on the debasement of women. The overvaluation of motherhood in the book of Genesis, for example, has to do with the promise of God to increase the numbers of Israelites. Here, patriarchy serves imperialism. Dube argues that it is important to maintain a distinction between patriarchy and imperialism because the biblical promise is really to be understood as a "male game."[28] Nevertheless, women are not absent from this game; they are also its "active participants as fellow travelers, revolutionists, sellouts, benefactors and victims."[29] In the book of Exodus, the identities of Israelite women under colonialism change as they become the beneficiaries of colonialism. During the transition, gender roles are somewhat obscured as women are conscripted in the battle for conquest. However, as soon as the colonizing project is launched, gender roles for women return with a vengeance. Thus, their position is ambivalent. On the one hand, they are repositories of impurity that can jeopardize male power and, on the other hand, repositories of purity for the nation as a whole. Yet, as Dube points out, colonizing women who are able to share in the victories of colonizing men are not oppressed in the same way as colonized women. Dube's analysis alerts us to the theological discursive context in which such ambivalences towards women circulate.

In her critical literary analysis of biblical texts, Dube maintains that biblical texts create and sustain such ambivalences. Biblical texts therefore, have to be read with reference to the imperial contexts in which they functioned and continue to function ambivalently. Thus, any reading of a scriptural text also must acknowledge the rhetorical context of collaboration and complicity between the text and its historical and contemporary colonizers, the goal of decolonization. Decolonizing readers such as African feminists, also called *Semoya* Readers,[30] are part of the African Independent Churches that arose as a protest movement against white-male-only or male-only leadership. In these churches, liberation was cast as a wider struggle against colonialism, capitalism, racism, and cultural proscriptions of women's roles. The name *Dikereke tsa Semoya* or, Churches of the Spirit, draw on pneumatology and understand the Spirit or *Moya* as central to its ecclesial theology. Women have leadership roles in these churches and seek theological legitimation for their calling from the Spirit of God. Even such a pneumatological basis for women's leadership in churches is often received with hostility, leading the women to challenge biblically based arguments against such leadership. Dube writes:

> The Spirit that reveals and gives one a vocation and power operates with a significant independence from the written word. This point was outlined by Bishop Virginia Lucas when asked, "Why are you a female church leader when the Bible seems to suggest otherwise?" She responded, "I have been asked this question several times before. I always tell people that when God spoke to me through the Sprit, God never opened the Bible to me. Instead, God's Spirit told me to begin a church and heal God's people, which is what I am doing."

Thus, feminist postcolonial African theologians engage multiple fronts: domestic patriarchy not identical but similar to colonial or imperial oppression; the persuasive apparatuses of cultural and textual products of patriarchy and imperialism; the creative resistances to these that arise in the humane visions of women resisting both forms of oppression; and, finally, the realization that women labor under multiple oppressions in the colonial and postcolonial contexts.[31] The net result of such a multipronged engagement with the multiple oppressions of domestic and global tyrannies leads African postcolonial feminist theologians to envision a goal of liberating interdependence in view of the "interdependence of males and females, Two-Thirds World and One-Third World economic/political systems, black and white races, Christian and non-Christian cultures, the past and present and so on."[32] Freedom in this context is interdependence and interliberation, through a method of rhetorically "twinning biblical stories with indigenous stories."[33]

SPECTRAL DEMOCRATIC VISIONS

Andrea Smith's ethnographic presentation of Native American negotiations with U.S. nationalisms exemplifies what Pheng Cheah calls a "spectral nationalism." Smith is one of the more astute and creative scholars of religion and anthropology and is currently an associate professor in the Department of Media and Cultural Studies at the University of California, Riverside. Her book *Native Americans and the*

Christian Right[34] presents an example of the haunting of the nation's freedom. Freedom in the context of contemporary native resistance is also freedom from restrictive forms of recognition circulating in the public sphere and a freedom from the cultural and political amnesia of the U.S. nation-state's emergence. That is, "American" modernity obscures a colonial tradition of genocide and mass killing in the name of progress. Concomitantly, Smith issues a ringing challenge to progressive "Left" critical theory, which is unable to account for the complex negotiations between religion and politics evident in the activism of Evangelical Christianity and Native Americans. That is, Smith is arguing that identity politics which pits (good) Native Americans against (bad) Evangelical Christian nationalist accounts cannot reveal the ways in which Native Americans may negotiate with U.S. nationalist ideology. Like Cheah, her argument is that the nation-people and its identity are critical to refashioning the nation-state, particularly by challenging global economic systems that prefer to mark Native American resistance as simplistic "cultural politics."[35] Even Native American feminism issues a challenge to any presumption that feminism is "modern" and pitted against "tradition." As she argues, "what is remembered as traditional is political."[36] Instead, Native American feminism should be seen as a form of "traditioning." That is, it is traditional for native peoples to be responsive to changing contexts. Feminist Native Americans therefore can and do ally with Evangelical Christian groups because neither group is homogenous. Further, both groups are influenced by arguments for gender egalitarianism.

The assumption that native peoples are only invested in minority cultural particularity over and against majority WASP (White, Anglo-Saxon, Protestant) culture obscures the political and theoretical contributions of native scholar activists and complex negotiations made in cultural and political venues. The problem here is who defines whom as an "agent of political change"[37] and what exactly connotes such activity. A critical notion illuminating her method is "ontopraxy," which is based both in an alternative view of freedom and agency giving rise to alternative views of coalition building.[38] She defines ontopraxy as incorporating relationality and praxis, revealing the complex negotiations of culture and politics. Smith, like Spivak, in asking the question of the agent of political change reiterates a question that Spivak, drawing on Ngũgĩ wa Thiong'o's "Who decolonizes and how?" has often volleyed at forms of postcolonial theory. Like Cheah, Smith is invested in the heterogeneity of political negotiations and how the specter of global financialization functions to distinguish the particularity of native peoples in their strategies of resistance.

Not only is the cultural difference of native peoples centered in her work, it is the centering of native women's activist scholarship (ontopraxy) that textures her constructive proposal to think beyond the multicultural nation-state. Smith asserts: "It becomes clear that native feminisms do not just intervene in the sexism of native organizing or the racism and colonialism in feminist movements; they also *challenge the framework of liberation itself* by recasting how we understand nation, sovereignty, and nationalist struggle."[39] Like Cheah, she deplores the sidelining of terms such as *nation* and *sovereignty* in postcolonial cultural studies. The site of a double haunting now, the United States' claims to nationalism and sovereignty ignore the genocide and erasure of women activists seeking to provide alternatives to nation-state rhetoric.

These original critical visions of *nation* provide a different frame for freedom. *Sovereignty*, a contentious term in Native American politics, is disarticulated in native women's writing. By disarticulation, Smith means that the notions of "nation" and "sovereignty" are unyoked from their nationalist associations and rearticulated in view of a political and emancipatory purpose on behalf of those forgotten in nationalist narratives. Quoting Ingrid Washinawatok from the Menominee nation: "Our spirituality and our responsibilities define our duties. We understand the concept of sovereignty as woven through a fabric that encompasses our spirituality and responsibility. This is a cyclical view of sovereignty, incorporating it into our traditional philosophy and view of our responsibilities. There it differs greatly from the concept of western sovereignty which is based on absolute power. For us, absolute power is in the Creator and the natural order of all living things; not only in human beings.... Our sovereignty is related to our connections to the earth and is inherent."[40] Here, autonomy, freedom, and sovereignty are disarticulated from their Euro-American strangleholds of control and dominance to one of interresponsibility and interrelationship with the land and its creatures. Significantly, a spiritual foundation bears up native visions of sovereignty. Native women activists see spirituality as "inextricably linked" to their political work. Sovereignty is a political and spiritual vision: "it is the dream of living outside the constraints of both US colonialism and multinational capitalism."[41] Such a vision of nation challenges right-wing views of "nation." Race and gender play a significant role in the rethinking of nationalist projects. As Cheah had warned, liberation visions of freedom in postcolonial contexts are not simplistically married to idealist notions of freedom. Smith provides subtle examples of how race and feminist politics in the nation ally in ways that perform deconstructions of "autonomy" and "freedom," "tradition," and "modernity."

A spectral *différance* haunts such negotiations. Quoting Dorinne Kondo: "'Even when colonized peoples imitate the colonizer, the mimesis is never complete, for the specter of the 'not quite, not white' haunts the colonizer, a dis-ease that always contains an implicit threat to the colonizer's hegemony.' ... The very act of mimesis challenges the hegemonic rules of the colonizers. And on the other hand, oppositional practices are never free of reinscribing that which they contest."[42] Thus Native Charismatics can be understood to perform whiteness even as they resist it. So, even as the evangelical Christian Right in the United States seem to disavow their own social embeddedness and ignore their white and cultural privilege, the politics of inclusion that leads native evangelicals into the conversation is reshaping that very conversation by calling attention to negotiations between the two groups. Thus, native evangelical Christianity is now developing theologies of mission that, "on the one hand, seem to be mimicking their oppressors by attempting to join the missionizing project, on the other, the attempt to begin missionizing is also a strategy to stop white Christians from continuing their mission work in Native communities."[43] Supporting the rights of native peoples and their sovereignty includes the right of native peoples to be Christian in their particularity. Such particularity includes strategic alliance with groups such as the Promise Keepers to allow for a "broader impact on the politics of race in evangelical communities than they might otherwise have."[44]

Native American arguments for sovereignty echo Cheah's assertion that contemporary postcolonial studies ought not to jettison terms such as *sovereignty* and *nation*. Coalitional politics like the alliance with the Promise Keepers provide alternate visions for American democracy by presenting native visions of freedom as strategic alliance, enabled by a traditional emphasis on right relation and response to context. Sovereignty and nation, for coalitional politics, means going beyond the nation-state. Founding narratives for the nation-state perform the "colonizing trick" of forgetting the genocide that underwrote the nation-state. Because the nation-state of the United States could not have come into existence without the genocide of native peoples, we should theorize U.S. democracy as if Native American genocide was foundational to it. Participatory democracy is only ever actualized when the memory of genocide is kept alive. Nevertheless, if the nation-people argue for sovereignty, what is it that they mean? Sovereignty here refers to the process of decolonization that Smith asserts is "a political practice that is rooted in building mass-based movements for social change"[45] that is simultaneously a struggle against imperialism and capitalism. Here is where we can note the connection to what Pheng Cheah and Spivak argue as important to postcolonial politics. Sovereignty for native activist women in particular is not a rule of law, but a law of kinship. It is a spiritual concept: "an active, living process within this knot of human, material and spiritual relationships bound together by mutual responsibilities and obligations,"[46] a freedom for others. Rhetorically, sovereignty is no longer a violent enactment of neocolonialism, but a continuing-to-live people's response to the violence of the nation-state and that of globalized capitalism. Another connection that resonates between Spivak and Smith in particular has to do with their unease with institutional academic contexts that demand that categories such as "postcolonial" reflect its assumptions about colonial histories and contexts. In Smith's view, when a capitalist academy commodifies its capitalist notion of postcolonial knowledge, then it simply becomes a tool of the nation-state. "Postcolonial" in her view is an empty category if we ignore the complex alliance and strategic coalitions that attempt to engage oppositional groups in surprising and novel ways.

"POSTCOLONIAL THEOLOGY"

This essay has taken an indirect path in developing the notion of "postcolonial theology." As is now clear, if we were to take freedom as a touchstone for theological thought, postcolonial contexts would not be homogenous or the same. Consequently, no simple affirmative answer can be provided to the question of what is postcolonial freedom. It is, first of all, a notion embedded in Western modernity and its colonial enterprise in which freedom for some was won on the backs of others. Second, such (after colonialism) freedom when tied to the emergent nativist politics was not a freedom at all, because it was freedom that reflected the interests of domestic elites, a false nationalism. Third, colonialism morphed into forms of neocolonialism to be observed in economic globalization that rhetorically constructs geopolitical identities, on the one hand, and, on the other, curtails the freedom of those that attempt to resist such global capitalism. Rather than a simple reversal or a simple absence, it is an active process of decolonization of metaphysics, language, thought, and practice in view of the poorest women. It is not an abstract idea as we see in Dube and Smith who clearly present their analyses from identifiable ethnic, gender, race, class, sexuality, and theological perspectives. Indeed, participative and representative democracy is for all of them, the key to resisting newer forms of colonial violence and the frame in which postcolonial freedom must be articulated.

No positivist notion of freedom can be discerned in this analysis of Spivak, Cheah, Dube, or Smith. First, the difference between Spivak and Cheah is critical to grasping why a positivist account of freedom is impossible. Both, like Derrida, abhor ontopology. For Spivak, it is *critical* theory, specifically feminist in its orientation, which challenges "ontopology and identitarian culturalisms."[47] A feminist perspective on freedom is strongly critical of masculinist political theory, which can afford these occlusions in which the freedom for "woman" is subsumed into a general category of freedom. Woman as the subject *and* object of ethics infinitely complicates philosophy, politics, and cultural theory. Rhetorical and discursive strategies in context are better able to illuminate how freedom for women is inseparable from freedom for anyone else. This point is also made in Dube's work; gendered oppression, its domestic and global face, can only be met by careful attention to the way in which culturally influential texts construct women. Neither Dube nor Spivak is invested in identity politics. The force of their rhetorical analyses of freedom is aimed at dissolving binary metaphysics of Self and not-Self with a view to decolonization.

Cheah goes after ontopology in view of his desire to complicate the organic basis for nationalism. Drawing on Derrida he asserts that ontopologies only present an "outmoded doctrine of self-present place,"[48] that is, no place exists uncontaminated by global capital and its geopolitical interests. Such ontopologies result in the death of the nation-people; it simply plays into a mechanism of narrow social ascription, expertly managed by neoliberal capitalism. Freedom in his work is not dependent on nationalist identity alone, but arises in the contamination or haunting of the present by globalization. Thus we note that the simple identity politics of earlier postcolonial studies is replaced by a more complex tracking of identity. Simple oppositions and antagonisms depend on a metaphysics of presence, which Cheah unravels. The specter, which is the mark of radical finitude and death (instead of the Kantian transcendence of finitude), reveals that we are radically historical beings haunted by presence and nonpresence. It is attention to such historicity that creates the conditions for responsibility. Recall here Smith's assertion that the colonial trick of erasing the memory of genocide results in the loss of participatory democracy. Challenging the colonial trick needs more than a metaphysics of presence; the specter, because it inhabits a realm of presence and nonpresence, challenges narratives of past and future by showing how both contaminate the narrative of the present moment. Andrea Smith in her concluding chapter captures the urgent need for decolonizing rather than postcolonizing as a spiritual need: "what seems to make sovereignty a spiritual concept for many activists is that sovereignty as a political and spiritual vision is the dream of living outside the constraints of both US colonialism and multinational capitalism ... [sovereignty] is the substance of things hoped for, the evidence of things not seen."[49] Smith's point, like Cheah's is that native politics and emphases on sovereignty are not narrowly nationalistic, but express the desire and freedom of its forgotten people to address the concerns of the world at large. An eternity of past and future attends our freedom to be for others, the theological face of postcolonial freedom.

Notes

1 See, e.g., R. S. Sugirtharajah, *Voices from the Margin: Interpreting the Bible in the Third World* (Maryknoll, NY: Orbis, 1991); *Voices from the Margin: Interpreting the Bible in the Third World* (Maryknoll, NY: Orbis, 1995); *The Postcolonial Bible* (Sheffield, UK: Sheffield Academic Press, 1998); *The Postcolonial Biblical Reader* (Oxford: Blackwell, 2006).
2 See Leela Gandhi, *Postcolonial Theory: A Critical Introduction* (New York: Columbia University Press, 1998).
3 Kwok Pui-Lan, *Postcolonial Imagination and Feminist Theology* (Louisville, KY: Westminster John Knox, 2005).
4 Gayatri Chakravorty Spivak, *A Critique of Postcolonial Reason: Toward a History of the Vanishing Present* (Cambridge, MA: Harvard University Press, 1999), p. 4 (henceforth CPR).
5 Ibid., p. 81.
6 Ibid., p. 7.
7 Ibid., p. xi.
8 Ibid., p. 4.
9 Ibid., p. 4.
10 Ibid., p. 13.
11 See also Stephen Morton's analysis in *Gayatri Spivak* (Cambridge: Polity, 2007), p. 146.
12 Spivak, *CPR*, p. 26.
13 Ibid.
14 Ibid., pp. 26–8.
15 See ibid., p. 32n36.

16 Pheng Cheah, *Spectral Nationality: Passages of Freedom from Kant to Postcolonial Literatures of Liberation* (New York: Columbia University Press, 2003), p. 2.
17 Jacques Derrida, *Specters of Marx: The State of the Debt, the Work of Mourning and the New International* (New York: Routledge, 1994).
18 Cheah, *Spectral Nationality*, p. 395.
19 Chapter 1, "The Rationality of Life: On the Organismic Metaphor of the Social and Political Body," begins with a reflection on the "Myths of the Organic Community." *Spectral Nationality*, pp. 17–59.
20 Ibid., p. 67.
21 In an earlier version of *Spectral Nationality*, published as an essay, Cheah points to Frantz Fanon's postcolonial critiques of nationalism as a case in point. See Pheng Cheah "Spectral Nationality: The Living on [sur-vie] of the Postcolonial Nation in Neocolonial Globalization" *boundary 2* 26.3 (Autumn 1999): 225–52.
22 Ibid., 240.
23 Cheah, *Spectral Nationality*, p. 394.
24 Musa Dube, *Postcolonial Interpretation of the Bible* (St. Louis: Chalice, 2000).
25 Ibid., p. 57.
26 Ibid., p. 60.
27 Ibid.
28 Ibid., p. 73.
29 Ibid.
30 Ibid., pp. 39–43.
31 Ibid. p. 43.
32 Ibid. p. 198.
33 Ibid. p. 108.
34 Andrea Smith, *Native Americans and the Christian Right* (Durham, NC: Duke University Press, 2008).
35 Ibid., pp. 215–23.
36 Ibid., p. 177.
37 Ibid., p. xi.
38 Ibid., p. xiv.
39 Ibid., p. 255, emphasis added.
40 Quoted in ibid., p. 260. Ingrid Washinawatok, "Sovereignty as a Birthright," in *Indigenous Women Address the World*, ed. Indigenous Women's Network (Austin, TX: Indigenous Women's Network, 1995), pp. 12–13.
41 Smith, *Native Americans and the Christian Right*, p. 269.
42 Ibid., p. 110.
43 Ibid., p. 98.
44 Ibid., p. 109.
45 Ibid., p. 273.
46 Ibid., p. 261.
47 Spivak, *CPR*, p. 404.
48 Cheah, "Spectral Nationality," p. 392.
49 Smith, *Native Americans and the Christian Right*, p. 269.

Further Reading

Bilimoria, Purushottama, and Andrew B. Irvine, eds., *Postcolonial Philosophy of Religion*. Dordrecht, The Netherlands: Springer, 2009.

Burns, Stephen, and Michael N. Jagessar, *Christian Worship: Postcolonial Perspectives*. Sheffield, UK: Equinox, 2011.

Chia, Philip P., "The Sun Never Sets on 'Marx'? (Marx) Colonizing Postcolonial Theory (Said/Spivak/Bhabha)?," *Journal for the Study of the New Testament* 30.4 (2008): 418–88.

Hill, Johnny Bernard, *Prophetic Rage: A Postcolonial Theology of Liberation*. Grand Rapids, MI: Eerdmans Publishing Company, 2013.

Jong-Kumru, Wietske de, *Postcolonial Feminist Theology: Enacting Cultural, Religious, Gender and Sexual Differences in Theology*. Zürich: LIT Verlag, 2013.

Kinyua, Johnson Kiriaku, "A Postcolonial Analysis of Bible Translation and Its Effectiveness in Shaping and Enhancing the Discourse of Colonialism and the Discourse of Resistance: The Gĩkũyũ New Testament – A Case Study," *Black Theology* 11.1 (2013): 58–95.

Lartey, Emmanuel Yartekwei Amugi, *Postcolonializing God: An African Practical Theology*. London: SCM Press, 2013.

Runions, Erin, "Detranscendentalizing Decisionism: Political Theology after Gayatri Spivak," *Journal of Feminist Studies in Religion* 25.2 (Fall 2009): 67–85.

Rynkiewich, Michael A., *Soul, Self, and Society: A Postmodern Anthropology for Mission in a Postcolonial World*. Eugene, OR: Cascade, 2011.

Stanley, Christopher, *The Colonialized Apostle: Paul in Postcolonial Eyes*. Minneapolis, MN: Fortress, 2011.

Sugirtharajah, R. S., *Exploring Postcolonial Biblical Criticism: History, Method, Practice*. Malden, MA: Wiley-Blackwell, 2011.

Taylor, Mark Lewis, *The Theological and the Political: On the Weight of the World*. Minneapolis, MN: Fortress, 2011.

Part II

Contemporary Questions in Political Theology

The Contemporary Discipline and Traditional Sources

8 Scripture
CHRISTOPHER ROWLAND

Christian political thought begins in the fourfold foundation narratives in the New Testament with their distinctive eschatological character, in which Jesus was convicted of blasphemy by the Jerusalem elite and then executed as a messianic pretender by the occupying power, a victim of the complex political arrangements at work in a Roman colony. They continue the political mode found in the story of the liberation of the Hebrew slaves from captivity in Egypt.[1] It draws on material from the Jewish scriptures, inspired by its prophetic tradition (e.g., Isa. 61 in Luke 4: 18–21) as well as the ethic of its legal material (Matt. 21: 35–39), particularly the Decalogue (Rom. 13: 8–10) and its understanding of holiness (e.g., 1 Cor. 3:17; 6:19). The indebtedness to Jewish ethical teaching, however, does not explain what motivates Christianity's theological ethics. There can be no doubt about the contribution of the Jewish scriptures to Christian political thought, though from the genesis of Christianity the relationship to the Jewish scriptures has never been unproblematic. Indeed the description of *New* Testament bears witness to that fact.[2] The main concern in this essay is the elucidation of the distinctive contribution of that New Testament perspective to political thought. Apocalypticism and eschatology are, however, crucial to the understanding of the New Testament, though in the course of time those important features have been evacuated of their political potency, a process given additional impetus when Christianity was adopted as the religion of empire. The recovery of the countercultural, nonconformist elements of the early Christian story has been a feature of recent biblical theology, retrieving the political dimension of the messianic minority movement in late antiquity, whose views are found in the New Testament.

In this chapter I have attempted to explain the basis of Christian political thinking in the Bible, by pointing to the important role played by eschatology in much modern New Testament scholarship. I suggest that the way in which eschatology has been construed in most modern biblical scholarship has evacuated eschatology of its political dimension, and the recovery of the political vitality of biblical eschatology is necessary to understand the way in which the Bible is a "source" for Christian political thought and the presupposition of biblical political themes and their subsequent reception. The chapter focuses on the New Testament Gospels, the Pauline epistles and the Book of Revelation, illumined by politically aware interpretations by authors or groups of authors, to expound the significance of Christianity's political inheritance as a theological topos in its own right.

Modern biblical exegesis has largely reflected the supposedly narrow, religious character of biblical theology and as a result minimised the political element. This has been in part because of the hegemony of German biblical scholarship, pervaded with Lutheran "Two Kingdoms theology," which has tended to underline the "nonpolitical" character of the Christian gospel, from the early modern period onwards. Reinforcing this trend has been the approach taken to the apocalyptic and the eschatological strands, which are rightly believed to be central to the New Testaments writings. Paradoxically, the interpretation of these strands have contributed to the view that earliest Christianity was nonpolitical and other worldly, dominated by the expectation of the imminent "end of the world" and thus devoid of this-worldly political concerns. So, there has emerged a view that the Christian religion is separate from politics. The role of the Bible, particularly the New Testament, in political thought has been marginalised, and there has emerged a misleading contrast between Jewish and Christian messianism, with the latter being considered "spiritual," as compared with the "this worldly," political character of Jewish eschatological expectation.[3]

In Luther's Two Kingdoms theology the religious and the political are the means of effecting the divine economy for the world. Of course, it was not the case that Luther believed that life could avoid the latter by being caught up in the former, but it meant that the main preserve of the Bible was the religious, with the life of righteousness, rather than the secular world of everyday politics. Lutheranism famously has worked with a dualistic contrast between the sacred and the secular, in which the secular complements the sacred in the world. The influence of Lutheranism meant that biblical concepts like justification and righteousness were viewed from the perspective of the individual. The political character of such concepts, and indeed of the Kingdom of God, has been more widely recognised by biblical scholars.[4]

The roots of this dualism lie deep within the Bible, not least in its eschatology. That which is perfect is still to come (1 Cor. 13:10), when the New Jerusalem comes down from heaven to earth, in which nothing unclean dwells (Rev. 21:27; 22:3). This governs the outlook of Christian political theology in two major ways. First, its dominant mode has been the conviction that here we have no abiding city, for our citizenship is in heaven (Heb. 13:14; Phil. 3:20), so there is a pilgrimage through this fallen world of travail to the heavenly home. Second, the "this-worldly" eschatology, which characterised much of earliest Christianity and looked for God's kingdom on earth (Matt. 6:10) set up a tension between the imperfections of the present, in which Christians lived, with the age that is to come. So, not only did Christianity inherit from Judaism the dualism of pure and impure, holy and profane, but also added to that a tension between the "now" of salvation (2 Cor. 6:2) and the "not yet" which is to come when God will be all in all (1 Cor. 15:28; Rev. 21:1–5). The contradictions and tensions of that double form of dualism are at the heart of Christian identity in the New Testament.

The understanding of the eschatological in the New Testament can seem to eclipse the political, and so the latter has been to a large extent absent from New Testament exegesis. The assumption is that Jesus and the early Christians believed that the end of the world was coming and so there was no need to change society, only prepare for its coming and the sweeping away of the old world. Paul's words are used to justify that view: "I think that, in view of the impending crisis, it is well for you to remain as you are" (1 Cor. 7:26). The intensity of the hope for a new age is not in doubt, but, contrary to what Schweitzer and others suggest this was not some transcendent world, but this earth. Also, crucially, the key figures in early Christianity did not see themselves as mere spectators of eschatological fulfilment but agents in it. The political dynamic of messianism is just as apparent in the Pauline letters as in Paul's self-understanding and activity. The politics of his apostleship replicates Jesus's challenge to the Temple authorities in Jerusalem, in its departure from the established order of things and in its implicit claim to authority and the ability to authorize alternative views and practice. Paul expresses his conviction that he had been set apart as the apostle to the Gentiles, commissioned by the Messiah, to preach the good news to the nations (Gal. 1: 16) and that he and the communities he formed were living in a critical period of salvation history (1 Cor. 10: 11). The eschatological future is not just a horizon of hope for it acts as a stimulus to action and change.[5] Both Jesus and Paul (and Stephen, if Acts 21: 27–36 and 7: 47–54 are to be believed) provoked crises in, or about, the Temple in Jerusalem and as a result paid the price politically.

The following three sections outline how the political nature of Christianity has been recovered in recent thought.

THE RECOVERY OF THE POLITICS OF JESUS

At the very start of the extraordinary story of the quest for the Jesus of history, as told most famously by Albert Schweitzer, H. S. Reimarus's reconstruction of Christian origins viewed the New Testament Gospels through the lens of Jewish messianism and offered a reconstruction of the life of Jesus as a story of a failed Jewish Messiah, which was retold by disciples who put a theological gloss on a tragic tale.[6] Whether conservative or liberal scholar, nineteenth or twentieth century, the treatment of the Gospel accounts are largely devoid of political analysis and instead replete with discussion of nonpolitical treatments of doctrinal and theological themes. The Son of Man who comes with the clouds of heaven ceases to be a hallmark of Christian devotion, and the messianic enthusiasm of the Gospels, with its millenarian fanatic of the Schweitzerian interpretations, is gradually domesticated. The emergence of what we know as Christian theology lost touch with its apocalyptic and eschatological roots.

At the heart of the stories that early Christians preserved about Jesus is the political. He was convicted as a blasphemer (Mark 14:64) and was executed with the connivance of the Roman colonial governor of Judea, Pontius Pilate (cf. Luke 3:1) but with the active involvement of the Jerusalem priestly elite, who for a variety of reasons found him to be a political threat. While he resembled the holy men who frequented Galilee in the first century CE,[7] and another Jesus, who was also arrested, beaten, and set free, for predicting the demise of the Temple thirty years after Jesus was killed,[8] his activity was more like the prophetic figures described by Josephus[9] who looked back to God's deliverance of old and promised a new era of deliverance. Whether they, like Jesus of Nazareth, proclaimed the imminence, indeed dawn, of God's eschatological kingdom (e.g., Mark 1:15; Luke 11:20) is unclear. The activity of both Jesus and these prophets caused large crowds to gather, probably because people saw in their persons and their actions new signs of God's liberating activity, echoing past events recorded in scripture, and bringing the possibility of some improvement in their social and economic situation. Jesus preached against the Temple, something that attracted intense opposition when Jesus's prophetic predecessor embarked on the same activity (Jer. 7; Matt. 23; Luke 11:42–52). In addition, from the perspective of the authorities (in Jerusalem in particular), his actions as an exorcist and a troublemaker made him a threat to public order. According to the Gospels, emissaries were sent to Galilee to investigate (Mark 3:22), but it was when he got near to Jerusalem that his position became untenable. Whatever historical value we attach to a passage like John 11: 48–9, in which the Jerusalem priestly elite saw Jesus as a threat to its power and to political stability, it probably reflects the attitude of the ruling elite in Jerusalem towards Jesus.

According to the Gospels, Jesus was linked with John the Baptist, who was executed for subversion by Herod Antipas.[10] John's message of a decisive moment in God's purposes seems to have provided the context for Jesus's own activity and helps explain his convictions about his peculiar place in the divine economy. Jesus moved from Galilee to Jerusalem, the metropolitan centre of ancient Jewish religion focused on the Temple. He was already in conflict with scribal religion, and the volatile atmosphere of Jerusalem at Passover time, a festival particularly linked with political liberation, also led to attempts by the priestly elite hierarchy in Jerusalem, the local elite that managed the Roman colony, to take action against him. As the result of what seems to have been a defection from Jesus's group, Jesus was captured and died as a failed messiah at the hands of the Roman colonial power, an example to others who would pretend to such grandiose ambitions.

This brief summary of the subject matter of the New Testament Gospels suggests that, however we interpret his intentions, the effect of the life of Jesus, as remembered and told by the first Christians, is thoroughly political. At the very least we have a nonconformist with eschatological beliefs, which put him in a different position to a mere prophet of doom. Yes, a harbinger of a new age, but also one who believed that he was an agent of its dawning. If he had been more cognizant of traditional values, of the Temple and its life, as at present constituted, he might have been more acceptable. But the memory of him was of one who was at odds with the politics of his day. That central fact was encoded in the basic texts of Christianity, an inspiration for those who would follow in Jesus's footsteps. Even Paul, who seems to have had little concern with Jesus's career, found himself by his words and deeds at odds not only with those who shared his beliefs about Jesus, but also he experienced the same kind of difficulties as Jesus when he went up to Jerusalem. So while the legacy of his Christology detracted from the story of the millenarian prophet in Jerusalem, Paul's actions continued that subversive character that is fundamental to the Christian story. Despite the fact that Christian theology and biblical imagery have served the needs of the politically powerful down the centuries – offering, for example, a justification of monarchy and hierarchy – the awkward facts surrounding the story of Jesus's life and death left a potent political legacy that could never be domesticated or offer an unqualified support for the ideology of the powerful.

Christianity began life as what was in effect a thoroughly political movement. The fact that this should have become attenuated is a cause of puzzlement, but it is a dimension of the Gospels that has been recovered in recent years. An influential book by the Mennonite historical theologian, John Howard Yoder, *The Politics of Jesus*,[11] in particular assisted this process of revolutionising the understanding of biblical politics. At first glance it is strange that it should come from the pen of a Mennonite theologian, whose experience had been in a church that had been at the margins of Christian life. Jesus is presented not only as a wide-eyed millenarian visionary, though that dimension is there, but also includes the strategic and the political. He is a creator of community inspired by the Jubilee ideas in the Torah, a counterculture of discipleship based on practices sketched in Matthew's Sermon on the Mount (Matt. 5–7) and Luke's Sermon on the Plain (Luke 7). Key to this, however, is Jesus's repudiation of violence when the political denouement finally comes in Jerusalem. What Yoder did in this remarkably influential book was to inject the discussion of the political as a central feature of the interpretation of the Bible, particularly the New Testament. What is more, as a powerful advocate for Anabaptism, he drew attention to the riches of his background, an approach that was eagerly embraced by Christians discovering for themselves a life of marginality with which Anabaptists had been familiar since their precarious existence in the sixteenth century and beyond. Yoder's Mennonite voice is one that has spoken to a generation that has seen the church's established influence decline in a hegemonic global capitalist world.

The story of Jesus sounds a discordant note in the midst of political order. Indeed, he seems to embody the spectre of pandemonium, as the forces of Beelzebub threaten to subvert the fabric of society (Mark 3:21–2). Even the Gospel of John, the supposedly "spiritual gospel," evinces a political challenge to the authorities.[12] Early Christians placed the story of Jesus in the context of hopes for a king, the Messiah, whose advent would hail a return to the divine purposes for creation. Unsurprisingly, the Messiah broke all convention, transgressing boundaries of holiness and acceptability, and ended up becoming a symbol of nonconformity to whom appeal was made by dissenters throughout subsequent history. But the reality on the ground was very different, with acquiescence to conventional patterns in gender relationships and with regard to institutions like slavery.[13] That situation reflected the fact that there is not immediately a new world order, for old and new orders exist concurrently until the fabric of the present age passes away. Yoder ably demonstrated the contradiction between radicalism and conservatism, which pervades the New Testament. Nevertheless he also embodied contradiction, between his rhetoric as a writer and apologist for nonviolence, on the one hand, and the abuse of power in his oppressive dealings with some women, on the other. Yoder's career reminds us not only of the way in which interpretations of the Bible reflect the political ethos of the interpreter but also the complex ways in which the interpreter is part of the hermeneutical process.

THE POLITICAL TURN IN PAULINE STUDIES

In the years since World War II and the horrors of anti-Semitism enacted in the Shoah, biblical study has witnessed a concerted attempt to locate Christian origins in Judaism. Anti-Judaism, which had characterised Christian thought down the centuries, was largely exorcised from biblical exegesis. The so-called New Perspective on Paul and the Third Quest for the Historical Jesus saw Second Temple Judaism as an indispensable part of the study. Notwithstanding attempts to relate early Christian texts to Greek literature, the Jewish context has been a *Leitmotiv*, which has dominated study. Questions of continuity and discontinuity cannot easily be ignored as the pendulum has swung so dramatically in one direction. But the political character of Judaism as a religion and the ongoing input of Jewish sources into emerging Christianity, including its political thought, have been prominent. The simplistic divide between Jewish political messianism and Christian spiritual messianism, for example, would find few adherents today. Locating Paul and Jesus within the politics of Second Temple Judaism and assessing the extent to which the problem posed by the new movement was political, as well as theological, has been one beneficiary of the renewed interest in Jewish studies, which is now *de rigueur* in biblical scholarship. Linked with this, there is a vibrantly self-aware Old Testament/Hebrew Bible discipline, which has gradually weaned itself away from dependency on the later New Testament.

The bursting in upon the world of the Apocalypse of Jesus Christ has become a cornerstone of understanding the Pauline message.[14] Its impact relativised the powers of this world and exposes the pretensions of the prevailing power and wisdom. There have been attempts to insert a political dimension into familiar New Testament texts. Thus, there has been quite a flurry of debate about Paul and empire.[15] Superficially, there does seem to be an implicit critique of the might of Rome in the eschatological hope of 1 Corinthians 15:25–8 and in particular the Christological hymn in Philippians 2:5–11, but the obstinate contrary example of Romans 13 gives even the most sympathetic interpreter pause for thought. Finding an overt critique of empire in the Pauline letters seems like special pleading. The Apocalypse, inspired by Daniel and other prophetic texts certainly has a political critique, but in the ecclesial orientation of the Pauline texts, there is lack of any overt attempt to confront the might of Rome – indeed the reverse. A realistic assessment would be that what we have in Paul's exhortation is an attempt to negotiate a *modus vivendi* and wherever possible to "keep one's head down" (e.g., 1 Thess. 4:10–11) thus offering a better outcome than a deliberate confrontation with the religion of empire. To put it another way, it is a form of what became known as "Nicodemism,"[16] outward conformity and private radicalism. This is the other side of the early Christian martyr narratives, which present a more heroic, but probably partial, picture of early Christian experience.[17] The politics of Paul is to be found in the complex negotiation of community formation, in which the boundaries of a new political entity based on convictions about the coming of the Messiah create ambiguous relationships with those outside it (cf. 1 Cor. 8) and necessitate a mix of application of Jewish law and secular wisdom, in the forging of early Christian identity.

This is where sociological approaches to the Bible have been so illuminating, in drawing out the political character of much early Christian identity, in its countercultural attitudes and practice. The welcome discussion of Pauline theology and community formation by Gerd Theissen and Wayne Meeks, for example, picks up the Weberian and Durkheimian perspectives on the Pauline tradition. Along with the widespread recognition of the political dimension of key Pauline terms like *ecclesia* and *the Body of Christ* there has been a growing appreciation of the social dimension of early Christian belief and practice. That may also apply to the kind of advice given by Paul in Romans 13:1 to be subordinate to the ruling powers. It is the sort of instruction given by a politically pragmatic writer who is also aware that every empire has its time and season in the divine economy (Dan. 7). Like Daniel, Paul saw himself as a steward of the divine mysteries (1 Cor. 4:1) and could interpret the times and the seasons in human affairs for his contemporaries (Dan. 2). While Paul may think the time is near (1 Cor. 7: 26; Rom. 13:11–12), it is not part of the life of the people of God to participate in the overthrow of Rome. Their task is different – to bear witness to the coming reign of God and in this age demonstrate that they are children of light and have cast off the works of darkness (Rom. 13:11–14).

In the last decade the writings of the apostle Paul have assumed an important role as an inspiration for a group of philosophers, literary critics, and cultural commentators, for example, Giorgio Agamben, Slavoj Žižek, Terry Eagleton, and especially Jacob Taubes. The Pauline corpus has offered a framework for thinking about politics and cultural criticism. In other words, Paul's letters, specifically Romans, have been liberated from the ghetto of theology and biblical studies and begun to inform a political discourse from which it had largely disappeared.[18] The work of Jacob Taubes has been crucial in this and reflects his immersion in apocalypticism and the Pauline texts.[19] In *Occidental Eschatology* Taubes traces the history of apocalyptic radicalism from Daniel and the New Testament through Joachim of Fiore and the radical Franciscans to Muenzter and then onto Hegel and Kierkegaard. Here is a manifesto for a politics in which apocalyptic imagery offers the climactic sense of an ending and the possibility of a new beginning, an ultimate moment, therefore, in which a radically new dimension to life interrupts the normal and habitual.

Agamben, dependent as he is on Taubes and particularly his use of the messianic in the work of Walter Benjamin as an interpretative lens, develops discussion of the nature of messianic time. The Messiah provokes the crisis for law and convention, tradition is challenged, and an anticipation of Paradise is evoked. There is something countercultural about the ethos – an alternative, albeit embryonic political discourse – in which the Pauline letters indicate what messianic justice looks like in the nascent social groupings brought into being in the midst of actually existing social injustice.[20] Such justice is improvisational in character and resistant to falling back into a legal structure. Messianism means radical newness. Alain Badiou picks up on the epistemology of this and grasps something fundamental to the politics of the New Testament. Identification with the suffering Jesus confronting the political powers in Jerusalem is a political perspective of wider significance than the ecclesial. It is a political narrative, the contours of which are the framework for Christian political thought, and its eschatological features, as we have seen, marry the mix of anticipation and provisionality, which pervade the various writings in the New Testament. There is a grasp here of the nub of messianism and its disruptiveness, epistemologically and socially, but the Messiah's agent not only disturbs the regime of law as the patterns of this age are disrupted but can also resort to that law in the service of the practical politics of community formation (e.g., 1 Cor. 5–6).

This is the ethos that pervades the Pauline letters. Paul was not just a messianic thinker but one actively engaged in shaping and holding together embryonic communities, so that social cohesion takes precedence over human freedom, a theme particularly explored in 1 Corinthians 8–9 (cf. Rom. 14, esp. 14:19). If Paul's letters are anything to go by, at this stage of his career the cohesion of the community has the last word. It is the legacy of this priority that has been so fundamental for Christian politics. Yet in the midst of the resort to the precepts of the law, as a way of dealing with life in community, Agamben rightly points to the fact that the messianic moment is not words, such as we find in letters of the law, but the life of the messianic community – not a writing, but a form of life (cf. 2 Cor. 3:2).[21] It is no surprise, therefore, that the character of life in the messianic community, waiting for the consummation of the messianic times, emerges as *the* crucial issue in the Pauline corpus, even if Paul paradoxically resorts to law as the means of enabling the social cohesion he regards as crucial.

The messianic and community cohesion are a constant dialectic in the Pauline letters. The eventual priority of the community is unsurprising given the perhaps inevitable investment that Paul had in the "success" of the communities he had established to maintain some kind of credible identity. What constituted "the messianic" became tied up not only with the cohesion of a particular community but some kind of emerging uniformity *across* the communities (cf. 1 Cor. 14:33–37), for which end the apostle of the Messiah was a crucial broker. By the time that Paul writes Romans, the criterion of the work of the messianic spirit is that "the just requirement of the law might be fulfilled in us, who walk not according to the flesh but according to the Spirit" (Rom. 8:4). A certain ethical standard in large part determined by the Law of Moses becomes critical; "staying in" requires that.[22]

This may read as if ethics trumps eschatology, but that would be to misunderstand the Pauline corpus, and indeed the New Testament where ethics is intimately bound up with eschatology. Put another way, the messianic has to be characterised and thoroughly permeated by an ethical, altruistic, element. The problem with the Pauline corpus is that piety can easily seem to outweigh the political. The language about being conformed to Christ[23] minimises the political character of "taking up the cross" (Mark 8:34; Luke 14:27), which has a strong political tinge in the narratives of Jesus's life but is less obvious in the Pauline theological injunctions. The great merit of what Taubes and Agamben have written is that they grasp this fundamental point. What is distinctive about the messianic life is, according to Paul, above all social rather than the aesthetic or spiritual; it is something that is "shaken by experience."[24] It has become something of an exegetical commonplace that changing society is not necessary because the imminent eschatological crisis is at hand: "in view of the impending crisis, it is well for you to remain as you are ... the appointed time has grown short ... for the present form of this world is passing away" (1 Cor. 7: 26–31). Nevertheless the "impending crisis" did not mean that there should be no change; far from it, as the rest of 1 Corinthians (and elsewhere in the Pauline corpus) indicates. This is not about being ordinary members of society while inwardly living as if part of the age to come, as was the case with some later Christians.[25]

For Christians as with Jews, there was the necessity of distance and nonconformity in belief and practice, which Paul explores in 1 Corinthians 8–10. Messianic life may seem to be socially conservative, but that initial assessment conceals the complex mix of negotiating the time waiting for the impending crisis, which required the implementation of certain patterns of life, in order to characterise life as "the temple of the Holy Spirit" (1 Cor. 6:19). The impetus for the Pauline injunctions is intimately linked with the messianic dynamic and how that works itself out in lives lived in the midst of a world passing away. Being in the world means inhabiting the present age; not being of the world indicates that "our citizenship is in heaven, and it is from there that we are expecting a Saviour" (Phil. 3:20), and it is that pattern of messianic life in this age that is explored in the pages of the New Testament. Theodor Adorno's words capture something of the struggle involved in negotiating messianic existence: "perspectives must be fashioned that displace and estrange the world, reveal it to be, with its rifts and crevices, as indigent and distorted as it will appear one day in the messianic light."[26] For Paul this is not just about perspectives but action, seeking out what life in the crevices of this age might be like. Taubes rightly saw a connection between Benjamin's eschatology and that of Paul in their common despair in the face of the apparent futility of creation and the impossibility of bridging politics and messianism.[27] Where the Pauline texts differ from Benjamin is in the ambiguity evident in the hint that already there can be a foretaste of that which is to come in the politics of those tiny fledgling communities and their life.

The letters of Paul indicate the difficulties posed by such necessary improvisation; necessary for communities living "as if" a new age had come but recognising the culture of the old age as still very much a force to be reckoned with. In them we find Paul juggling the different parts of his life: apostolic prophet, community organiser, renegade Jew, and embryonic theologian. What Taubes and Agamben have understood so well is the messianic impulse that runs like a thread through the letters of Paul that have come down to us and the impact it had on the emergence of the nonrevolutionary, nonconformist, politics that characterised emerging Christianity.

RECOVERING THE APOCALYPTIC DIMENSION IN POLITICAL THEOLOGY

As we have seen, apocalypticism has become a significant heuristic component in interpreting the New Testament. In the main, it has been construed as an expectation of the imminent end of the age, a radical contrast between present and future, the hope for another world breaking into and overtaking this world, told in complex visionary imagery, whose origin was in a distinctive type of Judaism, often at odds with traditional forms of religion based on the Law of Moses or on the cult.[28] Apocalyptic is important, but *not* because it is a form of cataclysmic eschatology. Rather, its importance for our subject is that it offered a different mode of understanding – based on experience of the divine through vision, audition, or dream – that could bypass conventional channels of authority based on tradition. Thus, it is not only eschatological conviction that was important for the first Christians but an apocalyptic epistemology that was a means of demonstrating or endorsing convictions about the inauguration of the divine purposes.[29] Occasionally in the Synoptic Gospels (e.g., Mark 11: 28–33; cf. Matt. 21:23–27; Luke 20:1–8) and more in the Gospel of John (e.g., John 12:49) the issue of authority is mentioned. The Johannine Jesus speaks what he has seen and heard from the Father (John 8:38) as a result of an apocalyptic conviction, whose veracity is doubted by his enemies (John 9: 29). Such a claim to revelation as the basis of authority, and similar claims made by Paul (especially in Gal. 1:1–16) and of Peter (Acts 10–11), have far-reaching political significance.

Central to early Christian hope was the expectation of a new age *on earth*, a belief that was still widely held, at least to the end of the second century, as is evident in the writings of Justin Martyr, Irenaeus, Hippolytus, Tertullian, and Lactantius.[30] This is the type of belief presupposed in the Matthean version of the Lord's Prayer, where there is an earnest longing for God's kingdom to "come on earth as in heaven." The imminence of the fulfilment of their expectation is unclear, though their language does indicate that they believed that the process leading up to the consummation of all things had been set in motion. The consummation might occur in decades, even centuries, rather than weeks or months, if the eschatological schemes of 4 Ezra 5:20–28 and Syriac Baruch 25 are anything to go by. In the final chapters of the Book of

Revelation, the messianic reign takes place on earth and precedes the descent of the New Jerusalem from heaven to a restored earth.[31] Indeed, *the* apocalyptic text in the Bible, the Book of Revelation (the *Apocalypse of Jesus Christ*) typifies Christian hope and its political outlook, as Friedrich Engels rightly saw.[32] This is nowhere better seen than in its unmasking of the pretensions of the Beast and Babylon (Rev. 13 and 17) and the hope for the transformation of this world and its structures.

Important for the rehabilitation of the character of earliest Christian eschatology and the perspective of Joachim of Fiore was Ernst Bloch, who recognised the significance of utopian elements in a variety of cultures and noted the power of hope in both Marxism and the Judaeo-Christian tradition. His mammoth book, *The Principle of Hope* (1986),[33] explored the ways in which that longing for a future age of perfection has coloured the whole range of culture in both East and West. Bloch's approach to eschatology influenced Jürgen Moltmann,[34] for Bloch reminded Christian theologians of neglected aspects of the eschatological tradition and its political potential. In the light of Bloch's work it is not surprising that Christians and some Marxists influenced by this utopian/chiliastic tradition have been united in a common quest for change and a new social order based on peace and justice in this world. Bloch's most succinct statement of the centrality of hope in the Bible is found in *Atheism in Christianity* (1972).[35] A central thesis of the book is the way in which humans become gods, with Jesus the Son of Man being the paradigm for this eschatological humanity. It is a sustained exposition of an alternative "Exodus" pattern in the Bible, one that is not nostalgic but determined on the winding quest for full human potential for all. His subtitle, "The Religion of the Exodus and Kingdom," aptly summarises a challenge to the marginalisation of eschatology in Christian doctrine by a sustained exposition of biblical themes from both parts of the Christian canon, which look forward to the moment when "God will be all in all." Mainstream Christianity was content with an ordered status quo in this life, preferring to worship Jesus as Lord, the guarantor of earthly potentates, than the humble Son of Man. Here in Bloch's work the political significance of Christology is boldly and provocatively stated. According to Bloch there was always a different kind of Christianity, revolutionary in character, that called for change. It is characterised by an expectation of the imminent overthrow of the existing order and the substitution of a "new heaven and a new earth in which justice and peace would dwell." As with Thomas Muentzer it could be militant, but it often involved patiently waiting for the moment of change, perhaps even for divine intervention, taking the opportunity to practice a different kind of polity.

The Book of Revelation epitomises early Christian political discourse. Not only does it look forward to a different kind of politics when heaven comes to earth (Rev. 21–22) and sorrow and sighing flee away (Rev. 7: 16; 21: 3–4), but also in its apocalyptic genre, particularly in Revelation 13 and 17, it offers the most sustained political discourse in the New Testament, something that has down the centuries been recognised by interpreters[36] and that, along with Daniel, is being recognised more widely in modern discussions of its theology.[37] We shall explore this through the eyes of one of the most remarkable modern biblical interpreters, William Stringfellow (1928–85). Stringfellow was a lawyer in Harlem, a civil rights activist, and protestor against the war in Vietnam, who interpreted Revelation in that context. He worked with the disowned and dispossessed, in a predominately black and Hispanic subculture marked by poverty and lack of access to basic services. In *An Ethic for Christians and Other Aliens in a Strange Land* William Stringfellow in effect wrote a commentary on the New Testament Apocalypse whose purpose was to "treat the nation within the tradition of biblical politics – to understand America biblically – not the other way round, not (to put it in an appropriately awkward way) to construe the Bible Americanly."[38] At the heart of his method is this conviction: that the Apocalypse can assist one to understand a particular moment of time because it enables an enhanced vision of the reality that confronts one.[39] For Stringfellow, the Apocalypse does not offer a timetable about the end of the world but a template by which one can assess the theological character of the world in which one lives, an interpretative key to understand the cosmos under God and the situation of his nation in the 1970s and 1980s.

Stringfellow follows in a long tradition going back at least to the fourth-century Christian writer, Tyconius,[40] such a powerful influence on Augustine's classic interpretation of Christian doctrine in *The City of God*. In Stringfellow's Tyconian hermeneutics, Babylon and Jerusalem become types of two different kinds of religious communities. So, they are not only eschatologically future images, but they also assist readers with their understanding of reality here and now. Babylon is a description of every city, an allegory of the condition of death, the principality in bondage to death in time, the focus of judgement. Jerusalem is about the emancipation of human life in society from the rule of death. It is a parable, he writes, of the church of prophecy, an anticipation of the end of time.[41] How might theology speak to the Vietnam War and the struggle of African Americans against white supremacy? William Stringfellow tried to do that, and the "powers and principalities" mentioned in Ephesians 6:12 and elsewhere in the New Testament are seen to correspond to the forces of death at work within his own time and place, twentieth-century America.

Stringfellow's influence has been profound, and his example encapsulates much that is typical of modern Christian political thought.[42] Few could have boasted of being spotted and endorsed by Karl Barth, who noted, "the conscientious and thoughtful New York attorney William Stringfellow, who caught my attention more than any other person," and advised, "Listen to this man." Apart from anything else he was steeped in the Bible, but his influence on some of the pressing issues of his day was profound. He was at the forefront of the advocacy of women's ordination to the priesthood, and his opposition to the Vietnam War pervades his brilliant critique of that war and the asylum he offered to Daniel Berrigan, S.J. His advocacy of a theology of "the principalities and powers," in *Conscience and Obedience* influenced the work of Walter Wink, which has in turn been very influential on modern political theology.[43] Thinking biblically was the way in which he did his political theology, and we find it done without any of the inhibitions that characterise those brought up in the historical critical tradition. The biblical text is a lens through which his context is viewed. His is a model of the way in which premodern biblical hermeneutic works in modernity as Christians seek to make political sense of their own lives by locating their stories within the context of that larger biblical story. What is more, in Stringfellow's case, experience in the light of his daily involvement in human rights and related justice issues were the major inspiration of his biblically informed political theology.[44]

CONCLUDING COMMENTS

The centrality of apocalyptic discernment and eschatological hope to the theology of the New Testament has been the thesis of this chapter. They pervade the understanding of present political arrangements and the articulation of an appropriate response in the midst of a world that is passing away and in relationship to the hope for a different kind of polity when God's kingdom comes and God's will be done on earth as in heaven (cf. Matt. 6: 10). The climactic sense of an ending and the possibility of a new beginning, an ultimate moment, therefore, disrupt the normal and habitual. As William Blake put it: "If it were not for the Poetic or Prophetic character, the Philosophic & Experimental would soon be at the ratio of all things & stand still, unable to do other than repeat the same dull round over again."[45]

Jacob Taubes and Giorgio Agamben rightly turn to a very distinctive Marxist, Walter Benjamin (1892–1940), whose thinking was imbued with Jewish messianism.[46] Benjamin turned to messianic theology at the close of his life, on the run from Nazis at the beginning of World War II, though his friendship with Gershom Scholem had meant that messianism had for a long time been a part of his thinking. In his *Theses on the Philosophy of History*, written months before his tragic death, there is a grasp of the nature of messianic time, which few have matched – perhaps it is there in the Joachite tradition, or the millenarian politics of mid-seventeenth-century England.[47] Like the Book of Revelation, Walter Benjamin's words, in this his last testament, offer from within a situation of existential crisis a messianic perspective on political change. His words encapsulate elements from the New Testament and the character of its hope for a redeemed humanity, which problematise convention and the conformism that threatens to quench the vitality of biblical tradition.[48]

Notes

1 Michael Walzer, *Exodus and Revolution* (New York: Basic Books, 1984); and *In God's Shadow: Politics in the Hebrew Bible* (New Haven, CT: Yale University Press, 2012).
2 B. Jackson, "Why the Name New TESTAMENT?," *Melilah: Manchester Journal of Jewish Studies* 3 (2012): 50–100.
3 G. Scholem, *The Messianic Idea in Israel* (New York: Schocken, 1971), pp. 1–36. cf. J. Taubes, "The Price of Messianism," in *Essential Papers on Messianic Movements and Personalities in Jewish History*, ed. M. Saperstein (New York: New York University Press, 1992), pp. 551–8.
4 E.g., J. B. Davis, and D. Harink, *Apocalyptic and the Future of Theology with and beyond J. Louis Martyn* (Eugene, OR: Wipf and Stock, 2012).
5 C. Rowland, "Joachim of Fiore and the Theology of the New Testament," in *Joachim of Fiore and the Influence of Inspiration: Essays in Memory of Marjorie E. Reeves (1905–2003)*, ed. J. E. Wannenmacher (Aldershot, UK: Ashgate, 2013), pp. 35–52.
6 H. S. Reimarus, *Reimarus: Fragments*, ed. C. H. Talbert (Philadelphia: Fortress, 1970); A. Schweitzer, *The Quest of the Historical Jesus: A Critical Study of Its Progress from Reimarus to Wrede* (London: Black, 1911).
7 G. Vermès, *Jesus the Jew: A Historian's Reading of the Gospels*, 5th ed. (London: SCM, 1994).
8 Josephus, *Jewish War*, vi.281.
9 E.g., Josephus, *Antiquities of the Jews*, xx.97, 167, 185.
10 Ibid., xviii.116.

11. John Howard Yoder, *The Politics of Jesus*, 2nd ed. (Grand Rapids, MI: Eerdmans, 1972; repr. 1994).
12. D. Rensberger, *Overcoming the World: Politics and Community in the Gospel of John* (London: SPCK, 1989).
13. Yoder, *Politics of Jesus*, 162–211.
14. Davis and Harink, *Apocalyptic and the Future of Theology*.
15. K. Wengst, *Pax Romana and the Peace of Jesus Christ* (London: SCM, 1987); R. A. Horsley, *Paul and the Roman Imperial Order* (Harrisburg, PA: Trinity, 2004); S. Porter, and C. Westfall, *Empire in the New Testament* (Eugene, OR: Pickwick, 2011); I. Rock, *Paul's Letter to the Romans and Roman Imperialism an Ideological Analysis of the Exordium (Romans 1:1–17)* (Eugene, OR: Pickwick, 2012).
16. D. MacCulloch, *Silence: A Christian History* (London: Allen Lane, 2013).
17. C. Moss, *Ancient Christian Martyrdom: Diverse Practices, Theologies, and Traditions* (New Haven, CT: Yale University Press, 2012).
18. T. W. Jennings, *Outlaw Justice: the Messianic Politics of Paul* (Stanford, CA: Stanford University Press, 2013).
19. J. Taubes, *The Political Theology of Paul* (Stanford, CA: Stanford University Press, 2004); *Occidental Eschatology* (Stanford, CA: Stanford University Press, 2009).
20. Jennings, *Outlaw Justice*, p. 212.
21. G. Agamben, *The Time That Remains: A Commentary on the Letter to the Romans* (Stanford, CA: Stanford University Press, 2005), p. 122.
22. E. P. Sanders, *Paul and Palestinian Judaism: A Comparison of Patterns of Religion* (London: SCM, 1977).
23. Gorman, M., *Cruciformity: Paul's Narrative Spirituality of the Cross* (Grand Rapids, MI: Eerdmans, 2001).
24. Taubes, *Political Theology*, p. 74.
25. MacCulloch, *Silence*, pp. 163–90.
26. T. Adorno, *Minima Moralia: Reflections from Damaged Life* (London: New Left Books, 1974), p. 247.
27. Taubes, *Political Theology*, pp. 75–6, 134.
28. P. D. Hanson, *The Dawn of Apocalyptic* (Philadelphia: Fortress Press, 1975).
29. C. Rowland, *The Open Heaven: A Study of Apocalyptic in Judaism and Early Christianity* (London: SPCK, 1982).
30. B. Daley, *The Hope of the Early Church: A Handbook of Patristic Eschatology* (Grand Rapids, MI: Baker, 2010); Irenaeus, *Adversus Haereses*, v.33.3–4.
31. N. Cohn, *The Pursuit of the Millennium* (London: Paladin, 1957); A. Bradstock, and C. Rowland, *Radical Christian Writings: A Reader* (Oxford: Blackwell, 2002).
32. F. Engels, "On the History of Primitive Christianity," in *K. Marx and F. Engels: Basic Writings on Politics and Philosophy*, ed. L. Feuer (London: Fontana/Collins, 1959), pp. 209–35.
33. E. Bloch, *The Principle of Hope* (Oxford: Blackwell, 1986).
34. J. Moltmann, *Theology of Hope: On the Ground and the Implications for a Christian Eschatology*, new ed. (London: SCM, 2002).
35. E. Bloch, *Atheism in Christianity: The Religion of the Exodus and the Kingdom* (New York: Herder, 1972).

36 J. Kovacs, and C. Rowland, *Revelation: The Apocalypse of Jesus Christ* (Oxford: Blackwell, 2004).
37 C. Rowland, "Revelation," in *The New Interpreter's Bible, Volume XII* (Nashville, TN: Abingdon, 1998); A. Portier-Young, *Apocalypse against Empire: Theologies of Resistance in Early Judaism* (Grand Rapids, MI: Eerdmans, 2011).
38 W. Stringfellow, *An Ethic for Christians and Other Aliens in a Strange Land* (Waco, TX: Word, 1973), p. 13; Bradstock and Rowland, *Radical Christian Writings*, pp. 255–60.
39 Stringfellow, *An Ethic for Christians*, p. 152.
40 C. Rowland, and I. Boxall, "Tyconius and Bede on Violent Texts in the Apocalypse," in *Ancient Christian Interpretations of "Violent Texts" in the Apocalypse*, ed. J. Verheyden, T. Niklas, and A. Merkt (Göttingen: Vandenhoeck and Ruprecht, 2011), pp. 161–79; and on the background to Tyconius's hermeneutical method, M. A. Tilley, *The Bible in Christian North Africa: The Donatist World* (Minneapolis, MN: Fortress, 1997).
41 Stringfellow, *An Ethic for Christians*, 21.
42 A. Dancer, *William Stringfellow in Anglo-American Perspective* (Aldershot, UK: Ashgate, 2005).
43 E.g., W. Wink, *Naming the Powers: The Language of Power in the New Testament* (Philadelphia: Fortress, 1984).
44 C. Rowland, *The Cambridge Companion to Liberation Theology*, 2nd ed. (Cambridge: Cambridge University Press, 2007).
45 W. Blake, *There Is No Natural Religion*, b vii, in *The Complete Poetry and Prose of William Blake*, ed. D. V. Erdman (Berkeley: University of California Press, 1988), p. 3.
46 Agamben, *The Time That Remains*, pp. 138–45; Taubes, *Political Theology*, pp. 70–6.
47 Bradstock and Rowland, *Radical Christian Writings*, pp. 20–8, 109–48.
48 W. Benjamin, "Theses on the Philosophy of History," in *Illuminations* (London: Verso, 1970), Thesis VI, 247.

Further Reading

Agamben, G., *The Time That Remains: A Commentary on the Letter to the Romans*. Stanford, CA: Stanford University Press, 2005.
Bloch, E., *Atheism in Christianity: The Religion of the Exodus and the Kingdom*. New York: Herder, 1972.
Daley, B., *The Hope of the Early Church: A Handbook of Patristic Eschatology*. Grand Rapids, MI: Baker, 2010.
Davis, J. B., and Harink, D., ed., *Apocalyptic and the Future of Theology with and beyond J. Louis Martyn*. Eugene, OR: Wipf and Stock, 2012.
Jennings, T. W., *Outlaw Justice: The Messianic Politics of Paul*. Stanford, CA: Stanford University Press, 2013.
Meeks, Wayne, *The Moral World of the First Christians*. London: SPCK, 1986.
Rowland, C., *Christian Origins: An Account of the Setting and Character of the Most Important Messianic Sect of Judaism*, rev. ed. London: SPCK, 2002.

Stringfellow, W., *An Ethic for Christians and Other Aliens in a Strange Land*. Waco, TX: Word, 1973.
Taubes, J., *The Political Theology of Paul*. Stanford, CA: Stanford University Press, 2004.
Theissen, G., *A Theory of Primitive Christian Religion*. London: SCM Press, 2003.
Wengst, K., *Pax Romana and the Peace of Jesus Christ*. London: SCM, 1987.
Yoder, J. H., *The Politics of Jesus*, 2nd ed. Grand Rapids, MI: Eerdmans, 1994.

9 Augustinianisms and Thomisms
ERIC GREGORY AND JOSEPH CLAIR

INTRODUCTION

The standard image of Augustine and Aquinas that emerges in twentieth-century textbooks of political philosophy is that of two fundamentally opposed theological approaches to the political. Augustine, in one corner, is the clear-eyed realist, convinced that political society is *fallen*, mired in the consequences of original sin and the contingent necessity to restrain evil, vice, and sin. Aquinas, in the other corner, is the more cheerful Aristotelian, who emphasizes the inherent goodness and naturalness of political society and its beneficial purposes for human flourishing.[1] These contrasting visions continue to animate diverse Christian understandings of the limits and possibilities of politics.

One extraordinary feature of these two interpretive pictures is the way that each was able to achieve rapprochement with the ideals of political liberalism and their institutional expression in twentieth-century liberal democracies. By "political liberalism" we mean to refer, in a general way, to modern ideals of equality, liberty, and freedom that can take a variety of institutional forms, but are essentially ordered by limited government, individual rights, the consent of the governed, constitutionalism, and the rule of law. Crucially, most versions of political liberalism presume to be indifferent to the ultimate goals and purposes of citizens, provided that they respect the laws and tasks necessary for the operation of responsible government. Theological rapprochement with political liberalism can also take a variety of forms – ranging from a more rigorous attempt to narrate the achievements of liberal democracy as being indebted to specific Christian theological concepts, movements, or practices, to a less ambitious program of describing the ways in which Christian commitments can be reconciled with the ideals and institutions constitutive of liberal democratic life.

By the end of the century, the opposed interpretive pictures of Augustine and Aquinas were also able to inspire an opposite, shadow argument for Augustinian and Thomistic antiliberalism. The story of this reconciliation and its reversal in the last decades of the twentieth century epitomizes the story of political Augustinianisms and Thomisms, and in some ways tells the story of political theology in Europe and America in the twentieth century in miniature.

The Augustinian side of this story has received renewed attention in recent work in both political theology and discussions of religion in public life. While it is difficult to overstate the significance of various retrievals of Aquinas for contemporary moral theology (especially in terms of natural law, virtue, and the structure of human action) and important forms of modernity criticism, their relation to *political* theology has been largely implicit. Notwithstanding the influence of Alasdair MacIntyre and John Finnis, it is striking that few recent proposals in *political* theology adopt an explicitly Thomist perspective.

Now, at the beginning of the twenty-first century, it is time to reassess this narrative and hopefully begin a new chapter. Telling a new, more accurate story will require reexamination of the standard interpretive pictures and a reconstruction of each thinker's political thought in light of the demands of the present day. In this chapter, therefore, we argue for a revision of the standard interpretive pictures that brings Augustine and Aquinas closer together. Our argument creates a new vantage from which to imagine the application of their thought to the political challenges of the twenty-first century.

Road Map

In the first section of this chapter, we tell the story of the standard interpretive pictures and their early to mid-century harmonization with political liberalism, and conclude with the reversals these conciliations suffer in the closing decades of the twentieth century. In the second section we argue for a revision of these textbook interpretations that moves Augustine's and Aquinas's political thought closer together – specifically focusing on each thinker's understanding of the naturalness of political society and their compatible conceptions of political life and its role in human flourishing. *Naturalness* is a highly contested term in Augustine and Aquinas studies, especially given the thinkers' shared eschatological perspective that can be obscured by strong contrastive interpretations of the "natural" and "supernatural." Henri de Lubac's influential challenge to certain Neo-Thomist understandings of the opposition of the natural and supernatural remains central to contemporary theological debates, though strangely neglected in political theology. De Lubac's Augustinian Thomism, itself part of a longer tradition of mediation between our two figures, strikes us as a plausible and neglected voice for reflection on the naturalness of politics. In a final section we take these points of congruence just established and sketch a way toward an Augustinian-Thomist political theology, arguing that one can be both Augustinian and Thomist in one's political attitudes and activities.

Our argument, in short, is that Augustine has a stronger sense of the naturalness of political life than interpreters have seen, and that it is much more akin to Aquinas's than interpreters have suggested. The two thinkers fundamentally and primarily view political life as *temporal*: the relationship between the goods constitutive of temporal political life and the *eternal* goods of ultimate human happiness form both the primary distinction and primary bridge between church and political society. Augustine and Aquinas's shared eschatological eudaimonism provides the lens through which to examine political liberalism and liberal democracy as a contingent political arrangement susceptible to affirmation and critique.

THE STANDARD STORY OF TWENTIETH-CENTURY INTERPRETATIONS

Thomist and Augustinian Reconciliation with Liberal Democracy

Thomism

The task of reconciling Aquinas's political thought with liberal democracy gained new urgency after World War I. Neo-Thomist philosophers and Christian democratic parties in Europe and Latin America began developing and reformulating aspects of Thomist social thought in support of liberal theories of democracy and human rights. At the same moment in the United States, Mortimer Adler and Robert Hutchins interested a new generation of students in Neo-Thomism and Thomist political thought at the University of Chicago – as evidenced in the list of publications in the University of Chicago Press's Walgreen Foundation Series. Preeminent among these Neo-Thomist thinkers was Jacques Maritain (1891–1965), along with Yves Simon, Heinrich Rommen, Josef Fuchs, and others.

Maritain's work in this period focuses largely on Aquinas's understanding of the naturalness of political society.[2] Like others in this generation, he is responding to Pierre Rousselot's influential early-twentieth-century effort to find a place for Thomism in modern discussions of freedom and individual right.[3] For Aquinas, the natural common good achieved in political community stands apart from the supernatural, eternal good found only in God, by grace, and is partially glimpsed in the ecclesial community. Aquinas's strong sense of the naturalness of political life for human flourishing then becomes central to Maritain's approach in reformulating a Thomist endorsement of modern liberal democratic institutions.[4] For it is this conception of a natural common good that provides a positive view of political society and its role in human flourishing, without also assigning it an ultimate role. That crucial limit provided protection from the excesses of a theocratic European past and the threat of a totalitarian present. To assuage liberal anxieties about the perfectionist or communist tone of a privileged common good in the wake of World War II, Maritain increasingly emphasizes Aquinas's thick conception of personhood and agency as he constructs a corresponding theory of rights to protect individuals from the excesses of state authority.

Augustinianism

There was an initial effort in the interwar period by Gustave Combès and others to identify the consonance between Augustine and Aquinas on the naturalness of political life and its natural common good.[5] Henri de Lubac, for example, cites himself in fundamental agreement with Combes's reading.[6] But this program quickly came under fire and gave way to a Neo-Thomist rejection of Augustine's political thought on the grounds that it lacked a clear distinction between the natural and supernatural common good, applicable to religious and political life. This criticism is crystallized in the thesis of Henri-Xavier Arquillière's 1934 work: *L'augustinisme politique: Essai sur la formation des théories politiques du moyen-age*. Arquillière's argument is twofold: first, Augustine's political thought lacks a careful distinction between the natural and supernatural good (as that distinction can be applied to realms of social existence). And, second, Augustine's medieval inheritors – especially Gregory the Great, Isidore of Seville, Gregory VII, and Giles of Rome – all pursued the subordination and subsequent absorption of the civic order by the supernatural order of the church, citing Augustine's political thought as their model and authority in doing so. Thus "political Augustinianism" comes to designate, for Arquillière, the essence of Christendom's hierarchical organization of religious authority over temporal authority.

Although Arquillière's understanding of political Augustinianism is more about the historical reception of Augustine's ideas than interpretation of texts, it stands as an important chapter in our argument. For Arquillière's thesis is thoroughly shaped by, and represents,

Neo-Thomist views of Augustine's political thought prevalent in his time, especially those of Pierre Mandonnet and Étienne Gilson. The case of Gilson's Neo-Thomist criticism of Augustine's political thought is more nuanced than Mandonnet's. Yet both ultimately agree that Augustine is missing the appropriate distinction between natural and supernatural realms necessary to protect the political community from being subordinated to, or absorbed by, the ecclesial community and its authority. Perhaps this kerfuffle was partially a case of inter-Catholic theological rivalry or scapegoating in the wake of World War I. Nevertheless, Arquillière's line of thought signals the divergence between political Augustinianism and Thomism in the twentieth century, a divergence that has since sedimented.

Strikingly, no immediate inheritors of the debate made a concerted effort to revive Combès's harmonization of Augustine and Aquinas on the natural common good after Arquillière's critique. In the wake of World War II, Augustinians sought an alternative route for reconciling with liberal democracy and political liberalism – one that emphasized the inherent limits and follies of political life as a foundation for human flourishing. Rather than naturalness, Augustinians began emphasizing the genuine contingency of politics in Augustine's thought.

The first major response to Arquillière came from Henri Irénée Marrou who, in his 1957 Warburg Lectures, "Civitas Dei, civitas terrena: num tertium quid?," claims that it is not the naturalness of political society that secures its value, or guarantees its intelligibility, in Augustine's theology, but rather its *temporality*. Between the coming of Christ and the end of history, Marrou claims, there is the time and space of the present age (*saeculum*) wherein the two cities – earthly and heavenly – are intermingled on their way toward their final eschatological destinations. Directly against Arquillière's thesis, Marrou argues that it is the "mixed nature" of the political sphere – necessarily a mixture of ultimate religious identities – that makes the political sphere a *tertium quid*, namely the reality of a *saeculum* where the two cities overlap.[7] This third thing, Marrou suggests, is the heart of Augustine's ambivalent affirmation of the *temporal* common good found in political society. The "natural" does not name an autonomous category of value, for Augustine, but rather the primary description of the temporal, created goods constitutive of political society. Thus the meaning of these goods is subject to the vicissitudes of salvation history, apart from which their goodness is not ultimately intelligible. Marrou's argument is intended to correct Arquillière's thesis as it also highlights the misinterpretations of Augustine by his medieval political inheritors.

Writing at the same moment as Marrou – in the aftermath of World War II and the beginning of the Cold War – Augustinians in the United States such as Reinhold Niebuhr and Herbert Deane also highlighted Augustine's sense of the contingency of politics, except this time with darker hues. Not merely *temporal*, political life for Niebuhr's and Deane's Augustine was a contingent intervention of God's providential judgment *after sin* aimed to help restrain chaos and maintain order. Thus the *unnaturalness* of politics – for Marrou and realists such as Niebuhr and Deane – is ultimately rooted in Augustine's sense of its historical provisionality. This provisionality, such interpreters argue, also secures political society's immunity from the ultimate aims of human fulfillment.

These two avenues of thought – Marrou's sense of historical temporality and the realists' sense of postlapsarian contingency – are synthesized in what stands as the culminating point of the rapprochement between Augustine and political liberalism: Robert Markus's *Saeculum: History and Society in the Theology of St. Augustine*, published in 1970.[8] Markus makes an intuitive leap from the interpretive work of Marrou and Deane, presenting Augustine's political thought as the harbinger of secular political liberalism. Markus transitions from the time-bound sense of political temporality espoused by Marrou to a stronger thesis of neutrality. With Markus's Augustine, political society becomes a religion-free zone, given its limited ambitions for practical political arrangement without theoretical agreement on matters of comprehensive doctrine. Markus's precise understanding of *neutrality* and the limited role of religious argument in the public square finds further nuance in his later work, where he adopts a Rawlsian vision of "overlapping consensus" joined with Maritain's "democratic secular faith."[9]

For Markus, it is not merely the case that Augustine happens not to have espoused a view of the naturalness of politics like that found in Thomas Aquinas. Rather, the absence of a natural antecedent for political society brings us to the core of Augustine's political thought; for if political society is natural it is always open to – indeed it is waiting for – its fulfillment in the supernatural common good. But for Markus's Augustine, the political is an antiperfectionist institutional arrangement set up merely to secure physical survival. The temporal domain of the political remains neutral to religion and autonomous until the very end, in anticipation of an eschatological closure that is beyond human agency.

In Markus, we find the reversal of Arquillière's thesis. Augustine's political thought no longer threatens to absorb the temporal into the eternal (without an adequate distinction between the natural and supernatural). For Markus, there is simply too much eschatological deferral and historical ambiguity in Augustine's conception of the two cities to legitimate an interpretation like Arquillière's. Markus argues that the Neo-Thomist distinction between the natural and supernatural common good, applied to the institutions of church and political society, threatens to make politics a halfway house for human flourishing, tending toward religious authority, constantly in need of a grace that can perfect it.

Reversals
By the end of the twentieth century these reconciliations with political liberalism came under fire from within both Augustinian and Thomist camps. Critics declared that such mid-century harmonization with political liberalism had gone too far, overstretching and reifying the central political concepts of the natural (Aquinas) and temporal (Augustine) into a pristine, secular space, disconnected from the ultimate supernatural or eternal good. This line of criticism suggests that such rapprochements exhibit conceptual failures that promote accommodation to the practices of secular political life – practices that are immune to the sacred and inimical to the smaller forms of community necessary to pursue the common good. Indeed such practices are beleaguered by the demons of excessive individualism and technocratic capitalism that ultimately consume liberal democracies and must be resisted. Thus the alliance went too far, critics suggested, and dulled the critical edges of Augustine's and Aquinas's theology – the very edges that made them so helpful for reflecting on modern politics. Indeed, far from restraining the excesses of the nation-state or the market, such reconciliation is now thought to blind Christians to the ways these arrangements constitute a new (false) sacrality. The most strident critic of Markus's secular Augustinian liberalism and its corresponding account of the *saeculum* remains John Milbank. The most forceful challenge to the Neo-Thomist reconciliation with political liberalism is Alasdair MacIntyre.

Although there are immense debates in each camp about how precisely to render the natural and temporal in each thinker, it is taken for granted that Augustine and Aquinas are fundamentally opposed on the question of the naturalness of the political. For this reason the liberalism and antiliberalism divide in Thomism and Augustinianism has reached an impasse. Rather than rehearse the terms of the debate or choose sides it will be more useful to reexamine the standard interpretive pictures.

CORRECTING THE STANDARD INTERPRETATIONS: BRINGING AUGUSTINE AND AQUINAS CLOSER TOGETHER

Mid-century Augustinian liberals doubled down on the apparently *unnatural* aspects of politics – a merely historical excursion through the consequences of sin – rather than searching for the missing *natural* antecedent to political life in Augustine's thought and thus responding to Neo-Thomists on their own terms. Part of what made Augustine's political thought so attractive to mid-century interpreters was his strong sense of the *tragic* dimension of human existence: the fact that all are tainted by original sin and experience some measure of fated powerlessness in the face of evil.

Yet the political often must be carefully teased out of Augustine's theology, and the mid-century affinity for tragedy led to a fixation on those notoriously dark passages in *The City of God* that seem most like political theory and most helpful in diagnosing the horrors of the twentieth century. Take, for example, Augustine's response to Cicero's *De re publica* and his claims about the impossibility of true justice in this life (2.21; 19.21, 24); Augustine's comparison of emperors and superpirates (4.4); his claims about the similarity between the authority exercised by kings and slave owners (19.14–15); the vignette of a mournful judge lamenting his duty to access truth by torture (19.6); and so on. Note that the majority of these passages appear in Book 19 of *The City of God* – the *locus classicus* of political Augustinianism. And there are good reasons for the authority of this particular text. In many ways it is, as Oliver O'Donovan has called it, "a microcosm of Augustine's social thought."[10] It also provides the perfect length of assigned reading for Augustine's political theology in a survey course.

The problem, however, is that the narrow concentration on this text – and its few tenebrous images – led to a distorted perception of the character of Augustine's political theology as a whole and its interpretive and practical possibilities. If Book 19 was the ur-text for the shadowy postwar Augustine, its fourteenth and fifteenth chapters form the interpretive center of it all. It is important to note that these chapters – more than any other – are used to validate the claim that, for Augustine, political society is ultimately rooted in the consequences of original sin. What is more, this text is ground zero for those intent on trumpeting the difference between Augustine's and Aquinas's political thought. Let us briefly turn to a closer examination of Book 19 and the widely divergent conclusions Augustinians drew from it in the second half of the twentieth century.

Part of the reason *City of God* 19.14–15 is seen to provide such conclusive evidence that, for Augustine, political society is rooted in the consequences of original sin is that it provides his only account of political society as it would have existed in a state of innocence, before the fall. The passage appears in the context of Augustine's broader reflection on the *contingent* (in the negative sense of *contingent* denoting something unnatural and expressive of temporal or provisional evil) origins of the institution of slavery.

> [God] did not intend that a rational creature, made in his own image, should have lordship (*dominor*) over any but irrational creatures: not man over man, but man over beasts. Hence, the first just (*iustus*) men were established as shepherds of flocks, rather than as kings of men (*reges hominum*). This was done so that in this way also God might indicate what the order of nature requires, and what the desert of sinners demands. By nature, then, in the condition in which God first created man, no man is the slave either of another man or of sin. (*City of God* 19.15)

Augustinian liberals and antiliberals alike read this passage as a blanket statement about the origins of political *authority*, and further evidence of Augustine's view of political society as essentially coercive, aimed primarily to help restrain evil, vice, and sin. What is striking are the very different conclusions drawn from it for thinking about the application of Augustine's political thought to modern political life.

Robert Markus concludes from this passage that the authority that would have been exercised in a state of innocence would have been akin to the paternal authority of Old Testament patriarchs or of a Roman *paterfamilias* over his wife and children, rather than the political authority that a king exercises over his subjects. Markus argues further that, in this passage, Augustine is identifying political authority in general with the authority of masters over slaves, thus fundamentally casting the institutions and relationships necessary for political society into contingent darkness. The key here, for Markus, is that the family – and therefore the corresponding institution of the household – is in some sense *natural* in a way that political society cannot be, for Augustine. Whereas the family can be, hypothetically, ruled without domination, this cannot be true of political society. Its contingent origins in human sinfulness and providential judgment exclude it from both naturalness and the possibilities of nondomination. Markus claims that, for Augustine:

> Coercive power is part of the essence of political authority, without it the state is not a state.... Political authority, coercive power, and its [institutional] apparatus are what transform society into a state. Society, so we may summarize Augustine's view, has its origins in the order of nature; the state is a dispensation rooted in sin.... The terms in which Augustine came to formulate his views on politically organized society ... were those which he thought appropriate to the treatment of the institution of slavery, rather than those which he applied to the family.[11]

For Markus, the postlapsarian contingency of political authority, and thus political society more generally, serves to strengthen his overall rendering of Augustine as godfather of a low-flying minimalist liberal politics, committed to the relative autonomy, neutrality, and secularity of the political sphere.

Strikingly, John Milbank, Markus's opponent in all things pertaining to Augustine, shares precisely Markus's view of Augustine on politics and original sin. For Milbank, just as for Markus, *City of God* 19.14–15 reveals, "that Augustine regards the institution of slavery after the fall, and the institution of political power, as virtually one and the same event."[12] Both authors read Augustine's comments about kingship in 19.15 as evidence that he identifies political authority with the authority of masters over slaves. Both conclude that this type of authority is contingently rooted in the consequences of original sin. They then read backward, as it were, and lump political community and institutions into the same category as authority. The equation is complete. Thus, for Markus's and Milbank's Augustine, political society is entirely unnatural in comparison with the family and the institution of the household. It is unnatural in the sense that it is not part of the order of human sociality inherent in the grain of creation.

Yet this shared conclusion leads Milbank to a very different appropriation of Augustine's political thought. For Milbank, the origins of political society in sin supports an ambitious claim that, for Augustine, the church, the *ecclesia*, is the only truly *political* society, and that its arrival in history spells the undoing of pagan political thought and practice. At the climax of his argument, Milbank states very baldly that "[a]ll political theory in the antique sense is relocated by Christianity [beginning with Augustine], as thought about the Church."[13] And, what is more, "the Church itself, as the realized heavenly city, is the *telos* of the salvific process. And as a *civitas*, the church is, for Augustine, itself a 'political' reality."[14] For Milbank's Augustine, the goods constitutive of political society do not have their own natural integrity or intelligibility, nor do they have their own provisional secular (or time-bound) integrity, as they do for Markus. The realm of politics – that is, the "realm of the merely practical" – when "cut off from the ecclesial," Milbank concludes, "is quite simply a realm of sin."[15]

It is Augustinian liberals and antiliberals' shared sense of the *temporality* of politics – as fundamentally rooted in the murky origins of sin – that eliminates any *natural* antecedent for political society. We believe this connection between politics and the contingency of sin breeds confusion, either hardening the temporality of the political sphere into the rigid secularity of Markus or deflating it into Milbank's realm of the merely practical to be subordinated to the ecclesial. For without a presupposed *natural* antecedent in Augustine's thought, political society is doomed to swing between these interpretive poles of the purely secular space or the fragile temporal realm waiting to be swallowed by the *ecclesia*.

Markus and others present such a rendering of politics and sin in *City of God* 19.14–15 in direct opposition to Aquinas's understanding of the naturalness of politics. Aquinas treats the origins of political authority twice, first in his *Commentary on the Sentences* (44.q.2.a.2) and then again in *Summa Theologiae* (1a.96.3, 4). In both instances Aquinas is in direct conversation with Augustine's *City of God* 19.14–15. In Thomas's treatment of the question in *Summa Theologiae*, he argues that free political rule (as opposed to slave keeping) would have been necessary even in humankind's state of created innocence. To make this argument, Aquinas draws a simple distinction between two types of dominion: the authority of a master over a slave and the authority associated with "the office of governing free men" (96.4). The second type has membership in an original, prelapsarian goodness – with all its practical structures for the cause of ruling subordinated to the common good. The first type, by contrast, expresses merely a contingent, postlapsarian form of domination – the suppression of XX by YY. Aquinas is clear that both the household and political society can and should be governed by the first type of authority. In making this distinction, Aquinas thinks he is closely following Augustine's *City of God* 19.14–15, and is distancing himself from Aristotle's view of natural slavery in the *Politics*. In *Summa Theologiae* 1a.96.4, Aquinas says:

> The control of one over another who remains free, can take place when the former directs the latter to his own good or to the common good. And such dominion would have been found between man and man in the state of innocence for two reasons. First, because man is naturally a social animal; and in consequence would have lived in society, even in the state of innocence. Now there could be no social life for many persons living together unless one of their number were set in authority to care for the common good. Many individuals are, as individuals, interested in a variety of ends.... Secondly, if there were one man more wise and righteous than the rest, it would have been wrong if such gifts were not exercised on behalf of the rest.... So Augustine says, "The just rule not through desire of domination, but because it is their duty to give counsel"; and "This is ordained by the natural order, for thus did God create man." (*City of God* 19.14–15)

Markus, in a revealing appendix to his book, argues that Aquinas's insistence on the naturalness of political authority commits him to a view of freedom akin to what Isaiah Berlin calls "positive freedom" – that is, the notion "that one remains free, even in being coerced, provided that it is for his own or the common good."[16] Augustine, however, Markus claims, espouses an entirely negative conception of freedom in the sense that any coercion in the political sphere implies a diminution of liberty.[17]

On Markus's reading, political authority, for Augustine, remains entirely (and perhaps tragically) tethered to the judicial and penal operations of coercion. Aquinas is therefore merely mistaken, on Markus's account, insofar as he sees any positive role for political authority in the work of virtue cultivation or overall human flourishing. Aquinas's distinction of two kinds of rule is a pregnant one for understanding the *possibility* of noncoercive political relations bound by law. Note, however, that Markus's insistence on Augustine's protoliberalism (of a distinctive kind) is inflected in his interpretive debate around these texts. We believe he is mistaken. In particular, Markus's borrowed modern notion of freedom as noninterference distorts more than it reveals with respect to relevant differences between Augustine and Aquinas. Their accounts of freedom, and subsequent debates about whether politics is *essentially* coercive, simply do not map onto these distinctions. A more productive reading of these texts would emphasize Augustine and Aquinas's shared indebtedness to the republican tradition of political thinking on liberty and domination, as can be found in the work of Peter J. Burnell.

The full exegetical details of this interpretive debate are manifold and would require a lengthier treatment of their discussions of mastery and servitude, and their different accounts of the nature of law, east of Eden. Let it be sufficient to note that Aquinas saw his presentation of human sociality and the naturalness of political authority in *ST* 1a.96.3–4 as standing in fundamental agreement with Augustine's *City of God* 19.14–15. Consider the similarities of their approaches to political authority in these two texts.

First, the *natural*, for Augustine and Aquinas, signifies the order of creation as it existed in a state of innocence before the fall. Second, the question of the naturalness of political society for each thinker is not a question of the raw aggregate of individuals who form a civil community, but rather of the naturalness of the forms of rule or authority that govern such a community. Third, implied in each author's account of authority is a picture of the profound fabric of political authority, civil community, and the common good unique to political community. Both Augustine and Aquinas endorse a conception of political society as a mesh of roles, institutions, and obligations in which the accent mark in the formation of political community falls on the authority of political officials. Their analysis of political society centers on the virtues necessary to fulfill the role-specific obligations associated with political office and the direction and formation of citizens. Finally, Augustine and Aquinas both fundamentally agree that humankind's natural sociality expresses itself in a series of concentric "moral circles" extending outward from the individual to the family, civil society, ecclesial community, and ultimately to all human beings and God. Contra Markus, we believe this is the most plausible way to read *City of God* 19. Each of these spheres of community, in turn, is embedded in an institution (e.g., household, commonwealth, church) and plays a role in human flourishing. For both authors, then, the temporal common good of political society provides a genuine, albeit incomplete, form of happiness.

The clearest evidence of Augustine's understanding of the "naturalness" (in the sense of original created goodness) of political authority is found not in *City of God* 19.14–15 but in his advice to public officials in his letters. There we find an Augustinian account of political leadership. There we get glimpses of public officials fulfilling their role-specific obligations in a distinctively Christian way – a way that supports the public good and also openly directs it toward the eternal good. Indeed, the letters in Augustine's correspondence with public officials such as Marcellinus and Macedonius are now being recognized by many as the center, not the periphery, of Augustine's political thought (see especially Letters 138 to Marcellinus and Letter 155 to Macedonius). For it is in these texts that we find Augustine at his most practical, offering detailed descriptions of the ways Christian faith should influence the performance of one's public responsibilities. Robert Dodaro's work on Augustine has brought these neglected texts into the mainstream of dialogue about Augustine's political ethics, against scholars in the more "realist" tradition of Reinhold Niebuhr and Herbert Deane.

Augustine's focus in these texts is the public official's soul, not political regimes. His political language is that of virtuous rule, not church and state. The transformation of political society by Christian faith begins at the level of the political official's role-specific obligations – specifically as the virtues necessary to carry out these obligations in the governance of political society are reinterpreted in light of the theological virtues of faith, hope, and love.

Illustrative of this approach is Letter 155 to Macedonius, who was imperial vicar of Africa during the years 413–414 AD, in which he oversaw the administration of justice in all of Roman Africa. At some point during Macedonius's tenure at this post, Augustine appealed to him for clemency on behalf of a criminal condemned to capital punishment. Through their exchange of letters (152, 153, 155) we learn that Macedonius grants the appeal, and Augustine writes to thank him and congratulate him on his decision. The climax of Augustine's argument to Macedonius in Letter 155 is that Macedonius must now learn to practice the political virtues required by his office with the twofold goal of tending the people's temporal and eternal well-being:

> The source of happiness is not one thing for a human being and another for a city: a city is indeed nothing other than a like-minded mass of human beings. Take all your virtues: all the prudence with which you try to serve human affairs, all the courage with which you allow no enemy's wickedness to frighten you, all the moderation through which you keep yourself from corruption when surrounded by the rottenness of contemptible human habits, all the justice which you use to judge correctly in assigning to each his due. Suppose that you employ all these virtues in toiling and struggling merely for the physical security of those you want to do well.... Then neither your virtues nor the happiness that comes from them will be real.... If any of your governing, however informed by the virtues, is directed only to the final aim of allowing human beings to suffer no unjust hardships in the flesh; and if you think that it is no concern of yours to what purpose they put the peace that you struggle to provide for

them (that is, to speak directly, how they worship the true God, with whom the fruit of peaceful life is found), then all that effort towards the life of true happiness will not benefit you at all.[18]

Letter 155 to Macedonius turns out to be an extended discussion of the relationship between virtue and happiness as it is practiced and experienced in the life of a political ruler. It provides an insight into Augustine's understanding of the good use of political authority that goes well beyond *City of God* 19.14–15. It also reveals that political society is "natural," for Augustine, insofar as it is a constitutive element of the social well-being that human beings were created to pursue.

The analogue to Augustine's account of virtue and happiness in these letters to public officials is Aquinas's account of the way the infused theological virtues of faith, hope, and love orient human beings to the eternal common good and thereby help direct their use and experience of temporal goods.[19] Although we must pay attention to the relationship and differences between Augustine's and Aquinas's understanding of the limited natural and temporal qualities of the common good achieved in political life (especially through law), they are in agreement in their description of how the gifts of the theological virtues are necessary to orient human beings toward eternal happiness. A common link between Augustine's and Aquinas's political thought is their shared Neoplatonic framework in thinking about how the theological virtues reorient the practice of the cardinal virtues in temporal political life. Although scholars have begun tracing the Neoplatonic elements in Augustine's thinking about the theological and political virtues, more work needs to be done on these same elements in Aquinas's thought relative to more familiar accounts of Aristotelianism and natural law (especially Aquinas's account of whether or not cardinal virtues remain in heaven).

On Kingship: To the King of Cyprus (De regno) can also be read as Aquinas's (or at least a very early Thomistic) presentation of the ways that the infused virtues fundamentally reorient one's responsibilities for tending the temporal, political common good. The text, admittedly of disputed authorship, applies a Thomistic conception of the theological and political virtues in the instruction of an actual public official.

TOWARD A CONTEMPORARY AUGUSTINIAN-THOMIST *POLITICAL* POLITICAL THEOLOGY

In many ways, Augustine's age is closer to our own than Aquinas's, for the institutional relationship between church and political society, bishop and magistrate, was still very much in flux. For Augustine, the relationship of political life and Christian faith is a matter of virtue, worked out on the battlefield of the public official's soul. Although Augustine's statesmanship approach to politics can strike the contemporary mind as elitist and underdeveloped in terms of structural analysis, it holds principles that are transferable for a more popular, democratic Christian virtue ethics of citizenship. This democratic translation has been the trend in contemporary political Augustinianism since the work of Dodaro, Gregory, and Mathewes.

Twentieth-century attempts to construct institutional renderings of Aquinas's natural and supernatural common good, or Augustine's temporal and eternal good, that can be neatly applied to church and political society have run their course and climaxed in the stalemate of a liberal and antiliberal debate over secularity. These distinctions primarily apply, for each thinker, to the virtues and corresponding goods associated with them. Both Augustine and Aquinas think of political theology more in terms of virtue ethics than institutional analysis. Ultimately, political questions are questions about the transformation of the political (cardinal) virtues by faith, hope, and love. And these questions are, in turn, questions about what it means *to refer* the common good achieved in political life toward its ultimate end in God, who is eternal happiness.

Thus the genuinely constructive work that lies before political Thomists and Augustinians falls into three categories. First we must identify the political virtues – especially those most relevant to contemporary *democratic* life – and describe what their reorientation by faith, hope, and love might look like. Part of this description brings about the second constructive task of identifying exemplars – both past and present, statesmen and citizens – who embody these virtues and their transformation through faith, hope, and love. Once such virtues and embodied transformations can be identified, we will be in a better position to describe what the *referral* of the natural or temporal common good toward eternal happiness might amount to at the level of political practice.

Referral brings us to the grand question in Augustine's and Aquinas's political thought: what is the relationship between earthly happiness and the ultimate form of happiness found only with God in eternity? That is, what is the relationship between political and eschatological eudaimonism? And, how do we avoid the previous errors of absorption (Christendom) and separation (secularism) in answering such a question? Note that both the natural and supernatural distinction, and temporal and eternal one, can lead to these errors if broadly applied at the institutional level. The way to avoid the twin errors of absorption or separation is to focus not simply on institutions but on individuals; not on raw individuals, but socially coded individuals in their distinctive roles, as members of all levels of society and as tenders of particular common goods who are in need of specific virtues. Such virtues are always threatened by unjust social and political practices. Getting a grip on these questions is more fundamental to the political thought of Augustine and Aquinas than institutional questions of church and political society, and yet the two sorts of question are never ultimately disconnected. For both thinkers the church is the locus of virtue formation and of the relationships necessary for discernment, and political society is the place where political virtue must be transformed by faith, hope, and love.

Responding to such questions, no doubt, will be informed by the sort of philosophical and theological reflection characteristic of contemporary political theology, often at odds with much of political theory resistant to such questions (including the work of many self-identified Augustinian and Thomist political thinkers). Concepts like naturalness, necessity, coercion, domination, and the common good remain high on the agenda for any theological interpretation of politics. In fact, we have highlighted areas where the political implications of major developments in theological scholarship on these thinkers remain undertheorized. But, as the best critics of our actual politics rightly have noted, theory alone cannot support the type of social change required to transcend the distinctive challenges of modern political communities and their economic arrangements. Here, with MacIntyre, we share many of the concerns about abstraction and philosophical exclusion noted by critics of liberalism and its characteristic bureaucratic and procedural expressions. Further theorizing of theory's relation to practice, or even Augustine's relation to Aquinas on supernatural grace, also will not meet these challenges. Prophetic critique, moreover, risks its own moral and political hazards.

Despite many valid theological criticisms of their work, Augustinians and Thomists in the mid-twentieth century like Reinhold Niebuhr and John Courtney Murray sought to provide a genuinely *political* Christian political theory, attentive to the details of political structures and processes without sacrificing normative reflection on the demands of political leadership and citizenship.[20] Contemporary Augustinian-Thomists can, and should, still learn from these forebears and be grateful for their concerns about the political institutions of a free society. Their concerns, attentive to political theory and political science, stand in stark contrast with the ecclesial focus of more recent work in political theology. Our rejection of the "institutional level" opposition of Augustine and Aquinas serves a different purpose. It may be that the debate over political liberalism has truncated our receptions of their political theologies. In fact, in addition to emphasis on the distinctive liturgical practices for training Christian virtue, further work in political theology might best be served by attending in more focused ways to how Augustinian and Thomist perspectives can inform debates about issues like mass incarceration, immigration, and international law.

Caricatures have their pedagogical value, even in the formation of holiness. We do not deny differences between Augustine's more consistent Platonism, and Aquinas's debts to Aristotle. Their rhetorical style and their visions of politics took shape in radically different historical contexts. But the demands of contemporary politics require something more than sweaty Augustinian "pessimism" and serene Thomist "optimism," let alone Augustinian "grace" and Thomist "nature." Our effort to historicize and interrupt conventional pictures by bringing Augustine and Aquinas closer together is one attempt to open new ways of addressing such challenges without default recourse to familiar tropes. Dislodging their opposition, without collapsing their different construals of human agency confronted by proximate and final ends, might liberate and generate new imaginations for both political engagement and practical reasoning. Such a politics remains a human enterprise, adequate to our creatureliness in time, but no less divine.

Notes

1 This approach can be found in the essays by Ernest Fortin on Augustine and Aquinas in L. Strauss and J. Cropsey, eds., *The History of Political Philosophy*, 3rd ed. (Chicago: University of Chicago Press, 1987), pp. 176–205 and 248–75. More recently, Alan Ryan helpfully identifies the salience of their different historical contexts, but he still maintains that Aquinas "successfully erased Augustine's relentlessly negative view of earthly existence from ethical and political debate." Alan Ryan, *On Politics: A History of Political Thought from Herodotus to the Present* (New York: W. W. Norton, 2012), p. 225.
2 The key texts in Aquinas on the naturalness of politics are to be found in *Summa Theologiae* 1a.92.1; 96.3, 4.
3 Pierre Rousselot, *The Problem of Love in the Middle Ages: A Historical Contribution*, trans. and with an introduction by Alan Vincelette (Milwaukee, WI: Marquette University Press, 1998).
4 Jacques Maritain, *Scholasticism and Politics* (New York: MacMillan, 1940), pp. 179–97.

5. Gustave Combès, *La Doctrine Politique de Saint Augustin* (Paris: Plon, 1927), pp. 105–6.
6. Henri de Lubac, *Theological Fragments*, trans. Rebecca Howell Balinski (San Francisco: Ignatius Press, 1989), p. 245.
7. Henri Irénée Marrou, "Civitas Dei, civitas terrena: num tertium quid?," in *Studia Patristica. Papers presented to the Second International Conference in Patristic Studies held at Christ Church, Oxford*, Vol. 2, ed. K. Aland and F. L. Cross (Berlin: Akademie-Verlag, 1957), p. 348.
8. Robert Markus, *Saeculum: History and Society in the Theology of St. Augustine*, rev. ed. (Cambridge: Cambridge University Press, 1988).
9. Robert Markus, *Christianity and the Secular* (Notre Dame, IN: University of Notre Dame Press, 2006), p. 13 and pp. 67–8.
10. Oliver O'Donovan, "The Political Thought of *City of God* 19," in *Bonds of Imperfection: Christian Politics, Past and Present*, ed. Oliver O'Donovan and Joan Lockwood O'Donovan (Grand Rapids, MI: Eerdmans, 2004), p. 72.
11. Markus, *Saeculum*, pp. 205, 209.
12. John Milbank, *Theology and Social Theory*, 2nd ed. (Oxford: Blackwell, 2006), p. 406.
13. Ibid., p. 403.
14. Ibid.
15. Ibid., p. 406.
16. Markus, *Saeculum*, p. 230.
17. Ibid.
18. Letter 155.9–10, E. M. Atkins and R. J. Dodaro, eds., *Augustine: Political Writings* (Cambridge: Cambridge University Press, 2001), pp. 94–5.
19. Aquinas, *On the Virtues in General*, Article 9: "Do We Acquire Virtue through Acts?" and Article 10: "Do We Receive Any Virtues by Infusion?," in *Disputed Questions on Virtue*, trans. Jeffrey Hause and Claudia Eisen Murphy (Indianapolis, IN: Hackett, 2010).
20. Note Jeremy Waldron's recent call for *political* political theory in Jeremy Waldron, "Political Political Theory: An Inaugural Lecture," *Journal of Political Philosophy* 21.1 (March 2013): 1–23.

Further Reading

Burnell, P., *The Augustinian Person*. Washington, DC: Catholic University of America Press, 2005.
Deane, H., *The Political and Social Ideas of St. Augustine*. New York: Columbia University Press, 1963.
Dodaro, R., *Christ and the Just Society in the Thought of Augustine*. Cambridge: Cambridge University Press, 2004.
Finnis, J., *Aquinas: Moral, Political, and Legal Theory*. Oxford: Oxford University Press, 1998.
Gregory, E., *Politics and the Order of Love: An Augustinian Ethic of Democratic Citizenship*. Chicago: University of Chicago Press, 2008.
MacIntyre, A., *Three Rival Versions of Moral Enquiry*. Notre Dame, IN: University of Notre Dame Press, 1990.

Maritain, J., *The Person and the Common Good*, trans. J. J. Fitzgerald. New York: Charles Scribner's Sons, 1947.

Markus, R. A., *Saeculum: History and Society in the Theology of St. Augustine*, rev. ed. Cambridge: Cambridge University Press, 1988.

Mathewes, C., *The Republic of Grace: Augustinian Thoughts for Dark Times*. Grand Rapids, MI: Eerdmans, 2010.

Milbank, J., *Theology and Social Theory: Beyond Secular Reason*, 2nd ed. Oxford: Blackwell, 2006.

Murray, J. C., *We Hold These Truths: Catholic Reflections on the American Proposition*. New York: Sheed and Ward, 1960.

Niebuhr, R., *Christian Realism and Political Problems*. New York: Charles Scribner's Sons, 1953.

Simon, Y. R., *Philosophy of Democratic Government*. Notre Dame, IN: University of Notre Dame Press, 1993.

Weithman, P. J., "Augustine and Aquinas on Original Sin and the Function of Political Authority," *Journal of the History of Philosophy* 30.3 (1992): 353–76.

Issues

10 Liberalism and Democracy
CRAIG HOVEY

A. D. Lindsay, one of the twentieth century's most earnest Christian advocates for democracy, insisted that the democratic state is "at best only an analogy of the really democratic religious congregation."[1] This chapter approaches the related topics of liberalism and democracy by attempting to understand Lindsay's claim. It asks what is meant by calling Christian congregational existence "democratic," whether this in any way extends to forms of church life beyond the local level, how this analogy to the modern liberal state works, and if and where the analogy breaks down. We begin, however, with a brief account of what makes the modern democratic state *liberal*.

Liberalism is a political philosophy that seeks societal stability and unity in the absence of shared conceptions of the common good. It is therefore regularly associated with contemporary discussions of religious and other pluralisms and, especially in our day, is connected to the anxieties that set in when moral convictions previously thought to be self-evidently true and binding lose their obviousness. How then will a society composed of diverse individuals – people of various faiths and traditions – function for its betterment? Where there are differing, even competing, notions of justice among members of a society, for example? What institutional forms ought that society's justice system take?

The theory of justice advocated by John Rawls is a notable version of how political liberalism negotiates justice in the face of such diversity. In his book *A Theory of Justice*, Rawls proposes that individuals engage in a thought experiment: imagine standing behind a "veil of ignorance" in which the particular social and political goods that one's self-interest would otherwise prefer are hidden from view.[2] How might people in this situation then organize a society? Rawls argues that they will act to maximize justice and opportunity for all people on the basis that the interests of any person might be their own. They will, in other words, actually be guided by a more generalized self-interest in service of a theory of justice that Rawls describes simply as fairness. The location behind this veil of ignorance is what Rawls calls the "original position," that is, bare humanity as any person would be were they free of all attachments, history, and identity.

This original position has much in common with descriptions of the "state of nature" imagined by earlier theorists of political liberalism such as Thomas Hobbes. According to Hobbes's famous argument in *The Leviathan* (1651), without society, life is a constant state of war of every individual against everyone else and hence "solitary, poor, nasty, brutish, and short." Society, for liberalism, plays a salvific role for originally autonomous, free-associating individuals who find belonging, purpose, meaning, and community nowhere else. This characteristic move among liberal theorists is subject to ideological critique, especially as any state of nature is not an actual historical description of humans, but an imagined hypothetical one, a vision generated by the kind of deliverance from destructive, individual self-interest that a liberal civil society promises to bring.

It is worth noticing in both Hobbes and Rawls the implicit neglect or even hostility toward tradition in general as well as collectivities and communities other than liberal society, which in modern politics is identified with the nation-state. On these grounds, Lindsay's question is already provocative because it suggests an ecclesial basis for democratic politics against liberalism. What are the differences between these two kinds of democracy?

Hobbes's liberalism located equality among all people in what they most minimally share in common: their fear of death. Such fear is the natural corollary of the fact that life is originally under threat from other individuals as everyone has a right over everything (*jus in omnia*). In order to prevent war of all against all, individuals hand these rights over to the absolute sovereign. In Hobbes's context of the English Civil War, new notions of sovereignty seemed urgently to be called for, particularly notions grounded in some way other than by divine *fiat*. Here we notice that there are places where Lindsay's analogy between the Christian congregation and the democratic state are apt, and other places where they sharply diverge.

Under threat by the impending war of all against all, former political approaches based on the pursuit and discovery of shared goods give way to individual rights. Whereas Aristotle, for example, sought politics in terms of goods and ends (*teloi*) and his Christian interpreters (notably Thomas Aquinas) framed the highest ends for humanity in terms of beatitude and friendship with God, Hobbes stripped goods of all politically determinative force. The sovereign state does not exist to aid the polis in the pursuit of virtues shaped by a common human *telos*; instead, the state is both humbler and more ambitious.

On the one hand, the state appears humbly to limit itself to terrestrial matters (such as peace) in the face of the threat posed by one's neighbors. It does not claim authority on moral or religious matters, even though the spiritual lives of the people are subsumed under absolute sovereignty. On the other hand, if fear of death is the enemy from which Christians understand God in Christ delivers them, then Hobbes may be read as positing a much more ambitious, even pseudotheological, project, as William Cavanaugh has argued: the state claims its legitimacy from its role as a rival savior to Christ.[3]

We should note that for this theological critique of liberalism, the threat of "natural," original enmity is a creation myth that rivals Genesis. Rather than envisioning the original goodness of all things – including harmony among humans, between humans and the other creatures, and between creation and God – Hobbes describes a mythological state of nature complete with its own salvation history that concludes with the establishment of peace through absolute political sovereignty as the response to death's overwhelming foreboding.

One also notices that the principle for unity here is specifically fear of *violent* death, fear of being killed. Hence the real threat is a war of all against all, rather than simply the individual's feeling of mortality's crushing weight. Hobbes's own civil war context gave his state of nature story a kind of legitimacy. As it was clearly a function of his historical setting's urgency, however, much of the force associated with claims to naturalness disappears. Still, Hobbes needed to deal with a deep irony in how he saw politics relating to nature's original state as both solution and problem. As Pierre Manent summarizes, "what makes [individuals] enemies is what they have in common; and what makes them capable of living together is also what they have in common."[4] Rousseau and Locke later disputed the inevitability of violence as humanity's natural state; it is enough to notice at this point that for the founder of liberalism, violence both roots and establishes society while it also functions to judge the viability of all political proposals.

We should not be content, however, only to follow some recent critics in noticing these rival mythologies and salvation narratives. We must go on to ask what kind of Christian polity is here being substituted with a secular alternative. For Hobbes, such a polity was an overweening ecclesiastical situation that had been clumsily appropriated by the English monarchs since Henry VIII and, in radically different forms, prior to this. Lindsay's analogy, however, is focused on the political life of the Christian congregation, which partly has its own force in Christian reformist tendencies to make appeal to biblical and early Christian political concepts and practices. What are the concepts and practices that particularly cast Hobbes's proposal in sharp relief? Which specifically Christian democratic themes, doctrines, and customs are most at odds with Hobbes's liberalism? In what follows, I investigate three: the constitution of peoplehood, the locus of polity, and the hyperdemocratic impulse.

THE CONSTITUTION OF PEOPLEHOOD

Lindsay referred to the *congregation*; yet local and universal conceptions of the church are analogies to each other. This is not obviously true everywhere, to be sure, because congregational polities exist in which the universal church is located in and as the congregation. However, even here, some notion of what the church is contributes to the congregation's self-understanding, assuring it that it is in fact church. In traditional, sacramental, or quasisacramental understandings of what constitutes the church as church, a more balanced dialectic moves back and forth between local congregation and universal *ecclesia* (e.g., the Vatican II document *Lumen Gentium* teaches that the church is "*uti sacramentum*"). In admittedly various ways, every church polity gives an account of the congregation's relationship with the whole church that shows itself in analogies to modern democratic thought and political forms.

Given the democratic concern to locate governance under control of "the people," it is normal to ask to whom this actually refers. In practice, "the people" may identify a population's particular subset, demarcated from the rest, as bearing greater legitimacy when it comes to political questions. The irony may at times be great, especially because democratic theory purports to fortify an alternative to rule by some elite class. Nevertheless, and especially in revolutionary situations, "the people" are positioned in opposition to ruling elites with the implication that critics of the revolution are not only undemocratic, but are even in some sense nonpersons.[5]

According to liberalism in the tradition of Hobbes and Locke, peoplehood emerges most clearly when individuals come together and pursue common projects out of self-interest. As with any contract, the political conditions that unite people are not meant to outlast the projects to which the people devote themselves by so uniting. However, theological critics of liberalism, though not necessarily of democracy, note that descriptions of what constitutes a people – descriptions such as baptism – will often conflict with political descriptions such as nation-state citizenship. The second-century *Epistle to Diognetus* describes this tension:

> [Christians] dwell in their own countries, but simply as sojourners. As citizens, they share in all things with others, and yet endure all things as if foreigners. Every foreign land is to them as their native country, and every land of their birth as a land of strangers.[6]

If Christians confess a heavenly citizenship (Phil. 3:20), their attachments to, loyalties to, and identifications with political, ethnic, and other groups become less important. Eschatologically, they are provisional and withering away.

Moreover, ever since the political developments of the early modern period, the category of citizen in liberal thought may be theologically problematic if it evades the question of what makes a people by simply defining a group of those who have been politically authorized to govern themselves. These democratic relations, like those created by baptism, are not natural; they are forged by noncompulsory acts. The tautology is evident enough from history in which, for example, voting rights have sometimes been limited to one racial group.

Especially since the eighteenth century, questions about peoplehood have often coincided with questions about borders of nation-states. In principle, when liberalism is united to a capitalist economic system, the free flow of goods is promoted alongside the free flow of people. Tariffs and immigration policies that restrict these reveal that very often considerations other than pure economic and social liberty are in view. For example, the North American Free Trade Agreement (NAFTA, 1994) promotes migratory liberty for corporations but not for workers; businesses are entitled to seek more profitable locations for manufacturing goods while one of the chief factors for keeping costs low in these areas is enhanced by restricting the ability for working populations to seek better wages elsewhere. As it happens, then, "a people" is here an economic identity bounded by nation-state borders.

Nevertheless the opposite phenomenon may also be observed in practice, which points to a paradox in liberal equality. Especially where a principle of equality has struggled against inherited (Old World) social and economic statuses, the isolation of individuals from each other that liberalism pursues may serve democracy in an unexpected way, as

Alexis de Tocqueville noted of the American West in the 1830s, where less defined borders served to break down old privileges:

> It is in the West that one can see democracy in its most extreme form. In these states, in some sense improvisations of fortune, the inhabitants have arrived only yesterday in the land where they dwell. They hardly know one another, and each man is ignorant of his nearest neighbor's history. So in that part of the American continent the population escapes the influence not only of great names and great wealth but also of the natural aristocracy of education and probity.... There are *inhabitants* already in the new states of the West, but not yet as a *society*.[7]

According to Tocqueville, then, democratic equality flourishes so long as the collection of individuals has not existed long enough to reentrench old privileges. These thrown-together people who "arrived only yesterday" share "improvisations of fortunes." But they are not yet together *as a society* because societies in practice depend on a certain degree of entrenchment. Equality emerges out of disorder when the only ordering a society can imagine is the order of inequality, which itself points to an instability in uniting democracy with liberalism.

The "classic" form of liberal democracy, then, tends to be formal and procedural; this is its liberal aspect. Because it was founded on a deep suspicion of communities that seek goods, liberalism first conceives of humans as individuals for whom the fact of coming together to agree on something surpasses the content of their agreement. The formal qualities that characterize the ways that they organize their common life are the source of liberalism's *value*. But values of a deeper sort – the kind that premodern politics sought by associating the purpose of human life with the shape of the community, or the virtuous characters of citizens with the traits that make a good leader – impede the procedures of liberalism.

Michel Foucault characterized the modern political spirit as being obsessed with questions about sovereignty and rule. As much as liberalism has, in the last several hundred years, sought to replace one form of rule by another – substituting accountable parliaments for dynastic monarchies, establishing free elections as a formal safeguard against corrupt power grabs – these replacements preserve historic trends toward addressing questions about sovereignty and are, therefore, in Foucault's estimation, insufficiently radical. "What we need," he writes, "is a political philosophy that isn't erected around the problem of sovereignty, nor therefore around the problems of law and prohibition.

We need to cut off the King's head: in political theory that has still to be done."[8] In political theology, John Howard Yoder recognized something similar when he pointed out that questions about the best form of government are always Constantinian questions. What he meant was that such questions assume that the one asking the question already holds sovereign power, whether democratic or not, and has the capacity to do something about it.[9] Bringing together related insights from Tocqueville, Foucault, and Yoder leads to the conclusion that the most genuine democratic arrangements may be found among those who are least in a position to ask normative questions about whether democracy is superior to other styles of government.

Might it be the case, then, that genuine democracy is actually inimical to power and rule? The political theorist Sheldon Wolin echoes Tocqueville in using the term *fugitive democracy* to describe a nonpossessive and nonsovereign characteristic of emerging and fleeting associations between members of a society. Other associations taken for granted are disrupted in favor of new and surprising ties generated by shared priorities and concerns. For Wolin, this fugitive quality describes particular occurrences of democracy coming into view for a short time in service to a limited set of tasks. Democracy is a spirit that resists institutions, codes, and rules (including constitutions) and is therefore not a form of sovereignty; it is "an ephemeral phenomenon rather than a settled system."[10]

Can Christianity then conceive of this fleetingness of society as analogous to an eschatological reconfiguration of social relations that the church may begin to live within that society as an alternative to it? We notice resemblances with Christian congregational politics such as the leveling of privilege. The dominant social form for Christians has not tended to be society as a whole – whether the church is modeled on it or is held up as a possible substitute. It has, instead, been the family or household and, as an image, a nonhierarchical one. A household levels social status and economic relations; members of the same household are always members of the same class, for example, and those who are adopted will come to share the class of the household regardless of the class from which they originated. (The Greek origins of our word *economy* display this: *oikonomia* literally means "law of the household.") Christians call themselves brother and sister, sharing the same Father, and are therefore equal in dignity and in the inheritance they receive as siblings of Christ within God's family. By contrast, Christians are more than thrown together and, in hope, may persist as a new society ordered by God's creative charity beyond the short term. That Christianity often witnesses a tension between the conventions of institution keeping and the urge to provide fresh wineskins for the new wine of the gospel in various forms of radicalism is an understandable feature of this political dynamic.

The church as God's family also promises to reform society as a microcosm of the whole world. A people elect from every nation and thereby theologically understood to be the worldwide body of Christ threatens the givenness of borders and other *made* markers for defining identity. While one's identity as a political agent may be bound up with nation-state conceptions of citizenship, the universal church shows that one's most significant identity is not a political one thus conceived, nor should the meaning of "political" be restricted to such a narrow range.[11] What is properly or in the first order political about democracy is not what Lindsay maligned as "machinery of political democracy" but is instead what he called a "democratic common life." For the unity required for any such machinery to work must either result from something more fundamental than the formal structures or, where unity does not already exist, from the state's propaganda.[12] Individuals will therefore exercise a democratic life through organizations – "congregations" – that are smaller than the state that depends on them to make its machinery work. Of course, the church may or may not actually be of this kind of service depending on the nature of the state, whether or not the church is granted an independent life of its own, and whether state propaganda transgresses the truthfulness Christians practice embracing in their exercise of being the church.

What I have referred to as the constitution of peoplehood asked about those to whom "the people" refers as well as the means by which they are gathered together. Responding to both questions yields for Christianity a kind of democracy that is free from assumptions about sovereignty and therefore from being primarily concerned with building and maintaining institutions. It also holds forth a fundamentally noncompetitive politics that may embrace the goods of a people far beyond procedural considerations.

THE LOCUS OF POLITY

Two questions follow from the previous section. First, if Christianity amounts to its own polity called the church or the congregation, what capacities does it possess as the result of its own constitution for identifying the truthlessness of competing political bodies such as the state? And second, what is the nature of the common life of such a community?

Ancient democracy prized the moral quality of *parrhesia* (boldness in speaking the truth), particularly in Athens. What is striking is how early Christian language and organization both appropriated and modified the Greek political concepts it inherited surrounding *parrhesia*. Christians made use of *parrhesia* in conceiving of the character of the body that deliberates over political questions. The *ekklesia* was originally a nonreligious designation for the group of assembled citizens who concerned themselves with the good of the polis while the practice of speaking with *parrhesia* is what marked the *ekklesia* as a special assembly. An *ekklesia*, and hence democracy, was judged according to whether it was capable of producing people able to speak the truth with boldness. *Parrhesia* is a moral quality of a person, not a political character of an organization. Even so, a virtuous polis will be responsible for forming citizens who were capable of speaking in this way, which would on occasion include the necessity to speak fearlessly *against* the majority of citizens and the general drift of the polis.

Early Christians transformed *parrhasia* away from strictly denoting the right and impulse to speak freely in the assembly. It came to designate the bold preaching of the gospel. Now the church was the true assembly (*ekklesia*), not because it was a place where the truth of the common life of the polis was free to be spoken, but because the particular truth about Jesus Christ was proclaimed. The citizens of the heavenly city proclaim the good of the life of its citizens and, by extension, of all people and all nations. This is a powerful illustration of how the locus of polity is redefined in light of the gospel.[13]

Considering the role of *parrhesia* for premodern democracy also highlights a contrast with democracy in its liberal form. In Athens, worry about the loss of *parrhesia* – a loss for which the polis should ultimately be held responsible – began almost as soon as champions of Greek democracy identified its importance. Euripides's *Ion*, for example, not only upheld this key democratic virtue; it also served as a warning to the audience of his day that Athens was already in danger of undervaluing it and hence losing democracy altogether. *Ion* disconnects the truth-telling virtue from sovereignty by showing the human Creusa speaking out against Apollo's lies. As a virtue crucial for democracy, it embodies the necessity for a polis to cultivate the determination of its citizens to speak truth about what is good for the common life more so than the liberal idea of ensuring that a polis grants the right to speak freely. There is also a reverse to *parrhesia*: a genuinely democratic polis will enrich the people's readiness to welcome an uncomfortable truth from the minority, a *moral* quality that contrasts with liberal emphasis on majority rule (despite efforts to safeguard minority rights). Ancient democracy goes far beyond this; the majority must cultivate vigilance for truth that they may not now know, possess, or allow.

Christians adopted and adapted *parrhesia* for their own uses based in part on identification of a democratizing impulse at the heart of the church's constitution and life. What is its shape? In arguing that democracy is modeled on the Christian congregation, Lindsay further described how the priesthood of all believers has implied a principle of human equality, especially among Puritans and other radical Protestants who more readily than others saw equality rooted in a common baptism. Members of the body of Christ are baptized "into Christ" irrespective of race, gender, wealth, and social standing. The church's first council (Acts 15) was persuaded that God's Spirit alighted on both Jews and Gentiles alike just as the Holy Spirit's discretion alone explains the variety of charismata found throughout the church. What Yoder refers to as the rule of Paul where "everyone must be given the floor" is an ecclesial practice of hyperdemocracy, which I will discuss in the following section.[14] It is, for example, how the Friends run meetings, concerned especially with not overpowering an unconvinced minority through majority votes because doing so neither solves the problem nor convinces the unconvinced. Furthermore, if church members are understood to be animated and enlivened by the same Spirit that blows where it wills, then the procedures of centralized and bureaucratized democracies violate the democratic vision.

Yet the social and political implications of the Spirit's work – in baptism and in gifts – have been far from uniform. For example, in seventeenth-century colonial America, slave owners worried about evangelizing slaves for fear that, should the slaves be baptized, they would need to be freed. In September 1667, the Commonwealth of Virginia passed legislation declaring that "the conferring of baptism does not alter the condition of the person as to his bondage or freedom."[15] This was good news for slave owners, no doubt, who could now share the gospel with their slaves without hesitation and now "freed from this doubt may more carefully endeavor the propagation of Christianity by permitting children, through slaves, or those of greater growth if capable, to be admitted to that sacrament." There is no reason for the churches to think that baptism has radical economic and political correlates. Despite legislators' intentions, however, the democratizing and leveling thrust of this practice in time proved impossible to manage, as revealed in the movement for abolition. Other historical examples would reveal more direct associations between Christian baptism and democratic politics.

If baptism joins diverse members into one body – an *ecclesial* body, if not a body that is immediately *political* in other senses – then a kind of Christian realism about sin and corruption pulls in the opposite direction. Reinhold Niebuhr argued that Augustine's political thought takes seriously the human tendency toward limited self-interest, a tendency that democracy seeks to diffuse.[16] Here "one man, one vote" – a twentieth-century slogan often invoked in universal suffrage movements – might be thought less to do with empowering the otherwise politically disenfranchised as would be the case for the Spirit's accord with nonelites described in the preceding section. Rather, it has more to do with limiting the reign of self-love, particularly among those who would exercise its power over others excessively. Checks and balances found in certain modern democratic forms, especially constitutional ones, are sometimes praised for concretizing this realistic appraisal of humanity. By some accounts, liberalism's separation of church and state is not unrelated to this realism.

At the same time, there exists a range of ways in which these impulses work themselves out within the many churches and denominations. Some defend hierarchy as Thomas Aquinas did, seeing it as an analogy to the order of beings in the created order, some lesser and some greater. What is Christian about this arrangement is that those with more power are given it for the sake of those who have less. While this strikes modern, democratic sensibilities as paternalistic, dependence of some people on others inscribes a kind of hierarchy. Yet it is a hierarchy of charity and service rather than of worth, a point that has been worked out by a number of thinkers following the Second Vatican Council, especially in liberationist and feminist circles.

Theorists in the tradition of political liberalism have often noted that although individuals are not equal with each other in their *actual* spiritual and physical capacities, they are equal in their *right* to them. One theological model for this conception of service is found in Jesus, whose self-emptying (kenosis) in the incarnation was displayed in welcoming and serving "sinners" while also deeming that the church's primitive leadership be comprised in large measure of nonelites such as uneducated fishermen. Augustine reflected on the fact that, where the good news is believed, it must owe to the power of what is proclaimed and the miraculous works that accompany it rather than the credentials of those who proclaim it.[17]

A related exegetical matter concerning the verb *kenoo* in Philippians 2:7 (Christ "emptied himself") turns on whether Paul here intends the incarnation – in which the cosmic hierarchy is upset – or whether he intends the cross and Christ's moral commitment to humility.[18] This debate over New Testament interpretation reflects a fundamental tension in subsequent political theology: that between hierarchy and equality. Where political hierarchy is seen to be analogous to God's ordering of the cosmos, Christ's kenosis is likely to translate into a moral injunction for the powerful to be as a shepherd to their flocks even while they are charged with upholding what God has ordained. However, where political hierarchy is understood to conflict with the "upside down" quality of God's kingdom in which the last will be first (Matt. 20:16), Christ's kenotic act is likely to translate into a more ontological upending of the order of things brought by the incarnation.

On the question of the nature of the community's common life, it is notable that, in our day, liberalism and democracy have become nearly synonymous. Premodern democracy had tended to be relatively small scale, hence its analogue in the churches being the *congregation*. The local assembly is not only the most common unit of public deliberation, but is also the model of a universal society. This understanding has been worked out theologically in at least two ways.

The first reflects the catholic and universal nature of the church centered on the Eucharist as the shared fellowship of all Christians worldwide. Yet because any one gathering of Christians for receiving the Eucharist is also the body of Christ, the presence of God to that gathering is not understood to be incomplete by including only the local congregation. The Eucharist is the principle of unity and the bishop is its office. Together, these ensure that the local feast being celebrated is a genuine instance of the union that the whole church is. The local congregation likewise participates in the life of the universal church by being an actual instance of it. Therefore, the local congregation is not merely part of a more important whole; rather, local sacramental acts are determinative practices dignified in their status before God.

Recent scholarship shows that the significance of the congregation has shifted over time, identifying the mystical body of Christ exclusively with the Eucharist rather than the more complex interplay of the Eucharist together with the congregation gathered around it (and gathered by it). Henri de Lubac argued this thesis in his work *Corpus Mysticum* where he traced the change in this term's meaning from the fourth to the thirteenth centuries.[19] The Eucharist migrated away from sacramentally associating both the individual with the local community and the universal church through the body of Christ. The dialectic between the congregation and universal church broke down. While *corpus mysticum* once referred to the Eucharist and *corpus verum* referred to the ecclesial body, de Lubac documents how these two terms changed place with each other. By the end of the twelfth century they had reversed so that the presence of the sacramental body came to denote what is real while the reality of the church is a mystery. The church as a visible social body, created and sustained by God, became subordinated and more recently even became redundant in the face of the emerging secular body politic. De Lubac shows how the Eucharistic language that had formerly bound the church as a community comes instead to be applied to society as a whole and eventually to nation-states and liberal democracy. This shift is partly the product of and partly responsible for the ascendency of modern liberal politics.

Wolin and Cavanaugh developed de Lubac's argument along parallel lines. As late-medieval and early-modern political thought eventually led to the prominence of the nation-state as the principle of unity for thinkers like Rousseau, Hobbes, and Locke, the church's own claims to unity begin to pose a threat to the unity nations seek (see Chapter 12). The modern individual is thus rescued for liberty from the traditional groups to which they belonged. Cavanaugh describes the "state as savior" for this reason – it holds forth a new vision for redemptive community characterized by democratic belonging. But for Cavanaugh, the ability for the modern, liberal state to claim deliverance for individuals depends on the locus of public devotion "migrating" away from the church. The political landscape has become dense with alternatives to the church's unity, whether it is in the form of monarchs or nation-states or dreams for generating a worldwide economy in equilibrium. This migration, however, began much earlier when theology lost the connection between the local congregation and the Eucharist, which is to say, the time when the local *was* universal. This shifted focus paved the way for democracy to be reconceived on a larger scale: as a *system* as opposed to a *vision*.

A polity's locus is the *place* where it lives its common life. Christian communities practice baptism, Eucharist, and speaking the truth with *parrhesia*, all of which sit uncomfortably with their place in liberal orders. Equality is both necessary for and derives from the common lives of congregations that understand their peoplehood through baptism. Christian unity exceeds that of nation-states in the intensity of both its local and worldwide expressions when they are held together sacramentally and not sacrificed to surrogates. The specific truthful speaking of the gospel replaces general, truthful speech as the mark of where the democratic virtue of the polis will be found. Taken together, this is the church's locus – the heavenly city locates the earthly city just as heavenly citizenship discloses the nature of citizenship more narrowly defined.

THE HYPERDEMOCRATIC IMPULSE

The unquestionable ideal of the church's theocratic orientation might appear to set it at odds with democracy: the church strives to be guided by the will of God, not the will of the people. However, South African theologian John De Gruchy distinguishes between the democratic system and the democratic vision, though he argues that both owe something to Jewish and Christian thought and practice.[20] The democratic vision is one that De Gruchy describes as being threefold. It is a vision for a society that promotes the equality of all people while also respecting the ways that people differ; it likewise depends on and advances genuine freedom for all people while social responsibility of one form or another prevails over individual self-interest; and it also seeks justice for all people commensurate with the vision of equality such that, for example, economic disparities are overcome. At its best, such a vision shapes procedural questions, determines institution building, funds civic participation, and guides public life.

According to De Gruchy, the fact that this democratic vision always outpaces the concrete forms that democracy takes in any historical circumstance not only implies a kind of messianic eschatology, but also indicates something of a *hyperdemocratic impulse* influenced first by ancient Israel's prophetic tradition. Samuel warned Israelites about the abuses of monarchical power concentrated in the hands of a human ruler rather than God reigning as king (1 Sam. 8); Amos warned of God's judgment on greed and lack of compassion and economic justice and envisioned a plumb line against which to measure Israel's own attempts at a just society; specific kings came under the rebuke of other prophets such as Nathan and Elijah; and still others like Isaiah and Jeremiah described Judah's coming destruction as evidence of God's displeasure. The dynamic of warning, judgment, destruction, and restoration is initiated by exodus in which God makes a people and instructs them in righteousness and justice; it is carried out in exile and a prophetic declaration of God's promises and expectation that they will be guided by a vision that seems to outpace concrete reality. As an eschatological vision, it is one that God will cause to prevail on the earth. Human sociality will finally be characterized by the exact correspondence of reality with vision.

With Christ, the Christian vision of the kingdom of God fulfills the prophetic tradition. A distinctive aspect of the kingdom is its emergence within history in the person and ministry of Jesus Christ. Here, the liberation of Israel from Egypt is fulfilled in individual bodies of lepers and in despised members of society ("sinners," prostitutes, and tax collectors); equality is presumed and made evident in Jesus's disregard for established patterns of hierarchy and political and religious authority; and justice is achieved by the kingdom's preference for the poor and "the least." This clearly supplies a kind of democratic vision.

Where the gap between any political vision and concrete reality suffers the accusation of being utopian, there is usually a severely secularized version of this Jewish and Christian eschatology. It has either become a flight of fancy, ultimately inimical to everyday life (Marx, Freud), or else has been rendered unreachable for the simple reason that transcendence has been erased. Liberal democracy may be especially guilty of the latter because it lacks a theologically identifiable *telos* and so, as I will argue, represents an idolatrous model of social relations.

Liberalism's proceduralism may be interpreted as the result of disaffection with a democratic vision or eschatology. Yet not all *actual* democratic forms fit the procedural model. When small communities or organizations form to pursue common goods – a community-based youth sport league, an advocacy group for nonviolence, an after-school program – they are refusing to act like the individuals that liberalism assumes they will or indeed must be if democracy is to flourish with the aid of liberalism. Moreover, their unity around a pursuit of some good is irrespective of liberalism's attention to base self-preservation. This is at once an empirical challenge to liberal theory – we might ask whether that theory correctly described human nature and natural human behavior – and a demonstration that nonliberal forms of democracy may exist and flourish within a liberal democracy when they are unsupported or even positively discouraged by liberal thought forms.

Because liberalism suspects that anything *shared* that goes beyond the most basic factors will tread on individual freedoms, it discourages nonprocedural democratic forms. These violate the supposition that there exists only the individual and the state where the state, in turn, functions to safeguard individual liberties. Against this, where there exists a plurality of communities aimed at achieving goods, liberalism concerns itself with unity; freedom solves the problem of pluralism. For many in the West, perhaps most prominently in the United States, this is the meaning of citizenship, what it means to belong to the nation-state. What is an American? It is someone who believes that freedom solves the problem of pluralism (perhaps adding: and is willing to fight for it).

Liberalism asks how a society of moral strangers is going to live together peacefully. Its response has been to give these strangers the freedom to pursue their moral lives within whichever communities of moral friends they happen to belong to. Liberal freedom is the freedom to do pretty much whatever you want, recalling the way that *parrhesia* moves from a moral quality of people to an institutionally guaranteed right to free speech.

However, in thinking that a liberal society has solved the problem of pluralism with freedom, citizens may permit themselves to live most of the time believing that there is much less disagreement than there actually is. The back-and-forth between pluralism and freedom functions as a very powerful myth that reinforces belief in liberal politics. When freedom fails to deal with the problem of pluralism as it has promised, forms of disagreement normally disguised by the power of the myth now come to the fore, provoking unease. Debates in the United States over "Obamacare" show what happens when the myth begins to outlive its usefulness, or simply when a people are confronted with parts of it that are wearing thin.

What Obamacare debates showed is not just disagreement over health care, but *disagreement over disagreement*. Opponents of health-care reform legislation did not simply disagree with the legislation. They actually found it useful to draw attention to the *fact* of disagreement, thus compounding it. The fact that there was opposition became a way of pointing to what happens when American society tries to answer questions about the common good as though this nonliberal project were part of its charge. The unpleasantness of the debate indicated to some that discussing questions of the common good disrupts the good peace that usually results from neglecting them. Instead, what is good is letting smaller communities of moral friends (such as private hospitals) decide among themselves. The state exists only to grant these groups the freedom to do so. The greater the discord, then, the stronger the case that democracies should keep from talking about forbidden topics, that we should not try to gain consensus on topics we have learned to avoid in the name of peace.

This sort of disagreement runs deep in the United States. It accounts for the strong distinction between what Andrew Manis refers to as two competing notions of civil religion.[21] Most people will immediately think of what Manis calls the *exclusivist/homogenous civil religion* that, in a particularly extreme form, identifies the scope of citizenship narrowly as being for "us," distrusts outsiders, and points to a particular Christian American heritage. This exclusive/homogeneous civil religion prevails if it can both get by most of the time thinking that it has prevailed (strengthened by the myth) and immobilize the alternative when it arises by demonstrating how it threatens homogeneity. Nevertheless, many proponents of American health-care reform had a fundamentally different set of ideas about what America is: what Manis calls the *pluralist civil religion*. For these, America is not a fragile house of cards that is always threatening to collapse at the slightest overreaching or at every attempt to find agreement among moral strangers. Instead, for these proponents America requires a spirited give-and-take among moral strangers that may often be a long and drawn-out process. This vision of America is reinforced by stories of struggle like civil rights and the abolition of slavery.

The thing to notice is that the homogeneous/exclusive civil religion believes that what makes America great is the distance-preserving solution ("freedom") that has been set forth to address the problem of pluralism. Struggle, then, is a sign that something has gone wrong and that it is about to break apart. The pluralist civil religion, by contrast, finds greatness in America's system of open collaboration and persuasion that goes along with the beneficence of pluralism. Conflict is not a sign of disruption, but an indication that something is going well – that society is converging on what is good. Citizens discern through their struggle that they are on their way to a better (by definition more progressive) society, one steadily being purged of injustice.

These are two different visions for how a society of moral strangers ought to get along. But a particular phenomenon occurs when those devoted to the homogeneous/exclusivist vision find themselves not only opposing a particular health-care proposal but also safeguarding the particular form that unity must take according to that vision by pointing to societal conflict as evidence that unity is under threat. Those with a pluralist vision, however, interpret the conflict in a more sanguine way, as Martin Luther King Jr. said in his famous "Mountaintop" speech in support of striking sanitation workers in Memphis in 1968: "the greatness of America is the right to protest for right."[22] Without the struggle for democracy to approach its hyperdemocratic vision, rights are interpreted to be mere procedures.

Versions of nonstatism, such as Christian anarchism, represent other instances of the Christian impulse toward hyperdemocracy. Christian anarchists in particular explicitly reject the state as a bearer of legitimate authority on grounds that it usurps a role to which God alone has the right. When it depends on the use of force for ensuring its survival, furthering its economic ambitions, or assuring social conformity, the state discloses its fundamental opposition to the peaceable kingdom that Jesus announced. Christian anarchism may be seen as a school of thought ultimately critical of democracy in its move to transcend it.

Some Anabaptist renunciations of "the sword" come closest to a democratic vision that strives to take the political import of Jesus's teaching at face value. For example, according to Yoder, a Mennonite, the church's refusal to grasp the reins of sovereign power does not mean that it is refusing "politics," but only that *hoi poloi* must be rescued from its undue sovereign associations. The politics of Jesus (also the title of Yoder's 1972 book) is not so much a disposition against traditional political power, but a radical alternative to it that depends on a different polity and is oriented to a different *telos*. For this same reason, Christian anarchists reject the charge that they must supplant the prevailing form of government with a rival. For some, including theorists like Jacques Ellul, Vernard Eller, and the Catholic Workers, noninterference by the affairs of the state represents the proper relation between church and state by encouraging the church's political activity in areas that, in liberal orders (owing to Hobbes), tend to be the state's domain.

Here religious liberty, for instance, arises not from a theory of the state's neutrality with respect to all faiths, but from Christianity's own reflection on its evangelical mission. If as a corollary to the human freedom required to hear and respond to the gospel the Christian must be free to preach it, then this freedom must be understood as an internal quality of the good news rather than its condition for flourishing.[23] The habit in the West of conceiving of religious liberty as a matter of "church and state" privileges the question from the side of the state by asking whether and how sovereign power must be construed in order to permit and tolerate a variety of religious practices. When asked from the church side, however, the Christian anarchist understands that she is asking a theological question that presents freedom as a human good able to be seen against the background of humanity's end as beatitude and friendship with God.

As a posture, nonrevolutionary Christian anarchists cultivate a principled indifference to the state. Ellul approvingly cites the Russian exile Nicolas Berdyaev: "The death of one man, of even the most insignificant of men, is of greater importance and is more tragic than the death of states and empires. It is to be doubted whether God notices the death of the great kingdoms of the world; but he takes very great notice of the death of an individual man."[24] This is the key characteristic of hyperdemocratic Christian anarchy. The curtain is pulled back, revealing that Caesar is just a man and even the queen needs to be saved. Human pretenses do not impress God and, with practice and discipline, Christians can likewise learn to be unimpressed.

Whatever shape it takes, Christianity's hyperdemocratic impulse is guided by a vision of human community and life with God that shares with biblical prophets the hope that God is bringing this about. It thereby surpasses liberal proceduralism and impatience, both of which result from a deficient or absent eschatology. Where peace alone is the goal of a diverse society, genuine differences risk being overlooked, neglected, and disdained as "peace, peace" is prematurely declared when in fact there is no peace (Jer. 6:14), an admission made more honestly in light of a more complex *telos*. The alternative is not only truncated vision but also an impulse that is less than fully democratic.

CONCLUSION

The contemporary challenges facing ecclesial polities are only instances of what may be increasing levels of wider dissatisfaction with modern democratic forms, especially those that theorize and formalize democracy at significant remove from local levels. It is possible that Lindsay's focus on the congregation as opposed to larger ecclesiastical forms may derive from this significance of scale. Theological objections to liberalism notwithstanding, it is not surprising that today's prodemocracy movements typically have in their sights much smaller social bodies than the nation, recognizing the greater likelihood that at these levels, people will be better represented and the diverse segments of the populace will be heard. Even so, the church's democratic vision need not be limited by liberal imaginations because the constitution of peoplehood, the locus of polity, and the hyperdemocratic impulse will always surpass the formal aspect of the organization of people. And a people's yearning for a vision beyond the current state of affairs will be best sustained by practices of living together that are undergirded by hope that God's kingdom is not far off but is at hand.

Notes

1 A. D. Lindsay, *Religion, Science and Society in the Modern World* (London: Oxford University Press, 1943), p. 19.

2 John Rawls, *A Theory of Justice* (Cambridge, MA: Harvard University Press, 1971).
3 William T. Cavanaugh, *Theopolitical Imagination: Discovering the Liturgy as a Political Act in an Age of Global Consumerism* (London: T&T Clark, 2002), p. 39.
4 Pierre Manent, *An Intellectual History of Liberalism*, trans. Rebecca Balinski (Princeton, NJ: Princeton University Press, 1994), p. 29.
5 Vernard Eller, *Christian Anarchy: Jesus's Primacy over the Powers* (Grand Rapids, MI: Eerdmans, 1987), p. 21.
6 *The Epistle to Diognetus*, ch. 5.
7 Alexis de Tocqueville, *Democracy in America*, ed. J. P. Mayer and Max Lerner, trans. George Lawrence (New York: Harper and Row, 1966), p. 47–8, emphasis added.
8 Michel Foucault, "Truth and Power," in *Power/Knowledge Selected Interviews and Other Writings 1972–1977*, ed. Colin Gordon (Harlow: Pearson Education, 1980), p. 121.
9 John Howard Yoder, *The Priestly Kingdom: Social Ethics as Gospel* (Notre Dame, IN: University of Notre Dame Press, 1984), p. 154.
10 Sheldon Wolin, *Politics and Vision*, exp. ed. (Princeton, NJ: Princeton University Press, 2004), p. 602.
11 E.g., see William T. Cavanaugh, "The World in a Wafer: A Geography of the Eucharist as Resistance to Globalization," *Modern Theology* 15.2 (April 1999): 181–96.
12 A. D. Lindsay, *The Churches and Democracy* (London: Epworth, 1934), p. 48.
13 Craig Hovey, *Bearing True Witness: Truthfulness in Christian Practice* (Grand Rapids, MI: Eerdmans, 2011), chs. 4–5.
14 John Howard Yoder, *Body Politics: Five Practices of the Christian Community before the Watching World* (Scottdale, PA: Herald, 1992), p. 69.
15 Virginia Slave Laws Digital History: http://www.digitalhistory.uh.edu/disp_textbook.cfm?smtID=3&psid=71 (accessed July 27, 2015).
16 Reinhold Niebuhr, "Augustine's Political Realism," in *The Essential Reinhold Niebuhr: Selected Essays and Addresses*, ed. Robert MacAfee Brown (New Haven, CT: Yale University Press, 1986), pp. 126–41.
17 Augustine, *The City of God*, ed. and trans. R. W. Dyson (Cambridge: Cambridge University Press, 1998), XXII:5; pp. 1113–14.
18 Sarah Coakley, "Kenosis: Theological Meanings and Gender Connotations," in *The Work of Love: Creation as Kenosis*, ed. John Polkinghorne (Grand Rapids, MI: Eerdmans, 2001), pp. 192–210.
19 Henri de Lubac, *Corpus Mysticum: The Eucharist and the Church in the Middle Ages*, trans. Gemma Simmonds (Notre Dame, IN: University of Notre Dame Press, 2007).
20 John De Gruchy, *Christianity and Democracy* (Cambridge: Cambridge University Press, 1995).
21 Andrew M. Manis, *Southern Civil Religions in Conflict: Civil Rights and the Culture Wars* (Macon, GA: Mercer University Press, 2002), esp. p. 193f.
22 Martin Luther King Jr., "I've Been to the Mountaintop," *The Words of Martin Luther King, Jr.* 2nd ed. (New York: Newmarket, 1996), p. 93.
23 Yoder, *Body Politics*, p. 67.

24 Cited in Jacques Ellul, *Jesus and Marx: From Gospel to Ideology*, trans. Joyce Main Hanks (Grand Rapids, MI: Eerdmans, 1988), p. 172.

Further Reading

Cavanaugh, W. T., *Theopolitical Imagination: Discovering the Liturgy as a Political Act in an Age of Global Consumerism*. London: T&T Clark, 2002.
De Gruchy, J., *Christianity and Democracy*. Cambridge: Cambridge University Press, 1995.
de Tocqueville, A., *Democracy in America*, ed. J. P. Mayer and M. Lerner, trans. G. Lawrence. New York: Harper and Row, 1966.
Eller, V., *Christian Anarchy: Jesus's Primacy over the Powers*. Grand Rapids, MI: Eerdmans, 1987.
Hovey, C., *Bearing True Witness: Truthfulness in Christian Practice*. Grand Rapids, MI: Eerdmans, 2011.
Lindsay, A. D., *The Churches and Democracy*. London: Epworth, 1934.
Manent, P., *An Intellectual History of Liberalism*, trans. Rebecca Balinski. Princeton, NJ: Princeton University Press, 1994.
Niebuhr, R., "Augustine's Political Realism," in *The Essential Reinhold Niebuhr: Selected Essays and Addresses*, ed. R. M. Brown. New Haven, CT: Yale University Press, 1986.
Rawls, J., *A Theory of Justice*. Cambridge, MA: Harvard University Press, 1971.
Wolin, S., *Politics and Vision*, exp. ed. Princeton, NJ: Princeton University Press, 2004.
Yoder, J. H., *The Priestly Kingdom: Social Ethics as Gospel*. Notre Dame, IN: University of Notre Dame Press, 1984.
  Body Politics: Five Practices of the Christian Community before the Watching World. Scottdale, PA: Herald, 1992.

11 Capitalism and Global Economics
PHILIP GOODCHILD

> If anyone strikes you on the cheek, offer the other also: and from anyone who takes away your coat do not withhold even your shirt. Give to anyone who begs from you, and if anyone takes away your goods do not ask for them again.... If you lend to those from whom you hope to receive again, what credit is that to you? Even sinners lend to sinners, to receive as much again. But love your enemies, do good, and lend, expecting nothing in return. Your reward will be great, and you will be children of the Most High; for he is kind to the ungrateful and the wicked.
>
> (Luke 6:30, 34–35)

While the foundation of Christian political theology in the teachings of Jesus was directly economic, concerned with coats, shirts, begging, giving, credit, returns, and rewards, it has always been considered somewhat "unworldly." The offenses of such teaching to modern sensibilities are numerous: security of life and property is abandoned; the free distribution of wealth is to extend to those who are not productive, and even to enemies; competition and market valuation are undermined by offering something for nothing; and the fundamental human drives for pleasure, wealth, power, and survival are renounced. What relevance can such unworldly teaching hold for the "real world" of capitalism and global economics?

THE CRISIS OF RELEVANCE

"What after all are these churches now if they are not the tombs and sepulchres of God?"[1] – so Friedrich Nietzsche's madman announced a change in the nature of believing that had occurred by the end of the nineteenth century: to believe in God was henceforth to mourn a loss, to feel nostalgia for a living and vital presence. For simply being devout is no longer enough: in an era of capitalism and global economics, matters of wealth creation and good conduct seem above all to be technical matters, requiring worldly expertise. Both theists and atheists may find God of limited relevance to their career development. Any contribution of political theology would seem strictly limited by harsh economic realities. For what good would it do to offer advice on Christian principles to economic agents, to overthrow sinful structures of oppression, or to reconstitute a Christian economy of giving, within a broader context of market competition? Market forces will restore equilibrium: in the long run, only those corporations that maximise their self-interest through the rational and technical pursuit of profit will thrive and survive. The mystery of free market capitalism is its power to spread itself universally: to appropriate land and resources, to incorporate workers and productive enterprises, and to reorder societies around an instrumental rationality. Not only has free market capitalism overthrown its rival of state socialism, not only has it undermined anticolonial struggles for liberation, but it has eroded traditional religious cultures ordered around rituals, customs, festivals, and offerings in favour of material gain, freedom of choice, and monetary signs of wealth. It can no doubt do so again. Under free market capitalism, only the rational pursuit of profit and growth counts, while other forms of belief and behaviour fade into relative insignificance – they do not grow. Whatever form it takes, Christian political theology experiences a crisis of relevance. As D. Stephen Long puts it:

> The problem in the modern world is not that people no longer desire theological truths but that theology does not matter. I mean that in the most literal sense. Theology has no flesh, no embodiment in daily existence. Instead, it is forced to the margins of everyday life to some sacred noumenal realm which is neither rational nor irrational.[2]

This disembedding of theology from practical, "real world," economic life has resulted in a condition where Christian commitment may express a personal preference, but such preferences make little difference to the overall distribution and performance of roles. Citizens of all faiths and none may often be largely indistinguishable from each other. This secular age, where religious belief is at best an option or a longing for "spirituality," differs markedly from preceding ages, where disbelief was almost inconceivable. As Charles Taylor helpfully explains, in premodern times God had a theoretical relevance in explaining the source, meaning, and order of the cosmos, yet also a practical relevance as the source of moral and spiritual fulfilment, and even a social relevance as the authority that undergirds trust and social cooperation: "we are linked in society, therefore God is."[3] It was inconceivable that people could reason, desire, and trust without grounding their hopes in an anticipated unity of metaphysical, moral, and social aspiration: a personal God. The mere existence of reason and order, desire, and mutual cooperation were evidence of the fruitfulness of an orientation towards God. Yet times have changed, and a division of labour is in accord with the demands of efficiency and effectiveness: in the modern world, science provides a basis for theoretical knowledge, the market for the practical aspirations of producers and consumers, and the state upholds society with law and the enforcement of contracts. Commitment to God is no longer required for science, economics, or the state.

What, then, is the role of political theology? In the twentieth century, three broad approaches developed that have been introduced in earlier chapters in this volume. One option is to take the institutions of the state and the market as offering a framework for free human agency: it is then the duty of a Christian social ethics to advise governments, individuals, and civil society organisations on their responsibilities and duties of care for others. A second option is the "option for the poor": markets and states have been constituted to legitimate or overlook the dispossession, exploitation, and marginalisation of the poor; and it is the duty of liberation theology to unite and empower the poor in the overthrow of unjust and exploitative economic structures. A third option is metaphysical, contesting the modern presuppositions of the preceding options: both the anthropology of individual liberty that underlies much Christian social ethics as well as the conception of politics as a clash of forces that underlies the struggle for liberation. Ecclesial political theology laments the rise of individualism and the consequent reduction of liberty to the negative freedom of unrestrained market choice, as well as the rise of a politics based on competing interests and the consequent reduction of political strategy to manipulation of the state monopoly of violence. It emphasises the role of the church as a polis, a community for the formation of character, founded on the peaceful relations of gift exchange dramatised in the Eucharist.

Each of these options may lay claim to a healthy realism: it ought to be admitted that personal, corporate, and state responsibilities are significant realities in the contemporary world, just as sinful structures of oppression and exploitation are best identified by their victims and need to be overthrown; similarly, the modern configuration of science, market, and state rests on deeply impoverished conceptions of humanity, justice, power, and authority. One cannot help but feel the live force of each of these three rival versions of Christian political theology – the liberal, the socialist, and the ecclesial. If Christian political theology exhibits the kind of the fragmentation and confusion famously diagnosed as being present in moral philosophy by Alasdair MacIntyre,[4] so that each talks past the others in vivifying its own moral claims, this may perhaps be less a symptom of the pluralism inherent in the "postmodern condition" than a consequence of the fact that Christian commitments appear to be somewhat irrelevant to personal and corporate conduct in a capitalist global economy. For far from the global economy exhibiting moral confusion, it may be characterised as transmitting a greater disciplining of human conduct and aspiration than ever before, if only around economic imperatives. The power of ideas, whether in the form of morality, politics, or metaphysics, so crucial in shaping ancient, medieval, and modern civilisations, seems to have had its day: transformative ideas are now found in technology, marketing, and management. Christian political theology experiences a crisis of relevance because the individual decisions, social structures, and political cultures that have made the modern world are no longer the live sources of its power. Once capitalism has spread to a global economy, then economic imperatives take precedence over all others.

The perceived crisis of relevance may only be challenged when political theology comes to deal directly in economic terms. Indeed, a theological reading of the contemporary global economy may claim a greater realism than any purely secular alternative. The aim of this chapter is to introduce several inversions of perspective. First, "free market capitalism," with its inexorable economic imperatives described by global economics, is simply inaccurate as a description of the global economy. Nevertheless, this viewpoint is an ideological illusion, a necessary component in the workings of the global economy. Second, the power that imposes economic practices and imperatives is not strictly economic, but spiritual, best understood through a "theology of money." Third, this spiritual dimension is present in global finance, which is a manipulation of time as much as it is of money. Here the practical endeavour to turn time into money masks the inherently theological dimensions of living through time. Fourth, it is only in the most radical and "unworldly" pronouncements of Jesus that the direct relevance of political theology to the global economy can be discerned. Because this approach is founded in the "unworldly" teachings of Jesus, it is with their superior realism that we must begin.

LIFE AS GIFT OF TIME

Economics has been characterised as the study of "how people make decisions under conditions of scarcity."[5] In practice, such decisions are delimited to acts of exchange: the buyer who offers the highest price successfully obtains the scarce item. In practice, value in exchange is measured in terms of money, and money is always scarce: there are always more purchases, investments, and philanthropic uses of money that could be made. The themes of scarcity and exchange delimit the concerns of economics to the kinds of goods that can be yours insofar as they are not mine, and mine insofar as they are not yours: they are *competitive* goods, and moral choices are reduced to those between self-interest and altruism. These are goods that may be appropriated, and they are largely rights and material benefits. Alongside these, we should note the existence of *cooperative* goods, "goods that can only be mine insofar as they are those of others, that are genuinely common goods":[6] environmental benefits such as clean air; state benefits such as security and law, social practices, institutions, forms of knowledge, and learning; and even markets. These are goods that one inhabits or participates in, goods that cannot become the object of individual appropriation. They are studied outside economics in science, politics, ethics, and metaphysics. But where are we to place money, or at least the value embodied in money? Money is, of course, an object of competition and appropriation, and yet money only holds value insofar as it is a social institution, that is, as it is collectively valued by others. It appears to be at once a competitive and a cooperative good. Yet might it not also point to a further class of goods? I can only realise the value of money when I spend or invest it, when it is no longer mine, whereas when I save money I can do nothing with it. What about those goods whose value can only be mine insofar as I renounce possession of them?

Jesus's hard sayings on lending without return, giving to anyone who begs, and not asking for goods once they have been taken, may seem counterintuitive when applied to competitive goods such as shirts. Cooperative goods, by contrast, demand reciprocity in order to be effectively established; they are both gift and obligation. Jesus's sayings ask us to look for a class of supererogatory goods, gratuitous or *theological* goods, where we "only possess what we renounce; what we do not renounce escapes from us."[7] Such goods would be characterised by the paradox of chiasmic inversion: "For those who want to save their life will lose it, and those who lose their life for my sake, and for the sake of the gospel, will save it. For what will it profit them to gain the whole world and forfeit their life?" (Mark 8:35–36) Life, here, does not belong to the "world": it does not consist in the abundance of one's possessions (Luke 12:15). Yet neither does it consist straightforwardly in home or community, in dwelling and participation, without a prior renunciation (Luke 18:29–30). In the Sermon on the Mount, the most unworldly and uneconomic conclusion, *"Therefore* I tell you, do not worry about your life, what you will eat or what you will drink, or about your body, what you will wear" (Matt. 6:25), is prefaced by a threefold account of what constitutes a life:

> Do not store up for yourselves treasures on earth, where moth and rust consume and where thieves break in and steal; but store up for yourselves treasures in heaven.... For where your treasure is, there will your heart be also.
> The eye is the lamp of the body. So if your eye is healthy, your whole body will be full of light.
> No one can serve two masters.... You cannot serve God and wealth. (Matt. 6:19–24)

Life consists in *investment*, "storing up treasure," whether through expenditure of time in endeavour, expenditure of time in waiting, or investment of one's heart's desire; life consists in *attention*, so that the health of the eye illuminates the body; and life consists in *devotion*, whether to God or to wealth. In each case, the life one receives is the life that one gives: "For with the judgement you make you will be judged, and the measure you give will be the measure you get" (Matt. 7:2). These are the chiasmic or theological goods, received only insofar as they are given.

Insofar as it is life that is given as investment, attention, and devotion, then Jesus's sayings on giving without return simply recall us to an ontological necessity: we can only live our desire by investing it, live our time by spending it, live our lives by paying attention, and order our lives by service, whether in the service of pleasure, fame, power, status, wealth, others, or God. So the theological dimension of political economy concerns how life should be lived forwards, in freedom and responsibility, giving due attention to that which matters and to that which is decisive. It concerns how the time that is given is to be invested or spent – and, unlike money, time can only ever be given, never lent at interest or even in expectation of return. This theological dimension of spending time is occluded when the economy is reduced to exchange, as though time did not matter and wealth is conceived in terms of values recorded in accounts. Yet it remains present under conditions of crisis or uncertainty where economic activity consists in an investment of credit. For it is in moments of crisis, when the "world" falls apart, that the direct relevance of the most radical and "unworldly" of Jesus's pronouncements to the contemporary economy can be discerned: economic life is constituted by *credit*, by the offering of investment, attention, and devotion.

CREDIT AND FINANCE: ON TIME AND MONEY

There is a sense in which credit is a theological good. Of course, when granted as an advance of money, credit seems like a good that can be appropriated. By contrast, when "credit" is conceived as creditworthiness, a reputation for honesty, integrity, and solvency, then it seems like a cooperative and communal good. But the actual act of issuing credit is an irreversible donation of time, attention, and trust that only exists insofar as it is donated. We may therefore distinguish between *credit* and *exchange*, between uses of time and uses of money.

The simplest kind of credit arrangement is a deferral of payment – time is required for buying before merchants can sell, for investing in capital before production, or for paying wages in advance of income from sales.[8] In some circumstances, time is all that is required to facilitate economic activity by delaying settlement of an exchange – such as in hire purchase. Yet a more efficient and advantageous credit arrangement is an advance of money – still deferring the time at which settlement of the debt takes place, but enabling the money to be spent in the meantime by the recipient. If one buys a commodity on credit, a financial intermediary advances the money and becomes the creditor, while the retailer simply transacts an exchange. So where credit relations involve an ongoing relationship, bound by risk, uncertainty, and responsibility on both sides, an exchange relation is instantaneous, redeeming one party from the credit commitment with its risks and responsibilities. The time of credit brings responsibilities; money, by contrast, brings freedom. Thus the creation, monitoring, and settlement of debts have an intrinsically different temporal structure to the exchange of debts for money.

One finds these two kinds of relations throughout the financial sector: there are "primary markets," where investments are agreed; futures and derivatives created and sold; and new kinds of assets are invented, and these operate as a series of over-the-counter transactions between privileged representatives of financial institutions who engage in private business based on their networks of trust. The most useful resource for any broker is their book of contacts. It is important to emphasise that in practice such transactions are nothing like the "markets" described by economic theory – business is conducted behind closed doors or over the telephone without transparency or publication of prices, and with limited opportunities to compare prices.[9] Credit relations are formed within social relations of prestige, privilege, trust, and patronage. Indeed, many of these derivative transactions are straight swaps, having no need of or recourse to money. Only subsequently are these debts and securities bought and sold on the secondary markets, the public financial markets that approximate more than any other market to those of economic theory because of their liquidity.

What is the essential difference here? Credit relations are affected by uncertainty, and so rely on privilege and trust to ensure that behaviour will be predictable. Exchange relations, by contrast, enable the pricing of risk, and more accurate levels of insurance – the pricing of options (for example) turns time and risk (as volatility) into money. To the extent that risk can be priced, a security has a determinate value, it can be freely bought and sold at that value, and advances of money can substitute for temporal commitment: it has *liquidity*. The more confidence in the price, the more liquid the asset; and the more liquid the asset, the more confidence in the price, and the more likely that investments will be made. The aim of much financial activity such as securitisation, therefore, is to turn long-term, illiquid investments as credit relations into liquid assets that can be traded on the market.[10] Here it is the confidence in liquidity that makes a market possible. Selling, of course, means exchange of the asset for a more liquid one: money. Money is a liquid asset because it is regarded as a safe store of value; money, in turn, is a safe store of value because it is a liquid asset that can be exchanged for anything else.

Notice, then, that it is a *faith* that makes markets possible; and this faith is inherently unrealistic because it represses the temporal reality of credit. There is a contradiction between the illusions that one must implicitly accept as a participant in financial markets – that markets are efficient, risk can be priced, debts should be repaid, financial agents are free, and wealth is private property – and a broader picture of sudden breakdown and default, where credit, which is a measure of the degree of trust and cooperation at work in economic life, is subsequently perceived as debt, an obligation and a cause for discipline and austerity. One represses the reality that financial investments are ongoing temporal relations of risk and responsibility, and that the pricing and liquidity of risks merely passes them on, without in any way reducing the underlying uncertainty. In this respect, secondary markets that increase overall investment also increase overall risk. Similarly, this faith represses the reality that the financial sector is structured by ongoing credit relations rather than simply by private ownership and exchange of assets, so that default does not merely result in a loss of wealth for some, but spreads by contagion. Furthermore, one represses the reality that the market only exists as an act of will, an affirmation of faith, and that risk is only priced accurately insofar as there remains a market. What remains uncertain is whether there will be any buyers at all, or that an asset will have any price. In the global financial crisis of 2007–8, the perception that "bad debts" were no longer liquid and could not be priced led to a contraction of credit, when financial institutions struggled to finance their long-term lending with short-term borrowing. There was a shortage of time, not money. It is this possibility of crisis that is the root of the enduring presence of unpriceable uncertainty. And behaviour in uncertainty is guided by faith, not by confidence: theology is required when markets fail.

What, then, is the ultimate aim or purpose of finance: Is it to save time or to make money? To offer liquidity, or payment of money in advance, is a strategy to save time because the advance can be reinvested prior to the final settlement. Yet to offer deferral of payment is to allow someone time to make money. Both time and money seem to be in reciprocal presupposition; neither is fundamental. The ultimate purpose of finance is investment – the investment of labour, psychic energy, attention and ingenuity as well as of socially approved value in productive activities and relations. Investment of credit is then something more than balancing a rate of return against a perception of risk: it is an investment of oneself, one's evaluations, and socially recognisable credit in something that one takes as mattering in conditions of extreme uncertainty.

There is, however, a striking reversal when freedom to evaluate and invest becomes constrained by debt. An advance of money may promise the freedom to spend it as we please, but once accepted credit turns into debt. Freedom is bought only at the expense of the demand to make money to repay debts. For those under pressure to repay debts, the entire world is viewed from the perspective of its capacity to yield money[11] – what counts as real, important, and decisive is that which yields a rate of profit or can be exchanged for the permanent, unpayable debts of a central bank. For in promising one seeks to make oneself a master of one's own time, but in practice we master ourselves only by becoming subservient to the record of our promise. Liberty conceived as the capacity to enter contracts is merely the power to subject oneself to the power of debt – in seeking to preserve our freedom we kill it off. Those who seek to save their lives will lose them, while those who lose their lives will gain them. In this respect, we can therefore distinguish between two theologies of finance: the theology of a debtor, who seeks to spend time and money in saving time and money, and the theology of a creditor, who has time and money to invest in what seems to be worthwhile. Public discourse and economic behaviour grounded in debt theology is all around us. What we are less practised in is credit theology, a discourse and practice based on spending lives, time, and money on that which is worthwhile. This is where a Christian political theology may become relevant: it promises redemption, the forgiveness of debts, and the restoration of grace and credit.

CAPITALISM AND THE GLOBAL ECONOMY

Do we really live in a system of global free market capitalism? The global economy, insofar as it is mediated by temporal relations of credit, cannot be reduced to exchange. Yet this is precisely what is done whenever it is conceived as a *market*, a meeting place for buyers and sellers where prices are determined by the balance of supply and demand. A price represents a future exchange value with anticipated hindsight: a price is an estimate of what an exchange value will prove to have been. Time is calculated in terms of money; credit is reduced to exchange. All the calculations of neoclassical economics rest upon such a conceptual reduction.[12]

Theologians, by contrast, can afford the time to take an interest in real life rather than in abstract models of markets. Such markets as there are tend to undermine their organising principle. Markets coordinate relations between strangers; they operate through competition; competition leads to winners and losers; success leads to capture of market share; numbers of participants in the market shrink; and the remaining relationships are forged as contracts between privileged competitors. As a consequence, a large proportion of global distribution takes place within multinationals rather than in open markets. Here relations are planned and hierarchically ordered: the vast majority of economic decisions are planning decisions.[13] So the ideal of a market is often more relevant in guiding decisions than any mechanism of the market is in determining outcomes.

Capitalism, in turn, can be considered to be an economic system where private enterprises drive the economy through saving, accumulation, innovation, and investment.[14] Yet today's capitalists bear little resemblance to those early Puritan industrialists described by Max Weber whose saving and investment were driven by their Protestant work ethic and salvation anxiety.[15] Saving is less significant than borrowing. For in a consumer society, investment and production are driven by so-called markets, consumer preferences enabled by consumer credit and manipulated by marketing strategies. Furthermore, when the activities of government typically constitute about 40 percent of gross domestic product, and government spending is funded by debt, then saving is no longer driving the economy. More significantly, saving is no longer a precondition for investment that is typically funded by borrowing. It used to be the case that one could only borrow the savings of others. Following financial deregulation, however, banks lend money first, and seek out reserves later. But the very act of lending money creates money through fiat, and adds new deposits to the banking system. The fundamental point is that in reality, in the system as a whole, lending is not limited by supply. There is no balance between supply and demand for credit, for credit creates its own supply of deposits. While the demand for credit may be unlimited, if credit is rationed this is because of risk: it is much more prudent to lend against collateral than to lend to a start-up company that will probably go bust. So what is true at a microeconomic level, that all economic entities including banks must balance their books, is not at all true at a macroeconomic level, where all banks may be highly leveraged. Leverage casts the economy adrift from the moorings of free market capitalism: it is the possibility of leverage across the financial sector as a whole that enables the financial economy to drive the productive economy by borrowing rather than saving, extending into the household sector to create a society based on debt; it is the possibility of leverage across all sectors of the economy that allows the possibility of financial crisis.[16]

At the level of real world institutions, the component of the economy that exceeds free market capitalism is the credit and banking system, the basis of money and finance. The overall level of debt in the economy is identical to the overall level of credit: it is a measure of trust, mutual cooperation, interdependence, and economic and financial activity. Such credit is the engine of global growth: when credit is expanding, there is more money available for investment and consumption. When credit contracts, however, debts have to be repaid with the debts of others, and there is a struggle to accumulate this scarce resource. An invisible hand has pulled the lever, converting economic competition from an engine of global growth into a war of all against all. For leaving real assets aside, net financial assets across an economy must amount to zero. In practice, then, there is no substantial money in the financial sector, including no true store of value and no true market: there are only debts, and the swapping of debts issued by one institution for another. Rather than the fiction of an entirely horizontal framework of market exchange between peers, the reality is a hierarchy based around a triangular relationship between three kinds of institutions and their apparently liquid debts – central banks who lend currency reserves, sovereign states who issue treasury bonds, and clearing banks (and other central banks) who hold reserve accounts at the central bank while offering clearing services and loans to others and operate at considerable leverage.[17] The basis for money is not liquidity on an open market, but a closed network of privileged institutions. The contractual relations between these institutions consist simply of swaps and debts, and if all such debts were settled there would be no financial system at all. At the apex of this system, the debts of the central bank can be continually refinanced and never repaid because they are liquid, and therefore not presented for repayment; they remain liquid, however, because they are required for the clearing operations of other banks; and they remain secure because central bank reserves never leave the central banks but are simply transferred between accounts of privileged institutions.

In the long run, it is faith that enables people to take on debts, it is faith that obliges people to repay debts, and it is faith that guides the moral conduct of repaying debts and balancing budgets. A faith in "free market capitalism," in saving and investment, in the justice of market pricing, and in fulfilling economic obligations is an essential component of the global economy. Capitalism, therefore, is best understood as a belief system and a set of accounting practices for moral self-discipline, rather than as an economic order based on saving and investment or a social relation between owners and workers: capitalism is the "social system in which capital is measured as an accumulated quantity in terms of exchange value."[18] The real economy is governed by a faith, rather than by a market mechanism or by a logic of capitalist growth.

THEOLOGY OF MONEY

Let us return to the striking reversal that occurs when credit, as freedom to evaluate and invest, is replaced by its mirror image, debt, as contractual obligation. Debts are conceived when relations of credit are given precise measurement, in terms of money, as well as a precise period for repayment. Once a debt has been repaid it will have proven to have been a simple exchange, when the elements of trust and risk are forgotten. Yet debt only appears as exchange with anticipated hindsight; while underway and under risk, its reality is more than can be counted in terms of money. This difference is acknowledged in communal societies that work on the basis of trust: they work most effectively when favours are not reciprocal, when debts do not exactly cancel each other out, for then each member of the community remains obliged to all others to offer further favours.[19] We owe almost everything we are to others, but it is difficult to imagine what it might mean to pay back our parents or become square with humanity.[20]

This natural system of mutual credit and enduring obligation is disrupted when credit is objectified as a finite and redeemable debt: freedom from social obligation may be bought by repayment, while failure to repay obligations, the very asymmetry that makes society function, is now regarded as unjust, or even criminal. As soon as unpaid debt is turned into a criminal offence in the name of justice, as soon as credit is detached from the real relations of trust between individuals, as soon as one falls victim to predatory loan sharks, then fear of recrimination can turn economic relations into a war of all against all. For one who is indebted by predatory lending there is a complex mixture of shame, righteous indignation, and frantic urgency to prevent debts from compounding: the world is reduced to a collection of potential dangers, potential tools, and potential merchandise – even human relations become a matter of cost-benefit calculation.[21] According to David Graeber, "by turning human sociality itself into debts, they transform the very foundations of our being – since what else are we, ultimately, except the sum of the relations we have with others – into matters of fault, sin and crime."[22]

The justice that demands the repayment of all debts may be a source of sin. There is an inherent relation between debt and a theological understanding of "sin," which names not simply an individual error or misdeed, but an entire perspective that possesses us and blinds us to what is true.[23] Wolfhart Pannenberg explains that sin "precedes all human acts as a power that dwells in us, that possesses us like our own subjectivity as it overpowers us." In summing up Protestant conceptions of sin, he notes that we engage in sin because it deceives us: "All of us sin because we think we can attain a full and true life thereby."[24] To sin is to be deceived about the true nature of wealth. For human choices, economic or otherwise, are limited by the things present to consciousness, yet we struggle to bring everything to consciousness so as to make it an object of choice. As Pannenberg puts it: "All that we can choose is the way in which we will be ourselves, at least within limits, and mostly indirectly by way of the objects and activities to which we devote ourselves, and always in admixture with illusions because we never have ourselves before us as objects, except partially."[25]

While the conception of capitalism outlined in the preceding discussion is primarily an ideology, grounded in a faith, it is the power of this ideology to be imposed upon us that requires a theological analysis as sin.

In my previous work, I have argued that this power is best conceived as a fourfold theology of money.[26] First, because money is both the measure of prices and the means of payment, it becomes effective demand, the means for the realisation of all other values. Whatever is valued in principle, the acquisition of money, or simply preserving the health of a fragile economic system, must come first. Money becomes the supreme value, because it is that which must be sought first, so that all other values may be obtained. It gives value to all other values.

Second, because money is merely a promise, the value of money is nowhere evident. Its value is transcendent, taken on faith; money is a sign of a value that is never seen.

Third, money measures the prices of assets, and the value of assets are based on speculative projections about their future value. Even when the value of assets crashes, the new value is no more real than the old because it depends on new expectations about the future. Value is composed essentially of speculative projections about the future, faith in the promise of what is to come.

Fourth, if money is created as a debt, then it includes an obligation to expand economic activity to repay the debt. Where common sense tells us that the goal of modern political life is the creation of wealth to improve standards of living, experience tells us that the goal of modern economic life is making profits. It is not a question of greed. All of us are dependent on individuals, corporations, and governments who are in debt, and there is a universal obligation to repay debts, and take out more debts, in order to prevent our fragile financial system from collapsing any further. The obligations of debt are the ultimate political obligations.

It is worth pausing to explore the theologico-political significance of this momentous occurrence in human history. Money has displaced God as the measure of the value of values. Where God decrees absolute values, money measures all values in terms of a potential rate of profit, and thus in terms of the production of more money. Money substitutes itself for all evaluation, producing a perspective of evaluation used by all in accounting, but which belongs to no one. The highest values are devalued.

The promises upon which we base our existence are the promises of others, for money is composed of the promises of central banks, governments, and commercial banks. We treat others as debtors rather than as creditors. This is the fundamental gesture of secularisation: time is regulated by debt, rather than by faith, hope, and charity. One consequence is the liberation of those with wealth from mutual obligations in society – wealth offers a secular redemption from social obligations. Wealth brings power to make one's desires effective, as well as freedom to choose which desires to exercise. Yet, in reciprocal relations of trade, goods and services are always provided by others. The one with wealth to spend has the power to command the promises of others. Where most people conform their work to the desires of others in order to obtain money, the power of complete self-determination belongs to those with wealth alone. The secular ideal of individual freedom is an ideal facilitated by money. Nevertheless, the freedom conferred by wealth remains an ideological illusion because it is dependent on others to produce and maintain it. Offering such freedom, money easily replaces God as the supreme value, the source of all values, the object of trust, and the source of universal obligation. Where God requires conversion of the soul, money lends itself to effecting the heart's most urgent desires.

Thus, on the one hand, money is that which gives mastery and has the power of making demands effective. On the other hand, money is that which places one in a position of helpless expectation. Money is the condition for entrepreneurial innovation, enabling true activity; however, money works on one's behalf in and through the labour of others. Debt is freely created through entering a contract; by contrast, credit is offered as an advance or opportunity, existing independently of whether the offer is accepted. The power of money, therefore, while it appears to be entirely subject to the human will, is that which calls into being the human will. It emerges from the imagination to become desire and then obligation. Its power consists in a promise of a vision of prosperity combined with the threat of exclusion from a share in society for those without wealth. Hence the one who believes money can do anything for them is the one who may be suspected of doing anything for money. Money is an evaluative perspective through which all reality may be seen; as a promise, this perspective imposes itself upon the world.

CONCLUSION

What, then, is the significance of such a political theology for capitalism and global economics? It offers the basis for a thorough and radical critique. It demonstrates how such matters remain truly theological, while secularisation is merely a mask for something more sinister. It gives an account of economic life that is neither grounded in the pessimism that humans are largely self-interested individuals in competition, nor in the optimism that humans are largely participatory members in a community that serves the common good. Instead, it regards humans as subject to the influence of spiritual forces in their most material interactions. It demonstrates how economic activity is largely constrained by debt. It invites us to consider how we may offer our lives as credit, and how we may treat others as creditors, in and through our economic relations.

It may be objected, of course, that this analysis of the global economy and human condition in terms of time, credit, and money could, in principle at least, be accepted by nonbelievers. In what sense, then, is this a political *theology*? Where is the specific difference afforded by Christian commitments and beliefs, by the intervention of grace, by participation in the sacramental community of the church? Yet this is precisely the intention of a kenotic, incarnational theology: theological concepts have to be taken from the realms of canonical texts, dogmatic formulae, and metaphysical abstractions and gain meaning from their application to life, however much they then unsettle the judgements of "the world." So far as this analysis conforms to reality, then it is capable of acceptance by all; so far as it fails, then it may be subject to effective external critique.

Nevertheless, the intention here is also to draw attention to a dimension of economic life that may be called "theological," and it is in this respect that it remains a political theology. It draws attention to the "theological" goods, the gifts of grace that are only received insofar as they are given away. Credit, investment, attention, desire, and life all possess this feature. The theological dimension of political economy concerns how life should be lived forwards, in freedom, responsibility, and uncertainty, where conduct is invariably guided by a kind of faith. When everything is reduced to accounts, what is overlooked is the experience of the economic subject as holding a particular perspective on reality, having unfulfilled desires, enduring hopes, and networks of trust. Instead of taking the value of values for granted, it is a relation to a future judgement of value that is crucial for economic behaviour. This future orientation takes us beyond the world of productive processes and the exchange of equivalent values. For in the very disciplining of life in relation to money, whether in seeking profits, recording accounts, or living in debt, the services one seeks from money become a reason for the spiritual service of money.

Beneath the appearance of free market capitalism we find a theology of money; beneath the nature of contemporary money we find the structure of credit; within the structure of credit we find the faith through which people invest themselves and their lives. Theology, therefore, lies at the heart of the global economic order in its most technical and worldly aspects. There is no crisis of relevance. There is merely a need to distinguish between bad theology and good theology, between sin and redemption, between counting others' debts and giving and receiving credit. Christian political theology should enable us to do precisely this.

Notes

1. Friedrich Nietzsche, *The Gay Science*, sec. 125, trans. Walter Kaufmann (New York: Vintage, 1974), p. 181.
2. D. Stephen Long, Nancy Ruth Fox, with York Tripp, *Calculated Futures* (Waco, TX: Baylor University Press, 2007), p. 72.
3. Charles Taylor, *A Secular Age* (Cambridge, MA: Harvard University Press, 2007), p. 42.
4. Alasdair C. MacIntyre, *After Virtue: A Study in Moral Theory*, 3rd ed. (Notre Dame, IN: University of Notre Dame Press, 2007).
5. Nancy Ruth Fox in Long, Fox, and Tripp, *Calculated Futures*, p. 34.
6. Alasdair C. MacIntyre, *Dependent Rational Animals: Why Human Beings Need the Virtues* (London: Duckworth, 2009), p. 119.
7. Simone Weil, *Gravity and Grace*, trans. Emma Crawford and Mario von der Ruhr (London: Routledge, 2002), p. 34.
8. Massimo Amato and Luca Fantacci, *The End of Finance* (Cambridge: Polity Press, 2012), p. 28.
9. Brett Scott, *The Heretic's Guide to Global Finance: Hacking the Future of Money* (London: Pluto Press, 2013).
10. Amato and Fantacci, *The End of Finance*, p. 71.
11. David Graeber, *Debt: The First 5000 Years* (New York: Melville, 2011), pp. 318–19.
12. See Steve Keen, *Debunking Economics*, rev. and exp. ed. (London: Zed Books, 2011).
13. Richard Werner, *A New Paradigm in Macroeconomics* (Basingstoke, UK: Palgrave Macmillan, 2005), p. 329.
14. Richard Duncan, *The New Depression: The Breakdown of the Paper Money Economy* (Singapore: John Wiley and Sons, 2012), p. 133.
15. Max Weber, *The Protestant Ethic and the Spirit of Capitalism*, trans. Stephen Kahlberg (New York: Oxford University Press, 2011).

16 George Cooper, *The Origin of Financial Crises: Central Banks, Credit Bubbles and the Efficient Market Fallacy* (Petersfield, UK: Harriman House, 2008).
17 See L. Randall Wray, *Modern Money Theory* (New York: Palgrave Macmillan, 2012), and Josh Ryan-Collins, Tony Greenham, Richard Werner, and Andrew Jackson, *Where Does Money Come From? A Guide to the UK Monetary and Banking System* (London: New Economics Foundation, 2011).
18 Philip Goodchild, *Theology of Money* (London: SCM, 2007), p. 84.
19 MacIntyre, *Dependent Rational Animals*, p. 100.
20 Graeber, *Debt*, p. 62.
21 Ibid., pp. 318–19.
22 Ibid., p. 387.
23 Wolfhart Pannenberg, *Systematic Theology*, Vol. 2, trans. Geoffrey W. Bromiley (Edinburgh: T&T Clark, 1994), p. 262.
24 Ibid., p. 263.
25 Ibid., p. 260.
26 Goodchild, *Theology of Money*.

Further Reading

Amato, M., and L. Fantacci, *The End of Finance*. Cambridge: Polity, 2012.
Bell, D. M., *The Economy of Desire: Christianity and Capitalism in a Postmodern World*. Grand Rapids, MI: Baker Academic, 2012.
Cassidy, J., *How Markets Fail: The Logic of Economic Calamities*. London: Penguin, 2010.
Chang, H.-J., *23 Things They Don't Tell You about Capitalism*. London: Penguin, 2011.
Cooper, G., *The Origin of Financial Crises: Central Banks, Credit Bubbles and the Efficient Market Fallacy*. Petersfield, UK: Harriman House, 2008.
Duchrow, U., and F. J. Hinkelammert, *Property for People, Not For Profit: Alternatives to the Global Tyranny of Capital*. London: Zed Books, 2004.
Goodchild, P., *Theology of Money*. London: SCM, 2007.
Graeber, D., *Debt: The First 5000 Years*. New York: Melville, 2011.
Long, D. S., and N. F. Fox, *Calculated Futures*. Waco, TX: Baylor University Press, 2012.
Polanyi, K., *The Great Transformation: The Political and Economic Origins of Our Time*, 2nd ed. Boston, MA: Beacon Press, 2001.
Sung, J. M., *Desire, Market and Religion*. London: SCM, 2007.
Wray, L. R., *Modern Money Theory: A Primer on Macroeconomics for Sovereign Monetary Systems*. Basingstoke, UK: Palgrave Macmillan, 2012.

12 Political Theology as Threat
WILLIAM T. CAVANAUGH

Companions are generally not adversaries. Those who pick up the *Cambridge Companion to Christian Political Theology* will probably expect to find therein a certain friendly disposition to political theology in some form. But educated readers today can hardly be unaware that political theology is considered a threat in some circles, a bane to human civilization. Especially since prominent terror attacks in Western countries signaled the beginning of the twenty-first century, political theology has often been held in contempt. For many observers, the rise of fundamentalism is especially worrisome because of the volatile mixture of politics with theology. Anytime the merely mundane questions of how to organize a society politically get sidetracked by supramundane questions of the will and law of God – so the story goes – the irrationality and transcendence-seeking passions of religion can only lead to confrontation and chaos. Combining politics with theology is like dropping bullets into the cup of the raving lunatic on the street corner.

Letters to the editor and op-ed pieces commonly treat some version of this story as obvious. They are encouraged by polemics from the "new atheists," Christopher Hitchens, Sam Harris, Richard Dawkins, and the like. Rather than address the idea of political theology as a threat in its crude form, however, I would like to take it in its most sophisticated form, and examine the much-discussed argument of Mark Lilla in his book *The Stillborn God: Religion, Politics, and the Modern West*. Lilla is professor of humanities at Columbia University, a learned and thoughtful scholar. His book has won acclaim in part because it straddles academic and lay audiences. It is entertaining, lucid, and organized around a central metaphor – the Great Separation – that provides easy access to the central claim of the book. What is being separated in the Great Separation is precisely "politics" and "theology." And Lilla thinks that that separation is a good and necessary thing.

In the first two sections of this chapter, I unpack Lilla's argument, paying particular attention to his use of the term *religion* and its relationship with politics. In the next two sections, I critique his argument and show that the Great Separation is both an historical myth and theoretically incoherent. There is no reason to suppose that "religious" politics are any more inherently dangerous than "secular" politics, because there is no *essential* difference between the two. The religious/secular distinction is not simply a universal fact about human life, but is an ideological tool that can be used to privilege certain kinds of politics and anathematize others.

THE GREAT SEPARATION

Lilla begins his book by speaking in the name of "we." We had thought that the battles over revelation and dogmatic purity were relics of the past, but we now find ourselves confronted by enemies who take this sort of thing with deadly seriousness.

> We are disturbed and confused. We find it incomprehensible that theological ideas still inflame the minds of men, stirring up messianic passions that leave societies in ruin. We assumed that this was no longer possible, that human beings had learned to separate religious questions from political ones, that fanaticism was dead. We were wrong.[1]

Exactly who is this "we" is unspecified, other than the occasional "we in the West." The assumption seems to be, however, that all of "us" are equally puzzled by the persistence of political theology, which puts the contributors and many of the readers of the present *Cambridge Companion* in the peculiar place of not recognizing ourselves as part of the "we." "Political theology is a primordial form of human thought,"[2] Lilla tells us, but "we in the West find it difficult to understand the enduring attraction of political theology."[3] We are separated from political theology by four centuries of political thought that has had no need of reference to the divine. "We live, so to speak, on the other shore. When we observe civilizations on the opposite bank, we are puzzled, since we have only a distant memory of what it was like to think as they do."[4]

The book appears to open, then, with a rather stark separation between Lilla and his friends in Manhattan, reading the *New York Times* over an espresso macchiato, and the contributors to this volume, like me, who are still drawing pictures of bison on cave walls. But Lilla claims to be more nuanced than this. He casts his argument as a corrective to Western triumphalism, chiding those who complacently assume that secularization is simply the fate of all humanity, discovered first in the West but an historical inevitability as sure as the eventual triumph of science over obscurantism of all kinds. Lilla sets himself against such quasieschatological accounts of modernity.[5] "[I]t is we who are different, not they,"[6] says Lilla. Most of the world throughout most of history has seen politics and theology as inseparable. We are the odd ones who have undertaken this fragile experiment in separating the two. And there is nothing historically inevitable about it; the Great Separation is the result of some thoroughly contingent responses to problems that uniquely plagued Christian Europe. Lilla has in fact taken heat from sympathetic critics like Christopher Hitchens[7] and Rebecca Goldstein who think that Lilla has conceded too much on this point. As Goldstein puts it, "Lilla offers a cogent explanation for why Christian Europe got to the Enlightenment first. It doesn't follow that the Enlightenment's solution to the political problems religion universally poses is not a thing to be universally recommended."[8]

Lilla claims in his introduction that "[t]his book contains no revelations about the hidden course of history, identifies no dragons to be slain, has nothing to celebrate or promote, and offers no plan of action."[9] Despite his attempts to appear evenhanded and nonnormative, however, it is hard to read the book as anything but a sophisticated defense of the Great Separation. Lilla has more to promote than the normative conclusion that we must recognize the contingency of the Great Separation. As Goldstein comments, "One can read Lilla's story and draw precisely the opposite normative conclusions from the ones he asks us to draw: that the West's experimental testing and retesting of political theology, trying to see if there is any safe way of mixing politics and religion, has delivered an answer from which all may learn."[10] Indeed, Lilla's very attempt to present us as different, ours as a fragile experiment, exudes a definite Western exceptionalism that any reasonably alert reader would find hard to miss, and it is a short step from such exceptionalism to recommending our path as the ideal for all.

Lilla tries hard not to say that all other civilizations must follow our path. The choice, he says, is not between "the West and the rest," quoting Samuel Huntington's contentious phrase. The choice is rather between "two ways of envisaging the human condition. We must be clear about those alternatives, choose between them, and live with the consequences of our choice. That *is* the human condition."[11] There are only two choices, and there are "real dangers in trying to forge a third way between them."[12] Regardless of what is wise for other civilizations, Lilla makes clear what "we in the West" have chosen: "We have chosen to keep our politics unilluminated by the light of revelation."[13] This choice to reject political theology apparently encompasses all of "us" in the West, and it is total and irrevocable. Lilla has written a scathing dismissal of historian Brad Gregory's book *The Unintended Reformation* for its argument that the secularization of the West and the withering of Christianity as a public reality was not inevitable, that a world where theology mingles with politics and economics and science was not and is not impossible in the West.[14] For Lilla there can be no compromise and no plurality of types of politics; we have made our choice against political theology, and it is the only road open to us now.

The first chapter of Lilla's book presents Christian political theology as a worthy but inherently unstable way of approaching political life. Since time immemorial people have engaged in political theology, and the kind of politics it rendered depended upon the kind of God that was worshiped. The immanent God of pantheism, the absent God of Gnosticism, and the transcendent God of theism each produced a certain stable kind of political order. The Christian God, however, destabilized political order, because the transcendent Hebrew God became immanent in Jesus, and then, after his ascension, reigned *in absentia* like the Gnostic God. Different Christian schools of political thought stressed one or another of these attributes of God, leading to irreconcilable and conflicting political theologies.[15] Unlike Islam, Christianity was never directly political, and so Christian political thinking in the Middle Ages was a confused grab bag of metaphors and images.

> Withdrawal into monasticism, ruling the earthly city with the two swords of church and state, building the messianic New Jerusalem – which is the true model of Christian politics? For over a millennium Christians themselves could not decide, and this tension was the source of almost unremitting struggle and conflict, much of it doctrinal, pitting believer against believer over the very meaning of Christian revelation.... All politics involves conflict, but what set Christian politics apart was the theological self-consciousness and intensity of the conflicts it generated – conflicts rooted in the deepest ambiguities of Christian revelation.[16]

Lilla goes on to say that these conflicts "reached a crisis in the Protestant Reformation and the bloody religious wars that followed,"[17] but he has inflated the usual tale of liberalism born in the sixteenth- and seventeenth-century "Wars of Religion" by tracing this crisis back to the nature of Christian political theology. But this is not enough; the "Wars of Religion" become a verdict, not only on Christian political theology, but also on the combination of religion and politics – political theology – as such: "Hanging in the balance was the very legitimacy of the primordial form of argument that has existed since the beginnings of civilization, and that we have called political theology. The crisis in Christian politics was the trigger of a much larger intellectual crisis with implications extending far beyond a few European kingdoms."[18]

Despite his claims to his argument's contingency and modesty, then, Lilla raises the stakes well beyond contingent events in European history to a general argument about the possibility of any politics that takes theology seriously; hence the stark choice he offers us. The brevity and sketchiness of his one chapter on Christian political theology leaves the reader with the distinct impression that he was never really very interested in – or knowledgeable about – the details of Christian theology. Lilla never attempts any historical account of the "unremitting struggle and conflict" over doctrine that supposedly characterizes the whole of the medieval period, nor does he explain how such conflicts resulted in violence. How and where exactly did arguments over Christology and the Trinity lead to war? How and where exactly did the "withdrawal into monasticism" spark conflict with other models of Christian politics? There was unquestionably a great deal of conflict and violence in medieval Christendom, and there was undoubtedly a diversity of political theologies, but Lilla provides no evidence that the latter was the cause of the former. At this point of the argument, innuendo suffices to establish the "greatest lesson" of Christian history: "that entering into the logic of political theology in any form inevitably leads into a dead end."[19] The six subsequent chapters of the book, which are quite detailed and lie within Lilla's area of expertise, map the attempts of modern political philosophers to escape political theology once and for all.

RELIGION AND POLITICS

Significantly, when Lilla turns to discussing the philosophers who pioneered the Great Separation, he turns to talking about "religion." The Bible, Lilla points out, is silent about religion. There is no attempt in the Bible to explain why "man" is religious, what are the varieties of religious experience, and so on. The Bible has no conception of religion as a characteristic of human beings in general. The other "religions" of the world are explained in terms of idolatry; there is the worship of the true God, and there is the worship of false gods, but they do not together fit under the general rubric of human religious behavior.[20] Thomas Hobbes and other early modern thinkers, however, began to examine religion as a universal human phenomenon. This, for Lilla, is a decisive breakthrough. Early modern Stoics were not merely interested in Christian theological-political struggles. According to Lilla, they wanted to answer "the deeper question: what is it about religion that allows it to be distorted and misused in this way?"[21] Hobbes similarly began with questioning the nature of religion as such, but he thought that the Stoics' ideas about religion were too optimistic. The relationship between religion and violence was not accidental, according to Hobbes, but embedded in the very nature of religion.

Lilla's Hobbes is an unambiguously anti-Christian thinker intent on destroying the Christian conception of humans as made in God's image. The subject of theology is not God but man. Religion is born of human desire and ignorance. Humans have desires they do not know how to satisfy, so they turn in fear to gods for solace. But solace soon turns into fear of God. Because of their ignorance, they turn to prophets and priests to discern God's will, but the prophets and priests, also being ignorant, disagree. "A bidding war for souls gets under way, frenzy takes hold among believers intoxicated by bizarre superstitions and fanatical, intolerant claims."[22] The resulting violence is so difficult to contain because the stakes are so high: eternal life or eternal damnation. As Lilla puts it, "men fight to get into heaven."[23] Hobbes' solution was to establish the complete authority of one political sovereign, "the earthly God," who would swallow Christianity into a civil religion to serve the good order of the state.

For Lilla, Hobbes's system is not a political theology, despite the overtly theological terms in which Hobbes writes of his ideal sovereign. According to Lilla, we need not accept the absolutist implications of Hobbes's politics or Hobbes's extremely negative view of religion to appreciate Hobbes's accomplishment in "successfully changing the subject of Western political discourse." Hobbes has pointed the way out of the "labyrinth" of political theology. From now on, we can "discuss religion and the common good without making reference to the nexus between God, man, and world. The very fact that we think and speak in terms of 'religion,' rather than of the true faith, the law, or the revealed way, is owing in large measure to Hobbes."[24]

"Religion," and its relationship to politics, is the subject of the rest of Lilla's book. Lilla works his way through some other canonical figures of Western philosophy and shows that, although subsequent figures had a more sanguine view of religion, Hobbes had successfully changed the subject from God to religion as a human phenomenon. "By the nineteenth century continental Europe would be awash in nostalgia for its religious past and in dreams of a new, improved religious future. Not because Europeans had shifted their orientation back again, to the God of Abraham and his Messiah, but because so many had come to feel that the modern Epicureans had not given religion its due as a human phenomenon."[25] Here "Europeans" seems not to mean the ninety-some percent of Europeans who were practicing Christians in the nineteenth century, but rather the philosophers from that era that Lilla likes to read. Rousseau and Kant, for example, pointed in different ways to a post-Christian moral religion that was based not on revelation but on the workings of the human mind. Unlike Hobbes, who hoped that religion would fade to political irrelevance, Rousseau and Kant thought that religion was a universal human impulse that must be harnessed for the sake of a well-functioning social order.[26] Hegel similarly located religion in the human mind, but went further in advocating a grand mythology of shared spirit that would serve as the basis of service to the State. This latter line of thinking was born of the Great Separation that Hobbes made possible, but for the "children of Rousseau," as Lilla calls them, religion was not the problem. Christian political theology needed to be abandoned in favor of a religion purified by reason that would serve as a foundation for the political order.[27]

Though Lilla is sympathetic with these attempts to treat religion as something more than just the combination of ignorance and fear, ultimately he thinks that they undermined the Great Separation. They are based on "the fantasy that politics could still be connected to the grand themes of biblical faith ... without jeopardizing the principles of the Great Separation."[28] The children of Rousseau may have been right that religion can sustain hope and build community. "But as that lesson was learned, another was lost – that religion can also express darker fears and desires, that it can destroy community by dividing its members, that it can inflame the mind with destructive apocalyptic fantasies of immediate redemption."[29] The children of Rousseau opened the door for the recrudescence of political theology in the nineteenth and twentieth centuries, first in the form of German liberal theology, and then in the form of Karl Barth's and Franz Rosenzweig's reactions against liberal theology. Liberal theology tried to unite orthodox biblical theology with the romantic glorification of community, resulting in a thoroughly accommodationist nationalism; "in the end this liberal theology did what all political theologies eventually do: it sanctified the present, putting God's seal of approval on the modern European state."[30] Barth and Rosenzweig reacted against liberal theology's idolatry and emphasized the transcendence of God, the eschatological breaking in of God in history, and the necessity of human decision to follow God's commands. Lilla acknowledges that Barth and Rosenzweig did not think of redemption in political terms, and he recognizes Barth's role in forming the Confessing Church to resist the Nazi regime. Nevertheless, Lilla thinks that the theological discourse of "shock," "crisis," "decision," and so forth that Barth and Rosenzweig created was easily appropriated by the false messianism of Nazism.

> The generation that Karl Barth's *Romans* helped to form had no taste for compromise with the culture that their liberal teachers celebrated and that committed suicide in the Great War. They wanted to confront the unknown God, the "wholly other," the *deus absconditus*. They wanted to live in the paradox, feel the eschatological tension embedded in creation. They longed to inhabit a chiaroscuro world of "either-or," not "yes, but." They wanted to experience the moment of absolute decision and to have that decision determine the whole of their existence. Well! They did experience it.[31]

And it is here that Lilla chooses to end his story; Hitler is the face of political theology reborn. The last two figures Lilla introduces in the book are Friedrich Gogarten and Ernst Bloch. The former is a friend of Barth who turned propagandist for the Nazis, the latter an atheist who used biblical rhetoric to support Stalinism. The successors to Barth and Rosenzweig, according to Lilla, "fueled by messianic expectation and cultural despair, brought the modern Western argument over religion and politics to an inglorious close, by returning it to where it began."[32]

Where it began, of course, is in the violence and despotism of religion that Hobbes had sought to escape by making the Great Separation between religion and politics.

WHAT IS POLITICAL THEOLOGY?

So a book that "identifies no dragons to be slain" ends by playing the Hitler card. This strikes me as both disingenuous and grossly unfair. To insinuate that Karl Barth, one of the most significant Christian critics of Nazism, is somehow implicated in the rise of Nazism indicates a prejudgment that one simply cannot distinguish false gods from the true one, a judgment Barth would have considered both blasphemous and stupid. To end the story of political theology in the 1930s is also to ignore the tremendous postwar proliferation of political theologies. To think that "the modern Western argument over religion and politics" ended in World War II is to ignore Dietrich Bonhoeffer, Dorothee

Sölle, Johannes Baptist Metz, Gustavo Gutiérrez, Jon Sobrino, Rosemary Radford Ruether, John Howard Yoder, Stanley Hauerwas, and the host of other political theologians who do anything but what Lilla says "all political theologies eventually do": sanctify the present. A book about political theology that claims to be relevant to the present but doesn't cite any political theology written in the last eighty years is not to be taken as the final word on the subject, to put it mildly.

The problem with Lilla's book goes deeper than his ignorance of political theology; the deeper problem is in identifying what counts as political theology and what does not. Political theology is identified with appealing to God when answering political questions,[33] or it appeals "at some point to divine revelation."[34] Throughout much of the book, however, political theology is the bringing together of politics with religion, even when religion is seen as an entirely immanent human phenomenon. And sometimes the net is cast wider, such that not only political theology but "political messianism" or "cosmology" or "larger historical drama" comes under scrutiny. "Only with effort and a great deal of argument can people be trained to separate the basic questions of politics from questions of theology and cosmology.... As we have seen throughout this book, the temptation to break the self-imposed limits of the Great Separation and absorb political life into some larger theological or historical drama has been strong in the modern West."[35] Political theology is not just reflection on politics in light of Christian revelation, but also includes Rousseau's and Hegel's slippery-slope constructions of religion without appeals to revelation, Adolf Hitler's political messianism, and the atheist Ernst Bloch's justification of the atheist Stalin's totalitarian regime.

It would help if Lilla would identify what does *not* count as political theology, but – despite Lilla's assurances that "we" are separated by four centuries and a body of water from civilizations on the "other shore" – the only figures in the book that have gotten the Great Separation right are Hobbes, Hume, and Locke. All subsequent history – everything after the eighteenth century – Lilla tells as a story of backsliding into political theology. Besides a few references to "liberal democracy," Lilla gives no real indication as to what a purely mundane politics looks like on this side of the Great Separation, as we scratch our heads and marvel at the primitives on the other shore. Lilla even acknowledges that American political language is messianic, but somehow we remain free of the taint of political theology: "Political rhetoric in the United States, for example, is still shot through with messianic language, and it is only thanks to a strong constitutional structure and various lucky breaks that political theology has never managed to dominate the American political mind."³⁶

In order for the Great Separation to be something more than the gap between "Politics That Mark Lilla Likes" and "Politics That Mark Lilla Does Not Like," Lilla must show that a pure politics shorn of dangerous religious passions is an historical reality. He relies on the common legend of the European "Wars of Religion" of the sixteenth and seventeenth centuries as the moment at which Europeans finally realized that religion needed to be removed from politics for the sake of peace. According to Lilla, this historical moment is when Europeans asked "Why should disagreements over the Incarnation – or divine grace, or predestination, or heresy, or the sacraments, or the existence of purgatory, or the correct translation of a Greek noun – why should such disagreements threaten the peace and stability of a decent political order?"³⁷ The problems with this tall tale begin with the fact that no Great Separation resulted from the "Wars of Religion." In fact, the 1648 Treaty of Westphalia that brought the wars to a close recognized a Europe dominated by confessional states in which the state presided over established churches. Separation of church and state would not come for another century and a half, and then only on the other side of the Atlantic. Furthermore, the idea that "religion" was to blame for the wars ignores the obvious fact that Catholics and Protestants often collaborated against their own coreligionists. The Thirty Years War that brought the era to a close was, for its latter and bloodiest half, a war between the two great Catholic dynasties of Europe, with Catholic France and Protestant Sweden allied against the Holy Roman Empire. To narrate these wars as a product of quibbling over Greek nouns and not as a result of the state-building process – as "religious" and not "political" – is distorting, if not preposterous.³⁸

In response to critiques of his historical narrative, Lilla has stated that he intended to write only an analytical history of ideas, not a history of actual political transformations.³⁹ Setting aside the dubious desirability of a history of ideas that floats free of actual political and social and economic history, it is clear that Lilla does in fact make ample claims about how ideas and actual history intersect: Hobbes responds to the "Wars of Religion," Barth paves the way for Hitler, and the way "we" are – our contemporary politics – is all about the ideological choice we have made that put us on the opposite shore. Lilla must be able to show that the analytical separation of religion and politics is at least a coherent possibility in history, especially because he claims not only that "we" have made that separation, but that the separation is so decisive that we can scarcely think otherwise.

Lilla's narrative is driven by the idea that "we" have tamed the "messianic passions" that "inflame the minds of men" and "leave societies in ruin" by learning "to separate religious questions from political ones."[40] The notion that religion has a peculiar tendency to promote irrationality and violence is a common liberal trope. As Lilla rightly points out, the first thinkers to examine religion as a universal human phenomenon were early moderns like Hobbes. According to Lilla, such thinkers were thus able to understand religion's peculiar pathologies and isolate it from politics. But what Lilla does not grasp is that early modern figures like Hobbes did not so much *discover* the religion/politics distinction as *invent* it. Lilla regards the lack of analysis of religion in the Bible and in medieval Christendom as a peculiar form of blindness to one of the most salient and universal aspects of human life. But as a growing body of scholarship is making clear, the idea that something called "religion" can be separated out from the rest of life – politics, art, economics, social life – is a modern Western invention, not a universal truth about human life. In 1962, Wilfred Cantwell Smith went looking for an equivalent concept to religion in ancient, medieval, and non-Western cultures, and found none: there is in fact no "closely equivalent concept in any culture that has not been influenced by the modern West."[41] In Smith's wake, a host of other scholars has done detailed genealogies of the creation of the concept of religion in Europe and in lands colonized by Europe. Tomoko Masuzawa's book *The Invention of World Religions* concludes, "This concept of religion as a general, transcultural phenomenon, yet also as a distinct sphere in its own right ... is patently groundless; it came from nowhere, and there is no credible way of demonstrating its factual and empirical substantiality."[42]

Although Lilla acknowledges the historical contingency of the Great Separation, he nevertheless treats religion and politics as two universal phenomena to which there are only two approaches: either combine them or separate them. Lilla sees figures like Hobbes and Locke as the founders of modern Western politics because they are the first to try the latter approach. In reality, however, it was not the problem of religion that produced modern Western politics, but the other way around. Religion as a universal, essentially interior and nonpolitical human impulse was a creation of figures like Hobbes and Locke. By creating religion as an essentially apolitical impulse that springs from the inner psychology of the human individual, the theorists of the Great Separation could claim that church authorities should stick to the care of souls and stay out of the business of government and commercial enterprise. As Brent Nongbri argues in his 2012 book *Before Religion: A History of a*

Modern Concept, the new concept of religion was a product of a political move, "*isolating* beliefs about god in a private sphere and *elevating* loyalty to the legal codes of developing nation-states to loyalties to god."[43]

As Nongbri goes on to point out, "These provincial debates among European Christians took on a global aspect since they coincided with European exploration and colonial activities in the Americas, Africa, and elsewhere."[44] Even though local cultures had no separation of "religion" from "politics," the classification of the local culture as a religion served the interests of the colonists well. If "Hinduism," for example, could be seen not as the whole of Indian life, but as a religion, then what it meant to be Indian could be privatized and marginalized from the public business of government and commerce, which was administered by the British colonial authorities. For this and similar reasons, some native scholars in India, China, and Japan objected to the use of the term *religion* to classify the native cultures.[45] This remains the case today. As Richard Cohen points out, contemporary advocates of Hindu nationalism (*Hindutva*) reject the confinement of Hinduism to "religion." "The proponents of Hindutva refuse to call Hinduism a religion precisely because they want to emphasize that Hinduism is more than mere internalized beliefs. It is social, political, economic, and familial in nature."[46]

The point of all this is that the choice with which Lilla presents us – either combine religion and politics or keep them separate – is already rigged in favor of the latter because religion and politics are presented as two essentially separate universal human activities that only subsequently get mixed up together. Lilla acknowledges that most people throughout most of history have assumed that their worship life is inseparable from how society is organized, but he persists in assuming that religion and politics are identifiably distinct universal human phenomena. Lilla presents separating politics from religion as a difficult achievement, something like separating gold from its ore. The consequences are serious. In the West, for example, we speak of the "politicization" of Islam, as if Islam were a religion that was subsequently – and dangerously – mixed with politics. As John Esposito writes, to describe Islam as a religion already marks out Islam as an "abnormal" religion, precisely because it does not conform to the Western standard of religion as essentially apolitical.

> However, the modern notions of religion as a system of belief for personal life and of separation of church and state have become so accepted and internalized that they have obscured past beliefs and

practice and have come to represent for many a self-evident and timeless truth. As a result, from a modern secular perspective (a form of "secular fundamentalism"), the mixing of religion and politics is regarded as necessarily abnormal (departing from the norm), irrational, dangerous, and extremist.[47]

RELIGIOUS AND SECULAR

The claim that religion is a modern Western invention seems odd because religion in the West has been presented as having to do with the worship of God or gods, and such worship has been present in many cultures ancient and modern, Western and non-Western. This fact is undeniable. As Nongbri writes, however, "What is modern about the ideas of 'religions' and 'being religious' is the isolation and naming of some things as 'religious' and others as 'not religious.'"[48] To say that religion is a modern invention is to point out that the identification of a "religious" sphere of life separate from "nonreligious" or "secular" activities like politics, economics, sports, and so on is not simply an analytical description of different transcultural and transhistorical human activities but marks a normative choice about the correct way of organizing society.

Lilla assumes that there is a type of politics that is not religious – as opposed to political theology – and that the West has definitively embraced this form of politics over the past four hundred years. He believes, furthermore, that the West is less prone to violence now that we have rejected combining messianic religious passions with "secular" politics. There are a number of significant problems with this tale. As José Casanova points out, the separation of church and state that first took root in the United States was not a separation of religion and politics. Separating church and state in early America owed a great deal to dissenting Christian sects who wanted the government off their backs, but did not at all accept the terms of the Great Separation. Indeed, from abolition to temperance to women's suffrage to civil rights, some American social and political movements have been deeply intertwined with biblical faith.[49] The Enlightenment provides one important strand of American politics, but not the only one.[50]

More crucial, however, is the question of whether liberalism has in fact produced a separation of religion from politics and a diminishment of violence. Is the abandonment of Christian theological politics in the West an abandonment of theological politics, or merely, in John Bossy's phrase, the migration of the holy from one location to another? The question is particularly fraught because the boundary between religious and secular is fluid. In Lilla's own analysis, the divide between the two sides of the Great Separation shifts, depending on what Lilla wants to condemn and what he wants to commend. One side of the Great Separation is occupied by "religious" politics, which Lilla usually identifies with politics that make reference to God or revelation. But when it suits his purposes, atheist ideologies such as Stalinism and Nietzscheanism or ideologies of the *übermensch* such as Nazism appear on the opposite shore from the mundane and rational politics Lilla finds so congenial.

So can atheist ideologies count as "religious" too? If Lilla were to make this move, he would have plenty of company. Faced with the obvious fact that atheist ideologies caused tens of millions of deaths in the twentieth century, for example, Christopher Hitchens simply declares that totalitarianism is a type of religion too, thus adding atheists like Stalin and Kim Jong Il to his indictment of the violence of religion.[51] Lilla does not directly claim that totalitarianism is religious, perhaps because he recognizes that such a move would scramble the line between religious and nonreligious politics upon which the Great Separation depends. Lilla instead uses Christian theological terms like *messianic* and *eschatological* to describe totalitarianism, and associates Nietzscheanism and Nazism and Stalinism with figures like Gogarten and Bloch who supported those causes by drawing on biblical themes (even though Bloch was also an atheist).[52] Lilla is trying to have it both ways: he wants the Great Separation between religious and nonreligious politics to remain intact, but he also wants all the kinds of politics he doesn't like to end up on the opposite shore. Thus does Karl Barth the Nazi fighter, who is clearly on the religious side of the Great Separation, find – undoubtedly to his great surprise – that he has dragged the Nazis with him to his side of the river. As Casanova points out, one could surely draw a much more direct and plausible line from Hobbes's Leviathan to totalitarianism; Carl Schmitt, who was for a time the Nazis' favored legal theoretician, was a dedicated disciple of Hobbes.[53] To do so, however, would challenge the neat tale of separation that Lilla has constructed.

The idea of Stalinism and Nazism as religions is not implausible. There is a significant body of scholarship on various forms of Marxism and fascism as religions, and there is an English-language journal dedicated to the study of "political religions."[54] Such scholarship abides by a "functionalist" view of religion that defines religion not in terms of the substance of beliefs in gods or transcendence but rather in terms of how it functions in people's lives. The large body of scholarship on nationalism as a religion, for example, considers it irrelevant that people do not actually claim that nations are gods; the real question is to what they give their devotion. Pledging allegiance to the flag, ritualized singing of hymns to the nation, and especially giving one's life for one's country are all markers of religion for functionalists. One must take a functionalist approach in order to include atheistic ideologies on the religious side of the Great Separation. The problem for Lilla is that, if one applies functionalism consistently, the separation between religion and nonreligion upon which the Great Separation depends breaks down very quickly.

What do "we" do when we discover that we have "an elaborate and well-institutionalized civil religion in America" that, in sociologist Robert Bellah words, "has its own seriousness and integrity and requires the same care in understanding that any other religion does"?[55] If, as even Lilla admits, American politics is "shot through with messianic language," then perhaps political theology is not such a distant memory to us. Lilla might want to blame political theology in the West on the residue of Christian influence, but liberal democracy is perfectly capable of generating its own political messianism. As political scientist Colin Dueck writes, the United States goes to war "either for liberal reasons, or not at all."[56] At least since Woodrow Wilson, American military interventions have been launched under the missionary banner of spreading "freedom" – meaning open elections and open markets – to the world. The United States' National Security Strategy issued in the wake of the 9/11 attacks makes the political messianism of liberalism explicit: "These values of freedom are right and true for every person, in every society – and the duty of protecting these values against their enemies is the common calling of freedom-loving people across the globe and across the ages."[57] The document goes on to say that "our best defense is a good offense."[58] The Great Separation between fanatical, violent religion and modest, peaceful liberalism begins to look dubious when such evangelical zeal and the world's largest military apparatus are deployed on behalf of liberal democracy.

The great Hobbesian Carl Schmitt saw clearly that political theology was never rejected by the West; theology rather migrated from the church to the state. Thus Schmitt's famous lines from his 1922 book *Political Theology: Four Chapters on the Concept of Sovereignty*: "All significant concepts of the modern theory of the state are secularized theological concepts not only because of their historical development – in which they were transferred from theology to the theory of the state, whereby, for example, the omnipotent God became the omnipotent lawgiver – but also because of their systematic structure, the recognition of which is necessary for a sociological consideration of these concepts."⁵⁹ Paul Kahn's 2011 book *Political Theology: Four New Chapters on the Concept of Sovereignty* updates Schmitt's basic insight for the contemporary United States. As Kahn shows, ritualized nationalism, the invocation of states of emergency, the threat of nuclear destruction, the language of "sacrifice," and the way that the president embodies the people as in the Body of Christ – all can only be understood if our politics is understood theologically. The Great Separation that Lilla describes simply never happened; as Kahn writes, "the state is not the secular arrangement that it purports to be. A political life is not a life stripped of faith and the experience of the sacred, regardless of what we may believe about the legal separation of church and state."⁶⁰

Despite this demolition of Lilla's historical tale, however, Kahn regards the sacred as entirely of human making, and he stridently differentiates the kind of political theology done by people who believe God's will is relevant for political life from the kind of theological analysis of politics that he does. "The latter is an entirely secular field of inquiry, while the former expresses a sectarian endeavor that is no longer possible in the West."⁶¹ For Kahn, political theology is a secular analysis of the sacred structures people – including liberal democrats – continue to invent for themselves. Kahn, then, does not go far enough, because – like Lilla – he continues to regard the religious/secular boundary as simply part of the way things are. To say that American nationalism is a religion is to leave the religious/secular boundary intact. The real point goes deeper: the religious/secular distinction is a thoroughly contingent construction of Western societies undertaken for certain political purposes.⁶² There is no reason that we should accept as fact the fanciful idea that Christianity occupies a religious realm of fantasy and fanaticism while secular ideologies describe a mundane and sober "real world." Secular politics continues to try to fill a God-shaped hole that modernity has left. The most rational explanation for this persistent longing for God might just be the existence of God.

That Christians generally view the separation of church and state as a positive gain does not mean that the separation of theology and politics need follow. There are indeed noxious forms of Christian political theology just as there are destructive forms of secular political theology. People kill for all sorts of things: gods, flags, oil, freedom, the invisible hand of the market, and so on. The fact that people spontaneously worship all sorts of false gods does not necessarily mean that true worship is impossible. This is the basic biblical approach to idolatry. What needs to be separated is good political theology from bad political theology.

The idea that we can and must make a Great Separation between theological politics and sensible politics is a piece of bad political theology.

Notes

1. Mark Lilla, *The Stillborn God: Religion, Politics, and the Modern West* (New York: Knopf, 2007), p. 3.
2. Ibid., pp. 3–4.
3. Ibid., p. 4.
4. Ibid.
5. Ibid., pp. 5, 305–6.
6. Ibid., p. 5.
7. Christopher Hitchens, "God's Still Dead: Lilla Doesn't Give Us Enough Credit for Shaking Off the Divine," *Slate*, August 20, 2007, http://www.slate.com/articles/news_and_politics/fighting_words/2007/08/gods_still_dead.html (accessed July 27, 2015).
8. Rebecca Newberger Goldstein, "The Political and the Divine," *New York Times*, September 16, 2007, http://www.nytimes.com/2007/09/16/books/review/Goldstein-t.html?pagewanted=all (accessed July 27, 2015).
9. Lilla, *Stillborn God*, pp. 12–13.
10. Goldstein, "The Political and the Divine."
11. Lilla, *Stillborn God*, p. 13.
12. Ibid., p. 307.
13. Ibid., p. 309.
14. Mark Lilla, "Blame It on the Reformation," *New Republic*, September 14, 2012, http://www.newrepublic.com/article/books-and-arts/magazine/107211/wittenberg-wal-mart?page=0,0 (accessed July 27, 2015); Brad S. Gregory, *The Unintended Reformation: How a Religious Revolution Secularized Society* (Cambridge, MA: Harvard University Press, 2012).
15. Lilla, *Stillborn God*, pp. 24–35.
16. Ibid., pp. 51–2.
17. Ibid., p. 52.
18. Ibid., p. 53.
19. Ibid., p. 54.
20. Ibid., pp. 66–9.
21. Ibid., p. 74.
22. Ibid., p. 84.
23. Ibid., p. 85.
24. Ibid., p. 88.
25. Ibid., p. 108.
26. Ibid., p. 159.
27. Ibid., pp. 218–20.
28. Ibid., pp. 299–300.
29. Ibid., p. 260.
30. Ibid., p. 300.
31. Ibid., p. 285.
32. Ibid., p. 278.
33. Ibid., p. 3.

34 Ibid., p. 307.
35 Ibid.
36 Ibid., p. 307.
37 Ibid., p. 58.
38 I analyze the myth of the "Wars of Religion" at length in ch. 3 of my book *The Myth of Religious Violence: Secular Ideology and the Roots of Modern Conflict* (New York: Oxford University Press, 2009).
39 See Lilla's response to José Casanova on the Immanent Frame blog, http://blogs.ssrc.org/tif/2007/12/07/the-great-separation/ (accessed July 27, 2015).
40 Lilla, *Stillborn God*, p. 3.
41 Wilfred Cantwell Smith, *The Meaning and End of Religion* (New York: Macmillan, 1962), pp. 18–19.
42 Tomoko Masuzawa, *The Invention of World Religions: Or, How European Universalism Was Preserved in the Language of Pluralism* (Chicago: University of Chicago Press, 2005), p. 319.
43 Brent Nongbri, *Before Religion: A History of a Modern Concept* (New Haven, CT: Yale University Press, 2012), p. 6.
44 Ibid.
45 See ch. 2 of my book *The Myth of Religious Violence*, and Nongbri, *Before Religion*, ch. 6.
46 Richard S. Cohen, "Why Study Indian Buddhism?," in *The Invention of Religion: Rethinking Belief in Politics and History*, ed. Derek R. Peterson and Darren R. Walhof (New Brunswick, NJ: Rutgers University Press, 2002), p. 27.
47 John L. Esposito, *The Islamic Threat: Myth or Reality?*, 3rd ed. (New York: Oxford University Press, 1999), p. 258.
48 Nongbri, *Before Religion*, p. 4.
49 José Casanova, "The Great Separation," The Immanent Frame blog, December 7, 2007, http://blogs.ssrc.org/tif/2007/12/07/the-great-separation/ (accessed July 27, 2015).
50 William T. Cavanaugh, "Messianic Nation: A Christian Theological Critique of American Exceptionalism," in *Migrations of the Holy: God, State, and the Political Meaning of the Church* (Grand Rapids, MI: Eerdmans, 2011), pp. 88–108.
51 Christopher Hitchens, *God Is Not Great: How Religion Poisons Everything* (New York: Twelve, 2007), pp. 231–47.
52 Lilla, *Stillborn God*, pp. 251–95.
53 Casanova, "The Great Separation."
54 See the summary of this literature in Cavanaugh, *Myth of Religious Violence*, pp. 109–13.
55 Robert N. Bellah, "Civil Religion in America," in *American Civil Religion*, ed. Donald E. Jones and Russell E. Richey (San Francisco: Mellen Research University Press, 1990), p. 21.
56 Colin Dueck, *Reluctant Crusaders: Power, Culture, and Change in American Grand Strategy* (Princeton, NJ: Princeton University Press, 2006), p. 26.
57 Introduction to "The National Security Strategy of the United States of America," September 2002, http://www.state.gov/documents/organization/63562.pdf (accessed July 27, 2015).
58 Ibid.

59 Carl Schmitt, *Political Theology: Four Chapters on the Concept of Sovereignty*, trans. George Schwab (Cambridge, MA: MIT Press, 1985), p. 36.
60 Paul W. Kahn, *Political Theology: Four New Chapters on the Concept of Sovereignty* (New York: Columbia University Press, 2011), p. 18.
61 Ibid., p. 124.
62 See Talal Asad, *Formations of the Secular: Christianity, Islam, and Modernity* (Stanford, CA: Stanford University Press, 2003), pp. 187–94.

Further Reading

Asad, T., *Formations of the Secular: Christianity, Islam, and Modernity.* Stanford, CA: Stanford University Press, 2003.

Cavanaugh, W. T., *The Myth of Religious Violence: Secular Ideology and the Roots of Modern Conflict.* New York: Oxford University Press, 2009.

Dueck, C., *Reluctant Crusaders: Power, Culture, and Change in American Grand Strategy.* Princeton, NJ: Princeton University Press, 2006.

Gregory, B. S., *The Unintended Reformation: How a Religious Revolution Secularized Society.* Cambridge, MA: Harvard University Press, 2012.

Kahn, P. W., *Political Theology: Four New Chapters on the Concept of Sovereignty.* New York: Columbia University Press, 2011.

Lilla, M., *The Stillborn God: Religion, Politics, and the Modern West.* New York: Knopf, 2007.

Masuzawa, T., *The Invention of World Religions: Or, How European Universalism Was Preserved in the Language of Pluralism.* Chicago: University of Chicago Press, 2005.

Nongbri, B, *Before Religion: A History of a Modern Concept.* New Haven, CT: Yale University Press, 2012.

Scott, P., and W. T. Cavanaugh, eds., *Blackwell Companion to Political Theology.* Oxford: Blackwell, 2003.

Shedinger, R. F., *Was Jesus a Muslim? Questioning Categories in the Study of Religion.* Minneapolis, MN: Fortress, 2009.

Ends

13 Good Rule

PETER J. LEITHART

For the first millennium and a half of church history, Christian political thought was an effort to evangelize politics. This involved an effort to infuse the truth and demands of the gospel into political life. Rulers were expected to follow Jesus's teachings and Jesus's self-giving example was held up as an *exemplum* of royal conduct. Kings were supposed to exhibit the fruits of the Spirit in political as well as personal life. It also meant placing political history within the framework of the evangel, the history of redemption that culminates in the Father's gifts of the Son and Spirit. Though this effort continued into the modern era, political thought took a different path after the Reformation. Secular theorists examined political questions without reference to Jesus, his teachings, or the work of the Spirit. Christian thinkers often followed suit, confining the gospel to a "strictly soteriological" realm and viewing politics as a sphere of justice *rather than* love and mercy.

It is common to suggest that two strands run through the history of Christian political reflection. On the negative side are realists and "Augustinians" who, stressing the sinfulness of man, see civil government primarily as a postlapsarian restraint on sin. On this view, government does not aim to cultivate virtue, much less to instill the fruits of the Spirit, and kings are not expected to govern based on the specific values of the Christian gospel. Against this is the "Thomist" or "idealist" view that civil order is natural to man, that men are social creatures who come to a perfection of virtue only in political society.

This distinction is barely evident in patristic or early medieval writing on political themes. In patristic writings from the Latin West and Byzantium, in late patristic encyclopedists, and in advice books (the *speculum regiae*, or "mirror of princes") of the Carolingian era, "realist" and "idealist" strains are jumbled together without any theoretical apparatus to sort things out. Scholastics were more deliberate and systematic, but scholastic writers still exhibit the same mixture of realist and idealist strains. All were devoted to the evangelization of politics

GOOD NEWS OF GOOD RULE

The promise of "good rule" is one of the main themes of the Christian gospel. Jesus announced that the reign of God was breaking into creation, and this reign came to fulfillment in Jesus's own ascension to a heavenly throne. "Jesus is Lord" (*kurios*) is the fundamental Christian confession, inspired by the Spirit (1 Cor. 12:3). In a world of many lords (1 Cor. 8:5), there is only one *kurios kurion* (Rev. 17:14; 19:16). As commentators have pointed out (at least) for decades, *kurios* was in the apostles' time a title reserved for Caesar.[1] To call Jesus *kurios* was, at least, to relativize Caesar's claims, perhaps to challenge and subvert them. In an apocalyptic vein, the gospel announces that Satan, "prince of this world" (*ho archon tou kosmou*), has been "cast out" (John 12:31). In this, Jesus fulfilled the hope of Israel's prophets, that One from the line of David would come to establish his throne in justice and righteousness (Isa. 9:7) as the one shepherd to feed and guide the flock of Israel: "I, Yahweh, will be their God, and my servant David will be prince among them" (Ezek. 34:23–24; 37:25). Good rule *is* the good news: The time is fulfilled, and the bad rule of Satan and Caesar has given way to the reign of the crucified and risen Jesus.

The prophetic promise was never about the Messiah alone. Already at the beginning of Israel's history, Yahweh promised that kings would come from Abraham's seed, and sealed that promise with circumcision (Gen. 17:6, 16; 35:11). After exile, Yahweh said that "nations will come to your light, and kings to the brightness of your rising" (Isa. 60:3). The age of light would recapitulate the great age of Solomon, when kings and queens came to learn wisdom from David's son (1 Kings 4:34; 10:1–10). Instructed by Yahweh's Torah on mount Zion, the nations – and, preeminently, their rulers – would beat their swords to plowshares and their spears to pruning hooks (Isa. 2:2–4). We can make the same point pneumatologically: the Spirit who clothes the Messiah is the Spirit of good rule, equipping the Servant of Yahweh with wisdom and understanding, counsel and strength, so that he can judge justly, deal fairly with the poor and afflicted, and strike the wicked down with the breath and words of his mouth. Anointed by the Spirit, the king exhibits royal wisdom in his an unquenchable zeal for justice (Isa. 11:1–5; 42:1–4). Jesus devotes considerable time and attention to his *twelve* apostles because they are being prepared as rulers of the renewed people of God. This comes to fruition at Pentecost when the Spirit who filled Jesus descends on the apostles.

Following Daniel 7, the Apocalypse recounts this dissemination of good rule. When John first enters heaven, he sees twenty-four angelic ancient ones (*presbuteroi*) crowned and enthroned (Rev. 4:4), while the martyrs languish under the altar where their blood has been poured, crying for vindication (6:9–11). By the end of the book, though, the martyrs have taken the thrones and share in God's judgment of the nations (20:4). In the messages to the seven churches, Jesus promises authority (2:25–27) and a throne (3:21) to the faithful who overcome. By the end of the book, the martyrs have received those gifts. Revelation moves from the unveiling of the anointed *One* to the reign of the anointed *many*.

These hopes should not be spiritualized out of political existence. Israel's hopes were not directed to a disembodied, apolitical future. They looked to the Creator to prove himself to be what Abraham confessed him to be, the Judge of all the earth who does what is just (Gen. 18:25). They expected a revolution in world order that would break the fangs of predatory rulers and rescue the helpless (Luke 1:52).[2] Jesus died on the cross to make the saints a new Adamic people, a kingdom and priests who reign on *earth* (Rev. 1:6; 5:10).

The Bible offers a number of detailed portraits of what good rule looks like. Deuteronomy 17 prohibits three of the most common practices of ancient kings: building an offensive force of horses and chariots; enriching the treasury with gold and silver; forming marriage alliances by creating a harem that has side benefits that are decidedly *not* political (vv. 16–17). Solomon violated all three prohibitions and fractured the kingdom (1 Kings 10–11). Instead of devoting himself to typical royal behavior, Israel's king was to write out a copy of the Torah with the aid of the priests, so that he could study it "all the days of his life." A king who renounced the normal forms of security could be secure only if he learned "to fear Yahweh his God, by carefully observing all the words of this law" (Deut. 17:19). The king's proper place was *among* the people, not lifted *above* them (v. 20).

Most of its political instructions in the Torah are given to judges rather than kings. Judges were to love truth, hate bribes, and be capable of making judgments in disputes (Exod. 18:21). Yahweh repeatedly warned not to take bribes, which blind the wise and pervert the judgment (Exod. 23:8; Deut. 10:17; 16:19). Judges must resist both the sentimentality that would unjustly favor the weak and the cowardice that would cower before the powerful (Lev. 19:15).

In the Psalms and prophets, these instructions from Torah are translated into a vision of good rule focused on protection of the vulnerable and suppression of violent oppression. The ideal king of Psalm 72 judges the people with justice when he vindicates the afflicted, saves the children of the needy, and crushes the oppressor (vv. 1–4). Rulers who rule well refresh the land like "rain upon the mown grass, like showers that water the earth" (v. 5). Good rule is quite literally as essential to the well-being of the land as regular rainfall: if the powerful confiscate the produce of the poor or invaders plunder the land, the people cannot survive. In Psalm 82, Yahweh addresses an assembly of "gods" (v. 1), but it is clear from the context that they are rulers. He rebukes them because they use their power to judge unjustly and show deference to the wicked (v. 2). They should instead judge in favor of the weak and fatherless, "vindicate the afflicted," by delivering the weak from the hand of the wicked (vv. 3–4). Jeremiah exhorted the kings of his day to administer justice by delivering victims from robbers (21:11–12) and promised that the Lord would raise up a Davidic branch who will do just that (23:5–6). Ezekiel's shepherd-king not only defends the weak when they are attacked but also searches for the sheep that wander, in order to feed them, bind the broken, strengthen the sick, and destroy the fat cannibalistic sheep (Ezek. 34:11–19). Rulers are called to restrain and punish crime, and to protect the weak. In the Hebrew Bible, however, these two responsibilities are seamlessly united: restraining the wicked *is* protection of the weak.

In scripture, wisdom is a royal virtue (1 Kings 3), and Proverbs is a virtual mirror of kings. Written mostly by Solomon to his son (1:8), it offers a detailed sketch of the wisdom of a ruler. All Israel, but especially her kings, were to "get" and "prize" wisdom (4:7) more than silver, gold, and precious gems (3:13–17; 16:16). Kings above all were to bind kindness and truth as garlands around their necks, trust in Yahweh, renounce self-regard, honor Yahweh, and submit to the discipline of the Lord (3:1–12). Kings above all had to retrain their words (10:8, 10), pursue mercy (11:17), reject the lifestyle of the sluggard (6:6–9; 13:4; 19:24; 20:4). Not only in their personal interactions, but also in political life, "a gentle answer turns away wrath, but a harsh words stirs up anger" (15:1). "Better is a little with righteousness than great income with injustice" is an axiom of public life, not merely a piece of pious advice (16:8). These few citations are, of course, representative. The entire book of Proverbs should be read as an advice book for good rule.

Throughout these scriptures, Yahweh who is Wisdom provides the model of good rule. He comes to Israel's rescue at the exodus, judging

Egypt with plagues to deliver his distressed people. He provides water and bread in the wilderness, guides them like a good shepherd to the Promised Land, and leads them in conquest of the Promised Land. Yahweh is what he expects all kings to be, Father of the fatherless, defender of widows and orphans (Psalm 68:5; 146:9), who will not leave the guilty oppressor unpunished (Exod. 34:7). His rule is like rain on mown grass, like the showers that refresh a parched land.

In New Testament terms, good rulers imitate Jesus, the incarnate Wisdom, by ruling as disciples of Jesus, following his commandments. Few Christian writers have put it as bluntly as Erasmus: "what Christ teaches applies to *no one more than* to the prince."[3] Erasmus has little use for the elaborate ceremonials and costumings of medieval kingship.[4] At best, these are signs of personal virtues. Erasmus stresses that the king's real adornments are moderation, frugality, and self-restraint. Kings are not members of the orders of Benedict or Francis, but the prince cannot forget that "the order in which he has made his profession is ... that of Christ himself."[5]

EVANGELIZED POLITICS

Though often mixed with themes drawn from Plato, Aristotle, Cicero, and other classical pagan writers, this biblical and evangelical paradigm of good rule was at the heart of Christian political theology for the first millennium and a half of the church's history. In this section, I illustrate that claim by focusing on several recurring themes. First, by typological interpretation of the Hebrew Bible, Christian writers defined kingship in Christological terms. Second, following Paul's injunctions to keep in step with the Spirit and produce the fruits of the Spirit, political writers emphasized that Christian rulers must cultivate and exhibit evangelical virtues. Third, following Jesus's promise that the Father rewards the generous, theologians encouraged generosity and benevolence. Finally, Christian rulers were to follow Jesus's own example by renouncing self-centeredness and regarding their subjects as more important than themselves. These various modes of evangelizing politics stand in some tension with each other. Typological interpretations of Joshua's conquest or David's wars do not always sit easily with exhortations to rulers to practice Christian virtues: If David's wars are types of spiritual battle, what guides a Christian ruler as he carries out *actual* wars? There is also variation over time. For obvious reasons, Carolingian writers apply biblical texts to political much more directly than pre-Constantinian writers. Yet there is a unified vision within this diversity: Jesus the Crucified is the risen King, and therefore politics can never be the same.

Against Trypho, Justin insisted that the royal Psalm 72 did not refer to the Jewish king Solomon but to "our Christ." The Psalm speaks of an "everlasting king," Jesus, who was "first made subject to suffering, then returning to heaven, and again coming with glory."[6] Psalm 45 too, an epithalamion for the king, points to Christ as the royal Bridegroom and object of worship.[7] Tertullian agreed: "In Solomon was no nation blessed; in Christ every nation."[8] Jerome's interpretation was less stark: He recognized Psalm 72 as a description of Solomon, but added that Solomon was a "type of the Savior."[9] Novatian saw Christ in Psalm 110's description of the king at the right hand, in Psalm 2's depiction of a king who inherits the nations, and in Psalm 72's celebration of the king's son who receives judgment.[10] Typological reading of the Old Testament redefined kingship in Christological terms. As Tertullian put it in a comment on Isaiah 9, Christ the King does not wear the sign of government on his head as a crown but on his shoulder as a cross. Jesus is the Lord who reigns "from the tree."[11]

Christian writers regularly stress that the king is not divine but only a man, made from the same mud and clay as everyone else. A truism to moderns, this was a revolutionary claim in the ancient world, where even civilized Romans considered their rulers divine.[12] Like other apologists, Theophilus of Antioch distinguished between civil respect owed to the emperor, and worship, reserved for God. The emperor was made "not to be worshipped" because "he is not God but a man appointed by God."[13] Tertullian ironically urged the emperor to attack or lay taxes on heaven. The fact that he cannot is a sign that great as he is, "he is less than heaven."[14] The church has rulers, but these are not, Origen claimed, men who "love power" but those who take on the responsibility of rule only reluctantly and with great humility.[15]

A Christian king especially is under authority, and should humble himself before the High King as David did before the ark. Augustine dismissed the notion that Christian emperors should be admired for the length of their reigns or their peaceful deaths. Instead, they are divinely favored if they are just; if they do not get puffed up by the "abject fawning" of courtiers; if they use their power to serve God and to spread "God's worship as far as possible"; if they fear, love, and worship God themselves from a devoted heart; if they are "slow to punish, prompt to pardon"; and if they inflict punishment as necessary for the good of the state rather than to "satisfy grudges against personal enemies." A king has to be master of himself before he can master people, and should "prefer mastery over their base desires" to lordship of nations. Christian rulers rule well when they "offer to their true God the sacrifice of humility and mercy and prayer" for their sins.[16]

Augustine was hardly the first to emphasize the need for kings to submit to the word of God. Tertullian already interpreted Isaiah 2 as a prophecy that nations will be judged "by the new law of the gospel" and that "minds that were once fierce and cruel are changed into good dispositions" by the word of God, as swords are beat into plowshares. He followed with an exhortation to kings to "hearken" to the Lord.[17] Reason, argued Clement of Alexandria, controls the passions and produces virtue, and he called the controlling agent over virtuous human beings "reflection." This is a form of kingship, which is called "politics" when it involves human rule over other humans.[18] Following Augustine's lead, Isidore's summary of the "justice of princes" begins with the comment that a prince should combine "the eminence of his position" with "his humility of mind."[19] Practically, the king's humility means that the king is "under law" as much as his subjects. He "should comply with his own laws" because he is "bound by them, and may not disallow in their own case laws which they uphold for their subjects."[20] Humility was not merely a personal but a *political* virtue.

The king's subjection to God and law is also expressed in his subjection to God's ministers who hold the priestly office. As is well known, the precise flow chart between bishop and king was a matter of considerable and contentious debate throughout the Middle Ages. The Carolingian writer Sedulius Scottus urged kings to be like Constantine, who encouraged zeal among the church's officers who are "under his direction."[21] Gregory VII, needless to say, operated by a different paradigm. In the swirl of debate, it is easy to miss an underlying continuity. Kings and bishops agreed on one thing: the king was a member of the body of Christ and the Eucharistic community, and that meant he was to that extent subject to the disciplines of the church and was required at least to be attentive to priestly counsel.

In the seventy-two aphorisms he offered as "Heads of Advice" to Justinian, Agapetos (ca. 530) applied evangelical commands and promises to imperial rule. Benevolence is a virtue of kings, and the dynamic of gift and return that Jesus describes applies to the king's public generosity. Following Jesus's promise that the heavenly Father rewards the generous, Agapetos urges Justinian to give: "In giving, we receive; in distributing, we gather. With this treasure in your soul, most generous king, give freely to all who ask you. You will receive your return many times over on that day when men are rewarded for their deeds."[22] Those who *seek* favors should be favored over those who bring gifts because doing favors puts "God in your debt, who takes what is done for them as done for himself, and requites with generous rewards."[23] Good rule is carried out under the demand for royal generosity and the promise of divine reciprocity.

Rulers do not rule, however, for their own enrichment or empowerment. They rule to provide public goods to their subjects. Civil authorities, Irenaeus said, exist to curb the "bestiality" of sinful humanity, yet the Lord establishes some rulers in authority "for the purposes of fear and punishment and rebuke." But the devil, who out of envy rebelled and seduces human beings to rebellion, has been defeated and "put ... under the power of men."[24] Reflecting simultaneously on Plato's *Republic* and the example of Moses, Clement of Alexandria saw a reciprocity between rulers and ruled. Rulers accommodate to their subjects, and the subjects defer to rulers.[25] Rulers act on behalf of their subjects even when they enforce law because "the greatest and most perfect good that one can do is to lead someone back from wicked courses to a virtuous and constructive life," which is "precisely what the law does."[26]

With his deep sense of human frailty and sin, Augustine also stressed the necessity of severe measures to "secure our tranquility." Kings make use of "the death penalty of the judge, the barbed hooks of the executioner, the weapons of the soldier, the right of punishment of the overlord."[27] Severity should be balanced with gentleness, and the harsh disciplines of the ruler coordinate with the mercy of the church. Augustine defends bishops' right to intercede on behalf of criminals. The king is the bad cop, but the bishop is the good cop whose "intercession ... works to restrain your severity."[28] Bishops intercede not because they approve of crimes, and in interceding they are not accomplices. Rather, they distinguish between the evil a man does and the man who does it, hating the first and loving the second. Ultimately, Augustine viewed these severities as part of the ruler's paternal care of his subjects: harsh measures were "the severity of the good father." The king was severe not to serve his own interests but to benefit his people. The severity and gentleness of the king are united in John of Salisbury's striking image of the "sword of the dove," a royal weapon that "quarrels without bitterness ... slaughters without wrathfulness and ... when fighting, entertains no resentment whatsoever."[29] Enforcing justice is, John argues, an act of mercy. Like a physician who must "employ harsher cures" to expel worse diseases, the king must administer "painful blows of punishment" and rage against evil to protect the body politic. Amputating a diseased arm is not easy, and in "tormenting the parts of the body of which he is the head, [the king] serves the law mournfully and he groans."[30]

Thomas's *De Regno* synthesizes these various themes in a typically systematic fashion. Rule by a single king is preferable to rule by many, but the rule of one wicked man is the worst possible government. The difference between a just ruler and a tyrant is the difference between private good and common good. Government ought to aim at the good of the whole community but the tyrant pursues his private good at the expense of the community. In pursuit of his own desires, he "oppresses his subjects in a variety of ways," trying to fulfill the different passions to which he is subject. He becomes like a predatory wolf (Thomas cites Ezek. 22:27) and creates instability and uncertainty. Tyrannies are ruled by ever-shifting, ever-expanding desires of the tyrant,[31] which means that they are not really ruled at all. Tyranny is morally corrosive because the tyrant is more suspicious of good men than of evil men and because the tyrant tries to prevent his subjects from becoming boldly virtuous enough to resist him.[32] Tyrants also disturb social harmony and mutual peace. To protect themselves from unified resistance, they "sow discord among their subjects, nourish strife, and prohibit those things which create fellowship among men, such as wedding-feasts and banquets and other such things by which familiarity and trust are usually produced among men."[33] Under a tyrant, men become fearful and servile. In this portrait of the tyrant, we can discern the outlines of Thomas's more positive vision of good rule, the "selflessness" essential to the just exercise of political power.

Ends are crucial for Thomas's political theory, as for his metaphysics. Tyrants aim to satisfy their own pleasure, and glory-seeking kings want to be highly regarded by men. Glory seeking is a vice, and has deleterious consequences on a political community, but Thomas displays the sanctified cynicism of Augustine in arguing that glory seeking at least has the virtue of keeping worse vices in check: an ambitious king will resist the desires that might lead him to luxury and cruelty because that would tarnish his reputation. That is a concession to the disorder of the fallen world. Thomas does not conclude that virtue and piety are therefore irrelevant to good rule. On the contrary, the true end of kings, like the true end of everything and everyone, is God: God is his reward because, as Paul teaches (Rom. 13), "a king governing his people is a minster of God" and ministers look for rewards to the lord they serve. God gives temporal rewards, but these rewards are distributed to both righteous and wicked kings, and so cannot be the final end of kingship.[34] Honor and glory are truly the rewards of a king, but Thomas argues that the only honor and glory that satisfies is that found in God's eternal rewards. Kings who seek this *eternal* glory can be confident they will receive it. Citing the *exemplum* of Solomon, Thomas adds that Christian rulers should also expect that "the glory of men, which they do *not* seek, shall follow them."[35] Pious kings, indeed, can expect greater rewards than most because they excel in the difficult arts of war and government. A king is Godlike in preserving good: "And it belongs to the office of a king studiously to procure the good of the whole community. A greater reward, therefore, is due to the king for good rulership than to a subject for good behavior."[36] This demonstrates the stupidity of tyrants, who reach for and may attain earthly rewards, but lose the greater heavenly ones. Tyrants are even worse off than that: they may even lose the best of earthly rewards – friends, the love of their subjects, stability, prosperity, and peace.[37]

Having set out at length the divergent ends of tyranny and good government, Thomas offers specific counsel about the duties of kings. Divine government provides the model: reason governs a man as God governs the cosmos, and in the political community the king rules by his individual reason. The king's duty is to be "to his kingdom what the soul is to the body and what God is to the world."[38] To grasp royal duties, therefore, Thomas considers God's actions in the world, which he summarizes as "creation" and "providence." The soul role in the body is also twofold, giving form to and moving the body. Only founding kings fulfill the first function of the soul, but all kings move the body politic.[39] God created the world and arranged particular things in their order – stars in heaven, birds in the sky, and fish in the sea. The founder of a city does the same with his realm.[40] Most kings, though, imitate God's providence, which they do in a variety of ways. Thomas identifies three threats to the preservation of public order: because men are mortal, one ruler must succeed another; some fail to carry out their responsibilities; and outsiders might attack and put the kingdom at risk. These three threats to order give rise to three duties of royal "providence": succession, restraint of evil, and protection against outside threats.[41] Kings aim not only at their own eternal reward, but have a duty to promote virtue among his subjects. As the king is subject to the government of the priestly office, so all other occupations and professions are subject to the king, and his aim is to bring those professions and occupations to their completion and perfection. He directs the whole to ensure that all are aimed, as he too is supposed to be, toward the common good of all. The king is responsible for establishing and preserving the "good life" among his subjects, a good life characterized by virtue and the satisfaction of bodily needs. To establish this life, the king has to ensure peace, guide those who share the bond of peace to act well, and provide a "plentiful supply of those things necessary to living well."[42]

As noted in the preceding text, this tradition is not without its tensions, but it is consistent in its overt and implicit reformulation of political categories in terms of the gospel. From early typological readings of Davidic Psalms through Augustine to Thomas, Christian political theologians have stressed that personal godliness, including apparently apolitical virtues like humility, is essential to good rule; they have emphasized the evangelical shape of political benevolence and focused on love and care for the poor; and they have insisted that a good ruler must imitate Christ in becoming a servant to promote the good of his people. Patristic and medieval political thought was not thoroughly evangelized by any means, but the gospel made a deep imprint on the Christian vision of good rule. Nowhere in this tradition do we find a dichotomy between "realists" and "idealists."

MOSAIC PRINCE

The Reformation shattered this somewhat uneasy consensus. Catholics and Protestants advanced not only different soteriologies but somewhat divergent political theologies. More radically, in some sectors of Protestantism, the unified vision of Christian civilization gave way to a split, sometimes radical, between civil government and church and a liberation of political from the gospel.[43] For many, "good rule" was no longer defined in terms of the gospel. In pointed contrast to Erasmus, Luther said that royal duties were obvious enough from the very institution of kingship. A king had no need to look to Christ to learn his duties as king.[44] Politics is not evangelical; it is a matter of law. Moses, not Jesus, is the model of good.

Catholic writers maintained the earlier tradition of evangelized politics. As late as the end of the seventeenth century, the classic vision of "evangelized" rule remained in play. Jacques Bossuet's *Politics Drawn from the Very Words of Holy Scripture* (1679)[45] was centrally a defense of the divine right of kings. But the converse of that position was that the king must aspire to "govern ... as God governs, in a way that is noble, disinterested, beneficent – in a word divine."[46] Bossuet considered Psalm 72 to contain the "vows" that Solomon made at his coronation, and the central thrust of the Psalm was to show that "nothing is so royal as to be the help of him who has none"[47] for "what good is it to be the strongest, if it is not to sustain the weak."[48] Like Thomas, Erasmus, and others, he contrasts the protective rule of the good prince with the tyrant whose aim is only to "feed himself."[49] Bossuet goes so far as to claim that the "general care of the people" is the foundation of the king's rights. In all the king's duties – "public works ... strongholds and arms ... decrees and ordinances" – he should seek the good of others more than his own.[50]

Calvin interprets Psalm 72 as a prophecy about the "spiritual kingdom" of Christ, the company of those who have been "called to the hope of everlasting salvation," but, like earlier theologians, he views the poem as a portrait of good rule. When David mentions the poor, he highlights the fact that "kings are armed with the sword to grant [the poor] redress when unjustly oppressed." While the Psalm depicts "the end and fruit of a righteous government," Calvin emphasizes that "kings can keep themselves within the bounds of justice and equity only by the grace of God," that is, "when they are governed by the Spirit of righteousness." Without this, government becomes "a system of tyranny and robbery." The image of rain on mown grass "elegantly and appositely" expresses the blessing of just kingship. Meadows are cut in the dry heat of the summer, and during that season the ground would be barren without rain. It provides a portrait of Christ who "by distilling upon the Church his secret grace, renders her fruitful," but it simultaneously teaches that the Lord "provides for the welfare of his Church, and defends it under the government of the king." With an eye on Anabaptist opponents, he adds (commenting on verse 11) that the Psalm indicates that "in the church and flock of Christ there is a place for kings, whom David does not here disarm of their sword nor despoil of their crown, in order to admit them into the Church, but rather declares that they will come with all the dignity of their station to prostrate themselves at the feet of Christ."[51] Calvin maintains a very traditional vision of evangelized politics.

Luther, by contrast, entirely ignores the political ramifications of the Psalm. It is a "prophecy concerning Christ and his kingdom" that will spread "throughout the whole world, over all kingdoms." In contrast to the old world, this is not a kingdom of death and sin but of "grace, righteousness, peace, and joy." These will be real, but "hidden in God." Outwardly the saints will "endure the most bitter hatred of the world, and its persecutions." Luther focuses on new worship mentioned in verse 15, turning it, strangely, into a polemic against Judaism.[52] The reign of Christ prophesied in the Psalm does not appear to have any concrete effects on real-life politics, and Luther's interpretation does not encourage a vision of "evangelized" politics. It is a hint of things to come: The gospel has been narrowed to a message of individual reconciliation with God, and the political ramifications have dropped out.

Luther's political writings expand upon this dualism of gospel and politics. When Jesus demanded meekness, he was "only talking about how individuals are to live in relation to others, apart from official positions and authority." Fathers and mothers need to follow the demands of the Sermon on the Mount in relation to neighbors and others, but not toward their own children, toward whom they relate in an "official" way. It is important that Christians "sharply distinguish between ... the office and the person. The man who is called Hans or Martin is a man quite different from the one who is called elector or doctor or preacher." An official is "two different persons in one man," and different requirements apply. Officials should be privately "meek toward everyone else," refusing to treat their neighbors "unreasonably, hatefully, or vengefully." Even in office, a ruler should not act "through personal malice or envy or hate or hostility." By contrast with private interpersonal relations, though, in government "we must be sharp and strict, we must get angry and punish" because "we must do what God puts into our hand and commands us to do for his sake."[53] A husband, judge, or ruler may fulfill his official duties because those acts are not his but God's, and God's ordination cannot be impure. But he must do so with a pure heart.[54] Luther acknowledges that Jesus's instructions have *some* implications for the conduct of politics. "Blessed are the peacemakers" implies that Christian kings will refrain from beginning war and will strive for peace, though he will be willing to fight in defense of his realm if devilish enemies attack.[55] In the main, though, a ruler is Christian not because of the way he rules but because of the intentions of his heart. Piety and politics have detached. Good rule is no longer evangelized rule. Indeed, for Luther, the very notion of an "evangelized" politics is an abominable mixture of two kingdoms that must be kept separate.[56]

Once this shift is made, it is natural that some conclude that the office of ruler is off-limits for Christians. After all, if you cannot – and *need* not – follow Jesus in your official capacity as a political ruler, then the pious thing to do would be to withdraw from public service altogether. When the alternative to withdrawal is schizophrenia, then many will choose withdrawal. Those who do not withdraw are condemned to alienation[57] because the exercise of power cannot be harmonized with profession of the Prince of Peace.

CONTEMPORARY IMPLICATIONS

Luther's dualism splits Christian political thought, disrupting the potent tensions of patristic and, even more, medieval political thought. On the one side are realists, best represented in the work of Reinhold Niebuhr. For Niebuhr, Christian love is self-sacrifice and submission, and can only lead to tragedy and slavery if it is applied in the public realm. Public expressions of Christian love can be harmful because "a saintly abnegation of interest may encourage the ruthless aggrandizement of the strong and unscrupulous." In the conflicted situations of political rule, "ruthless aggression must be countered by resolute defense."[58] The public realm is the realm of justice, and the public realm of justice exists only "because life is in conflict with life, because of sinful self-interest." Justice demands an assertion and coercive defense of rights that is "incompatible with the pure love ethic found in the Gospels."[59] Politics becomes impervious to evangelization because it is the realm of justice, a strange conclusion, given the New Testament repeated references to *dikaiosune*.[60]

On the other side are idealists, perhaps best exemplified by John Howard Yoder, Stanley Hauerwas, and their many followers. Yoder is capable of imagining a genuinely Christian ruler, a "Christian Constantine," as Hauerwas is capable of imagining the gospel infusing cultural practices to form small-scale outposts of "Christendom." R. R. Reno is no doubt correct that Hauerwas's attacks on "Constantinianism" are ad hoc efforts to call the church away from the "weightlessness of cultural accommodation."[61] Both, further, emphasize the political character of the church. Yet the work of Yoder and Hauerwas is pervaded by skepticism about the possibility of good rule, and even more about the historical fact of public authority conformed (albeit only in part) to the gospel. For all their opposition to the depoliticization of theology and the church, despite their hostility to Niebuhrian realism and liberal order, they reinforce the dualism of post-Luther political theology.

The tradition sketched in these pages is best maintained in the revived Augustinian political theology of recent years. For Oliver O'Donovan, political powers are not redeemed, but they are subjugated and to the authority of the Triune God. The church's political mission is thus to reveals the earthly "city's secret destiny," as it pursues its ultimate goal of "disclosure of the church as city."[62] From the vantage point of Christian theology it becomes possible to view political authority as a power to confer freedom, rather than as an obstacle to liberty.[63] Rulers are to judge, but as members of the church Christian rulers are to judge with gentleness.[64]

As Charles Mathewes points out, O'Donovan's discussion assumes an older paradigm of Christian ruler–Christian subject rather than Christian citizenship.[65] What happens when this tradition of "evangelized politics" translated into modern political settings, where monarchies have given way to variations on democracy? Though adjustments have to be made, the tradition has a good bit of staying power. The insistence that rulers must cultivate Christian virtues is quite directly applicable. Political humility has been conspicuous by its absence in the modern world, and the results are numbing. Over the past century, the horrors of political hubris are evident everywhere – millions slaughtered because of the Communist effort to remake Russian, Chinese, North Korean, and other societies; destruction and genocide inspired by Nazi racial pride; turmoil created or worsened by America policy makers who think that America can fix the world; vast expansion of a bureaucratic state confident that rationality and technology can heal every social ill; and statism that promises salvation through political power. Greed corrupts justice, as legislators reward wealthy donors and courts favor those who can buy the slickest legal counsel. Lack of sexual restraint is commonplace, if nothing else distracting attention, energy, and time from the work of rule. It is not difficult to answer the question: Would our politics be more stable, civilized, and responsive to public needs if politicians were full of the fruits of the Spirit?

Christian political thought has defined tyranny in implicitly Christological terms: a good ruler imitates Christ in his willingness to take the form of a servant and put the needs of his subjects ahead of his own; a tyrant grasps to maintain and advance his own interests. A tyrant need not be an Oriental potentate whose word is law, a bloodthirsty Stalin before whom the Politburo cowers, or an erratic Kim Jong-un. A member of a town council who uses his position to advance his own petty goals is, in Christian terms, a tyrant, albeit a pathetic one. The American system has virtually institutionalized tyranny insofar as it has made gaining and keeping power the main purpose of power. Congressmen, presidents, and senators are participants in a permanent campaign, and they evaluate their every vote, speech, and politic act with an eye toward the upcoming election. However idealistic they are when they arrive in Washington, politicians quickly realize that their main job is to keep their job. And here we can see that, though evangelized politics is a politics of love, it is not a soft politics. It imposes a stringent demand, that whatever their position in whatever political system, rulers must use their power like Jesus, who did not seek his own profit but the profit of many.

Notes

1. Ethelbert Stauffer, *Christ and the Caesars: Historical Sketches* (London: SCM, 1955).
2. Andrew Perriman, *The Future of the People of God: Readings Romans before and after Christendom* (Eugene, OR: Wipf and Stock, 2010).
3. Erasmus, *The Education of a Christian Prince*, trans. Lisa Jardine (Cambridge: Cambridge University Press, 1997), 13, emphasis added.
4. See Ernest Kantorowicz, *The King's Two Bodies: A Study in Medieval Political Theology* (Princeton, NJ: Princeton University Press), 1957.
5. Erasmus, *Education*, p. 19.
6. *Dialogue with Trypho*, p. 34; cf. ch. 64.
7. Ibid., p. 63.
8. *Against Marcion*, 5.9.
9. *Against Jovinianus*, 1.5.
10. *On the Trinity*, p. 9.
11. *Answer to the Jews*, p. 10. Texts cited in this paragraph are available at www.newadvent.org.
12. Henri Frankfurt, *Kingship and the Gods: A Study of Ancient Near Eastern Religion as the Integration of Society and Nature* (Chicago: University of Chicago Press, 1978) and S. R. F. Price, *Rituals and Power: The Roman Imperial Cult in Asia Minor* (Cambridge: Cambridge University Press, 1985).
13. *To Autolycus*, 1.11, in O. O'Donovan and J. L. O'Donovan, eds., *From Irenaeus to Grotius: A Sourcebook in Christian Political Thought* (Grand Rapids, MI: Eerdmans, 1999), p. 14.
14. *Apology* 30, in O'Donovan and O'Donovan, *From Irenaeus to Grotius*, p. 26.
15. *Against Celsus* 8.74, in O'Donovan and O'Donovan, *From Irenaeus to Grotius*, p. 45.
16. Augustine, *The City of God: Books 1–10*, trans. William Babcock (Hyde Park, NY: New City Press, 2012), p. 5.24.
17. *Against Marcion*, 4.2.
18. *Stromateis*, 1.24, in O'Donovan and O'Donovan, *From Irenaeus to Grotius*, p. 33.
19. *Sentences* 3.49, in O'Donovan and O'Donovan, *From Irenaeus to Grotius*, p. 207.
20. Isidore, *Sentences* 3.51, in O'Donovan and O'Donovan, *From Irenaeus to Grotius*, p. 208.
21. O'Donovan and O'Donovan, *From Irenaeus to Grotius*, p. 227.
22. Ibid., p. 186.
23. Ibid.
24. *Against Heresies*, 5.24, in O'Donovan and O'Donovan, *From Irenaeus to Grotius*, pp. 16–17.
25. *Stromateis* 1.25, in O'Donovan and O'Donovan, *From Irenaeus to Grotius*, p. 34.
26. *Stromateis* 1.27, in O'Donovan and O'Donovan, *From Irenaeus to Grotius*, p. 37.
27. Augustine Letter 153, in O'Donovan and O'Donovan, *From Irenaeus to Grotius*, p. 125.

28 O'Donovan and O'Donovan, *From Irenaeus to Grotius*, p. 127.
29 *Policraticus* 4.2, in O'Donovan and O'Donovan, *From Irenaeus to Grotius*, p. 284.
30 *Policraticus* 4.18, in O'Donovan and O'Donovan, *From Irenaeus to Grotius*, p. 288.
31 Thomas Aquinas, *Political Writings*, trans. R. W. Dyson (Cambridge: Cambridge University Press, 2002), pp. 12–13.
32 Ibid., pp. 13–14.
33 Ibid., 14.
34 Ibid., 24.
35 Ibid., p. 27; emphasis added.
36 Ibid., p. 28.
37 Ibid., pp. 30–4.
38 Ibid., pp. 36–7.
39 Ibid., p. 37.
40 Ibid., pp. 38–9.
41 Ibid., p. 44.
42 Ibid., pp. 42–4.
43 Oliver O'Donovan, *Ways of Judgment* (Grand Rapids, MI: Eerdmans, 2005), pp. 84–5.
44 Ibid., p. 85.
45 Jacques Bossuet, *Politics Drawn from the Very Words of Holy Scripture*, trans. Patrick Riley (Cambridge: Cambridge University Press, 1990).
46 Ibid., p. 62.
47 Ibid., p. 67.
48 Ibid., p. 71.
49 Ibid., p. 69.
50 Ibid., p. 84.
51 John Calvin, *Commentary on Psalms* (Edinburgh: Banner of Truth, 2009).
52 Martin Luther, *Commentary on the Sermon on the Mount*, trans. Charles Hay (Philadelphia: Lutheran Publication Society, 1892), p. 191.
53 O'Donovan and O'Donovan, *From Irenaeus to Grotius*, p. 596.
54 Luther, *Commentary on the Sermon on the Mount*, p. 59.
55 Ibid., p. 72.
56 O'Donovan, *Ways of Judgement*, p. 84.
57 Ibid., pp. 84–5.
58 Reinhold Niebuhr, *Faith and History: A Comparison of Christian and Modern Views of History* (New York: Scribner's, 1949), p. 184.
59 Reinhold Niebuhr, *Love and Justice: Selections from the Shorter Writings of Reinhold Niebuhr* (Philadelphia: Westminster, 1957), pp. 36, 49.
60 See Nicholas Wolterstorff, *Justice in Love* (Grand Rapids, MI: Eerdmans, 2011), pp. 62–72.
61 R. R. Reno, "Stanley Hauerwas," in *The Blackwell Companion to Political Theology*, ed. Peter Scott and William T. Cavanaugh (London: Blackwell, 2004), pp. 302–14.
62 Oliver O'Donovan, *The Desire of the Nations: Rediscovering the Roots of Political Theology* (Cambridge: Cambridge University Press, 1996), p. 286.
63 Ibid., p. 127.

64　Ibid., p. 200.
65　Charles Mathewes, *A Theology of Public Life* (Cambridge: Cambridge University Press, 2008), pp. 181–7.

Further Reading

Augustine, *Political Writings*, in *Cambridge Texts in the History of Political Thought*, ed. E. M. Atkins and R. J. Dodaro. Cambridge: Cambridge University Press, 2001.

Leithart, P. J., *Defending Constantine: The Twilight of an Empire and the Dawn of Christendom*. Downers Grove, IL: InterVarsity, 2010.

Milbank, A. J., *The Future of Love: Essays in Political Theology*. Eugene, OR: Wipf and Stock, 2009.

O'Donovan, O., *Ways of Judgment*. Grand Rapids, MI: Eerdmans, 2005.

O'Donovan, O., and J. L. O'Donovan, eds., *From Irenaeus to Grotius: A Sourcebook in Christian Political Thought*. Grand Rapids, MI: Eerdmans, 1999.

14 Eschatology and Apocalyptic
ELIZABETH PHILLIPS

Christian political theology has always been eschatological. This statement may come as a surprise to the casual theologian or politician who is likely to find the connection between eschatology and politics either irrelevant or potentially dangerous. Surely beliefs related to the return of Jesus to earth at the end of time, and the afterlife that follows, either have nothing to do with contemporary politics or could only have harmful influence in the political arena? Memories arise from Christian history of apocalyptic revolutionaries whose theopolitical movements punctuate the middle and early modern ages like flash paper, burning hot and bright but ever so briefly. Are not these the sorts of Christians for whom eschatology, and particularly apocalyptic, is politically normative? In fact, we find that from the Bible to Augustine to Aquinas to the beginnings of the academic discipline called "political theology," theological texts about politics have nearly always been saturated with eschatology and apocalyptic.

My exploration of eschatology and apocalyptic in political theology will proceed in three parts. Part 1 describes the centrality of eschatology in both the traditional sources and twentieth-century emergence of the discipline of political theology. Part 2 considers the eschatologies of nineteenth- and twentieth-century Protestantism in the North Atlantic, a context of great ferment in relation to the eschatological concepts of the millennium and the Kingdom of God. Part 3 takes these two discussions into account and asks how apocalyptic can function normatively in contemporary political theologies as it did within the canon of scripture.

ESCHATOLOGY IN TEXTS AND TRADITIONS OF POLITICAL THEOLOGY

Eschatology and Politics in Scripture
In the Jewish and Christian scriptures, eschatology and politics are unmistakably interwoven. Although convictions about the end of the

world and the afterlife do not seem to have entered into Jewish thought until the Maccabean period, and only the first hints of such beliefs can be seen in canonical books outside the Apocrypha, eschatology is not absent from the Hebrew scriptures. Within the prophetic books (and perhaps also some Psalms) there are both apocalyptic texts and nonapocalyptic eschatological texts, where we find messages of a coming age in which God will act decisively to transform human society and all of creation.

In the popular imagination of many Christians, all biblical eschatology is related to otherworldly realities and is marked by the judgment of individuals; Jewish eschatology is thought to share these themes and also to be marked by the expectation of a coming Messiah. In reality, for most of ancient Israel's history, prophetic eschatology was decidedly this-worldly and had very little to do with the fate of individuals or a messianic figure. Instead, these were visions of a coming messianic age in which the kingdoms of the world will be judged, peace and justice will be established, and human society will be transformed. During this age, God will act to gather the people of Israel (in some texts this includes a focus on Mount Zion and the Temple being rebuilt), judge Israel's enemies, and extend the blessings of Israel to the nations; all creation will be renewed, the people will be truly faithful to God, and nature will be fruitful and cooperative; and there will be no violence, either between people or other animals. Many of these themes come together in the following passage from Zechariah 8:

> [3]Thus says the Lord: I will return to Zion, and will dwell in the midst of Jerusalem; Jerusalem shall be called the faithful city, and the mountain of the Lord of hosts shall be called the holy mountain.... [7]Thus says the Lord of hosts: I will save my people from the east country and from the west country; [8]and I will bring them to live in Jerusalem. They shall be my people and I will be their God, in faithfulness and in righteousness.... [12]For there shall be a sowing of peace; the vine shall yield its fruit, the ground shall give its produce, and the skies shall give their dew; and I will cause the remnant of this people to possess all these things.... [16]These are the things that you shall do: Speak truth to one another, render in your gates judgments that are true and make for peace, [17]do not devise evil in your hearts against one another, and love no false oath; for all these are things that I hate, says the Lord.... [22]Many peoples and strong nations shall come to seek the Lord of hosts in Jerusalem, and to entreat the favor of the Lord.

Otherworldly visions entered into the tradition along with the apocalyptic genre, found in prototypical forms in Isaiah, Zechariah, Ezekiel, and Joel, and in its fullest sense in Daniel and several apocryphal texts. In an apocalyptic text, a story is told in which an otherworldly being mediates a revelation to a human seer, disclosing future events involving transcendent reality that is directly related to human temporal existence.[1] Most of these texts were likely written during social crises for communities that were oppressed or marginalized, and the visions often included the judgment and toppling of the powers under whom they were suffering.

The book of Daniel, set during the Babylonian exile, was likely written during a period of persecution under Antiochus IV Epiphanes (175–163 BCE). Daniel is visited by angelic mediators and given visions of a future of geopolitical powers in turmoil, all of them ultimately failing. These visions functioned to help the book's audience see their marginalization and suffering through eschatological faith and hope: they could be assured that just as the kings of Babylon faded away, so too would contemporary oppressors, because God ultimately controls human history and God's people will be vindicated: "But the holy ones of the Most High shall receive the kingdom and possess the kingdom for ever – for ever and ever" (Dan. 7:18).

The "Kingdom of God" is a central theme in biblical eschatology. It entered the Hebrew canon fairly late, especially in Daniel, but became central to much of the New Testament, particularly the eschatology of the Gospels. In all the synoptics, Jesus's ministry opens with an announcement of the kingdom (Matt. 4:17; Mark 1:14–15; Luke 4:21). Each of the Gospels has a particular emphasis in relation to the kingdom: its urgent imminence in Mark, its less urgent but no less awaited *parousia* in Luke, the judgment that it will bring in Matthew, and that which is already realized in John. Many Christians who have heard these texts, and indeed prayed daily for the kingdom to come, have been inured to its blatantly political meaning. We should not forget that, even from its earliest beginnings in scripture, the Kingdom of God "is the most political of Christianity's doctrines."[2] In Jesus's proclamations of the kingdom, the political visions of the prophets and seers of Israel are constantly implied, if not directly quoted.

In the Gospels, eschatological teachings about the already-not-yet kingdom are interspersed with hints of apocalypticism, especially in Mark's famous "little apocalypse" in chapter 13. And the New Testament famously ends with the unmistakably apocalyptic and undeniably political text of Revelation. Like generations of Jews before them, early Christians under Roman occupation and persecution found in apocalyptic their ability to relativize an oppressive empire's pretensions of ultimate power in the light of God's sovereign reign over the cosmos.

Some New Testament scholars have also found apocalyptic theology not only in the texts most clearly identified with the apocalyptic genre, but also in perhaps the least suspected place: the letters of Paul. It has recently been argued that modern, European understandings of politics and justice so colored Christian interpretation of Paul as to create a contractual, instead of more appropriately "apocalyptic," framework for his theology.[3]

Eschatology in Augustine and Aquinas

Within the previous chapters of this companion, Augustine and Aquinas have been identified as two of the most influential political theologians in the Christian tradition. Alongside scripture, their writings have been the most consistently drawn upon (and critiqued) in the political theologies of the Christian West. And we find in their writings, as well, the absolute centrality of eschatology to political theology.

St Augustine's *De Civitate Dei* is widely considered to be the seminal postcanonical text in Christian political theology. Its retelling of human history as a tale of two cities, one limited to and by its orientation toward this-worldly reality, and the other eternal in its desires and *telos*, is a thoroughly eschatological tale of the already and the not yet. God's sovereignty is already visible within human history and the meaning of history has been made manifest in the Christ event; those whose lives are shaped by love for God live here and now in ways that participate in what is ultimate and eternal. Yet God's sovereignty is not yet visible in many earthly realities; those whose lives are shaped by love for self can only participate in fatally partial versions of all that is true and good. To the Roman pagans who are blaming Christians for the unraveling of the empire, Augustine's apologetic message is that in the Christ event history's meaning is already revealed, and anything good about the empire was a faint shadow of the true justice and peace that is eternal. To the anxious Christians who had equated God's sovereignty in history with the empire and its embrace of Christianity, Augustine's pastoral message is that the empire is not the Kingdom of God but merely one manifestation of the earthly city.

William Cavanaugh has argued persuasively that political theologies falter when they ignore the eschatological complexification of space and time found in Augustine's two cities. Modern political theologies have tended to map the roles of church, state, and civil society so that "the element of time has been flattened out into space,"[4] whereas

Augustine "did not map the two cities out in space, but rather projected them across time."⁵ We speak of "spatial carving up of society into spheres of influence" in ways that divide what is public and political from what it sacred and religious. By contrast, Augustine emphasized that "there is no division between earthly goods and heavenly goods, secular and sacred."⁶ Both cities make use of the same goods, but for different purposes, with different orientations.

> The reason that Augustine is compelled to speak of two cities is not because there are some human pursuits that are properly terrestrial and others that pertain to God, but simply because God saves in time. Salvation has a history, whose climax is in the advent of Jesus Christ, but whose definitive closure remains in the future. Christ has triumphed over the principalities and powers, but there remains resistance to Christ's saving action. The two cities are not the sacred and the profane spheres of life. The two cities are the *already* and the *not yet* of the kingdom of God.⁷

St. Thomas Aquinas, likewise, cannot be understood in relation to politics apart from an understanding of the pervasive role of eschatology in his thought. "Aquinas teaches that eschatology is not a highly speculative appendix to any systematic theology, but a dimension characteristic of and inherent in all God-talk."⁸ Although Aquinas was never able to complete his work on eschatology in the *Summa Theologiae*, eschatology nevertheless pervades the *Summa* as well as his "political" writings elsewhere (if indeed there is any coherence at all in parsing apart "the political" from anything else in premodern theology – or any theology, for that matter). The eschatological vision of beatitude – the taking up of all creation into perfect union with and glorification by God – is what rightly gives order to all of human life in history, including human government. The way governments can now be oriented toward this ultimate reality is through providing the conditions for the establishment of the common good. Equally, the way governments descend into perversions of their intended purposes is through the pursuit of some *telos* other than the common good. Tyranny arises when a government's *telos* is the private good of those wielding power instead of the common good of all those on behalf of whom they rule.⁹

Already in this volume, Joseph Clair and Eric Gregory have given readers ample reasons to question the commonplace caricatures of the differences between the political theologies of Augustine and Aquinas. Matthew Lamb has argued elsewhere that it is precisely in the common orientation of their eschatologies that we may best learn to see past the calcified stereotypes of Augustine as the pessimistic Platonist and Aquinas as the optimistic Aristotelian.[10] Lamb's contention is that both Augustine and Aquinas have a "sapential eschatology," that is, eschatology that "depends upon a faith-illumined knowledge and wisdom about the *telos* or end of the whole of redeemed creation."[11] Aquinas follows Augustine, who already "understood that the eternal divine presence creates and sustains the totality of time in all its concrete particularity and universality. Eternity does not denigrate time, but creates it." According to Augustine, especially in the *Confessions*, God is:

> the fullness of Being as Presence freely creating, sustaining, and redeeming the universe and all of human history in the Triune Presence. All extensions and durations, all past, present, and future events, are present in the immutable and eternal understanding, knowing, and loving who are Father, Word, and Spirit. The eternal God creates the universe in the totality of its spatio-temporal reality. There is no before or after in God's eternal presence.[12]

In both Augustine and Aquinas, "sapential eschatology overcomes tendencies toward instrumentalizing both nature and divine revelation," as it recognizes that "the revelation of eschatology in Holy Scripture supernaturally fulfills the finality of the created universe rather than simply destroying and negating it in a final conflagration, as if that were all."[13] In this way, Aquinas in particular builds upon patristic interpretations of eschatological and apocalyptic texts in scripture "as revealing the transformation of the whole of creation so that it fully manifests the divine wisdom, beauty, and goodness. This contrasts with those who view these passages as involving or portending widespread devastation or ultimate doom."[14]

This sapiential approach to eschatology, which holds together the doctrines of creation and eschatology through the category of *telos*, has already often been noted for its centrality to the political theology of Aquinas, because his work on both natural law and the common good are so dependent upon it. As Gregory and Clair have noted, similarities in Augustine often go unnoticed in political theology because of our preoccupation with a single book in *De Civitate Dei*. Matthew Lamb's attention to the *Confessions* draws us beyond this preoccupation, and demonstrates the same matrix of creation, eschatology, and teleology at work in Augustine.

Eschatology and the Emergence of Political Theology

Having noted the centrality of eschatology in the politics (and indeed politics in the eschatology) of scripture as well as two of the most authoritative theologians of Christianity in the premodern West, we are not then surprised to find that in modernity, when appeals to the authorities of tradition went decisively, if only partially, out of fashion, Christian eschatology became decidedly less political.

One key aspect of the emergence of political theology as a distinct discipline in the mid-twentieth century was a desire to bring eschatology and politics back into conversation within academic theology. Catholic theologians had long been in the habit of treating eschatology as an appendix to dogmatics, and even there it generally only dealt with what would happen at the end of time and in the life to come. "Eschatology" was a collection of brief descriptions of the second coming, the resurrection of the dead, final judgment, heaven, and hell. Protestant theologians, meanwhile, had been rejecting the importance of such external matters in favor of existential meaning. Eventually the task became the stripping of ancient trappings from the essence of Christianity, and eschatology was an obvious target for the demythologizers.

By the early to mid-twentieth century the doctrine of eschatology began to resurface. Protestant theologians like Schweitzer and Barth, and Catholics like Rahner and von Balthasar, brought eschatology to the center of their work. European political theology seized upon this renewal and insisted both that Christian politics must be eschatological and that eschatology must be political. Jürgen Moltmann boldly proclaimed that while the theologians had been tinkering with death-of-God theology and demythologizing, the Marxists had cornered the market (if you will permit me the ironic wordplay) on hope. In *Theology of Hope* (1964), Moltmann sought to answer the valid critiques of Marxism while rejecting its a-theological materialism. The biblical narrative of redemption, from the exodus through the resurrection of Jesus and pointing toward the coming kingdom, is the narrative of this hope – a hope for this world, within history.

Eschatology was also at the heart of Metz's new political theology. In *Theology of the World* (1968), he argued that Christian hope in the promises of God is neither a passive waiting on a future, otherworldly reality which is ready-made for us, nor is it the encounter with a purely existential present reality. Instead, Christian eschatology is "productive and militant" in relation to the "emerging and arising" future. "The eschatological City of God is now coming into existence, for our hopeful approach builds this city."[15] However, this is not a mere "militant optimism. Nor does it canonize man's own progress."[16] The eschatologically motivated church is not a separate society but "the liberating and critical force of this one society."[17]

Theologies of liberation also emphasized eschatology, many of them drawing on the work of Moltmann in particular, reinterpreting his message in the European context for application in their own contexts. An entire chapter of Gustavo Gutiérrez's groundbreaking work in Latin American liberation theology, *A Theology of Liberation* (1971), was dedicated to "Eschatology and Politics." Here, Gutierrez argued that,

> The life and preaching of Jesus postulate the unceasing search for a new kind of humanity in a qualitatively different society. Although the Kingdom must not be confused with the establishment of a just society, this does not mean that it is indifferent to this society. Nor does it mean that this just society constitutes a "necessary condition" for the arrival of the Kingdom, nor that they are closely linked, nor that they converge. More profoundly, the announcement of the Kingdom is realized in a society of fellowship and justice; and, in turn, this realization opens up the promise and hope of complete communion of all persons with God. The political is grafted into the eternal.[18]

James Cone, in *Black Theology and Black Power* (1969), rejected the otherworldliness of eschatologies that encourage the oppressed to embrace their current sufferings in light of future rewards. Instead, he argued, eschatology must relate future hope to present realities. "Black Theology insists that genuine biblical faith relates eschatology to history, that is, to what God has done, is doing, and will do for his people."[19]

Realized eschatology became a focus of feminist political theology in this generation. A conviction that traditional eschatology was premised upon a strict dualism of body and soul, earth and heaven, which valued only the latter, led many feminists to reject any notions of eternity and afterlife, interpreting the Kingdom of God as an entirely this-worldly reality. In *The Radical Kingdom* (1970), Rosemary Radford Reuther argued both that social radicalism in the West has historically been motivated by Christian eschatology and that the gospel of the Kingdom of God for today is a message of radical sociopolitical transformation.

In response to the interiorizing and demythologizing of eschatology in Europe, and to the spiritualizing otherworldliness of eschatologies in contexts of oppression in the Americas, the first generation of political theologians sought to reclaim both the centrality of eschatology in theopolitics as well as the centrality of theopolitics in Christian eschatology.

THE MILLENNIUM AND THE KINGDOM

The Millennium in Modern North-Atlantic Christianity
Intriguingly, while eschatology was on hiatus in most of academic theology – Ernst Troelsch famously commented that in nineteenth-century theology the office of eschatology was usually closed – North Atlantic Protestantism of popular practice was awash in millenarian eschatologies.

One way to describe variations in Christian eschatologies is by their interpretation and employment of the idea of the millennium: an eschatology is millenarian or amillennial depending on whether or not it focuses on the thousand years of peace on earth described in Revelation 20. Millenarian eschatologies can be either postmillennial (viewing the millennium as an age that human agency can usher in, which will end with the second coming of Jesus) or premillennial (viewing the millennium as an age that Jesus ushers in through his return to earth, and during which he reigns over earth). In very broad terms, postmillennialism has been associated with political optimism and activism for social transformation, while premillennialism has been associated with political pessimism and a fatalist view of the increasing social evils of the world during the present age.

To many British Christians in the nineteenth century, the extraordinary social upheaval surrounding the French Revolution, accompanied by the precipitous decline of the Catholic Church in France, seemed to chime with the events in the apocalyptic texts of Daniel 7 and Revelation 13. Many became convinced that the end was near, and new forms of premillennialism arose. By the 1830s there were numerous British conferences, periodicals, and societies focused on biblical prophecy. A movement of Anglican clerics in the beginning, by the second half of the century premillennialism was more concentrated in Baptist churches and in new, dissenting groups such as the Irvingites and Plymouth Brethren.

The nineteenth century was also a time of millenarian ferment in America, in ways that were perhaps more fragmented and diverse, including forms of postmillennialism, some from the continuing influence of Jonathan Edwards and others from the new Disciples of Christ movement, and forms of Adventism in Millerite, Mormon, and Shaker groups as well as the Oneida Community. "America in the early nineteenth century was drunk on the millennium. Whether in support of optimism or pessimism, radicalism or conservatism, Americans seemed unable to avoid – seemed bound to utilize – the vocabulary of Christian eschatology."[20] John Nelson Darby and other British premillennialists began to tour North America in the 1860s and the following decades saw an explosion of premillennialist conferences and the founding of premillennialist Bible institutes for the training of evangelical clergy.

British premillennialists and their American followers had a pessimistic view of the world, a deep conviction that everything – including the church – was getting worse. For them, God's dealings with humanity over the course of history could be described as a series of dispensations; in each dispensation God had used new means by which to reach humanity and to test their obedience. But every time humans failed the test and were judged by God. In the current dispensation, the test is whether Jesus Christ will be accepted as savior.

The literalist approach of dispensationalists to the Bible in general and prophecy in particular led to constructions of elaborate end-time chronologies. As the end of the present age winds down, immorality, apostasy, poverty, natural disaster, and war will all increase. Suddenly, at an unpredictable moment, the true church will be raptured. The Beast will rule over the revived Roman Empire and the Antichrist will be head of the apostate church. Jews, having returned to the land of Israel "in unbelief," will rebuild the temple, only to have it desecrated by the Beast when he turns on Jews and the church, demanding to be worshiped. There will be a Great Tribulation, characterized by unprecedented human suffering. A remnant of 144,000 Jews will accept Jesus as Messiah and evangelize the suffering world. Two-thirds of them will be martyred. The apostate church will be destroyed. Finally, the Empire of the Beast will attack Israel in the battle of Armageddon, but Jesus Christ will return as military victor to destroy the Beast's forces, judge the Gentile nations for their treatment of Israel, be accepted as Messiah by all surviving Jews and Gentiles, gather the remaining Jews of the world into the land of Israel, and establish the kingdom, ruling the world from Jerusalem for one thousand years.

Some approaches to dispensationalism focus only on its pessimism about the current age, and neglect the key fact that dispensationalist visions of the millennium are utopian. During the millennial age there will be absolute fairness, equality, and justice in all social and political structures and practices. Human bodies will thrive in an existence without illness or violence. The earth and all its inhabitants will thrive as the soil becomes more productive and animals no longer kill one another. Every aspect of embodied, social reality will be transformed.

The Kingdom of God in Dispensationalist Fundamentalism, Postmillennial Liberalism, and Reinhold Niebuhr

Soon after the turn of the twentieth century, Protestant eschatologies fell in line with emerging fault lines between liberalism and fundamentalism in America. Diverse forms of nineteenth-century evangelicalism, when faced with the perceived enemies of modernism and liberalism, coalesced into a more uniform fundamentalism, and dispensational premillennialism became the eschatology of choice for fundamentalists.

Historians of American Christianity have long debated the impact of dispensationalism on the theopolitics of fundamentalism and evangelicalism. Some have posited that dispensationalist eschatology single-handedly transformed the socially progressive and active evangelicals of the nineteenth century into the inwardly focused and socially conservative fundamentalists of the twentieth century.[21] Others have argued that the transformation was neither that stark nor attributable to eschatology alone.[22] While the latter, more nuanced argument has become something of a consensus, it is nonetheless agreed that the social fatalism inherent in dispensationalism contributed to the social inertia evident in some aspects of fundamentalism and evangelicalism in America.

Pessimism about the inevitable worsening of social evil, natural disaster, and theological error as the current age continues is an obvious contributor to inertia, and the one most widely discussed, but it is not the only relevant aspect of premillennialism. In its dispensational form, premillennialism teaches that the current age is actually a pause in divine time, a temporal parenthesis when God's plans are on hold. This is because Jesus Christ came to earth to announce and establish the Kingdom of God, but Jesus was rejected and the kingdom was postponed. We thus live in a mysterious age, not foretold by the prophets, during which the church exists. The prophetic time line will resume at the end of this age, when the true church is raptured and all end-time prophecies are fulfilled in the tribulation, second coming, and millennium. Israel collectively rejected Jesus and put the kingdom on hold, so we await every aspect of the social, embodied transformation of the kingdom until the millennium arrives, the kingdom is established, and all Israel is saved. In the meantime, the work of the church is to convince Gentiles to accept Jesus as savior, thus the current era is marked by individual, spiritual salvation instead of social transformation.

On the other side of the divide, postmillennialism was the eschatology of liberal Protestantism. Perhaps the most influential factor in the solidification of its prominence was the Social Gospel Movement.

Though most were not concerned with a literal thousand-year period, liberal Protestant postmillennialists viewed the coming century as the time in which God's intentions for society might be fully realized, especially through the reform of industrial labor. This postmillennial drive for social transformation, and its optimism in the ability of American Christians to establish the Kingdom of God on earth, would lead to the naming of what is still the leading popular magazine for liberal Protestants: *The Christian Century*.

In the theology of the Social Gospel, primarily shaped and articulated by Walter Rauschenbusch, the Kingdom of God as sociopolitical reality intended for the here-and-now was the central theme. Rauschenbusch said of the Kingdom of God, "This doctrine is itself the social gospel."[23] He defined the kingdom as "the Christian transfiguration of the social order," specifying that the "Church is one social institution alongside of the family, the industrial organization of the society, and the State. The Kingdom of God is in all these, and realizes itself through them all."[24] The Kingdom of God, on this view, was the progressive improvement of society, and the establishment of this progression was the purpose of the church. "The institutions of the church, its activities, its worship, and it theology must in the long run be tested by its effectiveness in creating the Kingdom of God."[25]

Reinhold Niebuhr, a frequent contributor to *The Christian Century*, was famously and deeply critical of all forms of turn-of-the-century optimism, and particularly the Social Gospel. His criticisms, however, were not eschatological. For Niebuhr, the error of the Social Gospel was its attempt to apply the ethic of Jesus to the social realm. "The ethic of Jesus was," he said, "a personal ethic," an ideal that is "too rigorous and perfect to lend itself to application in the economic and political problems of our day."[26] One of the main functions of this division between the personal and political in Niebuhr was his contention that the *agape* ethic of Jesus could only function interpersonally and is dangerous if applied sociopolitically, where coercive justice must be the norm. This marginalization of the politics of Jesus has rightly been the focus of many critiques of Niebuhr's work. In my view, it renders much of his work unusable in contemporary political theology.[27]

Perhaps surprisingly then, we find something rather more usable and fruitful in a slightly lesser-discussed corner of his work where he does explicitly treat eschatology and the Kingdom of God, in *Faith and History* (1949). In the chapter "The End of History," Niebuhr targeted the rather nonspecific (and not entirely accurately rendered) categories of "Platonism" and "utopianism." The former he identified with an annulment of history by the eternal, and the latter with an optimism in progressive improvement within history that denies the transcendence of the eternal.[28] Laying aside the possibilities for debating his interpretations of Platonism and utopianism, we find something interesting in his assertion that a key feature of Christian eschatology is that "[b]y the symbol of the resurrection the Christian faith hopes for an eternity which transfigures, but does not annul the temporal process."[29]

How much more interesting this insight might have been if applied to the most popular eschatologies of his day, dispensational premillennialism, on the one hand, and liberal postmillennialism, on the other. In dispensationalism, we see that the eternal purposes of God can only be accomplished within history when Christ comes to violently claim control over earth against and in spite of all human action to the contrary; it is utter divine annulment of human history preceding the millennium. In postmillennialism, we see an unchecked optimism in the ability of human action to fulfill God's eternal purposes in the present age, so that human politics rather than eternity transfigures our temporal existence.

Niebuhr also rightly relates the church to the sociopolitical content of the kingdom when he says, "it is that community where the Kingdom of God impinges most unmistakably upon history because it is the community where the judgment and the mercy of God are known, piercing through all the pride and pretensions of men and transforming their lives."[30] This is neither the church of dispensationalism, a parenthetical holding station awaiting the true meaning of history that has not yet arrived, nor is it the church of the Social Gospel, one institution alongside all the others that have analogous roles in fulfilling the meaning of history here and now.

According to Niebuhr, this church "must be sacramental." The sacraments "symbolize the having and not having the final virtue and truth," and through them the church can "express its participation in the *agape* of Christ and yet not pretend that it has achieved that love."[31] Precisely where Niebuhr was so wrong about Jesus of Nazareth, in relation to the content and function of *agape*, he is piercingly right about the presence of Christ in the sacraments. By that presence we are infused with love and hope, and by that presence we are made keenly aware of God as the source of true love and hope; these are divine realities in which we participate, not abilities that we can claim to have mastered. In the Eucharist, we find that "[w]hat lies between the memory and the hope is a life of grace, in which the love of Christ is both an achieved reality in the community, and a virtue which can only be claimed vicariously," and thus "the supreme sacrament of the Christian church ... is filled with this eschatological tension."[32]

IN SEARCH OF A NORMATIVE APOCALYPSE

Narrating Apocalyptic Politics

Many theologians would argue that the reason Niebuhr's eschatology is so helpful here is precisely because it is *eschatology* and *not* apocalyptic; all normative uses of apocalyptic engage in the annulment of history that he described.[33] I believe such theological dismissals of apocalyptic trade in a misguided narration of what "apocalyptic" is and how it functions politically.

In his famous and standard treatment of the "revolutionary millenarians and mystical anarchists of the middle ages," historian Norman Cohn (1957) described the apocalypses as texts that foretell "immense cosmic catastrophe" and that functioned in their original contexts as "nationalist propaganda."[34] On this reading, apocalyptic feeds a paradigm in which an existing demonic power must be overthrown by God's saints, who will then be in charge of the culmination of history.[35] Thus "apocalyptic" movements are those with a dualistic view of contemporary sociopolitical realities and which identify themselves with the good people of God who are being called, with great urgency, to overthrow the evil powers at work, in relation to some impending catastrophe and the end of history.

Note how little these descriptions of apocalyptic resonate with the descriptions of biblical apocalyptic with which this chapter began. What drives our identification of social and political movements as "apocalyptic"? Rather than identifying movements that resonate with apocalyptic texts and their original functions, we identify movements that we feel comfortable judging as fanatical in terms of their self-identification in relation to good and evil, and that in some way involve a conviction about the nearness of the end of time – even though neither moral dualism nor the end of time are identifying characteristics of the apocalyptic genre. In other words, perhaps it is much more the case that we define *apocalyptic* as a dualistic approach to sociopolitical realities in light of a belief in history's immanent end, because this is the theopolitics we have seen in so many disturbing sociopolitical movements. Perhaps we even then read this definition back into the original texts, making our conclusions inevitable: apocalyptic in all its forms is dangerous and should be shunned in normative political theology.

As one would expect, historical, anthropological, and sociological work on apocalyptic has moved on since Cohn. In his now standard historical text, Paul Boyer (1992) identified the widespread preoccupation with aspects of eschatology in modern America, which often appealed primarily to apocalyptic texts, not in terms of "apocalyptic" but "prophecy belief."[36] Boyer's more careful and informed overview of the apocalyptic genre and the apocalyptic texts of the Bible made it clear that what has so often been driving the imagination of the end in modern America is not that people's orientation to events has been "apocalyptic" in that it mirrors the orientation and function of the apocalypses of scripture. Instead, it has been the interpretation of these texts as literal prophecies of coming events and the reading of contemporary life in relation to this "prophecy belief."

It has also been widely recognized that when "apocalyptic" is used in the popular sense, as it was in Cohn, there is nothing peculiarly Jewish or Christian about it, and nothing that necessarily ties it to ancient apocalyptic texts. While there are clearly still groups of this sort who do appeal to the apocalyptic texts of scripture in both Judaism and Christianity, there are also these sorts of "apocalyptic" movements in many places in modernity and contemporary politics, in Islam, in new religious movements in both east and west, in supposedly "secular" discourses, and in Catholic movements that primarily appeal to contemporary Mariology rather than ancient apocalyptic. It is also recognized that some of these movements are obviously politically dangerous (the Branch Davidians, Aum Shinrikyo) while others carry on in relative ease within society (sects within Baha'i and Adventism).[37]

My argument here is neither that apocalyptic texts do not contain some jolting, destructive, and violent imagery – some clearly do – nor that Jews and Christians have not or do not today perpetrate politically abhorrent things that they directly relate to the apocalyptic texts of scripture – they clearly have and do. Nor is it that the ways in which "apocalypticism" goes wrong should not be a concern of normative political theologies – they should.[38] Rather, the point is that the use of the label *apocalyptic* in ways that bear no direct relationship to the overarching contents and functions of apocalyptic texts, nor necessitate any connection whatsoever with them, puts us in danger of falling into syllogistic ways of approaching apocalyptic in political theology: apocalyptic is the orientation of x, y, and z groups historically; x, y, and z groups were politically dangerous; apocalyptic in all its forms is politically dangerous.

Eschatology, Apocalyptic, and Creation

How then can we constructively articulate the normative employment of apocalyptic in political theology? Thus far we have considered the roles of eschatology and apocalyptic in scripture, Augustine, Aquinas, first-generation political theologians, nineteenth- and twentieth-century Anglo-American Protestantism, and narratives of "apocalyptic" movements. I suggest that at least four variables have been at work throughout these political eschatologies that have determined whether or not apocalyptic was being employed in constructive and faithful ways that should be embraced as normative.

(1) *Defining "Apocalypse"*: The first factor in whether apocalyptic is inherently divergent from normative political theology or central to it is one's definition of *apocalypse*.[39] Both popular movements that dangerously wield apocalyptic and scholars of theology and religion who value eschatology over-against apocalyptic because the latter is necessarily dangerous assume the popular meaning of *apocalypse*, which is the cataclysmic end of the earth and human history. Those who are able to imagine constructive theopolitical employments of the apocalyptic emphasize the original meanings of *apocalypse*: unveiling, revelation, disclosure. To embrace apocalyptic as a genre as well as a theological mode of reasoning about and relating to our common lives in this world is not, then, to long for an otherworldly future that eclipses and annuls this world and its history, which is the reasonable anxiety of those who oppose the apocalyptic in politics. Rather, it is to embrace an openness to seeing what is ultimate in the world and the social order through dramatically calling status quo power claims into question.

In her recent book about early Jewish apocalyptic, Anathea Portier-Young has described the function of early apocalypses in precisely these terms. She argues that the early Jewish apocalyptic visionaries did not engage in "a flight from reality into fantasy, leading to radical detachment from the world or a disavowal of the visible, embodied realm." Instead, they were resisting imperial domination and manipulation, "challenging not only the physical means of coercion, but also empire's claims about knowledge and the world." Through their apocalypses, "[T]hey did not flee painful and even devastating realities, but engaged them head on."[40] This engagement was both a matter of resisting imperial accounts of reality (epistemic manipulations) and resisting imperial ordering of life (bodily dominations). The apocalypses both "answered terror with radical visions of hope," and issued in programs of "radical, embodied resistance rooted in covenant theology and shaped by models from Israel's scriptures as well as new revelatory paradigms."[41]

(2) *Apocalyptic Analogies*: This leads us directly into a second variable: whether or not the uses of apocalyptic are analogous to the functions of those texts in their original contexts. Definitions of apocalypse as cataclysm have also often been wedded with an understanding of *apocalyptic* as literal readings of events in apocalyptic texts applied with urgency to current events. These employments of apocalyptic are dangerous because literal readings are in place at two levels: the texts are read as literal predictions of events, and contemporary politics are read as literal fulfillments of those predictions.

When the original function of apocalyptic texts is understood in terms of directly engaging oppressive powers by disclosing realities that transcend them and give oppressed communities hope, the task shifts from watching current events for signs of literal fulfillment of predictions to watching the world for analogous sites of oppression where analogous visions of resistance and hope should be employed.

The political theologians of the first generation of the discipline embodied many of the best aspects of apocalyptic in the ways in which they questioned status quo power arrangements in the Christianity of their contexts, and in the ways in which they often gave resistant voices to oppressed and marginalized communities. In the historical examples we have considered here, they are by far the best examples of apocalyptic analogy; which is ironic considering how many of them rejected the "apocalyptic" in favor of the "eschatological" along with most theologians of their day.

(3) *Eschatological Apocalyptic (and Apocalyptic Eschatology)*: However, these political theologies often fared less well in relation to a third variable, the relationship between apocalyptic and wider eschatology. In their rightful protests against both internalizing existentialist readings and spiritualizing futurist readings of eschatology, and against the devaluing of this world and the bodies in it, the political and liberative theologies of mid-century tended to opt for overrealized eschatologies. Normatively employed apocalyptic must be situated within the wider category of Christian eschatology and governed by its tension between the already and the not yet. Failure to understand apocalyptic in this context creates failure to be faithful in our political engagements, whether this failure is one

of inertia because the apocalyptic vision is of the unrealizable not yet or one of zealotry because the apocalyptic vision is of the urgent already.

On the one hand, dispensationalist convictions about sociality, embodiment, and politics inevitably worsening until their redemption, which will only be possible in the divinely controlled millennium, have led generations of Christians to believe that in this age the gospel's transforming power comes only in human hearts through individual conversion and salvation, and this must be the sole mission of the church; sociopolitical transformation exists only in the not yet. On the other hand, one of the most determinative dynamics at work in many "apocalyptic" groups whose politics most of us can agree are genuinely dangerous is the utter erasure of the not yet, so that certain aspects of the visions of some biblical apocalyptic (or indeed, regime-changing and earth-ending visions from any number of sources) are associated with a literalist and uncritical immediacy to current contexts. Because of this urgency, and the loss of all patience and prudence that is demanded of us by the not yet, "apocalyptic" reasoning involves jettisoning what is "normally" morally normative; because an unparalleled event is about to occur, normal moral reasoning must be abandoned.

But even if we grant that apocalyptic needs the already–not-yet tension of eschatology, can we argue that eschatology needs apocalyptic? Why hold on to these ancient and sometimes troubling texts and try to find normativity in them? I believe the contents of the canon give us our cue here. There is a reason why we have the peaceful visions of the messianic age in Isaiah along with the radical toppling of kingdoms in Daniel. There is a reason why in one Gospel the kingdom seems urgently imminent, in another Gospel it seems near but not so urgently near, and in another Gospel it seems already to be here. There is a reason why there are measured, pastoral texts on eschatology as well as the Apocalypse of St. John. The presence of all these types of texts and modes of eschatology in the canon alert us to the very many ways imbalance between or within them have caused problems in history, as well as how their interrelation can be fruitful, particularly politically.

(4) *The Doctrine of Creation*: Eschatology in general, and apocalyptic in particular, must also be grounded in the doctrine of creation, by which I mean, along with Augustine and Aquinas, an understanding of creation not as the point of the world's origin, but as the reality within which our world and its history exist. The

abundant, loving, life-giving goodness of God creates and sustains all that is, continuously. This understanding of creation makes the link between creation and eschatology clear: God's own life is the ever-present source and goal of our lives. We live from, in, and toward God.

It is important to ground eschatology in this understanding of creation for at least two reasons. First, the eschatologically visionary community must be drawn ever back to its conviction that the earth and all that constitutes our embodiment are good creations issuing from the Goodness of the Creator God. This grounding of eschatology prevents the apocalyptic strand from the tendencies that it can otherwise have that annul the world and devalue the body. Second, the meaning of political existence must be found in both the doctrines of creation and eschatology, held in relation to one another. Holding together the questions of how and why we are created as political animals and how our creation is intertwined with the creation of earth and all its other creatures, with questions of how our politics will be consummated in the eschaton and how all creation will be transformed and glorified, allows a coherent theopolitics to be formed in relation to both the source and the goal of politics, which are both in God.

Last Things and Things That Last, or Ends and *the* End
James William McClendon Jr. taught that eschatology was not simply the doctrine of last things, but the doctrine of things that last. Christian political theology has always been ordered by visions of the last things, and in its best employments theopolitical eschatology has focused on things that will last. Eschatologies that align themselves with the traditional sources of Aquinas and more recently highlighted aspects of Augustine, focus on these things that last: the wisdom, beauty, and goodness in and for which human sociality and all creation came into being and toward which it moves in anticipation of the eternal beatific vision in which all creation will be taken up into the infinite wisdom, beauty, and goodness of God. Eschatologies that emerged in the twentieth century after the era of the doctrine's neglect focus on these things that last: the equality, community, and freedom in and for which human sociality was created and toward which earthly powers must be pointed in light of the ultimate justice of the Kingdom of God.

And yet, practitioners in these two streams tend to be radically dismissive of one another. My argument in favor of the normative employment of apocalyptic in theopolitics is perhaps, in the final analysis, an argument in favor of attending to both streams with utter seriousness, without denying the weaknesses in both or the ways in which they cannot be reconciled to one another.

St. Augustine recognized that there are not so much "spiritual" things that will outlast "worldly" things, rather the things that will last, which are taken up into eternity, are all things oriented toward God and ordered by desire for and love of God. What happens in the end, according to both Augustine and Aquinas, is not the end of all that has gone before, but the judgment of the ends of all that has gone before.

Notes

1. This description is a paraphrase of several criteria agreed upon in the late 1970s by a working group of the Society of Biblical Literature and has since been published many places, especially in the writings of John J. Collins and Adella Yarbro Collins.
2. Peter Manley Scott, "Kingdom Come: Introduction," in *An Eerdmans Reader in Contemporary Political Theology*, ed. William T. Cavanaugh, Jeffrey W. Bailey, and Craig Hovey (Grand Rapids, MI: Eerdmans, 2012), p. 159.
3. Douglas A. Campbell, *The Deliverance of God: An Apocalyptic Rereading of Justification in Paul* (Grand Rapids, MI: Eerdmans, 2009).
4. William T. Cavanaugh, "From One City to Two: Christian Reimagining of Political Space," in *Migrations of the Holy: God, State, and the Political Meaning of the Church* (Grand Rapids, MI: Eerdmans, 2011), p. 57.
5. Ibid., p. 59.
6. Ibid., p. 57.
7. Ibid., p. 60.
8. Carlo Leget, "Eschatology," in *The Theology of Thomas Aquinas*, ed. Rik Van Nieuwenhove and Joseph Wawrykow (Notre Dame, IN: University of Notre Dame Press, 2005), p. 381.
9. St. Thomas Aquinas, *De reginine principum*, Book 1, ch. II.
10. Matthew L. Lamb, "Wisdom Eschatology in Augustine and Aquinas," in *Aquinas the Augustinian*, ed. Michael Dauphinais, Barry David, and Matthew Levering (Washington, DC: Catholic University of America Press, 2007), p. 259.
11. Ibid.
12. Ibid., p. 264.
13. Ibid., p. 265.
14. Ibid., p. 274.
15. Johannes Metz, *Theology of the World*, trans. William Glen-Doepel (London: Burns and Oats, 1969), p. 94.
16. Ibid., p. 97.
17. Ibid., p. 96.

18 Gustavo Gutierrez, *A Theology of Liberation* (Maryknoll, NY: Orbis, 1988), pp. 134–5.
19 James H. Cone, *Black Theology and Black Power* (Maryknoll, NY: Orbis, 1997), p. 126.
20 Ernest R. Sandeen, *The Roots of Fundamentalism: British and American Millenariansim, 1800–1930* (Grand Rapids, MI: Baker Book House, 1970), p. 42.
21 Timothy Smith called this "the great reversal," and his thesis was carried forward by Martin Marty and Timothy Weber. See Timothy L. Smith, *Revivalism and Social Reform: American Protestantism on the Eve of the Civil War* (New York: Harper and Row, 1957); Martin E. Marty, *Righteous Empire: The Protestant Experience in America* (New York: The Dial Press, 1970); Timothy Weber, *Living in the Shadow of the Second Coming: American Premillennialism, 1875–1925* (New York: Oxford University Press, 1979).
22 See especially George Marsden, *Fundamentalism and American Culture: The Shaping of Twentieth-Century Evangelicalism: 1870–1925* (New York: Oxford University Press, 1980).
23 Walter Rauschenbusch, *A Theology for the Social Gospel* (Louisville, KY: Westminster John Knox, 1997), p. 131.
24 Ibid., p. 145.
25 Ibid., p. 143.
26 Reinhold Niebuhr, "The Ethic of Jesus and the Social Problem," in *Love and Justice* (Louisville, KY: Westminster/John Knox, 1957), p. 30. Originally published in *Religion in Life* (Spring 1932).
27 See Elizabeth Phillips, *Political Theology: A Guide for the Perplexed* (London: T&T Clark, 2012), ch. 4.
28 Reinhold Niebuhr, *Faith and History* (London: Nisbet and Co., 1949), pp. 269–70.
29 Ibid., p. 269.
30 Ibid., p. 271.
31 Ibid., p. 273.
32 Ibid.
33 See, e.g., Charles Mathewes, *A Theology of Public Life* (Cambridge: Cambridge University Press, 2007).
34 Norman Cohn, *The Pursuit of the Millennium* (London: Temple Smith, 1970), p. 20.
35 Ibid., p. 21.
36 Paul Boyer, *When Time Shall Be No More* (Cambridge, MA: Harvard University Press, 1992).
37 See Thomas Robbins and Susan J. Palmer, eds., *Millennium, Messiahs, and Mayhem* (New York: Routledge, 1997). See also, Stephen Hunt, ed., *Christian Millenarianism from the Early Church to Waco* (Bloomington: Indiana University Press, 2001).
38 This has been a central aspect in my own work. See "Saying 'Peace' When There Is No Peace: An American Christian Zionist Congregation on Peace, Militarism, and Settlements," in *Comprehending Christian Zionism*, ed. Göran Gunner and Robert O. Smith (Minneapolis, MN: Fortress Press,

2014), pp. 19–31; "'We've Read the End of the Book': An Engagement with Contemporary Christian Zionism through the Eschatology of John Howard Yoder." *Studies in Christian Ethics* 21.3 (2008): 342–61.
39 I introduced this first variable elsewhere. See *Political Theology*, ch. 8.
40 Anathea E. Portier-Young, *Apocalypse against Empire: Theologies of Resistance in Early Judaism* (Grand Rapids, MI: Eerdmans, 2011), p. xxii.
41 Ibid., p. xxiii.

Further Reading

Cavanaugh, William T., "From One City to Two: Christian Reimagining of Political Space," in *Migrations of the Holy: God, State, and the Political Meaning of the Church*. Grand Rapids, MI: Eerdmans, 2011.

Cavanaugh, William T., Jeffrey W. Bailey, and Craig Hovey, eds., *An Eerdmans Reader in Contemporary Political Theology, Part III*. Grand Rapids, MI: Eerdmans, 2012.

Cone, James H., *Black Theology and Black Power*. Maryknoll, NY: Orbis, 1997.

Farley, Margaret A., and Serene Jones, eds., *Liberating Eschatology: Essays in Honor of Letty M. Russell*. Louisville, KY: Westminster John Knox, 1999.

Gutierrez, Gustavo, *A Theology of Liberation*. Maryknoll, NY: Orbis, 1988.

Hauerwas, Stanley, *Approaching the End: Eschatological Reflections on Church, Politics, and Life*. Grand Rapids, MI: Eerdmans, 2013.

Karras, Valerie A., "Eschatology," in *The Cambridge Companion to Feminist Theology*, ed. Susan F. Parsons. Cambridge: Cambridge University Press, 2002: pp. 243–60.

Kerr, Nathan R., *Christ, History and Apocalyptic: The Politics of Christian Mission*. Eugene, OR: Cascade Books, 2009.

Lamb, Matthew L., "Wisdom Eschatology in Augustine and Aquinas," in *Aquinas the Augustinian*, ed. Michael Dauphinais, Barry David, and Matthew Levering. Washington, DC: Catholic University of America Press, 2007: pp. 258–75.

Mathewes, Charles, *A Theology of Public Life*. Cambridge: Cambridge University Press, 2007.

Moltmann, Jürgen, *A Theology of Hope*. Minneapolis, MN: Fortress Press, 1993.

Phillips, Elizabeth, *Political Theology: A Guide for the Perplexed*. London: T&T Clark, 2012: ch. 8.

Portier-Young, Anathea E., *Apocalypse against Empire: Theologies of Resistance in Early Judaism*. Grand Rapids, MI: Eerdmans, 2011.

Schwöbel, Christoph, "Last Things First? The Century of Eschatology in Retrospect," in *The Future as God's Gift: Explorations in Christian Eschatology*, ed. David Ferguson and Marcel Sarot. Edinburgh: T&T Clark, 2000: pp. 217–41.

Yoder, John Howard, "Armaments and Eschatology," *Studies in Christian Ethics* 1.1 (1988): 43–61.

Index

Adler, Mortimer, 178
Adorno, Theodor, 13, 167, 173
Adventism, 282, 288
Africa, xii, 10, 23, 67, 79, 81–83, 113, 135, 144–45, 189, 247
African Americans, 29, 37–39, 171, 206
Agamben, Giorgio, 165–67, 172
Agamemnon, 5
Agapetos, 262
Althaus-Reid, Marcella, 32, 41
Anabaptism, 102–3, 113, 162, 214, 267
analogy of being, 123–25
anarchism, 4, 7–8, 127–28, 213–15, 287
anthropology, 9, 16, 115, 121, 138, 145, 220, 288
anti-Semitism, 163
Antiochus IV Epiphanes, 276
Apartheid, 3, 10
apocalypticism, xiv, 7–8, 91, 94–5, 99, 157–58, 165, 168–71, 242, 257, 274–93
Apocrypha, 275–76
apologetic, character of public theology as, 49–50, 58–59
apostles, 38, 46, 159, 257–58
Aquinas, Thomas, xiv, 49, 68–70, 77, 113, 123, 177–93, 198, 207, 274, 277–79, 289–93
  Summa Theologiae, 186, 278
  De Regno, 264–67
Aristotle, 5, 101, 176, 186, 190, 193, 198, 260, 279
Armageddon, 7, 283
Arquillière, Henri-Xavier, 179–82
Asia, 79, 133–34, 136, 142
Asian-American theologies, 37, 40, 61
atheism, 7, 169, 219, 236, 243–44, 249–50

Augustine, xiv, 4, 49, 69, 96, 102–4, 125–26, 170, 176–93, 207, 256–57, 261–64, 266, 274, 277–79, 289, 291–93
Augustinian theology, 179–93, 269
  City of God (also *De Civitate Dei*), 4, 170, 183–90, 277, 279
  Confessions, 279
Aum Shinrikyo, 288
authority, 59, 77, 125, 159–62, 168, 211, 221
  church, 3, 76–78, 118, 126, 180, 182, 246
  divine, 7, 55, 214, 258, 261, 269
  moral, 50
  public, 52, 76
  state, 8, 32, 118, 179, 183–90, 199, 241, 263, 268
autonomy, 12, 51, 68, 73, 89, 136, 140, 147–48, 185
  of the secular, 115–17, 119

Babylon, 169–70, 276
Badiou, Alain, 165
Baha'i, 288
Bakunin, Mikhail, 7
Balthasar, Hans Urs von, 113, 121, 280
baptism, 201, 206–7, 209
Baptist, 282
Barmen Declaration, 9
Barth, Karl, 10, 13, 49, 57, 97–99, 112, 114, 171, 242–45, 249, 280
base communities, 26–27, 31–32
Bellah, Robert, 250
Benedict xvi, 36, 81–2, 260
Benjamin, Walter, 165, 167, 172
Berdyaev, Nicolas, 214
Berlin, Isaiah, 187
Berrigan, Daniel, 171

297

Index

Berryman, Philip, 32
Bible, *see* scripture
black theology, xii, 38–39, 61, 281
Blake, William, 171
Bloch, Ernst, 169, 243–44, 249
Boff, Leonardo, 33–34, 36
Bonhoeffer, Dietrich, 10, 114, 243
Bonino, José Miguez, 35
Bossuet, Jacques, 266–67
Boyer, Paul, 288
Branch Davidians, 288
Byzantium, 5, 256

Câmara, Dom Hélder, 26, 79
Caesar, 4–6, 11, 215, 257
capitalism, 11–14, 33, 35, 41, 53, 55–57, 73, 79–80, 101, 110, 115, 120, 133, 139, 144, 147, 149–51, 182, 218–34
Caritas in veritate, 67, 81
Carolingian era, 256, 260, 262
Catholic Social Teaching, xiii, 27, 47, 67–84
Catholic Workers, 29, 214
Cavanaugh, William, xi, 118, 125, 199, 209, 277
Centesimus annus, 80
Chalcedon, 6
charity, 26, 30, 67, 70, 73, 76, 78, 80–82, 207, 232
China, 5, 13, 79, 247
Christian Right, 148
Christology, 102–34, 161, 169, 240
Christology, from below, 34–35
church
  black church, 38
  and colonialism, 25, 144–45
  and eschatology, 281–87
  and "good rule," 261–63, 266–67, 269
  and the Kingdom of God, 89–98
  and modernity, 48, 58, 103, 116, 162, 214, 239, 245–48, 250–51, 277
  as political, 9–10, 13–15, 17–18, 27–29, 53, 57, 71–83, 99–102, 124–28, 178–79, 185–92, 220
  polity as democratic, 197, 200, 203–10, 215
  and the poor, 28, 31, 33–34, 68, 104
  in postliberalism, 112, 115–22
  and race, 40
  and the sacraments, 200–1, 206–9, 233, 286
  See also baptism, base communities; state, separation of church and; ecclesia/ecclesiology
Cicero, 183, 260
citizenship, 4, 11, 69, 73, 139, 159, 167, 176, 188, 191–92, 219, 270
  in liberalism, 200–15
civil religion, 11, 45, 212–13, 241, 250
civil rights movement, 3, 38, 47, 79, 170, 213, 248. *See also* rights
civil society xiii, 47, 55–57, 61, 89, 117, 188, 198, 220, 277
class, 8, 13, 25–26, 32, 37, 38, 60, 74, 75, 76–77, 78, 82, 104, 120, 136, 138, 150, 200, 203
Clement of Alexandria, 262–63
coercion, 103, 184–85, 187, 192, 269, 285, 289
Cohn, Norman, 287–88
colonialism, xiv, 14, 23, 25, 34, 41, 46, 96, 133–51, 160–61, 206, 219, 247. *See also* postcolonialism
Combès, Gustave, 179–80
Comblin, José, 31, 41
common good, 44, 46, 49, 61, 100, 116–17, 120, 127, 128, 197, 212, 233, 241, 264, 265, 278–79
  in Augustine and Aquinas, 178–93
  in Catholic Social Teaching, 68–73, 75, 77–78, 79, 80–83
communism, 36, 47, 79, 120, 179, 270
community, 37–38, 57, 83, 112, 113, 182, 198, 208–9, 215, 223, 230, 233, 242
  action/organizing, 78, 211
  Christian/ecclesial, 9, 14, 50, 52, 58, 61–62, 74, 83, 99, 101, 170, 179, 180, 188, 208–9, 220, 233, 262, 286, 292
  global, 16, 61
  in liberation theology, 30–40
  in Paul, 163–168
  political, 72, 111, 127–28, 178, 180, 185, 188, 192, 198, 202, 211–12, 264–65
  virtue and, 104, 202
Cone, James, 38, 281
Confessing Church, 9–10, 243
conscientização, 25–27
Constantine, 6, 106n39, 262, 269

Constantinianism, 5–6, 15, 58–59, 100, 106n39, 113, 127, 203, 260, 269
contextual theology, 29, 34–37
continental philosophy, xi
creation, xiv, 50, 52, 291–92
　and beauty, 104
　care for, 4, 10, 16
　and eschatology, 121, 162, 243, 275, 278–79, 291–92
　and liberalism's myth of origins, 199
　and natural law, 68, 185, 188, 265
Critical Theory, xi, 13, 26

Darby, John Nelson, 283
Dawkins, Richard, 236
Deane, Herbert, 181, 189
debt, 81, 224–34, 263
decolonization, 77, 133, 135, 138–40, 143–46, 149–51
deconstructionism, 135, 139, 141, 143, 148
de Gruchy, John, 210
democracy, xiv, 10, 11, 15, 68, 77, 78, 101, 117, 126–28, 148, 150–51, 176, 178, 244, 250, 270
　Augustine, Aquinas and, 178–82
　liberalism and, 197–215
　public theology and, 46–62
demythologization, 280–81
dependency theory, 82
Derrida, Jacques, 135, 139, 150
Deus caritas est, 81
Disciples of Christ, 282
dispensationalism, 283–86, 291
Dodaro, Robert, 189, 191
Dorrien, Gary, 88, 91, 103
dualism, 8, 114, 119, 123–25, 128, 144, 158–59, 268–69, 281, 287
Dube, Musa, 135, 142–45, 150, 152
Dueck, Colin, 250
Dussel, Enrique, 35

Eagleton, Terry, 165
earth, 3, 5–6, 14–17, 23, 32, 95, 120, 147, 158–59, 168–71, 210, 223, 241, 258, 277–78, 281, 282, 283, 285, 289, 292
Eastern Orthodoxy, xii
ecclesia/ecclesiology, 42, 46, 50, 58, 61, 62, 68, 71–73, 75, 76–77, 82, 89, 93–104, 111–12, 115, 145, 164–65, 179, 180, 185–86, 188, 193, 198, 205, 220–21

　and eschatology in Radical Orthodoxy, 121–28
　and liberal democracy, 200–10, 215
　and Protestant social ethics, 93–104
　See also church
ecofeminism, 16
economics, 17, 218–34, 239, 246, 248
　and Christian socialism, 127
　and finance, 224–31
　gift, 219
　global, xiv, 138–40, 147, 209, 221, 227–29, 233
　industrial, 75
　See also capitalism, poverty
Edwards, Jonathan, 49, 282
Ellacuri'a, Ignacio, 35
Eller, Vernard, 214
Ellul, Jacques, 214
empire, 4–6, 10, 15, 25, 100–1, 157, 163, 164, 214, 245, 277, 283, 289. *See also* imperialism, Roman Empire
Engels, Friedrich, 169
England, 76, 88, 172
Enlightenment, 25, 57, 88, 115–16, 122, 136, 139–40, 238, 248
environmental justice, 14–17
epistemology, 55, 57, 89, 112, 115, 121, 123, 128, 141, 165
epistemic privilege, 134
Erasmus, 260, 266–67
eschatology, xii, xiv, 6, 9, 54, 71, 91, 93–95, 99–103, 121, 123–24, 126, 157–71, 177–78, 180–82, 191, 201, 203, 210–11, 238, 242–43, 249, 274–93
Esposito, John, 247
eternal/eternity, 12, 53, 68–69, 77–78, 96–97, 114, 124, 151, 178, 179, 182, 188–90, 191–92, 241, 265, 277, 279, 281, 286, 292–93
Eucharist, 126, 208–9, 220, 262, 286
Eurocentric theology, 29, 32–41, 142
Europe/European, xiii, xiv, 23, 25, 34, 69, 75, 77–79, 81, 83, 100, 136–37, 139, 177–79, 241–42, 245–47, 277, 281
　Christianity, xiii, 24, 27, 47, 238, 281
　political theology, xii, 3–18, 45, 53, 116, 280
Evangelicalism, 32, 49, 61, 146, 148, 283–84
exile, 210, 257–56

Index 299

existentialism, 9, 12, 55
exodus, 46, 143–44, 169, 172, 210, 259, 280

faith, 1, 3–4, 6, 9–10, 24, 26, 33–34, 38, 40, 50, 67, 69–70, 73, 80, 83, 89–90, 93, 101, 118, 181, 189–92, 225–26, 229, 231–34, 241–42, 248, 251, 276, 279, 281, 286
false-consciousness, 26
family, 51, 62, 70, 75–76, 82–83, 105n19, 120, 184–85, 188, 203, 285
feminism/feminist theology, xii, 12, 16, 36–39, 134–37, 142, 144–50, 281
Freire, Paulo, 25–27
Finnis, John, 177
Foucault, Michel, 202–3
France, 3, 76, 245, 282
Francis, Pope, 67, 72, 81, 83, 260
Frankfurt School, see critical theory
freedom, xiv, 3, 7, 11, 38, 47–48, 51, 54, 61, 68, 76, 93, 100, 116, 166, 176, 178, 187, 206, 219, 220, 223–24, 226–27, 229, 232–33, 250, 269, 292
    in Kant, 88–90
    in liberalism, 210–15
    in postcolonial theology, 133–51
    in Radical Orthodoxy, 117–23
Friends/Quakers, 206
Freud, Sigmund, 211
fundamentalism, xi, 50, 248, 284, 294

Gaudium et Spes, 9, 27, 67, 70, 72, 79, 82
gender, xiv, 37–42, 136–39, 143–47, 150, 162, 206
Germany, 3–4, 6–10, 12, 14–15, 76
gift exchange, 120, 127, 220
Giles of Rome, 179
Gilson, Ètienne, 180
globalization, 17–18, 36, 61–62, 134–35, 149–50
Gogarten, Friedrich, 243, 249
Goldstein, Rebecca, 238
gospel, 6, 18, 30, 31, 49, 53, 68, 71, 74, 76–77, 79, 83, 94, 101–2, 110, 158, 204–6, 210, 214, 222, 256–57, 262, 266, 268–69, 281, 291
Gospels, 27, 33, 89, 158, 160–62, 168, 269, 276, 291
Great Separation, 236–52
Gregory the Great, 179
Gregory VII, 179, 262

Gregory, Brad, 239
Gutiérrez, Gustavo, 13, 24, 28, 33–34, 36, 244, 281

Harkness, Georgia, 94–5
Harris, Sam, 236
Hauerwas, Stanley, 58, 71–2, 100–4, 112–14, 128, 244, 269
healthcare, 212–13
Hegel, Georg Wilhelm Friedrich, 90–91, 93, 97, 136, 165, 242, 244
hermeneutical circle, 29, 30, 34
hermeneutics, 12, 14, 29–30, 34–35, 38, 55, 111, 135, 163, 170–71
heteronomy, 140–41
hierarchy, 101, 115, 125, 127, 161, 207–8, 211, 229
Hinduism, 24, 247
Hippolytus, 168
Hispanic theologies, 39–40
Hitchens, Christopher, 236, 238, 249
Hitler, Adolf, 6–7, 74, 243–45
Hobbes, Thomas, 198–200, 209, 214, 240–46, 249–50
Holocaust. *See* Shoah
Holy Spirit, 126, 167, 206
Homer, 5
hooks, bell, 38
hope, 9, 70, 95, 96, 120, 123, 151, 159, 164, 168–69, 171–72, 189–92, 203, 215, 232, 242, 257–58, 267, 280–81, 286, 289–90
human dignity, 39, 49, 51, 68, 79
human rights, *see* rights
Hume, David, 244
Hunter, James Davison, 103
Huntington, Samuel, 238
Hutchins, Robert, 178

idealism, 114, 139, 148, 256, 266, 269–70
idolatry, 4, 11, 23, 34, 211, 240, 242, 251
immigration, 45, 61, 193, 201
imperialism, 5, 13, 40, 135, 138–39, 142, 144–45, 149
individualism, 46, 82, 92, 182, 220
Industrial Revolution, 76
Irenaeus, 168, 263
Irvingites, 282
Isidore of Seville, 179, 262
Islam, xi, 239, 247, 288
Israel, 210–11, 257–59, 275–76
    in decolonial theology, 143–44
    in dispensationalism, 283–84

Japan, 15, 247
Jerusalem, 72, 157–65, 169–70, 239, 275, 283
Jesus Christ, body of, 126, 164, 204, 206, 208–9, 262
  corpus mysticum and *corpus verum*, 208–9
  cross, 10–11, 32, 166, 208, 258, 261
  as king, 261–62, 266
  resurrection, 10–11, 102, 280, 286
  Quest for the Historical, 91, 163
  Sermon on the Mount, 14, 223, 268
Joachim of Fiore, 165, 169
John Paul II, 36, 72, 78, 80–81
John the Baptist, 161
John XXIII, 27, 68, 75–80
Josephus, 160
Judaism, 5, 8–9, 46, 90, 94, 157–64, 167–68, 172, 210–11, 261, 267, 274–76, 283, 288–89
judgment, 137–38, 181, 184, 210, 258, 261, 275–76, 286
just war, 6, 15, 69
justice, 3–4, 10, 14, 15, 24, 94, 103–4, 115, 121, 165, 169, 171, 183, 189, 197, 221, 229, 230
  in Aquinas, 69–70
  in Catholic Social Teaching, 68–83
  environmental, 14–17
  eschatology and, 275–92
  "good rule" and, 256–70
  in liberation theology, 28–40
  in public theology, 45–63
  in Rawls, 197–98
Justinian, 262

Kahn, Paul, 251
Kant, Immanuel, i, 88–91, 93, 97–98, 104, 134–43, 242
Kierkegaard, Søren, 165
King, Martin Luther, Jr., 38, 47, 49, 213
Kingdom of God, 11, 13–14, 89–93, 96–97, 125, 158, 211, 274, 276–77, 281, 284–86, 292
Kondo, Dorinne, 148
Kwok Pui-Lan, 41, 134

labor (industrial), 23, 25, 94, 145, 285
  and CST, 70, 76, 78
  and the Social Gospel, 94
Lactantius, 168
Lamb, Matthew, 278–9
las Casas, Bartolomé de, 24–25

Latin America, xii–xiii, 3, 13–15, 24–28, 32, 36, 54, 79, 178
Latina/o liberation theology. *See* Hispanic theologies
law, 5–7, 11, 46, 51–52, 68–69, 71, 75–77, 83, 89, 149, 164–66, 168, 170, 176, 187–88, 190, 193, 202–3, 220, 222, 250, 258, 262–64, 266
  moral, 46, 89–90
  See also natural law
Leo XIII, 67, 76–77, 80
LGBT community, 37
liberalism, 44, 51, 221
  Augustine, Aquinas and, 176–93
  Catholic Social Teaching and, 68, 71, 72, 73, 75–76, 78, 82–83
  democracy and, 197–215
  neoliberalism, 23, 32, 36, 41, 133, 135, 150
  political, xiv, 25, 51, 53, 55, 60, 111, 113, 115–22, 124–25, 127, 128, 239, 244, 246, 248, 250, 269
  postliberalism and, 57–60
  postmillennialism and, 284–87
  Protestant social ethics and, 88–104
  theological, 32, 242–43
liberation theology, xii, 12, 23–42, 45, 53–56, 79–80, 117, 220, 281
Lilla, Mark, 236–54
Lindbeck, George, 57, 112
Lindsay, A. D., 198–200, 204, 206, 215
liturgy, 6, 62
Logos, 5, 17, 52, 62
Long, D. Stephen, xiii, 116, 219
Lubac, Henri de, 72, 113–14, 121, 177, 179, 208–9
Luther, Martin, 49, 268. *See also* two kingdoms doctrine

Macedonius, 188–90
MacIntyre, Alasdair, 113, 177, 182, 192, 221
Malcolm X, 38–39
Mandonnet, Pierre, 180
Manent, Pierre, 199
Marcellinus, 188–89
Maritain, Jacques, 49, 178–79, 181
Markus, Robert, 181–82, 185–88
Marrou, Henri Irénée, 180–81
Marty, Martin, 45
martyrdom, 11, 33, 35, 70, 258, 283
Marx, Karl, 13, 33, 136, 211

Marxism, 13–14, 26, 33–35, 54, 56–57, 76, 80, 111, 127, 135, 169, 172, 249, 280
Masuzawa, Tomoko, 246
materialism
 in culture, 53
 in philosophy, 45, 110, 280
Mathewes, Charles, 191, 270
McClendon, James William, Jr., 100–4, 292
Medellín Conference, 28
medieval, 69, 93, 113, 116, 118–19, 121–23, 126, 128, 179–80, 209, 221, 239–40, 246, 256, 260, 262, 266, 269, 287
Meeks, Wayne, 164
Merton, Thomas, 12
Messiah, 17, 50, 159–66, 242, 257, 275, 283
messianism, political, 117, 123, 159–60, 163, 165, 167, 172, 243–44, 250
metaphysics, 88–90, 104, 111, 117, 119, 135, 150, 220–22, 264
Metz, Johann Baptist, 9–10, 14, 74, 244, 280
Milbank, John, 71, 102–4, 110–14, 118–19, 121–22, 124, 126, 128, 182, 185–86
millennial/millenarian 8, 54, 160, 161, 162, 172, 274, 282–86
Minjung theology, 3
Miranda, José Porfirio, 35
modernity, 48, 53, 57–58, 94, 171, 177, 238, 280, 284, 288
 and postcolonialism, 134–35, 140–42, 146, 148–49
 and postliberalism, 110, 115–28
Moltmann, Jürgen, xiii, 74, 169, 280–81
monarchy, 5–6, 10, 125, 127, 161, 202, 209–10
moral theology, 104, 177
Murray, John Courtney, 48, 60, 192
mysticism, 12

nation-state, 102, 124, 127–28, 135, 139, 141–42, 145–49, 182, 198, 201, 204, 209, 212, 247
nationalism, 11, 18, 94, 139, 145, 147, 149–50, 242, 247, 249, 251
Native American, 25, 135, 145–49
natural law, 93, 102, 177, 190, 279
 Catholic Social Teaching and, 68–70, 77
 public theology and, 46–49, 52, 58

natural rights, *see* rights
natural theology, 4–5
nature
 state of, 198–99
 and grace, 113–15, 119, 121, 123–26, 128, 193
Nazism, 3, 9–10, 13, 47, 74, 172, 243, 249, 270
neo-orthodoxy, 114
neoliberalism, 32, 36
Ngũgĩ wa Thiong'o, 142, 146
Nicaea, 6
Niebuhr, H. Richard, 99–100
Niebuhr, Reinhold, 45, 49, 95–97, 103–104, 181, 189, 192, 269, 284–87
Nietzsche, Friedrich, 218, 249
nonfoundationalism, 59, 112
Nongbri, Brent, 246–48
nonviolence, 14–15, 34, 163, 211
North America, 27, 32, 88, 96, 116, 201, 283
 and liberation theology, 37–40
Novatian, 261

O'Donovan, Oliver, 71, 102, 183, 269–70
Obama, Barack, 212
ontology, 110–11, 119–20, 122–24, 126–27, 135, 140
ontopology, 140, 150
oppression, 95, 190, 219–20, 259, 281
 and liberation theology, 23–26, 29–34, 36–39, 40–42, 54
 and postcolonial theology, 141, 145, 150
overlapping consensus, 59

Pannenberg, Wolfhart, 230–31
parousia, 8, 276
parrhesia, 205–6, 209, 212
participation, 68, 70, 72, 75, 79–80, 119, 123–24, 127, 129, 233
patriarchy, 38, 144–45
Paul, 38, 52, 82, 158–68, 206, 208, 260, 264, 277
 New Perspective on, 163
Paul VI, 77, 79
patristic, 49, 113, 123, 256, 266, 269, 279
Pax Romana, 5–7
peace, 4–6, 10, 14–17, 48, 53, 60, 63, 67, 70, 79, 82, 100–1, 103, 117, 118, 120–22, 124, 169, 189–90, 199, 212, 214, 215, 220, 245, 250, 261, 264, 266–68, 271, 275, 282, 291

peace churches, 14
Peace of Westphalia, 118, 245
Pentecost, 258
Pentecostalism, 32, 50, 61
Peterson, Erik, 6–7
Pheng Cheah, 134, 139–42, 145–52
Pickstock, Catherine, 111, 122, 126
Pius IX, 76
Pius XI, 77–78, 80
Plato/platonism, 190, 193, 260, 263, 279, 285–86
pluralism, xiii, 40, 44–48, 52–56, 59–63, 75, 197, 211–13, 221
Plymouth Brethren, 282
polis, 199, 205, 210, 220
Populorum progressio, 9, 79–82
Portier-Young, Anthea, 289
postcolonialism, xi, xiv, 33, 82
   in theology, 4, 104, 133–53
postliberal theology, xiv, 45, 51, 57–60, 71, 110–31
postmodernism, 33, 44, 51, 61, 62, 122–23, 221
   in theology, 114, 122–23
poverty, xiii, 3, 12–13, 23–36, 41, 53, 62, 115, 120, 170, 211, 257, 259, 266–67, 283
   in Catholic Social Teaching, 68–83, 115
   structural, 33, 75, 82
   See also preferential option for the poor
Pramodeya Ananta Toer, 142
praxis, 12, 26–31, 34, 39, 41–42, 55, 146
prayer, 12, 14, 30, 72, 168, 262, 276
preferential option for the poor, 31–32, 39, 68, 72, 78, 80, 115, 211, 220
principalities and powers, 23, 56, 171, 278
private
   behavior of rulers, 268
   enterprise, 227
   goods, xiv, 70, 117, 120, 264, 278
   property, 33, 35, 76–77, 80–81, 127, 225–26
   religious faith and practice, 3, 8–10, 12, 30, 44–45, 51, 94, 118, 247
Promise Keepers, 148
Promised Land, 31, 260
prophecy, 170, 262, 267, 282–83, 288
prophets, 3, 38, 160, 210, 215, 241, 257, 259, 276, 284

Protestantism, 8–10, 14, 46–49, 114, 146, 239, 245, 266
   conception of sin, 230
   eschatologies, 274, 280, 282, 284–85, 289
   Latin American, 32, 35
   radicals, 206
   social ethics, xiii, 88–105
   work ethic, 228
   See also Reformation
public theology, 3, 17–18, 44–63, 73, 116–17

race, 3, 29, 32, 34, 37–38, 78, 136, 138, 140, 144, 147–50, 206
Radical Orthodoxy, xiv, 110–29
Rahner, Karl, 9, 72, 114, 280
Ramsey, Paul, 102
rationalism, 88. *See also* Enlightenment
Rauschenbusch, Walter, 47, 94, 285
Rawls, John, 181, 197–98
realism, 47, 54, 74, 95–97, 112, 176, 181, 189, 207, 220–21, 256, 266, 269
Reformation, 46, 239, 256–57, 266
Reimarus, H. S., 160
religion and human nature 51
religious freedom, 47–48, 90
Reno, R. R., 269
Rerum novarum, 67, 75–77, 80–81
ressourcement, 113, 122
restorationism, 121–22
revelation 8, 29, 69, 77, 95, 121, 168, 237–39, 242, 244, 249, 276, 279, 289
revolution, 7–9, 13, 15, 96, 117, 139, 144, 200, 274, 287
   in America, 46
   in Columbia, 28
   in Cuba, 27
   in France, 282
   See also industrial revolution
rights, 51, 69–73, 75–77, 79, 94, 117–18, 120, 139, 148, 176, 178–79, 198, 201, 205–7, 212, 222, 231, 263, 266, 267, 269
   civil, 3, 38, 47, 54, 70, 73, 79, 170, 213, 248
   human, 11–13, 44, 46, 48, 51, 55, 57, 58, 59, 61, 68, 70, 76–77, 82, 93, 115, 171, 178
   natural, 13, 46, 77

Roman Empire/Rome 4–6, 10–11, 15, 35, 157, 160–61, 163–64, 179, 184, 189, 261, 276–77, 283
Rommen, Heinrich, 178
Rosenzweig, Franz, 242–43
Rousseau, Jean-Jacques, 199, 209, 242, 244
Rousselot, Pierre, 178
Ruether, Rosemary Radford, 244
Russian Orthodox, 6

sacraments, 200, 206, 208–9, 233, 245, 286
sacrifice, 4, 74, 251, 269
saeculum, 180–82
salvation, 10, 24, 26–28, 30–32, 35, 72–74, 78, 83, 94, 114, 118–19, 159, 167, 180, 199, 228, 270, 278, 284, 291
Satan, 7–8, 257
Schmitt, Carl, 6–8, 249–51
scholasticism, 77, 88–89, 99, 256
Scholem, Gershom, 172
Schweitzer, Albert, 159–60, 280
Scott, Peter, xi
scripture, xiv, 1, 16–17, 29, 30–31, 34–35, 40, 41, 44–46, 49, 50, 68, 72, 75, 77, 99, 100, 133–34, 157–72, 215, 240, 242–43, 246, 248–49, 251, 258, 260, 274–77, 280–83, 287–88, 291
citations and references:
Acts, 35, 159, 168, 206
Amos, 210
Colossians, 17, 19
Daniel, 164–65, 170, 258, 276, 282, 291
Deuteronomy, 258
Ecclesiastes, 16
Ephesians, 19, 171
Exodus, 143–44, 169, 258, 260
Ezekiel, 257, 259, 264, 276
Galatians, 159, 168
Genesis, 16, 144, 199, 257–58
Hebrews, 159
Isaiah, 17, 31, 157, 210, 257, 261–62, 276, 291
Jeremiah, 160, 215, 259
Joel, 276
John, 26, 161, 162, 168, 218, 223, 258, 276
Joshua, 260
Leviticus, 258
Luke, 35, 157, 160, 162, 166, 168, 218, 223, 258, 276

Mark, 33, 35, 160, 162, 166, 168, 218, 223, 258, 276
Matthew, 24, 31, 35, 126, 157, 159, 160, 162, 168, 171, 208, 223, 276
See also Sermon on the Mount
1 Corinthians, 11, 19, 157, 158–59, 164–67, 257
1 John, 17
1 Kings, 210, 257–59
1 Samuel, 210
Philippians, 159, 164, 167, 201, 208
Proverbs, 259
Psalms, 12, 259–67, 275
Revelation, 158–59, 164, 169–70, 172, 257, 258, 276, 282, 291
Romans, 3, 9, 52, 97, 157, 164–65, 243, 264
2 Corinthians, 159, 168
Zechariah, 275–76
in feminist theology, 38, 142–45
Hebrew Bible, 31, 143–44, 157, 163, 184, 259–61, 275–76
New Testament, xiv, 96, 157–71, 208, 260, 269, 276–77
sectarianism, xiii, 44, 62–63, 251
secularism/secularization, xi, xiii, 3, 6, 7, 10, 44–45, 48–49, 53, 62–63, 71, 103, 110–29, 133, 138, 158, 181–82, 185–86, 191, 199, 219, 232–33, 237, 239, 248–51, 256, 278, 288
Sedulius Scottus, 262
segregation, xiii, 38
Segundo, Juan Luis, 34, 110, 115–16
Sermon on the Mount, 14, 70, 162, 223, 268
sexism, xiii, 32, 36–38, 138, 147
Shoah, 8, 54, 163
Simon, Yves, 178
slavery, xiii, 24, 31, 38, 76, 120, 143, 144, 157, 162, 183–86, 206, 213, 269
Smith, Andrea, 135, 145–52
Smith, Wilfred Cantwell, 246
Sobrino, Jon, 35–36, 244
social ethics, xiii, 69, 88–105, 220
Social Gospel, 47, 94, 96–97, 284–86, 294
social justice, 3–4, 24, 46, 53, 57, 73, 76–78, 81, 94
socialism, 12–14, 17, 33, 78, 110–11, 115, 126–27, 219, 221
solidarity, 24–27, 30–33, 38–40
in Catholic Social Teaching, 68–72, 78–83
Sölle, Dorothee, 12, 55, 74, 243–44

Sollicitudo rei socialis, 80–82
South Africa, 3, 49, 210
sovereignty, xiv, 4, 7–8, 46, 89, 117, 123, 124, 127–28, 147–49, 151, 198–99, 202–5, 277
space, simple v. complex, 125–26, 277
Spivak, Gayatri Chakravorty, 134–39, 142–43, 146, 149–50
Stackhouse, Max, 56, 59
Stalin/Stalinism, 11, 13, 243–44, 249, 270
state, separation of church and, 3, 9, 47, 71–75, 126, 207, 245–52
statecraft, modern politics as, 71, 116–17, 125
Stoicism, 4, 93, 241
Strauss, Leo, 7–8
Stringfellow, William, 170–1
structural sin, 29, 33–34, 75
subjectivity, 88, 90, 143, 230
subsidiarity, 49, 69–70, 78, 125
Sugirtharajah, R. S., 41, 134
Sweden, 245

Tamez, Elsa, 36
Taubes, Jacob, 165–67, 172
Taylor, Charles, 90, 219
techne, 140–1
temple, 159–61, 163, 275, 283
temporality, 180–81, 186
terrorism, 3–4, 8, 23, 61
Tertullian, 168, 261–62
Theissen, Gerd, 164
Theophilus of Antioch, 261
Thiemann, Ronald, 58, 133
Third Reich, xiii, 7
Thomisim, xiv, 113–14, 119, 176–83, 190–93, 256
  Neo-Thomism, 177–83
Tillich, Paul, 10, 49, 114
Tinker, George, 25, 34
Tocqueville, Alexis de, 202
Torah, 162, 257–59
totalitarianism, 11, 179, 244, 249
Treaty of Westphalia. *See* Peace of Westphalia
Trinity, 6, 17, 90, 240
Troeltsch, Ernst, 90–94, 96–100

two kingdoms doctrine, 8, 10, 158, 268
Tyconius, 170
tyranny, 264–65, 267, 270, 278

United States, xiii, 3, 8, 17, 35, 37, 39, 45–48, 54, 57, 73, 147–48, 178, 181, 211–12, 244, 248, 250–51
unity, 69, 77, 83, 197, 199, 204, 208–9, 211, 213, 220
universalism, 11, 68, 92, 138
univocity of being, 119, 121

Vatican II, 9, 27–28, 48, 67, 72, 75–80, 83, 105, 200, 207
violence, xiv, 12, 14–15, 23, 58, 70, 75, 82, 101, 113, 118, 125, 136, 139, 149–50, 162–63, 240–43, 248, 275, 283
  ontological violence, 120–22, 199
  and religion, 60, 246, 249
virtues, 256, 259–66, 270
  cardinal, 69–70, 113, 190–93
  public, 62–63, 104, 188–93, 205, 210
  of solidarity, 80
  theological, 70, 74, 189–93

war, 6–8, 15, 48, 68–70, 170–72, 198–99, 228, 230, 245, 250, 265, 268, 283
Ward, Graham, 111, 117–18, 121–25, 128
wars of religion, 118, 239, 245
Weber, Max, 91–93, 96, 98, 100, 126, 164, 228
Wilson, Woodrow, 250
Wink, Walter, 171
wisdom, 257, 259–60, 279, 292
Wittgenstein, Ludwig, 57, 101, 112
Wolin, Sheldon, 203, 209
womanism, 39
World War I, 178, 180
World War II, 8, 74, 77–78, 163, 179, 243
worship, 4–6, 31, 62, 101, 169, 190, 239–40, 247–51, 261, 267, 283, 285

Yale school, 57, 111–14
Yoder, John Howard, 98–104, 113, 162–63, 203, 206, 214, 244, 269

Žižek, Slavoj, 165